Health Care Politics and Policy in America

Health Care Politics and Policy in America

Kant Patel
Mark E. Rushefsky

M.E. Sharpe
Armonk, New York
London, England

Library of Congress Cataloging-in-Publication Data

Patel, Kant, 1946–
Health care politics and policy in America / Kant Patel and Mark E. Rushefsky.
p.   cm.
Includes bibliographical references and index.
ISBN 1-56324-558-2 (hardcover : alk. paper). — ISBN 1-56324-559-0 (pbk. : alk. paper)
1. Medical policy—United States.
2. Medical care—Political aspects—United States.
I. Rushefsky, Mark E., 1945–
II. Title.
RA395.A3P285   1995
362.1′0973—dc20   95-4803
CIP

Printed in the United States of America

The paper used in this publication meets the minimum requirements of
American National Standard for Information Sciences—
Permanence of Paper for Printed Library Materials,
ANSI Z 39.48-1984.

BM (c)   10   9   8   7   6   5   4   3   2   1
BM (p)   10   9   8   7   6   5

To my parents.
—K.P.

To my children, Rachel and Leah.
If you have your health, you have everything.
—M.E.R.

Politics is how society manages conflicts about values and interests. . . . And no issues trigger battles over values and interests more quickly and acutely than do the source and use of money in health reform proposals.

—Lawrence D. Brown

Contents

List of Tables

Preface

Kant Patel has been involved in a number of joint projects. For Mark Rushefsky, this book is his first with a coauthor. Patel began working on the book while on a sabbatical in the spring of 1991. Rushefsky joined the project in 1994. It has been an interesting experience for both of us. We do not have the same kind of work habits. One of us (we won't tell you which one) is very meticulous and organized; the other is considerably more scattered and sloppy. This has sometimes led to noisy discussions and scampering to find things. This is the kind of book Felix and Oscar, the Odd Couple, might have written! One adjustment we did make was that the neat, meticulous one kept all the papers and files because the other misplaced his. Nevertheless, it worked out well, and we have future projects in mind. Of course, the fact that we share some common interests in professional basketball (and computer games) helped the relationship. Patel, who is from Houston, roots for the Houston Rockets. Rushefsky, from New York, is a lifelong, avid, irrational Knicks fan. This project somehow managed to survive the 1994 NBA finals when the two teams met. Because the Rockets won, Patel's name is listed first! Because the Rockets won again in 1995 (even Rushefsky approved), Patel's name will appear first in our next project.

Both of us have had a long involvement in health care, dating back to the 1970s. Rushefsky first became interested in health care when his wife, Cindy, began teaching childbirth classes in rural Rocky Mount, Virginia. She trained some of the nurses and the wife of the administrator of the local rural hospital (about ten miles along winding mountain roads from where they lived), and that hospital maintained rather than closed its maternity ward. That was fortunate for them when their second child, Leah, was born shortly after midnight on Halloween. They just made it that ten miles to the hospital. Had that hospital not maintained its birthing facilities, they would have had to go another twenty-five miles to Roanoke. Given the speed with which Leah was born (so fast that she beat the doctor to the delivery room!), Rushefsky half-jokingly says that had she not been born in Rocky

Mount, Virginia, she would have been born in Boones Mill (about halfway between Rocky Mount and Roanoke), which had no hospital.

Patel's interest in health care was developed more conventionally, as an academic. He has a lifelong belief that health care is a right! The two of us agree that the health care system has problems and that there is no text that addresses those problems from a political perspective. This book is an attempt to fill that gap.

Acknowledgments

As is typical of any book, this text is not the product of its authors only. We would like to thank Pauline Woods for her work on the bibliography and our graduate research assistant Julie Atwater for her invaluable help in finding journal articles for us and the really boring task of checking citations. Patel would like to thank the Faculty Leave Committee at Southwest Missouri State University for the spring 1991 sabbatical that made the initial research for this project possible. We would also like to thank Michael Weber, executive editor for social sciences at M.E. Sharpe, for his insightful judgment in supporting this project, as well as Esther Clark, his assistant. Thanks are also due to Eileen M. Gaffney, production editor, and to her staff for the copyediting. Of course, any remaining errors are ours.

Kant Patel
Mark E. Rushefsky

List of Abbreviations

AARP	American Association of Retired Persons
AFDC	Aid to Families with Dependent Children
AHA	American Hospital Association
AHCCS	Arizona Health Care Cost Containment System
AHCPR	Agency for Health Care Policy and Research
AMA	American Medical Association
AMPAC	American Medical Political Action Committee
APHA	American Public Health Association
CalPERS	California Public Employees' Retirement System
CCHP	Consumer Choice Health Plan
CON	Certificate of need
DNC	Democratic National Committee
DRGs	Diagnosis related groups
ERISA	Employee Retirement Income Security Act
FDA	Food and Drug Administration
FEHBP	Federal Employees Health Benefit Program
GAO	General Accounting Office
GATT	General Agreement on Tariffs and Trade
GDP	Gross domestic product
HCA	Hospital Corporation of America
HCFA	Health Care Financing Administration
HHS	Department of Health and Human Services
HI	Hospital Insurance
HIAA	Health Insurance Association of America

HMOs	Health maintenance organizations
HSAs	Health systems agencies
IOGs	Illness outcome groups
IPAs	Independent practice associations
JCAH	Joint Commission on Accreditation of Hospitals
MCCA	Medicare Catastrophic Coverage Act
MRI	Magnetic resonance imaging
NAFTA	North American Free Trade Agreement
NAIC	National Association of Insurance Commissioners
NCHSR	National Center for Health Services Research
NCI	National Cancer Institute
NFIB	National Federation of Independent Businesses
NHI	National Health Insurance
NIH	National Institutes of Health
NSF	National Science Foundation
OBRA	Omnibus Budget Reconciliation Act
OECD	Organization for Economic Cooperation and Development
OHTA	Office of Health Technology Assessment
OTA	Office of Technology Assessment
PAC	Political action committee
PPOs	Preferred Provider Organizations
PPRC	Physician Payment Review Commission
PPS	Prospective payment system
PROs	Peer review organizations
PSROs	Professional standards review organizations
R&D	Research and development
RVS	Relative value scale
SMI	Supplementary medical insurance
TEFRA	Tax Equity and Fiscal Responsibility Act
USPHS	United States Public Health Service

Chronology of Significant Events and Legislation in U.S. Health Care

1798   President John Adams signs into law an act providing for relief of sick and disabled seamen, which approved the establishment of the first Marine Hospital.

1799   The first Marine Hospital is established.

1847   The American Medical Association (AMA) is founded.

1863   The National Academy of Sciences is established to assist in caring for the Union Army.

1870   First Reorganization Act federalizes the Marine Hospital Service.

1872   The American Public Health Association (APHA) is founded. This organization is concerned with the social and economic aspects of health problems.

1878   The National Quarantine Act is signed into law. This legislation is designed to prevent entry into the country of persons with communicable diseases.

1899   The National Hospital Superintendent's Association is created. It later becomes the American Hospital Association.

1904   The Council on Medical Education is established by the AMA.

1912   The U.S. Public Health Service (USPHS) is formed from the Marine Hospital Service.

1921   The Sheppard-Towner Act is signed into law. It establishes the first federal grant-in-aid program for local child health clinics.

1928   The Sheppard-Towner Act is terminated.

1929   Blue Cross is established.

1930   The National Institutes of Health (NIH) is established to discover the causes, prevention, and cure of disease.

1934   The Federal Emergency Relief Administration (FEMA) gives the first federal grants to local governments for public assistance to the poor, including financial support for health care.

1935   The Social Security Act of 1935 is signed into law. The act provides for unemployment compensation, old-age benefits, and other benefits.

1937   The National Cancer Act is passed by Congress, establishing the National Cancer Institute (NCI).

1939   The Murray-Wagner-Dingell bill is introduced, proposing national health insurance.

1946   The National Hospital Survey and Construction Act (Hill-Burton Act) mandates the provision of federal funding to subsidize the construction of hospitals.

The National Mental Health Act is signed into law, providing federal grants to states for research, prevention, diagnosis, and treatment of mental disorders.

1951   The Internal Revenue Service rules that employers' costs for health care insurance premiums are tax deductible.

1952   The nongovernmental Joint Commission on Accreditation of Hospitals (JCAH) is established.

The Health Insurance Association of America (HIAA) is formed.

1960   The Kerr-Mills Act (The Medical Assistance Act) is signed into law, providing federal matching payments to states for vendor payments.

1965   The Medicare and Medicaid programs are passed as amendments to the Social Security Act of 1935.

1966   The Comprehensive Health Planning Act is signed into law. This legislation is an attempt to implement health care facilities planning through the states.

1971   Ralph Nader's Health Research Group is founded.

Senator Edward Kennedy introduces the Health Security Act, which calls for a comprehensive program of free medical care.

1972   President Nixon, in response to Kennedy's plan, introduces the National Health Insurance Partnership Act.

The Professional Standards Review Organizations (PSRO) are created through the Social Security Amendments of 1972. The PSRO creates a regulatory mechanism to encourage efficient and economical delivery of health care in the Medicare and Medicaid programs through peer review.

The Office of Technology Assessment (OTA) is established. This organization maintains, in part, a concern for medical technology assessment.

1973   The Health Maintenance Organization Act is signed into law. This legislation encouraged the development of HMOs in an attempt to induce competition in the health care market.

The U.S. Supreme Court legalizes abortion in *Roe* v. *Wade*.

1974   The Congressional Budget and Impoundment Control Act is signed into law.

The National Health Planning and Resource Development Act is signed into law. This legislation develops certificate-of-need requirements.

The Employee Retirement Income Security Act (ERISA) of 1974 is signed into law. This legislation is concerned with protection of private employee benefits.

1976   The Quinlan case (right-to-die) is decided by the New Jersey Supreme Court.

1981   The Omnibus Budget Reconciliation Act (OBRA) of 1981 is passed. This legislation affects growth rates in Medicaid, reduces the number of those eligible for welfare, and changes Medicaid policy.

The Health Care Financing Administration (HCFA) grants waivers to states to pay for home health care.

1982   The Tax Equity and Fiscal Responsibility Act (TEFRA) of 1982 is signed into law, giving states discretion to require Medicaid beneficiaries to pay nominal fees for medical services.

1983   The Prospective Payment System (PPS), a mandate of the Deficit Reduction Act of 1982, begins. This system classifies illnesses into categories for reimbursement.

1984   The Deficit Reduction Act of 1984 requires Medicaid beneficiaries to assign to the states any rights they had to other health benefit programs.

1985   Congress creates the Physician Payment Review Commission (PPRC), which is charged with making recommendations regarding payment systems.

1986   The Omnibus Budget Reconciliation Act (OBRA) of 1986 gives the states the option to extend Medicaid coverage to pregnant women and infants who are members of households with incomes as much as 100 percent of the federal poverty level.

1987   The Omnibus Budget Reconciliation Act of 1987 increases the income requirements of pregnant women and infants to 185 percent of the federal poverty level.

1988   The Medicare Catastrophic Coverage Act is passed.

The Pepper Commission Report is released, calling for coverage for long-term care and for universal coverage for those under the age of sixty-five.

1989   The Omnibus Budget Reconciliation Act of 1989 requires provision of all Medicaid-allowed treatment to correct problems identified during early and periodic screening, diagnosis, and treatment (EPSDT).

The Office of Health Technology Assessment (OHTA) is established. This office is responsible for advising the Health Care Financing Administration (HCFA) about technology as it is applied to Medicaid and Medicare programs.

The Agency for Health Care Policy and Research (AHCPR) develops guidelines on the appropriate treatment of common illnesses.

The U.S. Supreme Court, in *Webster* v. *Reproductive Health Services,* gives states the authority to regulate and thus restrict abortions in public clinics.

The Medicare Catastrophic Coverage Act is repealed.

1990   The U.S. Supreme Court rules on the Cruzan (right-to-die) case.

1993   Clinton unveils his Health Security Act.

1994   Congress fails to pass any health reform bill.

November elections result in Republican control of Congress.

1995   It is reported that the Medicare Hospital Insurance Trust Fund will go bankrupt by the year 2002.

Republicans adopt balanced budget target of 2002, calling for reductions in spending for Medicare and Medicaid.

President Clinton announces balanced budget target of 2005, with smaller reductions in Medicare and Medicaid.

President Clinton proposes federal regulation of private insurance.

1
Health Care Politics

Health care is the largest single industry in the country. Health policymaking in the United States involves a complex web of decisions made by various institutions and political actors across a broad spectrum of the public and private sectors. These institutions and actors include federal, state, and local governments in the public sector. In the private sector they include health care providers such as hospitals and nursing homes, health care professionals, and health care purchasers such as insurance companies, industries and consumers. In addition, a wide variety of interest groups influence and shape health care politics and policymaking.

These institutions and actors are involved throughout the policy cycle. The policy cycle includes getting problems to the government and agenda setting; policy formulation and legitimation; implementation, evaluation, and decisions about policy continuation; modifications and/or termination.[1] These institutions and actors interact at every stage of the policy cycle. No one institution or actor dominates any one stage of policy development. Each contributes to the process by providing input that often is designed to promote the institution's own interests.[2]

Some of the problems in health policymaking are rooted in this diversity of institutions and actors. Any decision designed to affect the health system generates immediate and heated responses. Any attempt to regulate the health care system also produces pressures from opponents of regulation who favor market-oriented approaches to delivery of health care. Government regulations have often been thwarted by those being regulated as well as by actors in the system who oppose a strong government role.[3]

The development of a comprehensive and consistent health care policy is made difficult, if not impossible, by the shotgun approach followed by many policymakers, such as the president and Congress. For example, Congress deals with most pressing problems one at a time and not in the framework of overall health care policy. Such an approach is often necessitated by the political realities of producing tangible results on a short-term basis

1

for the purpose of reelection. Consequently, health care policy in the United States is in a constant state of fluidity, lacks consistency, and often encompasses a mishmash of programs involving conflicting values. It is not too surprising that the American health care system is often described as scandalous and wasteful.[4]

Policymakers' discretion is often limited by a wide variety of restraints imposed by the policy environment. Just as a policy environment can help facilitate policymaking, it can also hinder policy development by the number and types of constraints it imposes on policymakers. The constraints imposed by the policy environment make it difficult for the government to resolve issues in a new or innovative manner.[5] The health policy environment can be thought of as a total matrix of factors that influence and shape the health policy cycle. These factors include constitutional or legal requirements, institutional settings, shared understandings about the rules of the game, cultural values of a society, political ideology, economic resources, and technological innovations and their impact on the cost and delivery of health care services.

This chapter has two goals: to provide a detailed and systematic analysis of the health policy environment that shapes health care policymaking, and to examine the role played by key actors in the health care field. Chapter 2 provides a historical perspective on the development of health care policy in the United States. The remaining chapters discuss contemporary issues in health care: Medicaid and Medicare; the problems of the uninsured; women, minorities, and children; cost containment; health care technology; and health care reform. These policy issues are examined from the perspective of the conflicting values of access, quality, cost, regulation, market approaches, and generational conflicts involved in the distribution of health care resources.

The Health Policy Environment

Constitutional Environment

Over two hundred years ago, the Founding Fathers established a constitutional system of government that had two purposes. First, it established a government with powers to act. But second, it attempted to prevent a tyranny of the majority. Having experienced the repressive measures of concentrated power under British rule, the Founding Fathers opted for a decentralized structure of government. The major features of the American system of government, discussed next, reflect these two conflicting objectives.

Separation of Powers and Checks and Balances

The Constitution created a system that disperses political power and decision-making authority among various branches of government. The powers of the national government are divided among the legislative, executive, and judicial branches of government. This is known as the *separation of powers*. The powers of the three branches are not totally separated, however, and thus it is more accurate to describe this arrangement as three coequal branches of government sharing powers. The underlying principle behind such a sharing of powers was that it would lead to *checks and balances*. It is based on the assumption that an attempt by one branch of government to assume too much power or abuse its powers would be checked by other branches. James Madison, one of the most influential delegates at the Constitutional Convention, argued in *The Federalist Papers* (No. 51) that "ambition must be made to counteract ambition."[6]

Such a constitutional arrangement creates constant competition among these institutions for preeminence in various policy areas. It necessitates lengthy negotiations and compromises and bargaining in policymaking between the president and Congress. This makes it difficult to formulate a consistent and comprehensive set of policies. The result often is a government of deadlock and inaction. The problem becomes more pronounced during the periods of *divided government*, when different political parties control the White House and Congress. Since 1948 we have experienced divided government 59 percent of the time (twenty-six out of forty-four years) and since 1969, 83 percent of the time (twenty out of twenty-four years).[7] During the first six years of the Reagan administration (1981–86) the control of Congress itself was divided, with Republicans in the majority in the Senate and Democrats in the majority in the House. In the health policy area, this necessitated a number of compromises between the president and Congress. For example, the Reagan administration proposed the consolidation of some thirty-five health programs into block grants. Congress authorized four block grants covering twenty-four programs accompanied by a 25 percent reduction in federal funding. Similarly, President Reagan proposed putting a cap on federal Medicaid dollars, but Congress refused.[8] Even during periods of unified government, as occurred after the 1992 elections, institutional jealousies and prerogatives made policymaking a problematic adventure (see chapter 8).

Federalism

The Constitution also creates a federal system of government in which governmental authority is dispersed and divided between the national and state governments. The controversy over whether power and authority should be more centralized in the national government or decentralized in state and local governments has been a perennial question in American politics. In addition, both the national and state governments have often delegated important functions to thousands of units of local government. As a result, it is difficult to find many governmental activities that do not, to some extent, involve all three levels of government. Thus, despite the increased role of the federal government in the health care field during the 1960s, overall authority over health policy remains divided and shared among the national, state, and local governments. This is especially true with respect to implementation of many health policies and programs. In fact, the Reagan administration's desire to decentralize authority led to an increased role for state governments in the implementation of health programs.[9] In 1995, the Republican-controlled Congress proposed shifting more authority over social programs, including health care, to the states.

A federal system of government adds to the fragmentation of authority and thus increases complexity, jurisdictional competition, delays, duplication, finger pointing, and often the dodging of responsibilities by different levels of government in the health policy cycle. Attempts to reconcile many different geographical interests become problematic and tend to perpetuate a belief in organized chaos and flexible rules over central policymaking authority. The problem of regionalism and localism is accentuated by the need to satisfy the demands of a diverse and heterogeneous society. Thus, no single institution representing the nation as a whole defines the public interest and serves the public good. The result is a health care system made up of multiple "little governments" and "little empires" that pursue their own goals and interests. This in turn generates health policies that are vaguely defined and designed to serve "special publics."[10]

Institutional Environment

The institutional environment consists of the rules, structures, and settings within which major institutions involved in policymaking and implementation operate. These include the legislative, executive, and judicial branches of government. Congress is the primary policymaking institution, while the executive is primarily responsible for implementing policies. The judiciary's principle responsibility is to resolve constitutional and legal conflicts. In the twentieth century, however, these areas of responsibility have become increasingly blurred, with all three branches of government sharing powers in the areas of policymaking, implementation, and adjudication.

Congress

[handwritten margin note: committee structure => decentralized pwr; competition b/w H. & S. and bargaining]

Policymaking in Congress takes place in an environment of decentralized and thus fragmented power structure where political power is dispersed among numerous committees and subcommittees in both chambers. This decentralization of power and authority in the committee structure has led some to describe Congress as a "kind of confederation of little legislatures."[11] One of the consequences of this in health policymaking is competition among committees within and between the Senate and the House. The second consequence for health policymaking is bargaining and compromises. Thus, health policy formulation in Congress occurs in numerous subsystems with little coordination.[12] In the 104th Congress (1995–96), the Republican majority is attempting to coordinate committee action under tight leadership control.

Senators and representatives are elected to represent their respective states and smaller congressional districts, which leads to an emphasis on pork-barrel politics to capture federal goods and services for their constituencies. This creates a tendency to promote state and local interests and less sensitivity to national interests and needs in health care policymaking.

The Executive

The Constitution assigns the president and the executive branch agencies (i.e., the bureaucracy), the role of implementing policies approved by Congress. During the 1960s, concerns about issues of access, quality, equity, and efficiency in the health care area led Congress to create many new programs, such as Medicare and Medicaid, to increase access. At the same time, concerns over spiraling costs have resulted in the creation of programs designed to contain rising health care costs through planning, peer review, regulation, and encouraging the development of new health care delivery organizations such as health maintenance organizations (HMOs).

Congress routinely delegates the authority for making many decisions to bureaucratic agencies. For example, Congress created the Occupational Safety and Health Administration (OSHA) and gave it the authority to write regulations concerning workers' health and safety in the workplace. In addition, Congress often passes laws that are vague, very broad, or both, leaving bureaucratic agencies a significant amount of discretionary power to fill in the details of the law. Congress uses its legislative oversight and budgetary powers to exercise control over bureaucratic agencies. But the fact remains that congressional *delegation of authority* and *discretionary power* enjoyed by bureaucratic agencies gives them a significant role in health policymaking and implementation.

[handwritten margin note: agency discretion]

As with Congress, power and authority in the bureaucracy is highly dispersed and fragmented. Various health policies are under the jurisdictions of many different federal agencies, which leads to _overlapping jurisdictions, authority, and responsibilities._ In addition, as we discussed earlier, a federal system of government necessitates that many federal programs are implemented either partially or totally by state bureaucracies. Such dispersal and fragmentation of authority creates competition and conflicts along both vertical and horizontal planes throughout the health policy cycle. Turf fighting over program implementation, authority, and resources becomes the name of the game. The health policy cycle operates in a dynamic environment of constantly changing alignments of bureaucratic agencies, congressional committees, policymakers, and various interest groups shaping and reshaping health policy.

The Judiciary

Courts and judges influence health policymaking and implementation through their interpretation of the Constitution and congressional laws. They make sure that implementation of laws meets constitutional standards and that administrative agencies discharge their assigned responsibilities. Federal courts are also responsible for enforcement of the Administrative Procedures Act, which governs administrative procedures in all federal agencies. In addition, individuals and groups who feel that the executive and legislative branches have failed to redress their grievances often resort to seeking help from the courts.

The federal courts, and the U.S. Supreme Court in particular, have come to play a significant role in policymaking in certain aspects of the health care field. The Supreme Court's 1973 decision in _Roe_ v. _Wade_ legalizing abortion was a major policy decision and a victory for groups supporting a woman's right to have an abortion. But a 1989 decision by the Supreme Court _(Webster_ v. _Reproductive Health Services)_ whereby the Supreme Court granted states authority to regulate and thus restrict abortions in public clinics also suggests that the Court's position may change with changes in the composition of justices on the Court. Whether a more conservative Supreme Court in the future overturns _Roe_ v. _Wade_ remains to be seen.

The impact of health care technology on the treatment and delivery of health services and the ethical concerns raised by medical technology have drawn state and federal courts into such varied topics as organ transplants, fetal tissue research, health care surrogacy, quality of life, and the right to die with dignity, among others (see chapter 7).

Political Environment

The political environment includes a shared understanding among policy-makers about how policy decisions should be made and the underlying values, political feasibility, electoral cycles, influence of organized interest groups, and political ideologies. The political environment itself is influenced and shaped by the constitutional/legal, institutional, economic, and technological environment of a given policy area.

Consensus Building

We have already discussed how the constitutional and institutional environments create diffused and fragmented systems of authority and responsibility in the health policy cycle. This in turn creates a political environment that is conducive to constant *bargaining and compromises* among major institutions and key actors in the health policy field. Since no single institution or actor is in a position to dominate the process, *coalition building* becomes inevitable. It also injects *log-rolling* (trading votes to secure favors) and *pork-barrel politics* (obtaining government projects for one's legislative district) into the policy adoption and implementation stages. One of the consequences of this is that the policymaking process is invariably driven toward *consensus building* among diverse and conflicting interests. This often results in contradictory policies or policies that contain conflicting values.[13] Thus, the policymaking process, instead of being a science of creating policy that solves a problem, becomes an art of creating a consensus that holds conflicting and diverse interests together in order to create majority support for that policy. The political logic of coalition building in order to create a consensus creates a situation in which any measure that is successful, be it congressional or presidential, will have been changed in ways its proponents did not foresee or desire.[14] Attempts at comprehensive change, as in the health care reform debate of the 1990s and other attempts at national health insurance, often fail. Thus, what change does come about is piecemeal and incremental, epitomized by Medicaid and Medicare.

Incrementalism

Policymakers also share decision-making values that favor *incremental* policymaking, that is, relatively small or incremental changes and modifications in existing policies. Thus, rather than consider all possible alternatives in a comprehensive manner, policymakers concentrate only on marginal values or relatively few alternatives that bring about marginal changes in existing policies.[15] Incrementalism is politically attractive to policymakers because small policy adjustments reduce the impact of negative and politically risky consequences. Nevertheless, incremental policymaking can also inhibit imagination, innovation, and fresh new approaches to the solution of problems.[16] Policymakers end up creating policies aimed at "satisfying" diverse interests, rather than problem solving.

Political Feasibility

Policymakers are also influenced and guided in their policy deliberations by *political feasibility*.[17] This involves judgment about whether it is possible to enact a policy given the political realities. One of the major political realities that policymakers face is the potential public reaction to a proposed policy. All the major institutions and actors involved in policymaking are influenced by considerations of political feasibility. This is especially true of elected public officials. Members of Congress are more apt to support and vote for a policy that is likely to be popular with their constituents than a policy that may produce a strong negative reaction from their constituents.

Electoral Cycle

Policymakers are influenced in their deliberations by the *electoral cycle* and the necessity of *reelection*. Thus, policy decisions are viewed from the perspective of potential electoral consequences. This is all the more true near election time. The policymaking process is driven by the need to produce short-term tangible benefits. The fact that the president, senators, and representatives not only have different constituencies to serve but a different length of term in office make electoral calculations a permanent fixture of the political environment. For example, during the 1980 primary campaign, Senator Edward Kennedy (D-Mass.), who was challenging the incumbent President Carter for the Democratic Party's nomination for the presidency, advocated a plan for universal national health insurance. When his proposal proved to be popular with the general public, the Carter administration was forced to propose a scaled-down version of a health insurance plan. President Carter went on to win the Democratic Party's nomination but lost the general election to Ronald Reagan. The issue of national health insurance also receded from prominence on the national policy agenda as a result of the Reagan administration's commitment to deregulation and decentralization in health care, as well as the economic realities of the federal budget deficit. Health care reform came back on the health care agenda as a result of a special senatorial election in Pennsylvania in 1991 and the presidential campaign of 1992 (see chapter 8).

Public Philosophy and Political Ideology

Political ideology is the set of political beliefs and values by which policy actors in all policy arenas operate.[18] Within the health care system it is possible to identify the ideology of the medical profession, health care administrators, planners, and policymakers. The term "public philosophy," in contrast, is a broader concept and can be defined as an outlook on public affairs shared by a wide coalition in a nation.[19] A public philosophy often may not be explicit, but the ideological debate on issues takes place within its confines.

The underlying principle in American public philosophy, resulting from constitutional guarantees of freedom of speech, expression, and petition, is that organized interests should have an important role in influencing public policies. The public philosophy in the United States was influenced greatly by the writing of John Locke, a seventeenth-century English philosopher. A central feature of Locke's argument is the belief that ultimate authority resides in the individual's inalienable right to seek his or her own self-preservation. According to Locke, people form a government to protect their natural right of self-preservation. For Locke, the right to self-preservation is closely associated with the right to acquire property. This Lockean idea pervades American political thought and institutions.[20]

The clearest integration of this Lockean idea is found in James Madison's *Federalist Paper* No. 10. According to Madison, a faction constituted a number of citizens united by a common passion or interest adverse to the rights of other citizens or to the permanent and aggregate interests of the community. Madison argued that factions were evil and could lead to tyranny. Yet, elimination of the causes of factions was not a solution because it could also destroy liberty. Therefore, Madison advocated controlling the effects of factions. Since the American society is composed of a large number of geographic, ethnic, racial, economic, and religious groups, the way to control the negative effects of factions, according to Madison, was to create a representative form of government. In such a representative government, public views can be refined and enlarged by passing them through the medium of a chosen body of citizens (legislature) whose wisdom can help determine the true interest of the country. Madison also asserted that a large republic was less susceptible to tyranny than a small one because in a large republic many different interests will exist, making it difficult for any one interest regularly to dominate all other interests.[21]

This in turn helped create a *philosophy of liberalism,* which argues that all interests should be able to penetrate the political arena. Theodore Lowi describes this philosophy as *interest-group liberalism.*[22] Such a political system is called a *pluralistic system,* which is characterized by many channels of access with various interest-groups exercising countervailing veto power. This system is justified in terms of equality and openness that guarantees political freedom, which in turn can be used to achieve social and economic freedoms.[23]

The decentralized governmental structure based on separation of powers, checks and balances, and federalism is designed to give interest groups access throughout the policy cycle. Thus, ironically, a Madisonian system designed to prevent a tyranny of the majority and control the mischiefs of factions (interest groups) also gives these factions many opportunities for devilment. To formulate health policy under such a system requires public officials and institutions to reconcile the conflicting interests of many organized groups. In theory, the role of the government becomes one of neutral arbitrator resolving conflicts among organized groups. The broad and diffused distribution of political influence across numerous and diverse interest groups blurs the distinction between public and private power.

Private interests battle with one another and define themselves in terms of the public interest. But because all interest groups do not have equal resources, those with more economic resources have greater access to channels of influence and thus more opportunities for engaging in mischief. As McConnell has persuasively argued, small groups monopolize political power by successfully defining their own narrow interests as the general public interest.[24] For example, for many years, the American Medical Association (AMA) based its opposition to national health insurance on the ground that socialized medicine would be against the general public interest because it would deprive patients of their freedom of choice and would lead to poor-quality medical care. In a pluralistic system based on the public philosophy of interest-group liberalism, private economic, regional, and constituency interests are justified as public interests by appealing to values of individualism, constitution, democracy, freedom, and equality, which make up an important part of American culture and belief systems. This is done by private interests as well as public officials. The consensus created from compromises and bargaining among competing interests gets defined as the public interest. The role of the government, according to the pluralistic formulation, becomes one of protecting these diverse and competing interests by creating a consensus through the give-and-take of politics.

Reforming the present health care system becomes difficult because every reform proposal gets trapped in pluralistic processes designed to safeguard all existing professional and organizational interests. Ideological conflicts between those who want to protect the professional monopoly and autonomy of the medical profession and those who want more health care planning and regulation are contained within a pluralistic institutional framework that prevents either side from generating enough power to bring about significant reforms designed to integrate and coordinate health care.[25] *Market reformers* blame bureaucratic interference and cumbersome regulations for the problems of the health care system and call for less regulation and more incentive-based reforms to increase and diversify health care facilities and delivery of services. The *libertarian ideology* of distributive justice is most evident in arguments for competitive market reforms. According to this ideology, increased reliance on market competition for allocative decisions would result in a more efficient allocation of resources than we now have. Republicans in general, and conservatives in particular, support this position. *Bureaucratic reformers* blame market competition for the defects of the present system and call for more regulation and planning. This argument is based on the *egalitarian ideology*, which emphasizes the just distribution of health care resources based on need. The concern is to provide equal access to decent-quality health care for everyone at a reasonable cost. Democrats in general, and liberals in particular, support this position.[26]

Thus the health care system exhibits a continuous conflict and strain between the values of efficiency, access, equality, rights, and freedom. This is reflected in the contradictions between people's expectations for equal access to decent-quality health care, the failure of the private sector to provide equal access, and the inability of the public sector to compensate for the inadequacies of the private sector.

Which health policies are pursued at a given point in time depends on which ideology is dominant at that time. During the 1960s and early 1970s, the dominance of egalitarian ideology resulted in bureaucratic reformers' success in creating health policies designed to increase access to health care and at the same time provide quality care at a reasonable cost through such policies as Medicare, Medicaid, health care planning, and regulation. The ascendancy of libertarian ideology during the 1970s, and particularly 1980s, led to the creation of health policies—supported by market reformers—aimed at cost containment and economic efficiency. This was attempted through deregulation, cuts in federal funds, encouraging development of alternative health delivery organizations such as health maintenance organizations, and the establishment of a prospective reimbursement system of hospital payment for Medicare patients through diagnosis related groups (DRGs). These policies were designed to induce diversity and competition in the health care system through market incentives.

Economic Environment

Decisions about health care policies are invariably intertwined with economics. Health care affects and is affected by the economic environment in a number of ways. The economic environment consists of a network of institutions, laws, and rules that deal with primary questions such as what goods and services to produce, how they should be produced, and for whom.[27] The economic point of view is also rooted in three fundamental assumptions: (1) resources are limited or scarce in relation to human wants; (2) resources have alternative uses; and (3) people have different wants and do not attach the same importance to them.[28] Because economic resources are limited and have alternative uses, decisions must be made with regard to how and for what purposes to use these resources. The concept of *opportunity cost* suggests that when deciding to use resources in a certain way, one loses the opportunity to obtain benefits of using resources in some other way.

The economic environment affects policy decisions in health care in a number of ways. At any given point in time, health policymakers are influenced in their decisions by the notion of *economic feasibility*. When an economy is growing at a healthy rate, making economic resources available, policymakers find it economically feasible to establish new programs. Such was the case during the 1960s and to an extent in the early 1970s, when a number of new programs designed to increase access to health care were created. But corresponding increases in health care costs, a slowed rate of economic growth, the massive federal budget deficits, and an executive branch dominated by a conservative political philosophy during the 1980s has not only made it economically difficult to establish new health care programs but made it possible to cut expenditures on federal health programs.[29] If one accepts the assumptions of scarcity of resources and the existence of competing goals, then the question faced by health policymakers becomes how to bring about the optimum distribution of health care resources.[30] What is needed is not simply cost containment but a cost-effective health care system.[31] Former secretary of health, education, and welfare, Joseph A. Califano, Jr., has argued that one of the major problems with the U.S. health care system is that it is less cost effective than health care systems in other industrialized countries.[32] In a constrained economic environment health policymakers are confronted with making choices and establishing priorities that are not easy to make. One of the major issues in health care is that of deciding how to value health. An environment of limited resources and constantly changing health care needs requires value judgments by policymakers about priorities.[33] How much of society's resources should be devoted to health care? What priorities should be assigned to different groups competing for the same health care resources? Should more priority be given to the health care needs of the elderly or those of infants and children? Should everyone be entitled to an organ transplant, regardless of cost or the ability to pay? In recent years, a constrained economic environment has increased concerns about values of cost-effectiveness and efficiency. It has prompted some states to attempt health care rationing. This has generated significant controversy and public debate over the conflicting values of efficiency, access, and equality.

Technological Environment

Dramatic advances in health care technology in the past thirty years have revolutionized the nature and delivery of health services in the United States. The rapid pace with which new biomedical technologies are developed and the swiftness with which they are adopted have transformed many hospitals into very complex and resource-intensive institutions and changed the very nature of medical practice.[34]

New health care technologies have been linked to the problems of cost and quality of health care in the United States.[35] Since every change in technology involves costs and benefits, the formulation of a good public policy depends on an accurate assessment of their relative magnitudes. The nature of technological change can have profound effects on resource requirements.[36]

The technological revolution in biomedicine also raises questions about what medical technology should be developed and what is the proper and appropriate level of medical intervention to treat an illness. Since health care costs make up an increasing part of the government budget, the role of the government becomes crucial with respect to allocation of health care resources. Should health care technologies be available to all persons on an equal basis? If not, what criteria should be used to decide who gets scarce health resources and who does not? Should government be involved in technology assessment and play a role in encouraging or discouraging the development of particular technology through its funding? Should the government establish legal and ethical guidelines not only with respect to biomedical research but also regarding application of biomedical technology? We explore these questions in chapter 7.

Key Health Policy Actors

The key policy actors in the health care system include a variety of public and private institutions and groups: health care providers, health care practitioners, health care purchasers, health insurers, and a variety of other groups. The remainder of this chapter examines the role of the key health policy actors.

Health Care Purchasers

In 1993 federal, state, and local governments combined spent $387.9 billion to fund health care services. This represents 43.9 percent of the total national health care expenditures of $884.2 billion during the same year.[37] This alone makes the federal, state, and local governments key actors in the health care system. Since health expenditures continue to climb and require an increasingly larger share of the budget, the role of all three levels of government in health care has also increased.

The Federal Government

Today the federal government is one of the major purchasers of health care. In 1993 the federal government alone spent $280.6 billion on health care, representing 31.7 percent of total national health care expenditures.[38] The majority of federal health spending is for health services provided to low-income individuals and others eligible through Medicaid, people over sixty-five years of age through Medicare, military personnel and their dependents, veterans, federal civilian employees, and Native Americans.[39] Of these, the major bulk of the expenditures is taken up by Medicare and Medicaid programs. Medicare accounted for 53.8 percent of total federal funding for health care in 1993, with Medicaid accounting for another 27.1 percent.[40]

The three major branches of government play a crucial role in the health policy cycle. The primary policymaking responsibility lies with *Congress.* Most federal programs are implemented by numerous bureaucratic agencies in the executive branch of government. This makes the *president* and the *bureaucracy* important actors, especially during the implementation stage of the health policy cycle. In recent years the *federal courts,* especially the U.S. Supreme Court, have become major actors in the health policy cycle. The number, frequency, and complexity of legal, constitutional, and ethical issues is on the increase as a result of advances in medical technology. The federal courts are increasingly called on to resolve some of these conflicts.

The *Department of Health and Human Services* (HHS) is headed by a secretary who is appointed by the president with Senate confirmation. He or she is responsible for administering federal health care programs and activities. It advises the president and Congress on legislative measures and carries out congressional mandates in the health care (and social services) field. The Department of Health and Human Services has five operational divisions, three of them in the health care area.[41]

The *Office of Human Development Service* provides leadership and direction in the areas of human services programs for the elderly, children and youth, families, Native Americans, disabled persons, and people living in rural areas. It recommends to the secretary policies designed to improve coordination of human services programs within HHS, with other federal agencies, state and local governments, and private-sector organizations. It also supervises the use of research and impact evaluation funds.

The *Public Health Service* is responsible for conducting medical and biomedical research; developing and administering programs to prevent and control diseases and alcohol and drug abuse; providing resources, expertise, and direction in the delivery of physical and mental health services; and enforcing laws in the areas of efficacy of drugs, protection against impure and unsafe foods, cosmetics, and medical devices. The Public Health Service performs these responsibilities through its various agencies, such as the Agency for Health Care Policy and Research, Health Resources and Services Administration, Centers for Disease Control, Food and Drug Administration, Indian Health Services, and Alcohol, Drug Abuse, and Mental Health Administration. Many of these agencies are further subdivided into different components. For example, the Alcohol, Drug Abuse, and Mental Health Administration has various components that include agencies such as the National Institute on Alcohol and Alcoholism, National Institute on Drug Abuse, and National Institute of Mental Health.

The *Health Care Financing Administration* is responsible for the oversight of Medicare and Medicaid programs. It is also responsible for implementation of quality-assurance provisions of the Medicare and Medicaid programs and professional review provisions.

State and Local Governments

Because of the federal system of government, state and local governments are important actors in the health care field. During 1993, state and local governments spent $107.3 billion on health care. In 1993, about 39 percent of state and local expenditures for health were accounted for by Medicaid.[42]

The public health programs of state health agencies and local health departments are primarily involved in four program areas. These include personal health, environmental health, health resources, and laboratory services. In addition, they perform general administrative and service functions. A sizable part of state health agencies' expenditures goes for maternal and child health, mental health, communicable disease, and handicapped children.[43] State governments have traditionally been involved in licensing and accreditation of health care providers, as well as insurance regulation. In recent years, state governments have also become involved in rate setting, negotiated or competitively bid fixed-price arrangements, and health care rationing to control health care costs. Some states have also been in the forefront of health care reform. We consider the role of the states more fully in chapters 6 and 8.

Industries

Large industries and firms are also major purchasers of health care. Many major industries and firms provide health insurance coverage to their employees as part of a benefit package. Today a majority of workers in the United States are employed by firms that offer health insurance.[44] Factors that seem to have a bearing on whether employers provide health insurance benefits or not are employer size, employee job tenure, wage level, full-time work status, industry, and union membership.[45] The health insurance coverage provided by employer group insurance plans also varies widely with respect to the scope of covered services, conditions of eligibility, and the share of employee's contribution to the plan.[46]

Major industries and firms have become key actors in the health care system because of the cost they incur in providing health insurance for their workers. A survey of 2,000 companies by Foster Higgins & Company, a New York consulting firm, set the average cost of medical benefits at $3,161 per employee in 1990. This represented a 22 percent increase over the 1989 average of $2,600. Similarly, from 1988 to 1989, the average cost of medical benefits jumped 46 percent, from $2,160 to $2,600.[47] Such dramatic increases in health care costs have made businesses more conscious of their costs and have led them to use a variety of cost-cutting measures such as managed care, increased cost sharing and cost shifting, and encouraging or requiring employees to enroll in prepaid group plans for health services.

Health Care Providers

The major health care providers include health care institutions such as hospitals, nursing homes, and pharmacies, as well as health care professionals such as physicians, nurses, and dentists. They are important actors in the health care system because they not only deliver health care services but also influence the way in which services are delivered and the type of services that are delivered. The major feature of the American health care system is its entrepreneurial nature. Pharmacies and manufacturers of pharmaceutical and medical equipment and suppliers are private, profit-making enterprises. Similarly, many nursing homes are for-profit institutions. Most physicians are private practitioners.

Hospitals

In 1991 there were almost 7,000 hospitals with 1.5 million beds. [48] Hospitals have become the primary setting for the delivery of health care services because most of the sophisticated medical technology and equipment are located there. Hospitals vary by purpose and ownership. Not-for-profit hospitals (those that are community run or church affiliated) provide short-term care. States run psychiatric hospitals. The federal government operates veterans' hospitals. There are also an increasing number of proprietary or profit-making hospitals.

Since the early 1980s, the number of health corporations that own profit-making hospitals, health care facilities, and health care suppliers has grown very rapidly. Corporate medicine has become such a major American growth industry that some refer to it as the medical-industrial complex. [49] Hospital Corporation of America (HCA) is the largest hospital management company. It owns about twenty-five psychiatric hospitals. Similarly, Humana is one of the largest acute-care chain hospital companies in the United States. [50]

Nursing Homes

Today there are about 25,000 nursing homes with about 1.5 million beds. [51] An overwhelming majority of nursing homes are proprietary, that is, operated for profit. A small number of voluntary or not-for-profit nursing homes are operated by charitable organizations, mainly religious. [52] Nursing homes generally provide long-term care, and most of the people they serve are elderly. A sizable portion of their revenues comes from the government. For example, in 1993, 60 percent of nursing home revenues came from the government, with Medicaid constituting 51.7 percent and Medicare 8.8 percent of the payment. [53] Nursing homes are also heavily regulated by state and local governments.

Physicians

Physicians are key actors in the health care system because they are the primary caregivers. They enjoy considerable professional autonomy. There

↕ generalists

are about 600,000 physicians in the United States.[54] A majority of them are specialists who conduct their practices in a hospital setting. Over the years, the number of generalists or family doctors has declined considerably.[55] Physicians play a pivotal role and occupy a unique position in the health care system. Since they not only diagnose an illness but also prescribe treatment, they control the supply as well as the demand for health care services. In the process, they exert substantial influence over the pattern of health resources utilization in general and hospital resources in particular.

In addition to these key actors there are a number of other health care providers, such as 1.5 million registered nurses, 150,000 dentists,[56] and others who play if not a primary then a secondary role in influencing the health care system and health care policies.

Third-Party Payers

The U.S. health care system over the years has undergone dramatic changes. One of the fundamental changes that has occurred since the early 1930s is the method of payment for health care services. Before the rise of the modern health insurance system, the nature of financial transactions between patient and health care provider was largely a direct one-on-one transaction. Under this system the patient paid for health services directly to the health care provider out of his or her own pocket. The birth of the modern health insurance system came in 1929 with the establishment of the Blue Cross plans for hospital insurance. A third-party-payer system was created under which a consumer paid predetermined monthly premiums to an insurance company. In return, the insurance company agreed to pay the health care provider for a specified range of health services received by the consumer. The Blue Shield plans, initiated by physicians, followed, based on a similar concept. Over the years, the number of private health insurance companies increased. Between 1930 and 1950, health insurance companies not only continued to cover more and more people under such plans but also expanded the scope of coverage. In 1965 the federal government entered the picture by creating two major insurance programs—Medicare for the elderly and Medicaid for the poor.

In 1991 more than 214 million Americans, or 84.1 percent of the population, were covered by private or public health insurance plans, or sometimes both, while 13.9 percent of the population, or 34.7 million people, were uninsured.[57] Of the 214 million insured Americans, 182.1 million were insured by private insurance companies.[58] The cost of providing health coverage has risen dramatically for private health insurance companies. In 1993 private health insurers spent an estimated $273.7 billion for medical care and disability claims, compared to $143.5 billion paid in 1986 and $73.4 billion in 1980.[59]

Such cost increases and pressure from employers have led insurance companies to look for ways to cut costs as well as increase the premiums they charge. Many insurance companies have begun to develop managed care systems. The concept of managed care involves arrangements with selected providers such as health maintenance organizations (HMOs) and preferred provider organizations (PPOs) to furnish a comprehensive set of health care services to its members, formal programs for ongoing quality assurance and utilization review, explicit standards for selection of health care providers, and financial incentives for members to use providers and procedures covered by the plan.[60] The role of health insurers is changing significantly.[61] This has led Robert M. Brandon, vice-president of Citizen Action, an advocacy group, to charge that health insurance companies are engaging in "cream-skimming and cherry-picking" that eliminate or penalize firms and employees that could put them at risk of high payments, rather than offering coverage to all at rates that pool the risk. The Health Insurance Association of America, an industry group, denies such charges.[62]

Consumers

The general public can exert influence on health care policies not only as purchasers of health care but also by the perceptions, attitudes, and values they bring to the health care system as consumers. In 1993 consumers spent $157.5 billion in out-of-pocket expenses for health services (17.8 percent) out of a total of an estimated $884.2 billion national health care expenditures.[63]

The public's perception of the American health care system is negative. A study examining the public's feeling about health care systems found that of the ten countries included in the study, the lowest degree of satisfaction with health care systems was in the United States and the highest was in Canada.[64] Surveys by the *Los Angeles Times* in March 1990, NBC in 1989, and Louis Harris & Associates in 1988 all showed that majorities of at least 61 percent of those polled supported establishing a Canadian-style comprehensive national health system. Despite escalating health care costs, the general public also shows a preference for more spending for health care, but they themselves do not want to pay the bill. They want the government to pay the cost of health care.[65] In 1987 a Harris poll asked a random sample of 1,250 Americans whether some limit should be set, say $5 million, on what we can afford to spend to save a life. Fifty-one percent of the respondents said that no limit should be set.[66] Surveys also show that

Americans want more health care, not less. About half of all Americans believe that the United States spends too little on health care. Polls also suggest that the public does not believe the increased health care costs have been matched by similar increases in the quality of treatment.[67]

Those who are dissatisfied with the current system cite the high cost of care and lack of access—lack of availability of health care or health insurance —as primary reasons for their dissatisfaction. While a majority of Americans express a preference for a Canadian-style national health system, many also think that a government-run system would adversely affect their freedom of choice and lower quality of care, and they express doubt that such a system would lower costs.[68] Public dissatisfaction with the current health care system leads many people to support a change, but they are also ambivalent about the options that would change the system.

Such perceptions and attitudes in the general public present interesting dilemmas and value conflicts for health policymakers. The general public does not want to pay the bill but wants more spending on health care by the government. On their part, health policymakers concerned with the impact of escalating health care costs on the budget want to contain costs and at the same time provide access to quality care for all Americans.

Interest Groups

The role of interest groups in American politics has been debated intensely from the time of the founding of the Republic. The philosophy of interest-group liberalism has accorded interest groups a dominant role in American politics. Proponents have praised interest groups for advancing the cause of American democracy by providing access for citizen participation in the political process. Opponents have argued that special interests are stealing America[69] and destroying democracy.[70] Regardless of how one feels about interest groups, there is no denying the fact that they have become important political power brokers in American politics.[71] Since the 1970s, American society has also witnessed a rise in the number of public interest groups, that is, citizens' lobbies, to counter the influence of special interest groups in American politics.[72] Public interest groups presumably champion the cause of the public interest or the common good, while special or private interest groups work to advance narrow causes for the benefit of their members.[73]

Health care affects everyone in society. A wide variety of interests— health care providers, purchasers, third-party payers, suppliers, consumers —are affected by what happens within the field of health care. Thus it is not too surprising that the number and variety of interest groups involved in health care politics and policymaking is very large.[74] For example, over

1,000 health-related groups are listed in the *Encyclopedia of Associations*.[75]

The universal nature of illness gives health care professionals such as physicians important psychological and political leverage. Given their unique position, they are able to influence developments in the health care field. The introduction of government-sponsored health insurance programs such as Medicare and Medicaid has also made hospitals and skilled nursing facilities important players. The technical nature of modern medicine gives drug and medical supply companies significant leverage in the health field. Similarly, insurance companies as third-party payers have also come to play an important role.[76]

One of the major ways in which these groups try to influence the political process is through their political action committees (PACs). According to an analysis by the Center for Responsive Politics, a Washington-based research group, health PACs accounted for 6 percent of all campaign contributions in the 1987–88 election cycle. Health PACs gave nearly $10 million to congressional candidates. The largest donor among health PACs was the political action committee of the AMA. Pharmaceutical and other health-product manufacturers were the next largest segment, followed by hospitals and nursing homes.[77] By the 1991–92 election cycle, the 199 health-related PACs had given almost $13 million in congressional elections.[78]

While it is impossible to discuss all the interest groups involved in the health care field, some of the major groups should be mentioned. Many of them are professional or trade associations of key actors in the health care field.

American Medical Association

The American Medical Association (AMA) is one of the largest and most influential health-related groups.[79] It is a professional association of physicians with a membership of about 283,000.[80] It is the voice of organized medicine and as such acts as an umbrella organization of American medicine. Its main functions include representing the interests of its members, providing scientific and socioeconomic information, keeping data on the profession, and developing and maintaining standards of professional education, training, and performance.[81]

The AMA has grassroots political power and is very active in lobbying Congress on health-related issues. It is very well financed. It has one of the largest political action committees. During the 1991–92 election cycle, the American Medical Political Action Committee (AMPAC) spent $2.3 million on contributions to congressional candidates, "with another $1 million in 'independent expenditures.' "[82] AMPAC ranked fourth among all PACs in overall spending and third in contributions to federal candidates.[83]

The AMA has acted as a voice of free enterprise and fee-for-service independent medical practice in the health care field. Much of its effort has been directed toward protecting the economic interests of its members and opposing policies that threaten those interests or threaten their professional autonomy. For example, for a long time the AMA has successfully argued against a national health insurance program because of the fear of losing its professional autonomy and a decline in physicians' income. But, the organization has articulated its opposition to national health insurance not on the ground of protecting self-interest but by using the rhetoric of defending free enterprise and patients' freedom to choose their own doctors. It has argued that adoption of national health insurance would lead to lower quality of health care and services. The AMA has not been above using scare tactics to achieve its objectives.

The AMA is not the only physician group that has attempted to influence the political process. PACs representing such specialists as pathologists, plastic surgeons, anesthesiologists, chiropractors, and emergency physicians also contributed funds to political campaigns.[84]

American Hospital Association

The National Hospital Superintendents' Association was created in 1899. The membership in this organization was limited to chief executive officers of hospitals. A few years after the organization's founding, its name was changed to the American Hospital Association (AHA). In 1917 it changed from an individual membership organization to an organization of institutions.[85] Today, the AHA represents individuals and health care institutions including hospitals, health care systems, and pre- and postacute health care delivery organizations. It has a membership of about 45,000. In addition to conducting research and education projects, it acts as the voice of hospitals and represents their interests in national health care legislation.[86]

Hospital and other health care groups' political action committees are relatively small compared to AMPAC, but they are increasing their political power by raising more money for their political activities. The AHA's political action committee's spending has been relatively small compared to AMPAC's; however, in recent years there has been a significant growth of PACs among state hospital associations.[87]

Health Insurance Association of America

The Health Insurance Association of America (HIAA) was founded in 1956 and has a membership of 350 companies. It represents the voice of accident

and health insurance companies. Through HIAA the health insurance industry attempts to present a united front. This has led some to criticize the
health cost-containment record of the insurance companies and suggest that
insurers have colluded to prevent cost containment.[88] It has been argued
that health insurers have advocated policies aimed at reducing the competitive pressures on themselves by investing resources in seeking legislation
designed to suppress competition.[89]

Among the health insurers, two of the major commercial insurers are
Blue Cross and Blue Shield. The Blue Cross plans were developed by the
hospitals through the AHA, while the Blue Shield plans were developed by
physicians through the AMA. In 1988, of the 182.3 million Americans
insured by private insurance companies, an estimated 74 million were covered by Blue Cross and Blue Shield.[90]

American Health Care Association

The American Health Care Association is a federation of state associations
of long-term health care facilities with a membership of 9,800. It provides
continuing education to nursing home personnel and promotes standards for
professionals in long-term-care delivery. The organization focuses on issues
of availability, quality, affordability, and fair payment in health care. The
American Health Care Association also maintains a liaison with government agencies, Congress, and other professional health care associations.[91]

Other Groups

A number of other groups represent hospital equipment suppliers and manufacturers of drugs and health care products and attempt to influence health
care politics and policies. The increased cost of providing health care to
employees has led many businesses and industries to form health coalitions
to search for solutions to spiraling health care costs. Such coalitions are
rapidly expanding in number.[92] Some of the major health coalitions include
the Alliance of Business for Cost Containment, the Coalition on Health
Care Costs, Quality, and Access, the National Leadership Coalition for
Health Care Reforms, and the Washington Business Group on Health,
among many others. A consortium of business groups representing small
companies called the Partnership on Health Care & Employment was
formed to oppose legislative proposals requiring all employers to offer
health insurance to its employees. It includes the chamber of commerce, the
American Farm Bureau Federation, the National Restaurant Association,
and about 350 corporations.[93]

The number of health-related public interest groups has also increased. One of the most active groups is Ralph Nader's Health Research Group, founded in 1971. Its main objectives include protecting consumers and increasing public awareness on a variety of health issues.[94] Similarly, the National Insurance Consumer Organization was established in 1980 to help consumers buy insurance wisely and to serve as a consumer advocate on public policy matters.[95] Public interest groups typically rely on methods such as coalition forming, litigation, lobbying, testifying before congressional committees, and participation in regulatory proceedings and such to influence health care policies.

Conclusions

Health care politics and policies in the United States are shaped by a variety of factors. Health policy reflects a combination of initiatives taken by institutions and actors in the public and private sectors. The health policy cycle is influenced and shaped by the constitutional, institutional, political, economic, ideological, and technological environment within which it operates. The public philosophy of interest-group liberalism combined with constitutionally guaranteed freedom of speech, association, and petition allow a variety of interest groups to promote policies for private profit and successfully defeat policies they perceive as harmful to their interests. Interest groups promote their narrow private interests using the rhetoric of the common good. The consensus created through compromise and bargaining between narrow private interests is often defined as the public interest. Such a policy process makes the establishment of a comprehensive national health policy highly improbable, if not impossible. The result is a series of health care programs and policies that often reflects conflicting values of access, equality, quality of care, and efficiency.

2
Health Care Policy in the United States

There are substantial differences in the health care systems of various countries. They differ with respect to financing, delivery of health care, and the role of the government. Today there are three primary models of health care. In a *mostly private* health care system, workers and their dependents are covered through private insurance, even though the insurance is generally bought through employers. Government provides public insurance programs for those not covered by private insurance. Health care is delivered mostly by private hospitals and doctors. The United States is an example of such a system. Other countries have a health care system that is *mostly public*. Health care is paid out of general taxation or through payroll taxes. It is provided by publicly owned hospitals and salaried doctors. Examples of countries with such a system include Great Britain, Sweden, and Italy. The third model of health care system is a *hybrid* model. In such a system, health care is mostly publicly financed, generally through payroll taxes, but is delivered by private hospitals and doctors. Germany, Japan, Canada, France, and Holland exhibit variants of this model. But it is important to keep in mind that none of the countries follows these models in their purest form. In reality, most countries incorporate public and private elements in their health care systems.[1]

As mentioned, the U.S. health care system follows the model of the mostly private health care system. A majority of Americans are covered through private insurance, usually bought through their employers. The government provides public insurance programs to cover the health care needs of groups such as the poor, the elderly, and veterans. Nevertheless, public insurance programs do not cover all uninsured Americans. A sizable number of individuals who cannot afford private health insurance for one reason or another are not covered by public programs.

The United States spends proportionately more money on health care than all other Western industrialized nations. Statistics compiled by the Organization for Economic Cooperation and Development (OECD) indicate that in 1989 health spending in the United States amounted to 11.8 percent of gross domestic product (GDP), compared to 8.7 percent for France and Canada, 8.2 percent for Germany, 6.7 percent for Japan, and 5.8 percent for Britain. Similarly, during the same year the United States spent $2,354 per person on health care, compared to $1,683 in Canada, $1,274 in France, $1,232 in Germany, $1,035 in Japan, and $836 in Britain. By 1993, the United States was spending almost 14 percent of GDP on health care, an average of $3,299 per person.[2]

Despite the fact that the United States spends proportionately more money on health care than most other Western countries, it does not rank very high on many health care indicators. For example, the United States has a higher infant mortality rate, 9.7 per 1,000 live births, than the countries mentioned above. It has the lowest life expectancy at birth, 71.5 years for males, among the same countries.[3] The U.S. health care system also has other problems. Health care costs continue to soar. The number of uninsured Americans continues to rise and is currently estimated to be around 37 million. Many hospitals in large cities are reporting long waiting lines in emergency rooms, with many Medicaid patients leaving in frustration without receiving treatment.[4] The City Hospital Visiting Committee, in its recent annual report, described hospital care in New York City's municipal hospitals as the worst in recent memory.[5] Rising malpractice insurance costs are forcing many of the nation's community health centers to cut or eliminate services for low-income patients.[6] Law enforcement officials in several states are investigating one of the nation's largest private psychiatric hospital chains, Psychiatric Institutes of America, on charges that it systematically misdiagnosed, mistreated, and abused patients to increase its profits from insurance claims.[7]

As mentioned in chapter 1, a majority of Americans express very low satisfaction with the U.S. health care system and believe that increased health care expenditures have not been matched by similar increases in the quality of treatment. The American health care system has been referred to as "broken,"[8] "sick,"[9] "a disgrace,"[10] "wasteful,"[11] "built for waste,"[12] and "scandalous."[13] It is not too surprising, then, that 60 percent of Americans believe that fundamental changes are needed in the U.S. health care system, while another 29 percent believe that the entire system should be rebuilt.[14]

In this chapter we examine the historical development of health care policies in the United States. We discuss private- and public-sector policy initiatives and various factors that have shaped health care policy. The major emphasis is on the development of federal health care policies and how these policies have attempted to address the goals of equity, quality, and efficiency. The chapter also briefly explores the roles of state and local governments.

Health Care in the Nineteenth Century

The progress of medicine, or the "healing arts," was very slow in the 1700s and 1800s. Neither health care or the biosciences received a great deal of popular support in the United States in the early 1800s. The biological sciences were not very popular with the general public. During the 1840s, a proposal for the establishment of a National Institute of Science, funded by the federal government, was rejected repeatedly by Congress. Finally, during the Civil War, the National Academy of Sciences was established in 1863 on the grounds of its usefulness to the Union armies.[15]

The American Medical Association was formed in 1847. During the latter part of the nineteenth century, physicians and pharmacists were the sole dispensers of professionally recognized health services. Most physicians were trained through apprenticeships with practicing physicians. Physicians also established "diploma mills" to train several students at a time. Later, private and public schools set up medical schools to train physicians. Physicians made their living treating patients for fees and received very little money from the government. The same was true of pharmacists, who later developed drugstores to supplement their income from prescriptions. Thus, private practice and fee for service became firmly established in the early American health care system.[16]

During the nineteenth century, public health activities were devoted to preventing the spread of communicable diseases and were confined primarily to major cities until the Civil War. In response to epidemics, a city board or commission was appointed to establish regulations for the maintenance of a sanitary environment. Only after the Civil War did state boards of health become popular. By the end of the nineteenth century, boards of health had been established within the governments of most large cities and at the state level. Their functions were limited to enforcement of sanitary regulations and control of certain communicable diseases. The scope of the health departments did not expand until the turn of the century.[17] Public health services were separated from the private practice of medicine, and public health officers were not allowed to practice medicine.

General hospitals, as we know them today, did not exist. Poorhouses and almshouses provided care for destitute persons. The origin of a hospital system in the United States is associated with the establishment of the first

Marine Hospital in 1799.[18] Both the army and navy had their own require-
ments for treating sickness, and they differed from the U.S. Marine Service.
Between 1830 and 1860, marine hospitals proliferated. During the Civil
War, the Marine Hospital System was very much neglected and the number
of hospitals decreased. In 1869, Congress reviewed the Marine Hospital
System and passed the first Reorganization Act in 1870. Under this law, the
Marine Hospital Service was federalized and formally organized as a na-
tional agency with a central headquarters.[19]

The building of mental hospitals also preceded the development of personal health services. Mental hospitals were and continue to be largely
publicly owned and operated.

The last quarter of the nineteenth century saw a steady advance in medical science. Antiseptic surgery was highly developed by 1875. The science
of microbiology was introduced, and techniques of vaccination were developed. The advent of anesthesia and antisepsis made general hospitals a
relatively safe place for surgery. The early general hospitals were established mostly by voluntary community boards and churches. The growing
economy made it possible for hospitals to obtain capital funds from philan-
thropists and operating funds from paying patients. Voluntary hospitals,
because of their charitable and nonprofit charters, were obligated to provide
care for the poor. Physicians began to admit patients to hospitals for surgeries. Patients paid for hospital charges and physicians' fees. In return, hospitals provided physicians with their facilities to provide free care for the
poor. In 1875 there were very few general hospitals in the country. By
1900, there were about 4,000 general hospitals in the United States.[20]

The Transformation of American Medicine: 1900–1935

During the first decade of the twentieth century, the process of consolidation of medical education and the transformation of American medicine
began to take shape. For a number of years, the American Medical Association (AMA) had been trying to force inferior medical schools to close in
order to reduce the numbers of institutions competing for philanthropic
support.[21] Reform of medical schools was the top priority of the AMA. The
Council on Medical Education, established by the AMA in 1904, elevated
and standardized requirements for medical education for physicians. In addition, in order to identify and pressure weaker institutions, the council
began to grade medical schools and later extended its evaluation to include
curriculum, facilities, faculty, and requirements for admissions.[22]

Philanthropic foundations often had power and influence, but they lacked
authority. Their financial power was limited by their fear that legislatures

that chartered them would restrict their power or tax them out of existence. Nevertheless, placing medical education on a more scientific basis had also become their top priority. Several foundations began to finance studies that recommended reorganization of medical education and medical care. The AMA Council invited an outside group, the Carnegie Foundation for the Advancement of Teaching, to investigate medical schools. Abraham Flexner, as a representative of the Carnegie Foundation, visited each of the medical schools in the country during 1909 and 1910. He saw a great discrepancy between medical science and medical education. His report, known as the *Flexner Report,* was published in 1910 and recommended adoption of the German model of medicine with scientifically based training, the strengthening of first-class medical schools, and the elimination of a great majority of inferior schools.

Following the Flexner Report, the process of consolidation of medical education proceeded at a rapid pace. By 1915, the number of medical schools had decreased from 131 to 95. Similarly, the number of graduates from medical schools dropped from 5,440 to 3,536. Mergers between class A and class B schools became common. The AMA Council became a national accrediting agency for medical schools, and many states came to accept its judgments regarding medical schools. The new system increased the homogeneity and cohesiveness of the medical profession and made the AMA a powerful force in American medicine.[23]

Another significant development during this period was the rise of the *third-party payment system* in American medicine. Prior to the 1930s, medical insurance programs were nonexistent. During the Great Depression of the 1930s, the income of hospitals and physicians declined. Many people could not afford to pay hospitals or physicians for their medical services. Realizing that they could operate better with a steady income, hospitals began to sponsor prepayment plans, which came to be known as the *Blue Cross plans.* Similarly, prepayment plans for physicians' services in the hospital, especially surgery, also began to appear. Sponsored by state medical societies, they became known as *Blue Shield plans.* Both the Blue Cross and Blue Shield plans were very successful. During the 1940s, the federal government encouraged the development of private, voluntary insurance plans. For example, Congress gave voluntary plans a financial boost by legislating that health insurance and pensions were fringe benefits and exempt from a wartime freeze on wages. Thus, employers could offer their workers health care fringe benefits by paying for part or all of the cost of their insurance premiums. A ruling by the Internal Revenue Service in 1951 that employers' costs for premiums were a tax-deductible expense made large-scale development of private health insurance viable.

The rise of third-party payment led to increases in visits to physicians and admissions to hospitals. The third-party payment system replaced the financing system based on one-on-one financial transactions between patient and physician. Third-party payers insulated health care consumers from the realities of health care costs, leading to overconsumption, a problem called "moral hazard" by economists. Physicians and hospitals prospered. Since insurance companies reimbursed hospitals for the charges and/ or costs of hospitals services received by the patient, third-party payments made hospitals financially secure and independent because they could count on a steady income. Physicians prospered because they were paid by voluntary health insurance according to generous fee schedules negotiated by the Blue Shield plans.

The Role of the Federal Government

The Beginnings: 1800s

During much of the nineteenth century, the role of the federal government in health care was limited to providing public health services. In 1798 President John Adams signed into law an act that provided for the relief of sick and disabled seamen. This led to the development of marine hospitals during the nineteenth century. The American Public Health Association (APHA), composed mainly of social workers, was founded in 1872. Its main concern was the social and economic aspects of health problems. Following the Civil War, Congress in 1878 passed a National Quarantine Act for the purpose of preventing entry into the country of persons with communicable diseases. The period from 1870 to 1910 witnessed the maturation of the government's public health services. Health boards and health departments became widespread features of local and state governments; their functions were limited to the enforcement of sanitary regulations and control of communicable diseases. The AMA began to attack all proposals designed to extend the role of government in health care.

Limited Federal Role: 1900–1930

During the late nineteenth and early part of the twentieth century, countries in Europe were establishing compulsory sickness insurance programs. Germany established the first national system of compulsory sickness insurance in 1883. Similar systems were established in Austria in 1888, Hungary in 1891, Norway in 1910, Britain in 1911, Russia in 1912, and the Netherlands in 1913. France and Italy required sickness insurance only in a few industries. Countries such as Sweden, Denmark, and Switzerland gave extensive state aid to voluntary funds and provided incentives for membership.[24]

The federal government in the United States, in contrast to happenings in Europe, took no action to subsidize voluntary funds or make sickness insurance mandatory. This partly reflected existing political conditions and institutions in the United States, where, as a result of the influence of the public philosophy of classical liberalism, government was highly decentralized and played a very small role in regulation of the economy or in promoting social welfare.

Health insurance became a political issue in the United States on the eve of World War I. The progress of a workmen's compensation law between 1910 and 1913 encouraged reformers to believe that adoption of compulsory insurance against industrial accidents would lead to the adoption of compulsory sickness insurance. But the progressive reformers' hopes of strengthening government and adopting compulsory sickness insurance were soon dashed. Their reform proposals were defeated by opposition from physicians and pharmaceutical and insurance companies. In addition, both labor unions and business, fearing competition from government in social welfare programs, failed to support the reformers. By 1920, the movement for compulsory sickness insurance had faded from the political agenda.

Under pressure from the labor movement and children's advocates, Congress passed the Sheppard-Towner Act in 1921. It established the first federal grant-in-aid program for local child health clinics. But many local health departments refused to accept these grants because the AMA and local medical societies strongly opposed the program. Congress allowed the program to terminate in 1928.[25] Thus, the federal government's role in health care remained very limited during the nineteenth and early twentieth centuries.

Expansion of Health Facilities and Services: 1930–1960

A number of significant developments took place in the health care field during the 1930s. One major development, as mentioned earlier, was the start of a third-party payment system with the establishment of the Blue Cross and Blue Shield insurance plans. This revolutionized health care financing and led to employer-based health insurance programs. A second development concerned advances in medical technology and the discovery of antibiotics. Antibiotics changed the focus of medical care from prevention of disease through inoculation and hygiene to cure of illnesses.[26] For the first time, sulfa drugs and penicillin gave physicians their true power to cure.[27] The third development was the shift from local control of health and welfare issues to state and especially federal government control. Workmen's compensation, pensions, unemployment insurance, and certain medical services came to be perceived by the people as the responsibility of the federal government.[28] This was because of the Great Depression and the economic problems of state and local governments. The problems facing the country were too small for any but federal solutions.

The establishment of the National Institutes of Health (NIH) in 1930, with a broad mandate for ascertaining the cause, prevention, and cure of disease, reflected the increased role of the federal government in health care in general and public health services in particular. It also paved the way for public funding of biomedical research through NIH and later through the National Science Foundation (NSF). In 1934, during the Great Depression, the Federal Emergency Relief Administration gave the first federal grants to local governments for public assistance to the poor, including financial support for medical care.

During the depression, there was also an increased demand for social insurance as differentiated from insurance against specific risks. Most Western countries had placed a higher priority on establishing health insurance programs as a natural outgrowth of insurance against industrial accidents. Old-age pensions and unemployment insurance programs received a lower priority in these countries. In the United States, with millions of people out of work as a result of the depression, unemployment insurance and old-age pensions received the higher priority. Thus the United States, rather than move in the direction of providing free medical care or reimbursement for its costs, as many Western European countries had done, attempted to supply more general social security benefits.

The *Social Security Act of 1935* provided for unemployment compensation, old-age pensions, and other benefits. The early planning of the legislation had initially included health insurance as part of the package. But the Roosevelt administration did not want to jeopardize the enactment of the entire law because of strong opposition to health insurance by the medical profession. Therefore, national health insurance was omitted from the final legislative proposal. The Social Security Act did extend the role of the federal government in health care by including provisions designed to strengthen public health services. These provisions called for federal matching grants-in-aid to states for maternal and infant care and diagnosis and treatment of crippled children. Federal grants were also made available for general public health purposes under the administration of the U.S. Public Health Service (USPHS), which had evolved in 1912 from the Marine Hospital Service.

In 1937 Congress passed the *National Cancer Act.* It established the National Cancer Institute (NCI) and set a national pattern for the federal support of biomedical research. The law authorized the NCI to conduct research in its own laboratories and to award grants to nongovernment scientists and institutions for training scientists and clinicians.

During 1935–36 the USPHS conducted a national health survey that revealed many untreated diseases in the population, especially in low-income groups. This led Senator Robert Wagner (D-N.Y.), sponsor of the Social Security Act, to introduce an amendment to the act that would have provided federal grants to the states for the organization of health insurance plans covering workers and their dependents. The onset of World War II postponed any serious consideration of such a plan.[29] Similar attempts at establishing a health insurance program under the Truman administration were defeated during the 1940s. The medical profession had succeeded in defeating proposals for any national health insurance.

After the war, the Truman administration called for the expansion of hospitals, increased support for public health, maternal and child health services, and federal aid for medical research and education. The administration's aim was to expand the country's medical resources and facilities, reduce the financial burden for their use, and in the process expand access to medical care.[30] One major problem was that no new hospital construction took place during the depression or World War II, a period of some sixteen years.

In 1946 Congress passed the *National Hospital Survey and Construction Act,* also known as the *Hill-Burton Act.* This program provided federal funds to subsidize construction of hospitals in areas of bed shortages, mainly in rural counties. State public health agencies were made responsible for surveying the hospital bed supply in each state and developing a master plan for the construction of new hospitals. They were also assigned the task of inspecting and licensing all hospitals and related facilities.

Physicians welcomed Hill-Burton funds and actively sought them for construction of new hospitals for reasons of prestige, convenience, and service. Many physicians did not have privileges to treat their patients in the limited number of hospitals that were in existence. These physicians, faced with a limited supply of hospitals and beds and restricted access to them, supported the construction of new hospitals in the hope that they would enjoy the privilege of treating their patients in newly constructed hospitals. In addition, local pressure favoring nearby facilities, tax-favored bonds, and assured income from insurance companies and later from Medicare contributed to the proliferation of hospitals.[31]

As the number of hospitals increased, a nongovernmental Joint Commission on Accreditation of Hospitals was established in 1952. Between 1947 and 1966, the number of voluntary, not-for-profit hospitals increased from 2,584 to 3,426. During the same period, state and local government general hospitals increased from 785 to 1,453. The total number of hospitals (for-profit, state and local government, and voluntary not-for-profit) increased from 4,445 to 5,736. The rate of hospital admission per 1,000 population increased from 54 in 1935 to 129 in 1960.[32]

Congress, in 1946, also passed the *National Mental Health Act.* This law provided federal grants to states for research, prevention, diagnosis, and treatment of mental disorders. During the 1950s, there was also further expansion of public health services at the federal level. The NIH greatly expanded support of biomedical research. By the end of the 1950s, the role of the federal government in health care had increased significantly compared to its role in the early 1900s. There was a corresponding increase in the role of state and local governments in the field of public health services.

Increasing Access to Health Care: The 1960s

From the 1920s to the 1950s, efforts at establishing a system of national health care or insurance for the entire population had failed because of charges from the medical profession and others that such plans would constitute "socialized medicine." The concept of socialized medicine went against the general public philosophy of classical liberalism, which advocates a limited role for government, and the specific philosophy of interest-group liberalism, wherein different interest groups exercise countervailing veto power over governmental policy decisions.

Faced with opposition to comprehensive change, advocates of a national system of health care or insurance changed their strategy and objectives. They began to advocate increasing access to health care for the needy. Rather than push for a universal coverage under which the federal government would provide health insurance to all on a compulsory basis, they began to push for a limited system of health insurance for specific needy groups such as the elderly. The elderly were a perfect target group for providing help because of their greater medical need, inadequate financial resources, and the loss of employment-based group medical insurance upon retirement. Additionally, the elderly were deemed worthy and were not stigmatized as a failed group, as were welfare recipients. The health care problems of the elderly would be faced by most of us; almost everyone grows old, after all. This new approach also accommodated the federal structure of government by emphasizing that such programs would be administered by state governments with the federal government providing financial aid to states.

The end result was the passage of the *Kerr-Mills Act* (also known as the *Medical Assistance Act*) by Congress in 1960. The law provided federal matching payments to states for vendor (provider) payments and allowed states to include the medically needy (i.e., elderly, blind, and disabled persons with low income who were not on public assistance). The act also suggested the scope of services to be covered, such as hospitals, nursing homes, physicians, and other health services. It also required each state to plan for institutional and noninstitutional care as a condition of federal cost sharing. State participation in the program was optional and states were left free to determine eligibility and the extent of services provided. Most important, the act established the concept of "medical indigency."

The Kerr-Mills program proved to be neither effective nor adequate.[33] It failed to provide significant relief for a substantial portion of the elderly population. An investigation by the Senate Subcommittee on the Health of the Elderly in 1963 revealed that only 1 percent of the nation's elderly received help under the program. The report also highlighted several other problems such as stringent eligibility rules and high administrative costs of state governments.[34] Clearly, the issue of financing health care for the elderly had not been resolved and remained on the political agenda.

The Kennedy administration, on assuming office in 1961, was committed to increasing access to health care for millions of Americans. Having won a narrow victory in the 1960 presidential election, however, President Kennedy was not in a position to push for a universal insurance program. He faced a Congress that was not very amenable to his legislative proposals. He hoped that the 1962 congressional elections would produce a more receptive Congress. But he was able to keep the issue of health care needs of the elderly alive and on the political agenda.[35] On 21 February 1963, Kennedy delivered his "Special Message on Aiding Our Senior Citizens." The message contained thirty-nine legislative recommendations. The key proposal was Medicare to meet the medical needs of the elderly. It had two objectives. One was protection against the cost of serious illness. The other was to serve as a base of insurance protection on which supplementary private programs could be added.[36] The assassination of Kennedy in November 1963 left the task of carrying on the battle for Medicare to his successor, Lyndon Johnson.

Lyndon Johnson adopted most of John F. Kennedy's unfinished legislative proposals and incorporated them into the Great Society's War on Poverty program. After civil rights, Medicare was second in priority with the Johnson administration. Johnson saw Medicare as an essential part of his War on Poverty.[37] Johnson won a landslide victory in the 1964 presidential election, which allowed him to claim a public mandate for his programs.

Equally important was the fact that Democrats also won major victories in congressional elections. The administration now had enough votes in the House and the Senate for the passage of its health care proposals.

Health insurance was at the top of the legislative agenda in 1965. The Johnson administration proposed hospital insurance for the elderly, financed through payroll taxes. Republicans offered a proposal for subsidized, voluntary insurance for the aged including coverage for physicians' services financed through general revenues. The AMA opposed both plans and advocated expansion of the Kerr-Mills program of matching grants to the states for vendor payments for the needy. Both opponents and proponents used traditional concepts, symbols, and clichés in the debate. Opponents, especially the AMA and insurance companies, opposed the Johnson administration's proposal on the grounds that it was compulsory, it represented socialized medicine, it would reduce the quality of care, and it was "un-American." The proponents defended the plan as designed to help the needy by providing them with access to medical care and thus compatible with American ideals of equity and equality.[38]

Congress in 1965 passed the *Medicare* program for the elderly and *Medicaid* program for the poor as amendments to the Social Security Act of 1935. This final product was a classic compromise between three competing proposals. It included a compulsory health insurance program for the elderly, financed through payroll taxes (Medicare Part A, the Johnson administration proposal), a voluntary insurance program for physicians' services subsidized through general revenues (Medicare Part B, the Republican proposal), and an expanded means-tested program administered by the states (Medicaid, the AMA proposal).

In addition to Medicare and Medicaid, a number of other health programs, such as Maternal and Infant Care (MIC), the Children Supplemental Feeding Program, and community health centers were created during the 1960s as part of Johnson's War on Poverty.

The principal objective of the Medicare and Medicaid programs was to provide equal access to health care for the elderly and the poor. Both programs dramatically increased access to health care.[39] Medicare helped alleviate substantial financially related barriers to equal access to health care that existed before the program's enactment.[40] It greatly expanded financial access to acute care for the elderly and disabled.[41]

In recent years, concern over rising health care costs and efforts at cost containment have led to tradeoffs between cost containment and access to health care. This created new problems and gaps in access to health care. The next section provides a brief overview of the federal government's efforts at health care cost containment. Chapter 6 provides a more detailed examination and evaluation of major policy initiatives undertaken by federal and state governments, as well as the private sector, to contain health care costs.

Efforts at Health Care Cost Containment: 1970s–1980s

The 1970s represented a decade of transition in the American health care system. Prior to this time, federal health care policy was shaped by a number of assumptions. One of the major assumptions was that the health care system suffered from too few health care facilities and services. The health care system needed more hospitals, physicians, technology, and biomedical research. Biomedical research was encouraged through federal funds for the National Institutes of Health, while new hospital construction was encouraged with federal funds provided through the Hill-Burton program. The second assumption was that one of the serious problems with the health care system was limited financial access to health care among disadvantaged citizens. The establishment of Medicare and Medicaid by the federal government was an effort to increase access to health care for the needy. The third assumption was that competitive markets and regulatory strategies do not work in the health care field.[42]

By the 1970s these assumptions had come under increased scrutiny. As we discussed earlier in the chapter, the Hill-Burton program led to a significant expansion in the number of voluntary, not-for-profit, and state and local government hospitals. Policymakers came to recognize that the health care system was too large. This was in sharp contrast to the assumption before the 1960s that the health care system was too small. By the 1970s there was an increasing concern with the nation's sizable surplus of hospital beds and physicians. There was a realization that one of the reasons for increased health care costs was unconstrained diffusion of biomedical technology and an excess supply of hospitals and physicians, which encouraged excessive tests and treatments. Similarly, while Medicare and Medicaid had increased financial access to health care for the elderly and the needy, increased access had also led to increases in health care costs. From the beginning, outlays for Medicare and Medicaid greatly exceeded initial projections. When Medicare was established, the federal government had deliberately chosen to reimburse physicians in a generous manner to win their political support.

By the 1970s health care costs had risen dramatically. Total national health care expenditure increased from $27.1 billion in 1960 to $74.3 billion in 1970. During this same period, federal health care expenditures increased from $2.9 billion to $17.8 billion, while state and local govern-

Table 2.1

Selected Health Care Expenditures, 1960–93
(in billions of dollars)

	1960	1970	1980	1990	1993[a]
National health expenditures	27.1	74.3	251.1	696.6	884.2
Federal health expenditures	2.9	17.8	72.0	195.8	280.6
State and local health expenditures	3.7	9.9	33.3	90.7	107.3
Hospital health care	9.3	28.0	102.7	256.5	326.6
Physician services	5.3	13.6	45.2	140.5	171.2
Medicare expenditures		7.1	36.4	109.6	151.1
Medicaid expenditures[b]		5.3	24.8	71.7	112.8

Sources: Katharine R. Levit, "National Health Expenditures, 1993," *Health Care Financing Review* 16, no. 1 (Fall 1994): 282–84. Medicare and Medicaid expenditures for 1970 are from Robert M. Gibson and Daniel R. Waldo, "National Health Expenditures, 1980," *Health Care Financing Review* 3, no. 1 (September 1981): 46.

[a]Figures for 1993 are estimates.

[b]Medicaid figures combine federal and state/local expenditures.

ments' health care expenditures increased from $3.7 billion to $9.9 billion. Similar increases were evident in hospital care and physician services.[43] From 1966 to 1970, Medicare expenditures increased from $1.6 billion to $7.1 billion, while Medicaid expenditures increased from $1.3 billion to $5.3 billion. Increases in medical care inflation outstripped overall inflation. (See Tables 2.1–2.3.)[44]

Policymakers' concerns began to shift from providing access and quality health care to containing rising health care costs. Ironically, there was an increased tolerance for government regulation of the health care system and at the same time encouragement of a competitive market strategy to contain health care costs. During the 1970s and 1980s, the federal government and the states undertook a number of regulatory and market-oriented policy initiatives in an effort to contain costs. These policy initiatives are examined in more detail in chapter 6, which discusses cost containment.

During its first two years in office, the Nixon administration proposed only moderate changes in the health care programs and proposed to hold the line on appropriations. In fact, President Nixon signed into law various acts designed to extend community mental health centers, migrant health centers, and programs designed to support training of health care personnel, among others.

Beginning in 1971, the Nixon administration sought to curtail health care programs. In his health message to Congress on 18 February 1971, Nixon

Table 2.2

Percentage Change in Health Care Expenditures
(average change per year)

	1960–70	1970–80	1980–90	1990–93
National health expenditures	17.8	23.1	30.4	11.7
Federal health expenditures	49.0	30.1	17.6	16.1
State and local health expenditures	18.1	29.8	16.2	16.7
Hospital health care	20.5	25.8	15.7	13.4
Physician services	15.1	22.6	17.0	11.0
Medicare expenditures		40.1	21.2	12.5
Medicaid expenditures[a]		37.7	19.7	33.4

Source: Calculated from Table 2.1.
[a]Medicaid figures combine federal and state/local expenditures.

argued that "costs have skyrocketed but values have not kept pace. We are investing more of our nation's resources in the health of our people but we are not getting full return on our investment."[45] Nixon sought curtailment in federal categorical grant programs and vetoed legislation designed to renew and expand these programs. He also relied on the strategy of impounding funds already appropriated. A struggle between the executive branch, headed by a Republican president, and a Congress controlled by Democrats ensued. The Democratic Congress was able to override some of Nixon's vetoes and the battle over impoundment of funds ended up in the federal courts. It also ultimately led Congress in 1974 to enact the Congressional Budget and Impoundment Control Act, which Nixon signed into law a few days before he resigned from the presidency in the aftermath of the Watergate scandal. Despite Nixon's conflicts with Congress, a number of cost-containment initiatives were begun during this time.

PSROs and HMOs

One of the factors often cited as responsible for increased health care costs was the overutilization of health care resources. The rising costs of Medicare and Medicaid created concern in Congress about the cost and quality of care provided in these programs. Congress created the *Professional Standard Review Organizations (PSRO)* through the Social Security Amendments Act of 1972. It created a regulatory mechanism to encourage efficient and economical delivery of health care in the Medicare and Medicaid programs through peer review. More than 200 local PSROs were created and

Table 2.3

Consumer Price Index, 1960–90

	All items	Medical care
1960	29.6	22.3
1965	31.5	25.2
1970	38.8	34.0
1975	53.8	47.5
1980	82.4	74.9
1985	107.6	113.5
1990	130.7	162.8

Source: U.S. Bureau of the Census, *Statistical Abstract of the United States, 1991*, 111th ed. (Washington, D.C.: Government Printing Office, 1991), 479.

staffed by local physicians to review and monitor care provided to Medicare and Medicaid patients by hospitals, skilled nursing homes, and extended-care facilities. They were given the authority to deny approval of payment to physicians who provided services to Medicare and Medicaid patients.

Senator Edward Kennedy (D-Mass.) in 1971 introduced the Health Security Act in Congress, which was backed by organized labor. The bill called for a comprehensive program of free medical care and would have replaced all public and private health plans in a single federally operated health insurance system. The act would have set a national budget, allocated funds to regions, and obligated private physicians and hospitals to keep within budget constraints.

In his remarks introducing the plan, Kennedy blamed the insurance industry for failing to control costs, providing partial benefits, and ignoring the poor and the medically indigent. He also recognized the political difficulty of his plan becoming a reality when he stated that "throughout our society today, there is perhaps no institution more resistant to change than the organized medical profession."[46]

Opponents immediately described the plan as socialized medicine, a pejorative term used to help polarize debate. In reality, it was not socialized medicine because the plan did not involve nationalization of health care facilities such as hospitals or require doctors to work on salary.

Nixon was interested in seeking reelection in 1972. The president felt compelled to respond to Kennedy's political challenge by proposing the National Health Insurance Partnership Act. It consisted of two parts. The Family Health Insurance Plan was a federally financed plan to provide health insurance for all low-income families. The second part, the National

Health Insurance Standards Act, would be financed by private funds and set standards for employer health insurance programs and required coverage of employees. But this plan could not win the necessary support for passage since up to 40 million persons would still lack coverage.[47]

Nixon was really not interested in starting a national health insurance program. The administration wanted some kind of plan to control health care costs that would look uniquely Republican. Nixon hoped to promote market-oriented reforms designed to encourage competition in the health care market as a way of controlling costs. He was interested in developing a health strategy that would create a more efficient health care system, balance the supply of health care resources and demands, and at the same time assure equal access to health care. The Nixon administration's key proposal was to provide federal funds for the development of *health maintenance organizations (HMOs)*. In 1973, nearly three years after Nixon first sent his proposal to Congress, the *Health Maintenance Organization Act* was passed. It was a much more modest plan than originally conceived and reflected the necessity of bargaining and compromises between the president and Congress. For example, the first Senate bill had authorized $5.2 billion over three years for start-up costs. The version signed into law authorized $375 million over three years for projects more limited in scope.[48]

HMOs are a system in which enrollees pay a fixed fee (capitation) in advance, and in return they receive a comprehensive set of health services. The Nixon administration believed that HMOs would promote competition with traditional health care delivery systems by creating incentives for shifting health services utilization from more costly inpatient services such as hospitals and skilled nursing facilities to less costly outpatient services such as visits to doctors' offices. We consider HMOs and market reforms in later chapters.

Controlling Costs by Planning

The federal government during the late 1960s and the 1970s also emphasized health planning to contain rising health care costs. The rationale for planning was based on the argument that there was an abundance of health care facilities and services—too many hospitals, hospital beds, and medical equipment. Unnecessary expansion and duplication lead to overutilization of health care resources. The *Comprehensive Health Planning Act* of 1966 was an attempt at health care facilities planning through the states. Comprehensive health planning agencies were to be established in every state and in local areas. Their principal focus was hospital planning. The law also established the goal of providing the highest level of health care attainable to every person. Thus the law attempted to synthesize the goal of cost containment with the goal of providing access and quality care to everyone.

In 1972 the federal government, through the section 1122 amendments to the Social Security Act, limited Medicare/Medicaid reimbursements to approved expansions. Congress in 1974 passed the *National Health Planning and Resource Development Act.* This law replaced the Comprehensive Health Planning Act and such other health planning programs as the regional medical programs and the Hill-Burton programs. The law required all states to adopt *certificate-of-need* laws by 1980. Certificate-of-need laws require hospitals to document community need to obtain approval for major capital expenditures for expansion of facilities and services. The law also established a network of *health systems agencies* at state and local levels to administer the certificate-of-need laws.

Despite these efforts, overall health care costs continued to soar. The Medicare and Medicaid programs were also experiencing dramatic increases in expenditures. A recession combined with inflation during 1974–75 made efforts at expansion in medical programs politically impossible. The movement for national health insurance was stalled despite the election of a heavily Democratic Congress in 1974. Having assumed the office of the presidency following Nixon's resignation, President Ford proposed a national health insurance plan in his first message to Congress in 1974. In his 1976 State of the Union address, however, he withdrew the administration's plan on the ground that it would be inflationary.

Jimmy Carter, as a Democratic candidate for president in the 1976 election, also pledged his support for a comprehensive national health insurance program. His support during the Democratic primaries was a response to a political challenge by Senator Edward Kennedy, who was also seeking the party's nomination. Carter's continued support for a national health insurance program during the general election partly reflected his desire to win labor's support for his election.

Nevertheless, after assuming office in January 1977, Carter was hampered by budget constraints and was less anxious to push for a national health insurance program. From 1971 to 1974, under the Economic Stabilization Program, economywide wage and price controls were in effect. Hospital prices were subject to control under this program; however, this had a limited effect in controlling hospital costs. In 1977, the Carter administration proposed a series of all-payer revenue controls on hospitals, known as the *hospital cost-containment proposal.* The Carter administration argued that controlling hospital costs was necessary because traditional market forces would not keep those costs down. The proposal was strongly opposed by the medical industry in general and hospitals in particular. It also did not receive enthusiastic support in Congress. After three years of legislative battles, the proposal was defeated in favor of a promised voluntary effort by hospitals to contain costs. During the 1980 Democratic primary season, Carter was again challenged by Senator Kennedy. The president promised a national health care program, but one that would be implemented only when the economy, reeling from energy shocks and high interest and inflation rates, stabilized. Thus, the second half of the 1970s represented a political stalemate in the health policy area. Opposing and conflicting interests prevented adoption of any systematic and comprehensive set of health policies.[49]

The Reagan–Bush Years

After having campaigned on a platform of antiregulation and less government, Ronald Reagan became president in January 1981. Reagan sought to reduce expenditures for social programs, including health care. His "new federalism" proposal of 1982 attempted to decentralize authority and responsibility, giving state and local governments more discretion.

During the first two years of the Reagan administration, Congress enacted significant changes in federal health programs to restrain budget deficits, provide states with greater authority over health funding, and at the same time reduce federal funding for some health programs. Funding for health planning and health maintenance organizations was eventually eliminated. The PSRO program was renamed Peer Review Organizations (PROs) and its funding was reduced from $58 million in 1980 to $15 million in 1983. The Reagan administration also succeeded in replacing twenty-one categorical grant programs in the areas of prevention, mental health, maternal and child health care, and primary care into four block grants. Funding for Medicare and Medicaid was also reduced.[50]

The Reagan administration proposed a swap (the new federalism proposal) in which the federal government would assume full responsibility for funding Medicaid in return for state governments taking over responsibility for Aid to Families with Dependent Children (AFDC) and the food stamp program. Intense opposition from state governments caused the administration to drop this proposal from its legislative agenda.

The biggest innovation of the Reagan administration was the introduction in 1983 of a *Prospective Payment System* (PPS), mandated by the Deficit Reduction Act of 1982, for reimbursement to hospitals under the Medicare program in the hope of reducing Medicare costs and making hospitals more efficient. As discussed earlier, when Medicare was created, it provided for a generous reimbursement to hospitals based on a retrospective, reasonable cost basis for services provided to Medicare patients. Under the new system, illnesses are classified into one of 468 diagnosis related groups (DRGs). Each category is assigned a treatment rate, and hospitals are reimbursed according to these rates. If hospitals spend more money on treatment, they have to absorb the additional costs. If they spend less money than the established rates, they can keep the overpayment as profit. The new system was phased in over a period of time and did not go into full effect until 1987.

By the mid-1980s it was also becoming clear that the Medicare program was unable to meet the health expenses of its beneficiaries. Their out-of-pocket expenses for services covered by Medicare were on the rise. In addition, the Medicare program did not provide coverage for certain basic services such as outpatient prescription drugs, custodial care, and most of the cost of nursing home care. The Reagan administration tried to address this problem of "medigap." In his 1986 State of the Union message, President Reagan unveiled his proposal for an expansion of Medicare. His proposal was passed by Congress in 1988 as the *Medicare Catastrophic Coverage Act*.

The law modified both program benefits and financing with changes to be phased in over a period of several years beginning in 1989. The act provided for coverage of outpatient prescription drugs such as home intravenously administered antibiotic and other FDA-approved drugs, as well as mammography screening for the elderly and disabled beneficiaries. The act also expanded coverage of inpatient hospital days from ninety days to an unlimited number of days per year. Similarly, the act increased the number of days of coverage for skilled nursing facility, home health care, and hospice coverage. The act also reduced the amount of deductibles and coinsurance for certain coverage. The new benefits were to be financed entirely by the beneficiaries themselves through supplemental premiums. The act increased monthly premiums for Part B of Medicare and increased the tax liability of higher-income beneficiaries.

The Medicare Catastrophic Coverage Act was very unpopular, particularly among the affluent elderly. One reason for their opposition was the fact that they would shoulder most of the burden of financing the proposed changes through increases in their taxes. Many elderly did not like the idea of paying additional taxes to finance the new coverage. A second reason for the opposition was the fact that many of the elderly were satisfied with the supplemental private insurance coverage they had purchased to cover the gaps in the Medicare program. Another major criticism of the act was that while it made modest changes in Medicare nursing home benefits, it did not extend Medicare coverage to long-term nursing home care.[51] Long-term care is the type of care most likely to devastate the elderly financially.[52]

Significant protests against the Medicare Catastrophic Coverage Act forced Congress to repeal the act in November 1989. This defeat of one of the most significant expansions in the Medicare program since its creation in 1965 is likely to make Congress, at least in the near future, less enthusiastic about reforms in Medicare or about undertaking any new initiatives with respect to long-term care.[53]

The Role of State and Local Governments in Health Care

The distribution of authority and responsibility between different levels of government within a federal system is a topic of continuous debate. Health care policy has not been exempt from this debate. Initially, the role of the federal government and state and local governments was very limited. In the previous section we discussed how the federal government became increasingly involved in health care policy and how it plays a major role today with respect to access, quality, efficiency, and cost containment. This section briefly discusses the changing role of state and local governments in health care in our federal system.

During much of the nineteenth century, the role of state and local governments was confined to public health activities. The role of local governments in public health was stimulated by the great epidemics of the late eighteenth and early nineteenth centuries. Municipalities established health boards or health departments to deal with problems of sanitation, poor housing, and quarantine. For example, health departments were established in Baltimore in 1798, Charleston in 1815, Philadelphia in 1818, and Providence in 1832.[54]

Similarly, the states' role in public health was initially limited to special committees or commissions to control communicable diseases. The first state health department was established in Louisiana in 1855. State governments also played a significant role in personal health care through the establishment of state mental hospitals.[55]

By the beginning of the twentieth century, state and local governments were active in the delivery of personal health services. During the first decade of the 1900s, state governments also began the regulation and licensure of hospitals. But it was not until the end of World War II that detailed state regulations and licensure procedures for hospitals became more common.[56]

During the 1960s and 1970s, state governments took on many new functions; some of them fundamentally changed the traditional public health activities of subnational governments.[57] The federal health programs of the

1960s dramatically changed the functions of state and local governments in health care. There was increased federal support for the delivery of health care services by institutions that traditionally served the poor (i.e., public hospitals and local health departments). The establishment of the joint federal-state Medicaid program also increased revenues available to public hospitals and local health departments. Thus, by the 1980s, state and local governments were not only heavily involved in traditional public health activities such as health monitoring, sanitation, and disease control but were also key participants in the financing and delivery of personal health care services, particularly to the poor through Medicaid and other programs. The traditional public health focus on sanitation and communicable diseases also expanded to cover a broad range of protection against man-made environmental and occupational hazards to personal health.[58]

State governments are heavily involved in the regulation and licensure of health care facilities, such as hospitals and nursing homes, and in licensing health care professionals such as physicians and nurses. They also regulate hospital costs and prices through hospital rate setting. Furthermore, they have become important purchasers of health care services, especially for the poor. Thus, state and local governments play an important role, not only in public health activities, but in health care financing, delivery, and regulation of services as well. This increased role is reflected in the fact that between 1979 and 1981 alone state and local government health expenditures increased by 35 percent.[59]

The new federalism policies of the Nixon administration and especially the Reagan administration created new challenges for state and local governments. The Reagan administration placed heavy emphasis on decentralization, increased sharing of responsibilities and authority, and giving state and local governments more discretion in the implementation of health programs. The diminishing federal responsibility in health care in the early 1980s resulted in increased cost shifting from the federal to state and local governments.

This has led some to argue that the Reagan administration's new federalism strategy was largely a means of cutting the federal budget rather than sharing responsibilities.[60] The increased discretion granted to state governments in the implementation of health policy raises the question of commitment, capacity, and progressivity of state governments. Conservatives have placed great emphasis on devolution of authority and financial responsibility back to the states, without much concern for adequate access to health care for all segments of the society.[61] This concern is heightened by some evidence that state and local governments may be even more susceptible to the influence of special interests than the federal government. Thus, compared to the federal government, some have argued that state governments are less likely to make decisions in the public interest.[62]

Recent federal budget reductions made in an effort to contain rising health care costs have left many states unable to meet the financial burden of meeting the health care needs of the poor under the Medicaid program. State governments have resorted to the practice of "bootstrapping." Thirty-seven states have passed laws that charge doctors, hospitals, and other Medicaid providers an extra tax. The idea is to force the federal government to pay more of the cost of the program because it reimburses states between 50 and 83 percent of the states' Medicaid costs. The more a state charges, the more it gets back.[63] The Bush administration announced new rules under which the federal government would no longer match spending by states for Medicaid if the state money comes from donations or special taxes paid by hospitals and nursing homes rather than a state's general revenues. According to state governors, these new rules would cut medical coverage for women and children.[64] The Clinton administration, headed by a former governor, has been somewhat more sympathetic to state concerns. More stringent Medicaid eligibility rules also have left a sizable number of poor people with no access to health care under the Medicaid program. Over the past ten years the number of Medicaid recipients has remained stable, while the poor population has grown substantially.[65] Thus, the Medicaid program is increasingly confronted with a tradeoff between cost containment and access to health care.[66]

This again raises a concern about the impact of new federalism initiatives on the issue of access to quality health care on the part of the elderly, the poor, and the uninsured. But the liberals' vision of a national health insurance program is likely to remain illusive, confronted with the reality of enormous federal budget deficits and the antitax mood prevalent in the country.

It should be pointed out, however, that states have become major actors in health policy reform, from regulation to rationing to innovative competitive strategies. We consider these changes in later chapters.

Conclusion

The United States remains the only major Western industrialized nation without a national health insurance system. Health care policy in the United States results from a combination of decisions made and initiatives undertaken by various levels of government and the private sector. Though the role of federal, state, and local governments in health care policy has expanded significantly in the twentieth century, the U.S. health care system remains a mostly private system. Policymakers in the United States have mainly followed a middle road between a totally private health care system and a publicly financed national health care system.

The federal government's health policy initiatives have focused on concerns about values of access (equality), quality of care, and cost efficiency. The federal role in health care has gone through three distinct stages. The first stage was characterized by policies designed to increase access through expansion of health care facilities, services, and resources. The second stage was characterized by policies specifically designed to provide equal access and quality care to needy groups such as the elderly and the poor. The third stage was characterized by policies designed to contain rising health care costs.

Nevertheless, with respect to providing equal access to health care, federal policies have never displayed or practiced a broad commitment to ensuring that all Americans receive needed health care. Instead, the federal government has always followed an incremental approach by creating specific policies such as Medicare, Medicaid, and numerous categorical grant programs targeted at narrowly defined groups or problems.[67]

Medicare, Medicaid, and other federal grant-in-aid programs have increased access to health care by removing some of the financial obstacles for certain needy groups. Problems remain, however, and recent evidence suggests the emergence of new difficulties. The demise of the Medicare Catastrophic Coverage Act has left many poor elderly with significant gaps in their Medicare coverage because they cannot afford to buy supplemental private insurance. This problem is likely to grow as the number of elderly in the population increases. One of the biggest problems is Medicare's failure to provide coverage for long-term care. Similarly, a significant number of poor people are not covered under the Medicaid program. More and more people are falling through the cracks in the health care safety net, as reflected in the increased number of uninsured Americans. Moreover, hospitals in many major cities are facing a crisis situation.[68]

Because government intervention in American politics takes place within the context of the public philosophy of interest-group liberalism and cynicism about government regulation, governmental input has tended to occur at the margin rather than the core of the problem.[69] Powerful interest groups have been able to exercise veto power over proposed policies. For example, since the 1920s numerous attempts by the federal government to establish some form of national health insurance that would guarantee health care access to everyone have been defeated by powerful interests such as the AMA and insurance companies. Such groups have successfully defended and protected their narrow and selfish interests, even if they have done so in the name of protecting the public interest by appealing to the value of freedom to choose one's doctor and by raising the specter of "socialized medicine," which they argue would lower the quality of health care. In recent years the issue of national health insurance has been pushed back on the legislative agenda because of an economic environment characterized by huge federal budget deficits and a protracted recession.

Both liberals and conservatives have had difficulty carrying out an ideologically faithful health care policy. Thus, for example, while the Nixon administration advocated a competitive market strategy and successfully pushed for federal support for the development of HMOs, it also had to accept increased federal government regulations in the form of peer review organizations. Similarly, the important innovation of a Prospective Payment System (PPS) for Medicare reimbursement under the Reagan administration relied on regulatory price-control mechanisms to encourage efficiency in the health care market. Both liberals and conservatives had to contend with powerful interest groups. For example, insurance companies, hospitals, and the medical profession have welcomed some regulatory relief, but they have not shown a great deal of enthusiasm for the conservative program of increased competition in the health care market.[70] Liberal efforts at major reforms to increase health care access have been successfully thwarted by these same interest groups.

The constitutional structure of separation of powers and checks and balances combined with the increased frequency of divided government have necessitated constant bargaining and compromises between the two houses of Congress and between the President and Congress. The federal structure of government has produced a continuous debate in health care policy over the proper distribution of authority and responsibility between the different levels of government. Different presidents have stressed different objectives in this regard. The Johnson administration in the 1960s placed more emphasis on increasing health care access by the federal government. In contrast, the Reagan administration in the 1980s emphasized deregulation and devolution of authority to state and local governments. The changing political climate and public mood and the desire to win election or reelection to office make short-term approaches to the solution of problems appealing. Under such circumstances, a comprehensive and consistent set of policies directed at long-term solutions to problems becomes difficult to attain.

We leave this chapter with a brief overview of the remainder of the book. Chapter 3 examines Medicaid. We explore Medicaid's structure and the coverage provided by the program, with an emphasis on its federal nature. We look at problems with Medicaid and new developments in the program. We explore gaps in Medicaid coverage and attempts by states to control costs.

Chapter 4 looks at Medicare and the problem of long-term care. The chapter describes Medicare, the primary program of health care for the elderly and certain categories of the disabled. It looks at the cost and financing problems, recent changes, and gaps in the program. The major gap is long-term care, the subject of the second part of the chapter. We discuss the participants in the long-term care industry and the financing of this difficult problem.

Chapter 5 has as its principal topics access and equity. In particular, we discuss two overlapping aspects. One is the uninsured. We look at the problem of those without adequate or any health insurance, the access aspect, and seek answers to the question of why this group has increased in recent years. We tie this answer to current pressures for health care reform. The second, related, part of the chapter looks at disadvantaged groups in American society, the equity aspect. Here we specifically concentrate on minority groups, women, and low-income persons. There is some overlap between low income and the other two sets of groups, as there is with these groups and the uninsured.

Chapter 6 spotlights perhaps the major driving force behind change in the health care field, the ever-increasing costs of health care. We explore explanations for cost increases and attempts at cost containment. This chapter highlights efforts at the state and federal levels as well as by the private sector.

Chapter 7's subject is technology and health care. Technology is one of the factors that has been implicated in health care cost increases. Some point to advances in health care technology in the United States as indicating the virtues of the system, while others suggest it is responsible for overuse of care. Technology also presents numerous ethical concerns. In this chapter we discuss the factors that have contributed to the growth of medical technology, cost of medical technology, the issue of technology assessment, and the ethical dilemmas raised by high-tech medicine.

Chapter 8 explores health care reform in the 1990s. For more than a decade, health care has seen considerable changes. We examine changes made by the states, the federal government, and the private sector. We examine the health care reform proposal of President Clinton and some of the politics surrounding the proposed changes. We also discuss market-reform concepts as an integral part of health care reform.

Chapter 9 summarizes the major issues and problems in health care discussed in the previous chapters and presents our prognosis and recommendations for change.

3
Medicaid: Health Care
for the Poor

The establishment of Medicare and Medicaid in 1965 was the end result of a lengthy debate during the early part of the twentieth century over the role of the federal government in financing health care. The debate among policymakers focused on two competing models. One was a universal coverage model, under which the federal government would provide health insurance to all people on a compulsory basis financed by taxes on earnings. The second model envisioned a more limited role for the federal government. This model would limit the federal government's role to providing assistance to needy groups in society. In the past, most federal laws dealing with health care had followed the second model.[1] The political environment—structure and processes—made such an incremental approach feasible. Thus, during the 1950s and the 1960s policymakers followed the same approach.

The 1950 amendments to the Social Security Act authorized matching grants to the states for direct vendor (provider) payments for treatment of individuals on public assistance. During the late 1950s, the debate focused on the problem of hospital costs faced by the aged. The cost of hospital care doubled in the 1950s. Support increased for addressing the problem of hospital costs of the elderly. The aged could be presumed to be both needy and deserving.[2] In 1960 Congress passed the *Kerr-Mills Act*. This act expanded federal matching funds to the states for vendor payments, and more important, it allowed states to include the "medically needy"—that is, elderly, blind, and disabled persons with low incomes who were not on public assistance. But many states moved very slowly or failed to move at all to take advantage of the Kerr-Mills Act.

The Democratic Party's sweep of the 1964 elections guaranteed further action with respect to the role of the federal government in health care. Lyndon Johnson was elected to the presidency with an overwhelming popular vote. The Democrats gained a two-to-one majority in the House of Representatives. This made it possible for Congress in 1965 to create the Medicare and Medicaid programs. Both were in the forefront of Lyndon Johnson's Great Society programs designed to help the poor and the disadvantaged.[3] Medicare was established as a program for the elderly, while Medicaid was a program for the poor. The final shape of both programs represented compromises among competing models and approaches. The Democratic plan for a compulsory hospital insurance program, financed through payroll taxes under Social Security, became Part A of Medicare. The Republican-supported plan of a government subsidized, voluntary insurance program financed through general revenues to cover physicians' bills became Part B of Medicare. The AMA opposed both plans and pushed a plan of its own to expand the Kerr-Mills program to the needy. An expanded means-tested program for the poor administered by the states became the Medicaid program.

The generally accepted political explanation for the creation of Medicaid is that the program was created almost as an afterthought to Medicare.[4] Medicaid was intended to "pick up the pieces" left over by Medicare. It was designed to cover deductibles and coinsurance for indigent Medicare patients. The program was intended to pay for services not covered or covered only inadequately by Medicare (i.e., outpatient and nursing home care), and to pay the cost of medical care of indigent persons other than the elderly.[5]

Although Medicare and Medicaid were adopted at the same time, there are fundamental differences between the two. The Medicare program has enjoyed public popularity and legitimacy because it is tied to Social Security, a program that is contributory in nature (i.e., through Social Security taxes paid by workers). In contrast, from the beginning, Medicaid has been burdened by the stigma of being a public assistance; (i.e., welfare) program. Medicare has uniform national standards for eligibility and benefits. In sharp contrast, Medicaid lets states decide on eligibility and benefit standards. Another major difference is that physician reimbursement under Medicaid is much lower than under Medicare or private insurance; as a result, very few physicians participate in the Medicaid program.[6] In addition, Medicare is financed and administered solely by the federal government, while Medicaid is financed by both the federal and state governments on a matching basis and is administered by the state governments.

Program Objective and Structure

Medicaid was established to increase the access of the poor to health care by providing them with financial assistance to meet their medical needs.

Even though the program was created by federal law, the intent was to encourage state governments to set up a "unified system of health care" for certain low-income individuals.[7] The federal government encouraged state participation and compliance with the program in several ways. The federal government provided matching funds to encourage states to expand their existing medical assistance programs. Today, the federal Medicaid matching ratio varies from a minimum of 50 percent to a maximum of 83 percent. Second, state governments were given the responsibility for establishing program requirements. Finally, states were given the option of making the administration of the program a local as opposed to a state responsibility.

Thus the Medicaid program was created as a partnership between different levels of government to improve access and quality of health care for the poor. The national government establishes broad program guidelines, promotes and monitors program development, and provides financial assistance through matching grants. State governments are given significant control over important aspects of the scope and structure of the program. For example, state governments enjoy discretionary authority for establishing eligibility standards, the nature and scope of benefits provided, and mechanisms used to reimburse health care providers.

Medicaid is an excellent example of how the federal structure of government shapes the dynamics of policymaking and implementation. On the one hand, the federal structure, with its multiple governments, shared authority, political autonomy, and constitutional ambiguities, has allowed states to act as laboratories for innovation and experimentation in the Medicaid program. On the other hand, the same federal structure of government produces overlapping jurisdictions and wastefulness and encourages the promotion of narrow and parochial interests that make it difficult to solve serious problems. It allows one level of government to pass the buck to another level by playing the federalism game.

Medicaid Coverage

The program's main target groups are children and mothers who receive Aid to Families with Dependent Children (AFDC), the elderly poor over the age of sixty-five, and disabled or blind persons who qualify for the Supplemental Security Income (SSI) program—a federal program for the aged, blind, or disabled. The federal government sets the income limits for the SSI program. Thus, state Medicaid programs are required to include all *"categorically needy"* persons—those receiving cash assistance under Old Age Assistance, Aid to the Blind, Aid to Families with Dependent Children (AFDC), and Aid to the Permanently and Totally Disabled.[8]

States may elect to provide coverage to people who are not required to be covered by federal law. State governments can receive federal matching funds for providing coverage to these optional groups. Such optional groups include *"medically needy"* families with dependent children whose incomes are above state AFDC limits and elderly persons who do not qualify for cash assistance but have large medical or nursing home bills.[9]

Mandatory benefits covered under Medicaid include hospital and physician services, family planning consultation, care in skilled nursing facilities, diagnostic services, and screening and treatment of children for various sicknesses and impairment. *Optional benefits* include prescription drugs, dental care, and nursing home care in intermediate-care facilities.

States are permitted to restrict the amount of services per beneficiary. For example, a state may limit the number of days in hospitals or number of visits to physicians per year that it would cover. States also enjoy significant discretion with respect to the method of payment to health care providers. Originally, under the Medicaid program, states had to pay hospitals according to the same principle used by Medicare—the "reasonable cost" principle—that is, all costs associated with the care of a patient. Today, states can use any method for reimbursement as long as payments are "reasonable and adequate." Similarly, in the Medicare program, physicians are reimbursed for their charges which are subject to screening for "reasonableness." But physicians are permitted to charge the patient more than the amount considered reasonable by Medicare. Under Medicaid, states can pay physicians according to the Medicare principle or on the basis of a fee schedule. All providers must accept Medicaid's reimbursement as payment in full. Because of the very low physician rate paid by many states, a large number of physicians refuse to treat Medicaid patients.[10]

Originally, Medicaid was viewed as a limited entitlement program. Over time, the scope of the program has expanded considerably. Today, Medicaid also pays for health care services for low-income "first-time" pregnant women who do not qualify for programs such as AFDC. In addition, Medicaid finances long-term institutional care for the elderly, disabled, and mentally retarded.[11] From 1984 to 1990, Congress imposed various federal mandates requiring states to expand Medicaid coverage to women and children.

Major Trends in the Medicaid Program

Growth in Program Costs

As the data in Table 3.1 document, the Medicaid program has experienced dramatic increases in overall program cost from the beginning. Total Med-

Table 3.1

Medicaid Expenditures, 1970–93
(in billions of dollars)

Year	Total	Federal	State/Local
1970	5.3	2.9	2.4
1975	13.6	7.6	6.0
1980	24.8	13.7	11.1
1985	39.7	21.9	17.8
1990	71.7	40.7	31.1
1991	89.9	54.5	35.4
1992	103.6	65.9	35.7
1993	112.8	73.2	39.6

Sources: For the years 1970 and 1975, Robert M. Gibson and Daniel R. Waldo, "National Health Expenditures, 1980," *Health Care Financing Review* 3, no. 1 (September 1981): 45–46. For the years 1980, 1985, and 1990, Suzanne W. Letsch et al., "National Health Expenditures, 1991," *Health Care Financing Review* 14, no. 2 (Winter 1992): 27–28. For the years 1991, 1992, and 1993, Katharine R. Levit et al., "National Health Expenditures, 1993," *Health Care Financing Review* 16, no. 1 (Fall 1994): 290–91.

icaid expenditures increased from $5.3 billion in 1970 to $ $24.8 billion in 1980. In the early years of the program, the primary reason for increases in program cost was the growth in the number of eligible recipients. Between 1981 and 1984, spending for Medicaid increased at a much slower rate than between 1978 and 1981. The average annual growth rate between 1981 and 1984 was 7.5 percent, compared to 16.1 percent between 1978 and 1981. Factors contributing to this slowdown were the recession, the reduction in federal matching rates, and the programmatic changes introduced in the Omnibus Budget Reconciliation Act (OBRA) of 1981.[12] But as a result of new federal mandates imposed by Congress between 1984 and 1990 that expanded Medicaid coverage, the annual growth rate increased again. By 1990, the total Medicaid cost had increased to $71.7 billion. From 1989 to 1990 Medicaid expenditures increased 21.3 percent. Even more dramatic was the increase that came during 1991 when the total program cost jumped to 89.9 billion. This represented an increase of 25.2 percent, the fastest annual growth in the history of the program. Factors that contributed to this dramatic increase were the expansions in Medicaid eligibility and a slowdown in the economy. Both factors caused additional individuals to qualify for coverage.[13]

The cost to the federal government alone increased from $2.9 billion in 1970 to $13.7 billion in 1980 and $40.7 billion in 1990. The federal spending in 1991 alone jumped to $54.5 billion, and by 1993 it had increased to $73.2 billion.

State governments have also experienced significant increases in their program costs. The combined cost of state and local governments for Medicaid increased from $2.4 billion in 1970 to $11.1 billion in 1980, $17.8 billion in 1985, and $31.1 billion in 1990. In 1991, the state share of the program jumped to $35.4 billion. By 1993, state and local governments were spending $39.6 billion. Needless to say, state-by-state program costs, eligibility standards, and benefit levels vary significantly among the states. The amount of optional services (those beyond the ones mandated by the federal government) and the mix of services provided by the state governments also varies a great deal. "The maze of eligibility rules is enough to make anyone sick."[14]

Overall, two characteristics have contributed to the steady growth in program expenditures. First, since Medicaid is an "entitlement" program, individuals who meet eligibility criteria are automatically covered. Thus, program costs increase any time the size of the population in need increases. Second, Medicaid, like other health insurance systems, pays health care providers and not the recipients who receive treatment. Thus, overall health care costs directly influence Medicaid expenditures. During the 1970s and 1980s, the cost of medical care increased annually by an average of 8.5 percent. Some of the increases in the Medicaid expenditures are attributable to general medical cost inflation.[15]

Despite the dramatic increases in spending for Medicaid, the program fails to insure millions of poor people who are ineligible to receive Medicaid because they do not fall into one of the eligible categories. It is not surprising that Medicaid is often called a monster.[16] Since its creation, the Medicaid program has occupied center stage in the debate over the proper role of the federal and state governments in meeting the health care needs of the poor.

Growth in the Number of Recipients

Medicaid has also experienced a steady growth in the number of recipients. Those receiving Medicaid nationwide increased from 17.6 million in 1972 to 21.6 million in 1980. By 1990, the number had grown to 25.3 million people. In 1993, the total number of recipients had increased to 33.4 million. Still, it is important to note that the number of recipients has fluctuated over the same period. In the early years of the program's history, the number of recipients increased because eligibility for Medicaid increased. Paul Ginsburg cites four main reasons for this: states increased their need standards for AFDC, making more people eligible for Medicaid; the number of female-headed households (i.e., those categorically eligible for AFDC), increased as this demographic trend continued during the 1980s; organizations mounted public information campaigns to increase awareness and participation in the program; and additional states initiated Medicaid programs.[17]

The number of recipients declined slightly and remained steady during the early 1980s but began to rise again beginning in the mid-1980s and has continued to rise during the 1990s (see Table 3.2). The decline in the number of recipients can be attributed to the fact that from 1980 to 1984, eligibility for Medicaid was either directly or indirectly limited. Medicaid coverage for poor and near-poor people declined from 53 percent in 1980 to 46 percent in 1985. Factors contributing to this decline included failure to update state income standards, changes in Medicaid eligibility policy, and federal and state changes in AFDC eligibility policy. The 1981 OBRA established new limits on both income and resources for AFDC and Medicaid eligibility. It also limited cash assistance and Medicaid for certain groups of potential beneficiaries.[18] By 1985, however, this downward trend in the number of Medicaid recipients was reversed, and the number of recipients began to increase. This was largely caused by new federal mandates imposed by Congress between 1984 and 1990. Most of these mandates significantly expanded Medicaid eligibility for women and children. Between 1989 and 1991, the number of recipients increased by 4.8 million with a significant portion of the increase attributable to federal mandates. For example, about one-half of the 3 million additional recipients qualifying for Medicaid between 1990 and 1991 were eligible because of mandated program expansions. The major beneficiaries of the mandated program expansions were children.[19] The changes introduced in the Medicaid program during the 1980s are discussed in more detail later in the chapter.

Changes in the Composition of Medicaid Clientele

Over the years, the composition of the Medicaid clientele has changed. This in turn has affected patterns of Medicaid expenditures and enrollments. Between 1972 and 1990, the number of elderly, blind, and some other Medicaid recipients decreased, while the number of disabled persons and children and adults in AFDC families increased. In 1972, disabled persons accounted for 9.2 percent of the total Medicaid population; in 1990, they accounted for 15 percent. In 1972, disabled persons accounted for 21.5 percent of Medicaid payments; in 1990, they accounted for 37 percent of the payments. Similarly, the number of children and adults in AFDC fami-

Table 3.2

Medicaid: Total Expenditures and Number of Recipients, 1966–93

Year	Total expenditures (in billions of dollars)	Number of recipients (in millions)
1966	1.3	—
1967	3.0	—
1968	3.4	—
1969	4.0	—
1970	5.1	—
1971	6.4	—
1972	8.0	17.6
1973	9.1	19.6
1974	10.6	21.5
1975	12.9	22.0
1976	14.5	22.8
1977	16.6	22.8
1978	18.5	22.0
1979	21.2	21.5
1980	24.8	21.6
1981	28.9	22.0
1982	30.6	21.6
1983	33.6	21.6
1984	36.0	21.6
1985	39.7	21.8
1986	42.9	22.5
1987	48.2	23.1
1988	52.1	22.9
1989	59.2	23.5
1990	71.3	25.3
1991	89.9	28.3
1992	103.6	30.9
1993	112.8	33.4

Sources: For 1966 through 1990, Katharine R. Levit et al., "National Health Expenditures, 1990," *Health Care Financing Review* 13, no. 1 (Fall 1991): 41. For 1991, 1992, and 1993, Katharine R. Levit et al., "National Health Expenditures, 1993," *Health Care Financing Review* 16, no. 1 (Fall 1994): 9.

lies on Medicaid increased from 62 percent of the total population to 68.2 percent in 1990. This group accounted for 43.4 of total Medicaid payments in 1972 and 37.2 percent of payments in 1990.[20] More than 13 million children received Medicaid benefits in the 1991 fiscal year, 16.2 percent more than in 1990. Today, children constitute the largest and fastest-growing component of the Medicaid population. Yet children are the least costly recipients covered by the program. The average payment per child is one-third the average payment for all recipients.[21]

Table 3.3

Medicaid's Share of Total Nursing Home Care Expenditures, 1970–93

Year	Total expenditures (in billions of dollars)	Medicaid share (in billions of dollars)	Medicaid share (in percent)
1970	4.9	1.4	28.0
1980	20.5	11.0	53.6
1985	34.9	16.6	47.7
1990	54.8	26.3	47.9
1991	60.8	31.0	50.9
1992	65.5	33.7	51.4
1993	69.6	36.0	51.7

Source: Katharine R. Levit et al., "National Health Expenditures, 1993," *Health Care Financing Review* 16, no. 1 (Fall 1994): 288.

The elderly, the disabled, and to a lesser extent, the blind are the most costly recipients covered by the program. The elderly and disabled averaged about $6,717 per recipient, while the blind averaged about $5,212 per recipient in 1990. The average for all recipients in 1990 was $2,568.[22]

There has also been a shift in the nature of the program. This shift has been away from an acute-care program for the disabled, poor adults, and children toward a long-term-care program for the elderly and chronically ill. In view of this shift toward long-term care, it is not surprising that elderly, blind, and disabled people are consuming a major share of Medicaid resources.[23] As the data in Table 3.3 reveal, Medicaid's share of total nursing home care expenditures has increased from $1.4 billion (out of total expenditures of $4.9 billion) in 1970 to $36 billion (out of total expenditures of $69.6 billion) in 1993. Medicaid accounted for 28 percent of total nursing home care expenditures in 1970. By 1993, Medicaid accounted for 51.7 percent of total nursing home care expenditures.[24]

The Medicaid Program in the 1980s

Two significant developments occurred in the Medicaid program during the 1980s. First, the Reagan administration introduced major changes in the early 1980s designed to decentralize Medicaid. State governments were given more autonomy and flexibility to attempt innovative approaches to providing health care for the poor and also contain rising Medicaid costs. Second, beginning in 1984–85, Democrats in Congress succeeded in imposing various mandates on the states designed to expand Medicaid coverage.

Reagan's New Federalism and the Medicaid Program, 1981–1984

One of the major goals of the Reagan administration was to restructure the role of the federal, state, and local governments through the concept of "new federalism." New federalism was designed to decrease the role of the federal government and increase the role of the state governments in domestic policy areas. The Reagan administration tried to restrict the open-ended matching feature of the Medicaid program by proposing to limit the growth rate of the federal government's annual contribution to Medicaid to 5 percent. Congress did not support this proposal.

The most important spending and policy shift affecting health care for the poor was incorporated in the *Omnibus Budget Reconciliation Act (OBRA)* of 1981. This legislation contained three major changes affecting the Medicaid program. First, the federal contribution to Medicaid was directly reduced by 3 percent in 1982, 4 percent in 1983, and 4.5 percent in 1984. Second, changes in the federal welfare eligibility policy reduced welfare rolls and thereby the number of eligible Medicaid recipients. Third, the law contained many fundamental policy changes with far-reaching implications in Medicaid itself.[25] For example, although Medicaid had historically followed Medicare's reasonable-cost reimbursement principle, the act allowed states to pay health care providers (hospitals, nursing homes) on a basis other than reasonable cost.

OBRA also authorized formal retreat from the principle of free choice about provider eligibility. The act gave states wide discretion, on approval from the secretary of health and human services (HHS), to limit Medicaid recipients' freedom to choose their doctors or hospitals. Other provisions made it easier to use new kinds of health care providers, particularly health maintenance organizations (HMOs). The law also granted states wide discretion in deciding who they would cover under Medicaid. It also authorized a provision allowing payment, through waiver from the secretary of HHS, for a wide range of home and community services that states could cover as an alternative to nursing home care. OBRA also allowed the states to buy laboratory services and medical devices via competitive bidding.

The *Tax Equity and Fiscal Responsibility Act (TEFRA)* of 1982 created new financing initiatives that allowed shifting costs to beneficiaries and third parties by granting the states discretion to require Medicaid beneficiaries to pay nominal fees for medical services.

In 1982 President Reagan, as part of his new federalism, proposed a swap of programs between the federal and the state governments. He proposed that the federal government take over full responsibility for Medicaid in return for state governments taking over food stamp and AFDC programs.[26] Reactions to the proposal were mixed. State governors liked the idea of the federal government assuming full responsibility for the Medicaid program, but they wanted to defer action on the AFDC–food stamp portion of the swap.[27] The reaction on Capitol Hill ranged from tepid to frigid. The majority of Democrats were hostile to the plan.[28] New York City's Democratic mayor, Ed Koch, termed the Reagan plan "a con job, a snare and a delusion, a steal by the feds."[29] Because of the controversy surrounding the proposal, the plan was dropped and never submitted to Congress.

The *Deficit Reduction Act of 1984* required Medicaid beneficiaries to assign to the states any rights they had to other health benefit programs. This allowed the states to collect from such programs any available payments for medical care for the covered beneficiaries.

President Reagan's new federalism initiatives posed a different challenge to the health policies established over the past fifty years. [30] The new federalism's emphasis on decentralization, with its focus on state- and local-level decision making, raised some fundamental questions. Could the state governments contain dramatically rising costs and provide access and quality care to the poor? How states respond to this challenge will shape the future course of Medicaid policy in particular and health care policy in general.

Congressional Expansion of the Medicaid Program: 1984–1990

By 1984, the 1981 Reagan initiative to prune the AFDC rosters was beginning to be challenged, and Congress began to ease eligibility standards. Since 1984, many incremental extensions of the Medicaid program have been aimed primarily at covering more low-income pregnant women, infants, and children. Thus, for example, under the *Deficit Reduction Act of 1984* Congress required states to broaden their Medicaid coverage to include more low-income women during their first pregnancy, pregnant women in two-parent families in which the principal breadwinner was unemployed, and poor children up to the age of five in two-parent families.

The impetus for further expansion came from a 1985 Institute of Medicine report which showed that every dollar spent on prenatal care saved $3.38 on care needed by low-birthweight babies. The *Omnibus Budget Reconciliation Act of 1986* gave states the option to extend Medicaid coverage to pregnant women and to infants up to the age of one year who are members of households with incomes of as much as 100 percent of the federal poverty level. The law also allowed coverage to be gradually implemented for children up to age eight in households with income less than the federal poverty level. By January 1989, twenty-nine states had adopted the option.[31]

The *Omnibus Budget Reconciliation Act of 1987* allowed states to expand Medicaid eligibility to include pregnant women and infants up to age one year who live in households with incomes of as much as 185 percent of the federal poverty level. States were also given the option of immediately covering all children younger than age five living in households with incomes that are less than the federal poverty level. The National Governors' Conference reported that as of January 1989, nine states were using the higher threshold established in the 1987 OBRA.[32]

In 1988 Congress passed a law to help avoid impoverishing the spouses of patients who receive Medicaid-financed nursing home care. The *"spousal impoverishment" benefit*—one of the few provisions to survive the Medicare Catastrophic Coverage Act repealed in 1989—substantially raised the amount of income that spouses could retain before handing the balance over to Medicaid to help defray the cost of a patient's nursing home care. The federal law allows states to let "at-home" spouses retain as much as $66,480 of the couple's combined assets and as much as $1,662 in monthly income.[33]

The *Omnibus Budget Reconciliation Act of 1989* required provision of all Medicaid-allowed treatment to correct problems identified during Early and Periodic Screening, Diagnosis, and Treatment (EPSDT), even if the treatment is otherwise not covered under the state Medicaid plan. The act also required periodic screening under EPSDT if medical problems were suspected. The *Budget and Reconciliation Act of 1990* required Medicaid coverage of children under age eighteen if the family income is below 100 percent of the federal poverty line.

President Reagan's new federalism initiatives posed a new challenge to the health policies established over the past fifty years.[34] The Reagan administration was willing to grant states more discretion when such discretion promised cost reductions.[35] The new federalism's emphasis on decentralization, combined with significant expansion of the program through federal mandates since 1984, raises a fundamental question: can the state governments contain dramatically rising costs and provide access and quality care to the poor? How states respond to this challenge will shape the future course of Medicaid policy in particular and health care policy in general. In the rest of this chapter we analyze how state governments have responded to the Medicaid program's decentralization and expansion during the 1980s.

State Governments' Responses: Innovations and Experimentations, 1980s

By the early 1980s, health care cost containment had emerged as a major issue for state and local governments. Confronted with more discretionary authority and the need to reduce Medicaid expenditures, state governments responded to new federalism initiatives in many different ways. The discussion that follows focuses on some of the major responses of state governments.

Cutbacks in Eligibility, Benefits, and Coverage

In response to federal cuts in matching funds, many states turned to strategies such as placing limits on income eligibility standards, reducing coverage of optional groups, and reducing the amount of services covered in an attempt to reduce state expenditures under Medicaid.

States selected options that were easy to implement and promised the quickest savings. Some states attempted Medicaid cuts by reducing the number of people on the program, reducing benefits for those covered, or both.[36] These are attractive options for state governments because state agencies are the ones that make such decisions, and they have the machinery to calculate the amount of savings that can be generated. Nevertheless, these are also the cost-saving methods that are most likely to affect low-income patients adversely.[37]

In a nationwide survey, the Intergovernmental Health Policy Project at George Washington University found that in 1981 alone more than thirty states reduced Medicaid benefits or limited Medicaid eligibility. Since January 1982, twenty-four states had restricted use of medical services by placing limits on the number of visits to doctors, emergency rooms, and out-patient facilities. Eleven states placed limits on the number of hospital days covered under Medicaid, while another eight states eliminated certain optional services.[38] Many states use a combination of stringent income criteria and limited optional service coverage to constrain enrollments and outlays.

By 1982, most of the states had made only small increases in AFDC benefit levels or none at all, thereby allowing inflation to raise earnings of employed welfare recipients above the eligibility ceiling. People between the ages of eighteen and twenty-one were declared ineligible for AFDC in several states. Some states, such as California and Washington, reduced patients' medically needy coverage by increasing the amount that recipients must "spend down" before Medicaid eligibility begins. Thus, by 1982 most states had reduced eligibility.[39] The number of total Medicaid recipients declined from 22 million in 1981 to 21.6 million in 1982. Reduction in Medicaid eligibility is an area where one of the goals of OBRA was realized by the early 1980s.[40]

Similarly, states have been active in reducing service coverage. States such as Illinois, Massachusetts, Michigan, Missouri, and Rhode Island have placed limits or increased existing limits on hospital days, eliminating weekend admissions, reducing the coverage of preoperative days, and ending payment for inpatient surgery when the service could be provided on an outpatient basis. California, Connecticut, Illinois, New Jersey, and North Carolina have directly limited physician visits to "lock in" overutilizing patients or to "lock out" providers found to provide too many services or poor-quality care. Several states also added controls on the number of nursing home days (in either skilled nursing or intermediate-care facilities) they will pay for. Several states extended limits on drug coverage. Other states placed limits on optional services such as dentists, chiropractors, and optometrists, or eliminated coverage for such services completely.[41]

As we discussed earlier in the chapter, federal mandates imposed between 1984 and 1990 designed to expand coverage to women and children dramatically increased the number of recipients. The end result is that despite state governments' attempts to reduce program cost and enrollments, both increased dramatically in the late 1980s and early 1990s. While federal mandates have helped increase access to the health care system, especially for poor women and children, they have also significantly increased program costs at both the federal and state levels of governments. Once again, we are faced with the often conflicting values of access versus cost.

Increased Use of Copayments for Medicaid Services

Use of copayments has also become common in many states. Several states today require copayments for many Medicaid services.[42] The assumption here is that copayments force the beneficiary to ask whether the care is really worth paying for and thus make him or her more cost conscious. Some view copayments as an ideal mechanism for eliminating services not highly valued by Medicaid recipients. Others fear that even small copayments will result in drastic reductions in the use of health care services by the poor. Some early studies have suggested that copayments indeed reduce expenditures on medical services. More important, the effects of copayments, at least with income-related upper limits, did not vary significantly with the family income of those participating in these studies. Thus, supporters of use of the copayment approach argue that the fear of reduced use of health services by the poor as a result of copayments is unfounded.[43]

Competitive Bidding: Contractual and Prudent Buyer Arrangements

Another approach—a competitive strategy—used by the states is to attempt a fundamental reform in their approach to Medicaid. This involves replacing a fee-for-service system with *negotiated* or *competitively bid fixed-price arrangements* for Medicaid services. For example, California relies on negotiated fixed-price arrangements. Selective contracting of hospitals by the California Medicaid program (Medi-Cal) was established in 1983. During that year the state negotiated all-inclusive per diem rates on an individual basis with eligible hospitals. Once the rate was determined, hospitals had to absorb costs that exceeded the negotiated level. Medi-Cal patients are required to go to a contracting hospital, and contracting facilities must treat patients coming to them. Contracting applied to more than half of California's hospitals and more than 75 percent of its Medicaid hospitalizations.[44]

The Arizona Health Cost Containment System (AHCCS), implemented in 1982, relies on provider bidding for the delivery of health care to the indigent. The Arizona Medicaid program puts out various types of care for per capita bids, and counties as well as private-sector providers compete for prepaid contracts. In such a prepaid, capitated system of health care, financial risk bearing is shifted, partially from the consumer and totally from the third-party insurer, to the provider. According to proponents, such a system internalizes economic incentives.[45] Competitive bidding is also becoming increasingly popular for health care services such as clinical laboratory services, home health care, and mental health care.[46]

An analysis of the Arizona system in 1985 revealed that, overall, a lower proportion of the poor were enrolled in AHCCS in 1984 than in county programs in 1982. Access to care increased for AHCCS enrollees in 1984 compared to county patients in 1982. But the study also discovered significant undercoverage of the medically indigent and the medically needy. The study concluded that AHCCS may be a viable alternative to conventional Medicaid programs, but poor persons who were financially ineligible for AHCCS were experiencing decreased opportunities for health services.[47] Thus it remains to be seen whether a competitive bidding approach helps contain costs without sacrificing access or quality of care.

The 1981 OBRA greatly expanded state authority by allowing states to purchase in bulk durable medical equipment, lab tests, and X-ray services. Some states are using bulk purchase arrangements for goods such as eyeglasses, hearing aids, and laboratory services. The objective is to buy from the lowest bidder, rather than reimburse every retail seller at his or her price.

Rationing of Medicaid Services

The state of Oregon is in the process of implementing an innovative approach to address problems of cost and access in its Medicaid program. In 1987 the state decided to stop financing most organ transplants for Medicaid patients and use the money instead for prenatal care for pregnant women. In 1990 the state produced a more revolutionary Medicaid plan. As we discussed earlier, a large number of poor people do not have access to Medicaid because they do not meet eligibility criteria. The state proposed that under its plan, Medicaid would cover all poor people in the state but may not cover all medical services. In other words, the plan proposed a tradeoff—increased access in return for reduced benefits. The state ranked most medical services as more or less economically worthwhile to treat under the plan. If money ran out before all services were covered, the lowest-priority services would not be covered. In March 1993, the HCFA under the Clinton administration, granted the state of Oregon a waiver from federal statutes to implement such a program. This is likely to encourage other states to adopt similar plans. Colorado is considering doing away with the Medicaid program and establishing its own health care program for the poor.[48]

Critics charge that the plan targets the poor—mainly women and children, who make up most of the Medicaid population.[49] They also argue that the meat-ax approach to health care will inevitably lead to gross misallocation of resources.[50]

Use of Medicaid Waivers for Home and Community-Based Services

Section 2176 of the 1981 OBRA allowed states to seek waivers from the Department of Health and Human Services (HHS) for a variety of home and community-based services provided to certain individuals—the elderly, the physically disabled, the developmentally disabled, and the mentally ill—who would otherwise require nursing home care. States that have approval from HHS can receive matching funds. The objective of section 2176 was to encourage a move away from the use of more expensive treatment in nursing homes and other long-term care facilities and toward less expensive home and community-based services when appropriate. The traditional purpose of the waiver process has been to allow HHS to conduct demonstrations on alternative delivery and financing schemes. The waiver provisions of the 1981 OBRA were based on early successes of demonstration projects in this area.

Such waiver programs have become popular with many states and have grown rapidly since their creation in 1981. In 1985, forty-two states were providing a broad range of health and social services under seventy-five waiver programs. The number of recipients had increased steadily under such waiver programs. For example, the number of aged/physically disabled recipients increased from 6,389 in 1981 to 45,934 in 1984. Similarly, the number of developmentally disabled and chronically mentally ill recipients increased from 10,000 to 21,823 during the same period.[51] But the popularity of waiver programs does not mean that all states find them cost effective. The waiver also provides states with a way to secure additional federal funding for services that otherwise would have to be funded entirely through state revenues.[52]

The Clinton administration has expressed its willingness to allow states more flexibility on Medicaid funds and has supported states' efforts at innovation and experimentation. For example, President Clinton has ordered the federal government to make it easier for states to use Medicaid funds to introduce new health care programs for the poor. The administration intends to ease paperwork requirements related to states' request for waivers in two ways. First, the Department of Health and Human Services will no longer be allowed to make numerous requests for information and clarifications on a state's waiver application. Second, HCFA has been ordered to develop a list of state programs already approved for waiver. The purpose of this is to allow other states seeking to start similar programs to adopt them immediately, without having to go through the paperwork themselves.[53]

Medicaid: Middle-Class Entitlement?

In recent years, Medicaid has come under attack on the grounds that the program is being misused by the affluent elderly. Critics of the program have charged that it is increasingly being used to provide expensive benefits, that is, nursing home care for middle-class and affluent elderly. The "spousal impoverishment" benefit has expanded Medicaid's role for the middle class. Many families have begun to see Medicaid as a middle-class entitlement, as a way to preserve the family's life savings and property in the event that one or both parents require high-cost nursing home care.[54] Middle-class and affluent elderly are also increasingly utilizing ways not sanctioned by the government to retain family wealth and at the same time take advantage of Medicaid benefits. Numerous techniques for sheltering assets or transferring them to family members as a prelude to getting Medicaid to pay the bills for nursing home care are employed. These include maneuvers such as joint bank accounts, holding property in joint tenancy, investing in irrevocable and nontransferable annuities, and paying family members for services such as shopping and transportation. An army of lawyers and financial advisers are counseling affluent Americans on how to shuffle, shed, or shelter an elderly family member's assets to qualify for Medicaid nursing home benefits. Such maneuvers, often called "Medicaid estate planning," are legal but run counter to the intent of the law. Today Medicaid pays about 52 percent of the nation's $69.3 billion nursing home bill. The Health Care Financing Administration has estimated that Medicaid's nursing home costs will grow two and a half times by the year 2000.[55]

The state of Virginia has tried to close some of these loopholes and gaps in the Medicaid program. The state's General Assembly rejected a proposed tax on hospitals, nursing homes, and doctors. Nevertheless, one of the measures approved would allow state Medicaid officials to recover up to $92,000 in assets transferred within four years of a patient's becoming eligible for Medicaid by going after the heir or recipient. Federal law bars transfers within two and one-half years of eligibility and allows states to extend that period.[56]

A few states are trying to find ways to allow more of the affluent elderly to benefit from the Medicaid program. Seven states have been trying to devise experiments that would allow these elderly to hang on to more of their assets and be entitled to Medicaid benefits provided that they bought long-term care insurance first. Under the experimental plan, elderly participants would contribute to the cost of their care in a more rational way by pooling risks. Such a plan, supporters argue, would save states money. The more middle-class people who buy long-term care insurance, the fewer who will "spend down" their savings and end up on Medicaid at public expense.[57]

New Approaches to Reimbursing Providers

Payments to Physicians

States have generally enjoyed significant discretion over Medicaid payments to physicians. The Medicaid program has traditionally paid physicians much less than Medicare or private insurers. For example, under the

Medicare program states are mandated to pay physicians "usual, customary, and reasonable" fees (UCR payment system). The Medicaid statute, however, never imposed any specific method of payment on the states except that the fee be high enough to assure reasonable access to care for Medicaid beneficiaries.

Through waivers, states have also been able to pay physicians a set fee or capitation payment rather than a fee-for-service payment. States also can establish case management programs linking patients to solo or group practice physicians or with an HMO.[58] States may, under a waiver program, enroll Medicaid patients in an HMO and restrict their use of other providers.

Several state Medicaid programs have imposed significant limits or ceilings on physician payment. Some states have turned to the use of fee schedules. The average Medicaid payment for a visit to a physician is estimated to be only 65 percent of the average charge for visits of other patients. Medicare pays about 84 percent on the average. The result is that many physicians do not accept Medicaid patients; the willingness to accept them varies with the level of Medicaid payments.[59] This raises questions about access of Medicaid recipients to physicians. When Medicaid cuts have to be made, state programs often attempt to impose further restrictions on physicians' fees. Such efforts are often misguided. In general, physicians' fees constitute a very small percentage of total Medicaid spending. Thus, trying to save money by limiting payments to physicians may not be the best way to reduce program costs. In fact, reduced physician participation may drive many beneficiaries to substitute services at a greater cost to Medicaid.

Payments to Hospitals

In contrast to physician payment, Medicaid has generally been required to pay hospitals on the same basis as Medicare, that is, a "reasonable cost" reimbursement method. With the 1972 amendments to the Social Security Act, however, there has been a gradual trend toward paying less than the actual cost. The amendments allowed states with approval from HHS to use alternate (to Medicare) payment methods for Medicaid.

The 1981 OBRA gave states more flexibility to develop and implement new Medicaid hospital payment methods as long as those payments were reasonable and adequate to meet the costs of "efficiently and economically operated facilities." The only requirements were that payment levels take into consideration the circumstances of hospitals serving a disproportionate number of low-income persons and that payments be sufficient to ensure Medicaid patients reasonable access to adequate-quality services.[60]

Faced with reduced revenues and increased health care costs, state governments have tried various strategies to contain costs. By 1982, seventeen states had legislation requiring the disclosure, review (such as HSAs and CON), or regulation of hospital rates or budgets. States such as California converted their hospital payment approach to selective contracting on the basis of price negotiated for services provided.

One major alternative payment method used by state governments is rate setting. Many states have adopted some form of hospital rate review or prospective reimbursement system. In some states, rate setting applies only to Medicaid, while in others the rate applies to all payers.[61] Rate-setting programs fall into three broad strategies to control Medicaid costs: multiple-payer rate setting, Medicaid-only prospective payment, and selective contracting.[62]

The state rate-setting strategy emerged in the mid-1970s in several eastern industrial states as a regulatory device in response to Medicaid's financial crisis. Limited prospective payment schemes for Medicaid reimbursement have been adopted in Kentucky, Missouri, Alabama, Georgia, Mississippi, and North Carolina.[63]

State rate-setting programs have produced mixed results. Proponents have argued that some mandatory prospective rate-setting programs have been successful in reducing hospital expenditures per patient day, per admission, and per capita.[64] Other studies have also demonstrated that states have achieved modest success in containing Medicaid payments to hospitals under different rate-setting strategies—multiple-payer rate setting, Medicaid-only rate setting, and selective contracting—with some being more effective than others.[65] States that use all-payer rate setting are able to force down hospital prices for all payers. In states where the payment systems apply only to Medicaid, savings appear to be temporary and may not be sustained over a long period of time.[66]

Increased Use of Managed Care and HMOs

In response to problems of cost and access, states have increasingly turned to managed care systems in the Medicaid program. More and more state governments are moving in the direction of "privatization" of their Medicaid programs. States and the federal government continue to fund the program jointly, but the day-to-day control of health plans for the poor is being turned over to HMOs and private insurers. Many states require Medicaid recipients to enroll in an HMO or other preferred provider organizations (PPOs). Case managers or primary-care physicians are assigned to watch Medicaid patients' health. They act as gatekeepers to control and coordinate the delivery of health services in a cost-conscious manner. The emphasis is on low-cost preventive care, outpatient services, and less reliance on emergency hospital care and costly specialists as a way of reducing costs.[67]

The 1981 OBRA gave states more flexibility to design managed care plans. In addition, HCFA allows states to experiment with innovative approaches to Medicaid through research and demonstration projects. In most instances, states must obtain a waiver of federal statutory requirements from HCFA. As a result, most states are rapidly developing managed care programs. According to a study by the General Accounting Office, Medicaid managed care enrollment more than doubled between 1987 and 1992 and included about 3.6 million beneficiaries nationwide, representing about 12 percent of the total Medicaid population as of June 1992. Thirty-six states were operating one or more mandatory managed care programs for Medicaid beneficiaries in February 1993.[68] States participating in managed care share a common approach but employ a variety of models. Some plans utilize a prepaid or capitated method. In this model, organizations providing health care are paid a per capita amount each month to provide or arrange for all covered services. Other states rely on primary-care case management (PCCM) models. Such models are similar to traditional fee-for-service arrangements except that providers receive a per capita management fee to coordinate a patient's care in addition to reimbursement for the services they provide.[69] All of the thirty-six states with managed care programs target their programs to the AFDC population. Other Medicaid populations are included by states to a varying degree.[70]

The results of managed care experiments by state governments to contain Medicaid costs have been mixed. Some studies have found that managed care can save money. One study examined twenty-five managed care programs and found that per-member costs were 5 to 15 percent lower than in conventional Medicaid programs.[71] Many other studies of managed care plans have demonstrated that to a large extent such plans have failed to improve recipients' access.[72] A General Accounting Office study concluded that "managed care plans have had mixed results in improving access to care, assuring the quality of services, and saving money."[73]

Managed care programs are plagued with other problems. In states that do not monitor HMO behavior, such plans may offer impressive marketing but poor care. Such HMOs are often referred to as "Medicaid mills." Some HMOs snap up the healthiest patients, leaving traditional Medicaid to deal with sicker people. In addition, paperwork is always a problem because many Medicaid recipients go on and off program rolls as their income and family status change.[74]

Recent Developments: Late 1980s and Early 1990s

The incremental expansion in Medicaid coverage for pregnant women, infants, and children through the 1986 and 1987 OBRAs, and the "spousal impoverishment" benefit of 1988 has led to a significant increase in the number of Medicaid recipients. The total number of recipients increased from 21.6 million in 1985 to 28.3 million in 1991. This expansion in coverage and the increased number of recipients, combined with the 1990–91 recession, has forced many states into a situation of fiscal crisis. According to a national survey conducted in 1991 by the National Association of Budget Officers and the National Governors' Association, the recession and Medicaid expansion mandates from the federal government forced more than half of all states to cut spending or increase revenues to avoid deficits in fiscal year 1991. Twenty-eight states faced total revenue shortfalls totaling $9.6 billion in 1991. Thirty-two states reported that their Medicaid spending would exceed their projections for the year.[75] According to a report by the General Accounting Office, expansion of Medicaid through federal mandates has improved coverage, but the fiscal problems faced by the states are likely to jeopardize further progress.[76]

State Taxes on Hospitals and Health Care Providers

In response, state governments have come to rely on a very controversial and growing practice known as *"bootstrapping,"* also called "FTF" for "Fool the Feds." The practice involves states ordering doctors and other health care providers to hike up their fees so that the cost can be passed on to Washington. Thirty-seven states have passed laws that charge doctors, hospitals, and other Medicaid providers an extra tax. The money then can be returned to hospitals in the form of higher Medicaid reimbursements. Since the federal government reimburses anywhere from 50 to 83 percent of state Medicaid costs, the more a state charges, the more it gets back. If hospitals are unwilling to play along with the "voluntary donation" scheme, the states can pull the same trick by charging "provider taxes." The state levies a uniform tax on all hospitals, doctors, and other health care providers. The tax revenues are routed back to the providers of Medicaid services in the form of higher Medicaid reimbursements.[77] According to Richard Kusserow, inspector general of HHS, such provider taxes and donation programs "may change the very nature of the whole federal-state partnership."[78]

In September 1991 the Bush administration proposed new rules intended to eliminate what it described as a "scam" used by the states to extract $3 billion to $5 billion a year from the federal government. Under the proposed rule, the federal government would not match spending by states for Medicaid if the state's money came from donations or special taxes paid by hospitals and nursing homes. The administration claimed that this practice of raising federal money by counting donations and taxes as part of a state's Medicaid share is a major reason for the explosion of the federal government's Medicaid costs. A statement issued on behalf of the National Governors' Association warned that if the proposed rules were adopted they could lead to the closing of hospitals, and women and children would lose eligibility for Medicaid.[79] After strong opposition from state officials, a deal was struck in which states could continue the program if every hospital is taxed by the method.

The new rules impose various requirements. First, health care–related taxes eligible for federal matching funds must be broad based, imposed uniformly, and include all members of a class, such as all inpatient hospitals, all physicians, or all HMOs and other prepaid entities. Second, these taxes cannot make up more than 25 percent of a state's share of Medicaid. Finally, the taxes cannot contain a "hold harmless" provision, which guarantees that health care providers will have the tax they paid returned to them.[80] Based on the above rules, Congress in 1991 passed a law that closed the "provider taxes" loophole. But the story did not end with the 1991 law. According to the rules published by the Health Care Financing Administration (HCFA) in August 1993, the provider taxes must be broad based and uniform. In addition, states must drop "hold harmless" clauses. Nevertheless, almost half the states continue to make the assessments. The HCFA sent letters to nine states claiming that they were violating the law. In another letter to twenty-three states the HCFA argued that their programs were neither broad based nor uniform. The HCFA has disallowed millions of dollars worth of claims made by many states.[81]

Increase in Number of Medicaid Lawsuits

The 1981 OBRA eliminated altogether the federal requirement for reasonable-cost reimbursement. As we discussed earlier, under this act, states are now required to pay only the "reasonable and adequate" rates needed to meet the costs of "efficiently and economically operated facilities." This is also known as the Boren Amendment, named after Senator David Boren (D-Okla.). States only have to consider the special needs of institutions serving a disproportionate number of poor persons and to assure "reasonable access" to services and "adequate quality."

State governments facing budget problems have begun to change their rate-setting formulas to reduce reimbursements to hospitals and nursing homes. This in turn has led hospitals and nursing homes to file lawsuits against states to force them to increase Medicaid payments to levels that more closely reflect what it costs to treat patients. Not only has the number of Medicaid lawsuits increased, but so have the legal and political complexities involved in such lawsuits.[82] In February 1990 a federal judge ordered the state of Pennsylvania to increase its reimbursements to Temple University Hospital, the state's largest provider of health care to the poor. The judge declared that Pennsylvania's Medicaid rates were arbitrary and that the rate-setting formula used by the state was simply a mechanism to keep the total medical assistance cost within the welfare department budget.[83] In a decision handed down in June 1990, the U.S. Supreme Court upheld the right of hospitals and other providers to sue the states for higher Medicaid payments.[84]

According to a survey of hospitals by the American Hospital Association, hospitals, on average, receive 78 cents for every dollar it costs to care for Medicaid patients. Judges in several cases have reached similar conclusions. In many states, judges have ruled that Medicaid payments to health care providers do not meet the standards of "reasonable and adequate" compensation under the law. Judges in several states have also concluded that states often base their payments simply on budget considerations. The result is that federal and state spending has increased by several billion dollars a year as a result of court judgments, settlements, and rate increases granted by states in anticipation of lawsuits.[85]

Despite various strategies attempted by the federal and state governments to control the cost of Medicaid, total Medicaid expenditures increased from $24.8 billion in 1980 to $112.8 billion in 1993. During the same period, the federal government's Medicaid costs increased from $13.7 billion to $73.2 billion, while state costs increased from $11.1 billion to $39.6 billion. Thus, despite many innovative approaches utilized by state governments, the overall cost of the Medicaid program continues to grow.[86]

Conclusions

Medicaid policy has, in a sense, come full circle. The Reagan administration, in the early 1980s, used the conservative rhetoric of decentralization as a way of giving states more discretionary authority and reducing Medicaid enrollment. In the process, the administration also attempted to reduce the federal costs of the program and pass along some of its financial burden to the states. The Democrats in Congress during the mid-1980s used the liberal rhetoric of equal access and quality of care to expand the Medicaid program incrementally through the use of federal mandates.

The decentralization of the Medicaid program by the Reagan administration in the early 1980s gave state governments greater flexibility to experiment with new approaches in delivering health care to the poor. The subsequent program expansion through congressional mandates significantly increased the number of recipients, as well as program costs. Concerned with the dramatically rising cost of a program that is consuming an ever-larger portion of state budgets, state governments have used the Medicaid program in innovative ways to respond to the access and health care financing issues. Some have experimented with service delivery, payment reforms, and outreach programs. These approaches have included rationing Medicaid services, the increased use of Medicaid waivers for home or community-based services, fixed-price arrangements with health care providers, hospital rate setting, and the bulk-rate purchase of equipment and services. More emphasis has also been placed on case management and managed care. Many states have established new programs designed to provide preventive and primary care. Today, many states are trying innovative ways to expand coverage and at the same time control rising costs.[87]

The results of these experiments have been mixed. While a few have been successful in containing specific costs, the overall cost of the program continues to rise both at the federal and state levels. Rationing in the Medicaid program leads to concerns about reduced access and limited choices. The same concerns arise in managed care programs. Reduction in payments to physicians has often made them more reluctant to accept Medicaid patients. Hospital rate-setting programs, especially those confined to the Medicaid program, in general have not been very successful.

Increased micromanagement of the Medicaid program by the federal government through congressional mandates has created additional problems for states. State governments' ability to fund the program at the current service level has been severely tested. The problem is compounded by a growing caseload, declining revenues, and balanced-budget requirements. States are being sued by hospitals and other health care providers over reimbursement rates. In a majority of cases states have been the losers. The crisis of escalating costs is not likely to be resolved until the problems of long-term care, reimbursement levels, and the uninsured are addressed in one form or another.

State governments alone are not likely to solve the problem of Medicaid and its cost because of fundamental impediments in the federal system. As Deborah Stone has argued, state governments lack sufficient autonomy from the federal government in the area of health care financing. Nor do they have sufficient power over private insurers, doctors, and hospitals. Federal law governing Medicaid limits the options available to state governments. The problem is too big and too complex for state-based solutions.[88]

Medicaid policy reflects the dictum that the more things change, the more they stay the same. The Medicaid policy process is driven to a significant extent by forces of federalism that often produce policies geared toward short-term, patchwork answers, rather than long-term solutions. All the new state experiments and innovations have failed to produce any consensus on how best to contain costs. These experiments have offered many different models of cost containment, but none that is satisfactory to all parties. It is clear that the program cannot continue on its current course given stagnant or declining resources on the one hand and pressure to provide coverage to more people on the other. Additional ad hoc, stopgap fixes are likely to produce more dissatisfaction with the program among groups such as policymakers, health care providers, program administrators, and advocacy groups. The Clinton administration, as part of a health care plan designed to overhaul the health care system, had considered a proposal to dismantle the Medicaid program and integrate low-income people into the same network of doctors, hospitals, and private insurance companies that serves more affluent people. The failure of the Clinton administration to bring about major health care reform leaves the future of the Medicaid program uncertain.

That uncertainty was compounded by developments in 1995. The Republicans, who regained control of Congress as a result of the 1994 elections, made two proposals regarding Medicaid. One proposal is to reduce expected Medicaid spending through the year 2002 by about $175 billion. The Clinton administration has proposed $55 billion in cuts in Medicaid over the same period. The other, related Republican proposal was to transform Medicaid into a block grant. A block grant proposal would provide the states with the funds to run the program (though at a lower level than under current law) plus the flexibility to run the program the way they want. Under the block grant proposal, states could, for example, require their Medicaid recipients to enroll in HMOs.[89] Given these proposals, Medicaid reform initiatives are likely to come from state governments. In any event, the two-tiered health care system we currently have—one for the rich and another for the poor—is likely to continue for the time being.

4

Medicare: Health Care
for the Elderly and Disabled

Medicare is the largest public-sector health care program in the United States, both in terms of dollars and numbers of people covered. It began as an alternative to national health insurance and remains one of the most popular government programs. Despite its popularity, it has often been a target for those who seek to curtail government spending. Further, significant changes in the course of the thirty-year history of the program provide lessons for the possible expansion of government provision of health care services. Finally, there are problems in the Medicare program relating to costs and coverage. Perhaps the most significant gap in Medicare is the lack of coverage for long-term care.

In this chapter, we closely examine Medicare. We begin by looking at its origin and structure. We then look at some of the changes and problems with the program and how those problems have been addressed. We close this portion of the chapter by examining proposed solutions. We next turn to the problem of long-term care and how that has been addressed in the United States. We look at some solutions to those problems and make some final conclusions about Medicare.

The Origins of Medicare

As mentioned in chapter 2, national health insurance (NHI) was first considered in the early twentieth century, during Woodrow Wilson's administration. But the onset of World War I, the linkage between NHI and Germany (which was the first to adopt NHI), and opposition to national health insurance on the part of the AMA killed the program.[1] During the development of what eventually became the Social Security Act of 1935, policy formulators (the Committee for Economic Security) considered and rejected adding a national health insurance provision. They believed, based on responses to the mere mention of national health insurance, that including national health insurance would sink the entire Social Security bill.[2] Beginning in 1939, bills for national health insurance were introduced in Congress (e.g., the Murray-Wagner-Dingell bill). As Marmor points out,[3] though the Democrats had a numerical majority, they did not have a "programmatic majority" to enact the legislation. That is, there was insufficient unity within the majority Democratic Party, a problem that has been repeated, most recently in 1994 (see chapter 8). The 1948 Democratic national platform called for national health insurance. Despite Truman's victory in that election, the Murray-Wagner-Dingell legislation died, never coming out of committee in Congress.

Advocates of national health insurance then tried an alternative strategy. The new strategy was incremental in nature, focusing on a group or groups that had reasonably high status but could not afford health insurance. The ideal group was the elderly.[4] Marmor describes the political strategy behind the new strategy:

> The concentration on the burdens of the aged was a ploy for sympathy. The disavowal of aims to change fundamentally the American medical system was a sop to AMA fears, and the exclusion of physician services benefits was a response to past AMA hysteria. The focus on the financial burdens of receiving hospital care took as given the existing structure of the private medical care world, and stressed the issue of spreading the costs of using available services within that world. The organization of health care, with its inefficiencies and resistance to cost-reduction, was a fundamental but politically sensitive problem which consensus-minded reformers wanted to avoid when they opted for 60 days of hospitalization insurance for the aged in 1951 as a promising "small" beginning.[5]

The above quote contains several important points. It shows the attempt to accommodate potential opposition, primarily the medical profession. It did this in several ways. It excluded coverage of physician services, though Medicare as enacted did include such coverage (but treated it differently from hospital care). It limited the number of hospital days covered, the "small beginning," a feature that remains an integral part of Medicare. Finally, it left the structure of American medicine alone. That structure was the private practice of physicians and the fee-for-service system.[6] Some of these features would eventually be changed in the 1980s and 1990s. But they were at least partly responsible for some of the problems that Medicare has faced. A final note: the attempt at political accommodation was also a feature of the Clinton administration's Health Security Act. In any event, the finance committees in Congress held hearings on Medicare from 1958 to 1965.[7]

In 1960 Congress passed the Kerr-Mills bill, which provided federal assistance (50–80 percent) to states to help with hospital care for the aged poor. In other words, Kerr-Mills was a welfare program, with all the accompanying problems and stigma of means-tested (income-based) programs. By 1963, many states had not even enacted programs to use Kerr-Mills.[8]

John F. Kennedy's campaign platform in 1960 included health insurance for the aged. Attempts were made to push a narrow program for the elderly from the beginning of the Kennedy administration. The conservative coalition (Republicans and southern Democrats) that had long opposed liberal legislation was able to delay enactment of the program, but the great electoral victory of Lyndon Johnson in 1964 accompanied by a large liberal Democratic majority in Congress allowed passage of a number of programs, part of the Johnson administration's Great Society. For our purposes, the important bill was Medicare, passed in 1965.

The law (Title 18 amendments to the 1935 Social Security Act) was broader than envisioned under the incrementalist strategy of the Truman administration. It included physician services and covered a large section of the aged population, not just those who were poor, but those covered by Social Security. Thus it embodied a social insurance concept, where subscribers made contributions, rather than assistance to the poor, which required means testing. Medicare would cover a large portion of the population, and virtually all would contribute and benefit.[9]

Program Objectives and Structure

Objectives

The original design or theory of the program has been aptly stated by Thompson: "If Washington paid mainstream rates to providers for delivering medical care to the elderly, they would receive increased amounts of needed care."[10]

The problem facing the elderly was that, for several reasons, they could not afford health insurance. First, health insurance was available to individuals and families largely through the workplace. As retirees, the elderly were (in most cases) no longer eligible to receive health insurance benefits. Second, because retirees were no longer part of a larger group through their job, they would not be able to gain the benefits of group insurance. Individual insurance rates are considerably higher than group rates. Finally, the elderly were (and are) more at risk of needing medical care (more likely to experience periods of illness, especially extended illness) and expensive care than those of working age. The combination of these three factors meant that few private health insurance companies would offer a policy to retirees, and those that were offered were prohibitively expensive. In 1963, only about 54 percent of the elderly (sixty-five years and older) had hospital insurance.[11]

Medicare resolved many of these problems. For example, from 1985 to 1987, 99.3 percent of those sixty-five or older were covered by insurance. Only 0.6 of a percent of those over sixty-five were covered for only part of that period, only 0.1 percent were not covered at all. By comparison, only 65.5 percent of those under eighteen years of age were covered for the entire period. Almost 30 percent were covered for part of that period, and more than 5 percent had no coverage whatsoever.[12] In 1992, over 12 percent of those under eighteen had no health insurance.[13] Clearly, Medicare had achieved its primary goal of providing health insurance for the elderly. Whether it was adequate is another story.

Structure

Medicare is open to those over sixty-five years of age, those disabled and receiving Social Security cash benefits, and those suffering from end-stage renal disease (ESRD, or kidney failure).[14] The program has two parts, hospital insurance and the supplementary medical program.

The hospital insurance program (HI, or Part A) covers inpatient hospital expenses for specified periods. Recipients are covered for up to ninety days for a benefit period and have a lifetime reserve of sixty hospital days. Payment is made for room and board in semiprivate rooms and for such hospital services as nursing and pharmaceuticals. Part A also pays for hospice services and limited skilled nursing care. Table 4.1 lists the services covered under Part A.

The other major portion of Medicare is the supplementary medical insurance program (SMI or Part B). This is a voluntary program, though most Medicare recipients subscribe to it. SMI covers a wide range of physician and outpatient services, including diagnostic and surgical procedures and radiology. It also covers outpatient services, including ambulance services, medical supplies, clinical services, and blood transfusions. Table 4.2 lists the services covered under Part B.

As important as what is covered is what is not covered. In three major areas, Medicare coverage is extremely limited. First, Medicare does not pay for prescription drugs unless a patient is hospitalized. Thus, a Medicare patient, unless otherwise insured, must pay the full cost of medication, which can be expensive. We address this gap later in the chapter in connection with so-called medigap policies and the Medicare Catastrophic Cover-

Table 4.1

Medicare Part A, Covered Services, by Place of Service

Type of covered service	Inpatient hospital	Skilled nursing facility	Home health agency	Hospice
Accommodations, semi-private, including special diets	X	X	—	X
Blood transfusions	X	X	—	X
Counseling	—	—	—	X
Dental services requiring hospitalization	X	—	—	X
Doctors' services	—	—	—	X
Drugs and biologicals	X	X	—	X
Durable medical equipment	X	X	X	X
Emergency services	X	—	—	—
Home health aides	—	—	X	—
Homemakers' services	—	—	—	X
Intern and resident services and teaching physicians in hospitals	X	X	X	—
Medical social services	X	X	X	X
Medical supplies and appliances	X	X	X	X
Nursing and related services, excluding private duty	X	X	X	X
Nursing, intermittent skilled nursing care	—	—	X	—
Occupational therapy	X	X	X	X
Other diagnostic services	X	X	—	—
Outpatient services	—	X	X	—
Physical therapy	X	X	X	X
Respite care and procedures necessary for pain control	—	—	—	X
Speech pathology	X	X	X	X
White blood and packed red blood cells	X	X	—	—

Source: John T. Petrie, "Overview of the Medicare Program," *Health Care Financing Review*, 1992 annual supplement, 1–12.

age Act of 1988. A second, related limitation of Medicare is catastrophic coverage, that is, coverage of hospital stays that exceed the specified limits. Finally, Medicare has extremely limited long-term-care coverage. We also address this issue later in this chapter.

Table 4.2

Medicare Part B, Physician and Outpatient Covered Services

Physican services	Outpatient services
Diagnostic tests and procedures	Ambulance transportation Ambulatory surgical centers Antigen and blood-clotting factors
Medical and surgical services, including anesthesia	Blood transfusions, blood and other components
Radiology and pathology services while hospital inpatient or outpatient	Certified registered nurse anesthetist Clinic services
Other services furnished in a doctor's office: X-rays Drugs and biologicals Blood and blood components Medical supplies Physical therapy Occupational therapy Speech therapy	Comprehensive outpatient rehabilitation facility Dialysis services Drugs and biologicals Durable medical equipment Emergency room services Independent clinical laboratory Laboratory tests billed by hospital
Chiropractic services (manual manipulation of the spine to correct subluxation)	Medical supplies Mental health services Nurse-midwife
Dental services that involve surgery on the jaw or the setting of fractures	Occupational therapy Physical therapy Physician assistant
Optometrists, excluding routine eye examinations	Portable diagnostic X-ray Prosthetic devices
Podiatrist services, excluding routine foot care	Psychological services Rural health services
Second opinions	Speech pathology Vaccines, hepatitis and pneumococcal X-rays and other radiology services billed by the hospital

Source: John T. Petrie, "Overview of the Medicare Program," *Health Care Financing Review*, 1992 annual supplement, 1–12.

Financing Medicare

Medicare is financed through a combination of subscriber and tax payments. The Hospital Insurance and Supplementary Medical Insurance programs are financed differently. We begin with the hospital program.

The bulk of funds for the hospital insurance trust fund comes from the payroll tax (1.45 percent), a part of the Social Security tax that employees and employers pay.[15] In addition, there are copayments when Medicare recipients use hospital services. There is a one-time deductible (paid before Medicare starts paying) equal to the average cost of one day in the hospital. For 1995, that amount was $716.[16] Medicare then pays for the entire cost of hospitalization for the next fifty-nine days. If the hospitalization lasts longer than sixty days, there is a deductible equal to one-quarter of a hospital day ($179) for days sixty-one through ninety. Each Medicare recipient has a reserve equal to sixty hospital days, which can be used past day ninety. The deductible is then half of the inpatient hospital deductible ($358) per day.[17] Under Part A, Medicare also pays for hospice and home health care with very limited deductibles. For example, those eligible for skilled nursing home services do not have to pay a deductible for the first twenty days. For the next eighty days, the deductible is $89.50 per day.

The Supplementary Insurance Program, or Part B, is financed through a combination of general federal revenues and Medicare subscriber premiums. Federal government revenues accounted for more than 73 percent of the trust funds in 1991. Premiums and tax contributions were approximately equal in 1971; since that time, tax contributions have dwarfed premiums. That is why, even given the cost increases in Part B copayments, SMI remains a bargain.[18]

Virtually all Medicare recipients (over 97 percent) are enrolled in the Supplementary Insurance Program (Part B). The 1995 premium (the amount paid each month) is $46.10 and is deducted from Social Security checks. Medicare pays 80 percent of physician charges as determined under the physician fee scale phased in beginning in 1992. The Medicare recipient is responsible for the other 20 percent. Physicians elect each year whether to accept full assignment, that is, whether to accept the Medicare fee schedule (participating). If the physician does accept the fee schedule, Medicare is billed by the physician and the recipient pays the balance (what is known as *balance billing*). Physicians do not have to accept full assignment. They can charge up to 115 percent of the Medicare fee schedule.

An example may help explain the fee schedule. Assume that you are a Medicare recipient who needs to visit a doctor. Your doctor would normally charge $200, given the services provided. According to the Medicare physician fee schedule, the visit is worth $118.[19] Medicare then will pay 80 percent of the $118, or $94.40. Now it gets complicated. Consider these two cases: In case 1, the physician accepts full assignment, or the $118. He or she then sends in the paperwork to Medicare and receives a reimbursement of $94.40. You, the Medicare patient, pay the balance, or $23.60, to the doctor. Now take case 2: The physician does not accept full assignment. He or she can charge up to 115 percent of the $118, or $135.70. The physician bills the patient for the entire amount. The patient pays the doctor and files for reimbursement from Medicare. The Medicare recipient receives $94.40 from Medicare and has to pay a net of $41.30. From the standpoint of the recipient, using a physician that does not accept full assignment would cost an additional $17.70, an increase in the copayment of 75 percent. It obviously pays the Medicare recipient to use physicians who accept assignment.

Over time, Medicare cost sharing has become a higher proportion of the elderly's income. In 1975, cost sharing was about 6.2 percent of the elderly's average median income. By 1990, that figure had risen to 10.2 percent.[20] The problem of cost sharing, or medigap, is considered below.

Medicare and HMOs

In the 1980s, Medicare began enrolling recipients in health maintenance organizations (HMOs) as a means of restraining cost increases while maintaining quality of care for recipients. In addition, it was hoped that Medicare recipients would gain access to the same range of services as other patients.[21] In 1986, over 467,000 Medicare recipients were enrolled in HMOs. This represented about 1.6 percent of Medicare recipients and about 2.2 percent of HMO subscribers. By 1993, Medicare HMO enrollment exceeded 1.5 million recipients. This represented 4.8 percent of Medicare recipients and just over 3.8 percent of the total HMO subscriber population.[22] Under the Medicare risk program, HMOs provide Medicare recipients with all Medicare covered services for a set payment (known as capitation). The capitation payment, 95 percent of what Medicare would normally pay, is calculated through a complicated formula. Therefore, Medicare should save 5 percent. The theory behind this provision was that

> HMOs, which act as insurers but have control over the set of providers from which members can choose and how much they are paid, have an incentive to provide care in the most cost-effective manner possible. This cost-effectiveness is achieved by reducing unnecessary services and providing health care in the least expensive but appropriate setting. The market power of HMOs can also help them negotiate favorable prices for provider services.[23]

A four-year evaluation found that these "risk" plans tended to enroll healthier than average Medicare recipients. Those enrolled in risk plans had 20 percent lower Medicare reimbursements than those not so enrolled. Further, they were less likely to be disabled or have chronic health problems than those enrolled in risk plans. Such a pattern of enrollment, called *favorable selection,* has often been charged to HMOs. The evaluation study estimates that given favorable selection, costs to Medicare were actually 5.7 percent higher than for the fee-for-service system.[24]

On the other hand, HMOs do tend to reduce the length of hospital stays over the fee-for-service system, though they do not reduce the number of admissions. For other services, HMOs tend to reduce the intensity of services (the number of services provided). The effects are greatest for those who are most seriously ill. Quality of care for HMO Medicare recipients was about equal to that of fee-for-service Medicare recipients.[25] Of concern is that some of these risk HMOs failed during the latter part of the 1980s. Oversight of the programs seem to have improved, as has the performance of the HMOs.[26]

Medigap

As can be seen from the above discussion, Medicare does not cover everything. Nor does it pay for everything it covers. This has created a situation known as *medigap.* The gap can be covered in several ways. First, for Medicare beneficiaries who are also eligible for Medicaid (i.e., low-income individuals), there is state buy-in coverage. In 1991, some 3.6 million (about 11 percent of Medicare recipients) were eligible for both programs.[27] States pay the premium under Part B and any cost sharing. What is covered under Medicare is paid for by Medicare and what is covered under Medicaid (such as prescription drugs or long-term care) is paid for by Medicaid.

Another solution is private supplemental medical insurance, so-called medigap policies. Such policies are provided by insurance companies or group organizations such as the American Association of Retired Persons (AARP). In 1990, 77 percent of those sixty-five and older had private health insurance.[28] Medigap policies raise the average cost of health care because policyholders pay the full cost of that insurance, which includes administrative and advertising costs plus profits for insurance.[29] Such policies, as might be expected, are expensive. Those most likely to have supplementary policies are those who are better educated, younger, in better health, have higher incomes, and are white.[30]

The 1980 amendments to the Social Security Act made it illegal knowingly to sell medigap policies that duplicate other policies. Of course the key word here is "knowingly." Nevertheless, analysis in 1987 suggested that while about 20 percent of Medicare recipients purchased more than one medigap policy, duplication was not a serious problem. There was duplication of policies that paid cash benefits or were specific to certain diseases. Between duplication and premium increases, some regulation was seen as necessary.[31]

In 1990 Congress passed legislation, as part of the Omnibus Budget Reconciliation Act (OBRA),[32] that regulated medigap policies. Earlier federal regulation over medigap policies was limited, requiring only minimal benefits. OBRA required insurers to obtain a written statement outlining the purchaser's insurance coverages.[33] Medigap policies could be offered in one of ten standardized forms developed by the National Association of Insurance Commissioners.[34] Perhaps more than the question of duplication of policies, Congress was concerned about the increase in medigap premiums. The increase in medigap premiums from 1989 to 1990 was 19.5 percent. Congress was also looking at medigap policies in the wake of the repeal of the Medicare Catastrophic Coverage Act in 1989 (see below).[35]

As a result of the mandated changes, Medicare recipients now choose from these ten standardized policies, labeled "A" (least comprehensive) to "J" (most comprehensive). The thirteen possible services that can be covered under the medigap policies are Part A hospital coinsurance for days 61–90; Part A hospital coinsurance for days 91–150; all charges for the Part A blood deductible; Part B coinsurance, skilled-nursing facility coinsurance for days 21–100; the Part A deductible; emergency care in foreign countries; the Part B deductible; excess charges under Part B; in-home health care following surgery, illness, or injury; prescription drugs; and preventive medical care.[36]

According to an analysis of medigap policies and insurance company practices by Consumers Union, agents try to sell Plan F, which is very profitable for them and perhaps unnecessary for consumers. The difference between Plan F and Plan C is one benefit, coverage of Part B excess charges. But since Congress has limited such charges, coverage for them is not, on the average, a wise investment.[37] Consumers Union also argued that insurance companies are selling what are known as "attained age" policies. Such policies have low premiums for the younger years, 65–69, but become increasingly expensive as the insured becomes older. The report compared Plan F policies from two different companies. In the first company, the premium depends on the age of the buyer at first purchase and then rises only with inflation. The second company has an attained-age policy. At age sixty-five, the second company's policy is $114 per year cheaper than the first company. But in the next fifteen years, the second company's policy would cost the insured $5000 more than the first company.[38] Despite Congress's attempt to tighten the medigap policy market, problems remain.

The new medigap policies have simplified some of the choices available to purchasers. More specifically, the most popular benefits are retained and in a hierarchical order so that a purchaser does not have to give up the basic benefits for other desired benefits, and the number of choices is limited to the ten standardized policies. They suggest that the new law and regulations promote the use of information about policies to make informed judgments. They also suggest that the legislation promotes market stability.[39] This experience with medigap regulations suggests how health care reform based on competition among competing plans might be structured.[40]

The Disaster of the Medicare Catastrophic Coverage Act

One of the more interesting episodes in the history of Medicare (and American health care policy in general) revolves around the Medicare Catastrophic Coverage Act of 1988. The notion of catastrophic coverage is that there may be medical expenses that can cause financial hardship or ruin to a family. Preventing financial ruin is one of the purposes of health insurance in the first place, certainly of the Medicare program. Such catastrophic expenses might include diseases such as cancer or AIDS that progress over a lengthy period of time and thus are very costly. Long-term care (to be considered in detail below) can also deplete the life savings of the average family in a couple of years.

As we have seen, Medicare does not cover everything. There is extremely limited long-term-care coverage, no coverage of prescription drugs outside of hospitals, and limits on hospital and physician services. Medigap policies were developed by the private sector to cover some of the holes in Medicare coverage. Nevertheless, there were (and are) Medicare recipients who cannot afford medigap policies (the low-income and disabled) and whose copayments would wreak hardship on families.

With this as background, the road toward the Medicare Catastrophic Coverage Act (MCCA) began in January 1986 with President Reagan's State of the Union address. The president discussed the problem of catastrophic expenses and suggested that coverage should be broadened for all sectors of the population, not just the elderly. Reagan also suggested that any solution should rely on the private sector.[41]

The president set up a commission headed by Otis Bowen, then secretary of the Department of Health and Human Services. The commission was supposed to look at both long-term and acute-care problems. Indeed, testimony before the Bowen Commission emphasized the problems of long-term care; however, the commission decided to focus on acute care for Medicare recipients as the easiest step that could be taken.[42]

The commission's original idea was to add a cap or limit of $2,000 on yearly expenses paid by Medicare beneficiaries. Once the limit had been reached, Medicare would pay Part A and B deductibles and coinsurance. The cost to the beneficiary would be $59 a month added to Part B premiums. The cost of this proposed expansion was $2 billion. Congress accepted the administration proposal as a framework for change. As is typical of congressional-presidential relations, this was seen as an opening bid by a Republican administration. The Democrats would try to expand benefits but keep the self-financing provisions.[43]

MCCA was passed in June 1988 with significant changes from the Bowen proposal of two years earlier. It eliminated limitations on hospital benefits including coinsurance, with the exception of a yearly deductible. It increased limits on stays in skilled nursing facilities. It increased provisions for home health care. It provided for a limit on Part B services (to $1,370 for 1990 and with adjustments to the cap in subsequent years). It provided for coverage of outpatient prescription drugs, with a deductible and coinsurance dropping to 20 percent by 1993.[44]

The act also included a self-financing provision. A surtax was assessed on Medicare beneficiaries in a progressive manner. That is, low-income recipients would pay $22.50 (if their tax liability was $150) with the highest surtax limited to $800 for an individual with income greater than $35,000 or $1,600 for a couple with incomes greater than $70,000 a year. The law also required that the surtax be paid beginning in 1989, though benefits would not begin until 1990.[45]

At first glance, there should have been considerable support for the new law. Groups representing the aging population, especially the American Association of Retired Persons (AARP), were enthusiastic advocates of the legislation. But there was opposition. The drug industry opposed the legislation, fearing the imposition of cost controls (a stance it also took in regard to health care reform in 1993–94). The National Committee to Protect Social Security and Medicare was against the financing package because it would require beneficiaries to pay for all the new benefits, rather than rely on a combination of taxes and beneficiary contributions.[46]

It was also true that MCCA had redistributive implications. As we have seen, those least likely to have supplemental medical insurance (medigap policies) are those at the low end of the income scale. They would have benefited more by the law than those at the high end. The progressive nature of the financing enhanced the redistributive effect.[47]

It also turned out that many Medicare beneficiaries did not understand the law, despite the considerable publicity that surrounded its enactment. A telephone survey of Medicare recipients documented this problem. For example, only 19 percent of the respondents knew that Medicare did not cover the costs of an extended nursing home stay. Few knew about the financing details or about the drug benefit. Once respondents were briefed about the new law, many were opposed. Indeed, those opposed held that opinion more strongly than those who favored it. The elderly were concerned about all costs, such as the deductibles for prescription medication. They also seemed satisfied with their medigap policies.[48]

From the standpoint of wealthier Medicare recipients, MCCA did not appear to be much of a bargain. They were more likely to have private insurance that already gave them what MCCA would do plus they were asked to make a larger contribution to the program. Thus they did not see themselves as benefiting, but as having to pay for the expansion nevertheless.

Apart from the opposition of the two groups mentioned above that financed mail campaigns against the law, it appeared that the new premiums would build up faster than anticipated, yet the costs of some benefits (particularly the drug benefit) had been underestimated. Town meetings held by Congress in the summer of 1989 demonstrated the discontent. Given all this, Congress repealed the law in November 1989, about eighteen months after it had been passed.[49]

Controlling Cost

From the beginning, a chief concern about the Medicare program was cost. Several dimensions of costs play a role. One that has been discussed earlier was costs to the Medicare beneficiary. Here we can look at the copayments and deductible that recipients have to make under Parts A and B and premiums under Part B. We have also looked, to a certain extent, at the problem of cost through HMOs and medigap policies.

The other major dimension of cost control is costs to the federal government. As Medicare became more expensive for a variety of reasons, federal administrators and policymakers sought for ways to curb those costs. Some of this could be done by raising premiums and deductibles for Medicare recipients. But by far the largest target of cost control was providers: physicians, hospitals, and so forth. From the beginning, the politics of Medicare revolved around the issue of provider payment, beginning with hospitals and then expanding to doctors.[50]

Consider, first, the increase in enrollments and expenditures in Medicare (see Table 4.3). Medicare expenditures in 1970 were about $7.3 billion, about 28 percent of public health expenditures and about 10 percent of total

Table 4.3

Selected Health Expenditures
(in billions of dollars)

	Total health expenditures	Public expenditures	Medicare expenditures
1970	74.3	27.7	7.3
1980	251.1	105.3	36.4
1985	434.5	175.1	70.3
1990	696.9	286.5	109.6
1993	884.2	387.8	151.1

Source: Katharine R. Levit et al., "National Health Expenditures, 1993," *Health Care Financing Review* 16, no. 2 (Fall 1994): 285.

health expenditures. In 1991 Medicare expenditures were almost $123 billion, representing over 37 percent of public expenditures on health and over 16 percent of total expenditures. One could argue that because Medicare only began in 1965, it would surely make large increases starting from such a small base. Nevertheless, doing similar calculations for 1980 to 1991 showed how much quicker Medicare was growing than the overall health sector. Overall health care expenditures increased by just a bit over 200 percent, public health expenditures increased by 214 percent, but Medicare expenditures increased by 227 percent. Considering the concern about overall increases in health care, such rapid increases in Medicare could not help but raise alarms.

One of the reasons for the increase in program expenditures was the increase in the number of Medicare beneficiaries. When the program began operation, in 1966, there were a little over 19 million enrollees. By 1972, that number had increased to over 21 million people. The 1972 amendments to the Social Security Act added the disabled and those suffering from end-stage renal disease (ESRD, or kidney failure). By 1991, there were approximately 34,870,000 Medicare enrollees, 3.1 million of whom were disabled and about another 65,000 suffering from ESRD.[51] That represents an increase of about 82 percent. Another reason is the growing generosity of Medicare in the sense that cost sharing on the part of Medicare recipients has become relatively smaller. In 1977, cost sharing amounted to about 18 percent of total expenditures; by 1990, that figured had decreased to 16.5 percent.[52] Other reasons include increases caused by general inflation, health care inflation over and above general inflation, and changes in the technology of health care.

When policymakers first seriously considered imposing cost-control measures on Medicare they focused first on hospitals. As is true for overall national health care expenditures, hospitals accounted for the largest single portion of Medicare expenditures. In 1990, hospital inpatient services were $56,716,000, approximately 56 percent of total Medicare payments. By contrast, physician services accounted for $39,222,000, approximately 30 percent of total Medicare payments.[53]

When Medicare began, it contained the usual compromise provision "that the federal insurance program would not interfere in the practice of medicine or the structure of the medical care industry."[54] But it was inevitable that the federal government would have to take steps as the program became relatively more expensive. One way to understand that inevitability is to consider the theory of imbalanced political interests and its application to Medicare.[55]

At the beginning of the program, Medicare amounted to a relatively small percentage of federal expenditures. In 1970, five years after Medicare was established, Medicare expenditures amounted to about 4 percent of federal expenditures. Hospitals and physicians were faced with concentrated benefits and costs of payment and regulatory policies. The program was too small in the early years for the federal government to pay much concern. Ten years later, however, Medicare had increased to about 6.4 percent and by 1990 almost 8.9 percent of federal expenditures.[56] As Medicare spending continued to increase faster than overall spending, the federal government developed its own set of interests in cost containment that would counterbalance provider interests.[57] Additionally, there was, and is, the continual concern that the hospital trust fund will be insolvent by the end of the twentieth century. In the early 1980s, the federal government looked at hospital cost containment in Medicare. During the latter part of the decade it turned to physician payments.

Prospective Payment System and Cost Containment

The strain on the federal health budget (mentioned above) laid the political foundation for federal regulation of hospital costs.[58] Proponents of regulation claimed that it could reduce waste and inefficiency without sacrificing quality of care.[59]

The Omnibus Budget Reconciliation Act of 1981 made minor changes in the Medicare program. It tightened limits on Medicare reimbursement to generate cost savings. The Tax Equity and Fiscal Responsibility Act (TEFRA) of 1982 established a limit on the rate of increase over time in Medicare hospital payment rates, incorporated a case-mix index based on diagnosis related groupings (DRGs), and provided incentive payments to hospitals defined as efficient. The law also directed the Department of Health and Human Services (HHS) to design a prospective payment plan for the Medicare program. The TEFRA system was replaced in 1983 by the Prospective Payment System (PPS) for Medicare reimbursement to hospitals.

The PPS for Medicare reimbursement was modeled after the New Jersey program.[60] Faced with health care cost increases, inadequate care for the poor, pressure on the state Medicaid budget, and rising hospital charges, New Jersey adopted in 1978 a prospective reimbursement mechanism for all payers based on 467 diagnosis related groupings (DRGs). Implementation of PPS in New Jersey was phased in between 1980 and 1982. The Health Care Financing Administration (HCFA) in the Department of Health and Human Services had been supporting research, development, demonstration, and evaluation in cost control since the early 1970s, and the New Jersey DRG system was one of its demonstration projects. The adoption by the federal government in 1983 of a prospective payment mechanism based on DRGs for Medicare reimbursement to hospitals was a natural outgrowth of the New Jersey experiment.[61]

The rationale behind replacing the retrospective payment system was that under that system hospitals had no incentive to economize in their use of health care resources in treating Medicare patients. If anything, such a system encouraged overutilization of health resources because hospitals were assured that they would be reimbursed for all reasonable costs incurred. PPS was based on the assumption that given built-in incentives hospitals would be forced to consider cost factors in treatment and would be encouraged to be economically more efficient. Thus, inefficient hospitals would be forced to close. An economically more efficient hospital sector would help contain increases in hospital costs. PPS was viewed as a method of influencing hospital activities, creating cost-containment constraints, and introducing incentives into hospital payments.[62] The cost-control incentive was the primary purpose in establishing PPS.[63]

Under PPS, hospitals are paid according to a schedule of preestablished rates linked to 468 DRGs. All major categories of diagnosis are classified into 468 categories. Each category is assigned a treatment rate, and hospitals are reimbursed according to these rates. There are economic incentives in the form of rewards and punishments built in to the system. If a hospital spends more money than the preestablished rate for a particular diagnostic treatment, the hospital must absorb the additional cost. If the hospital spends less money than the preestablished rate, it is still paid the preestablished rate, and it can keep the overpayment as profit. The Health Care Financing Administration (HCFA) was assigned the responsibility of establishing the DRG payment schedule. To safeguard against reduction in quality of care as a result of PPS, Congress assigned to Professional Review Organizations (PROs) the responsibility for monitoring the quality and appropriateness of care for Medicare patients. If a PRO finds inappropriate or substandard care, the hospital may be denied Medicare payment. If a pattern of inappropriate or substandard care is discovered, the hospital Medicare provider agreement may be terminated.

The shift in the Medicare payment method to hospitals from a retrospective reimbursement system to a prospective payment system based on DRGs was the most far-reaching change in the Medicare program since its inception.[64] The changeover to PPS was expected to revolutionize the economics of American health care.[65]

Assessing the Effectiveness of PPS

Has PPS succeeded in meeting the goal of cost containment? Some early results are encouraging but inconclusive. Any assessment of the impact of PPS must be viewed with caution, for two reasons. First, PPS was not immediately implemented in 1983 but was phased in over a period of time. The complete transition to a PPS system occurred in November 1987. Thus, sufficient time has not elapsed to make any definitive conclusions about the impact of PPS.[66] Second, it is very difficult to assess changes in hospital behavior using aggregate data. It is even more difficult to disentangle the effects of Medicare PPS from other influences on hospital costs, let alone measure the magnitude of any effects.[67]

The initial years of PPS showed some slowdown in the growth rate of hospital costs. The rate of increase for hospital expenditures averaged 3.2 percent annually for the first three years of PPS (1984–86) compared to an average annual growth rate of 7.8 percent for the three years before PPS (1981–83).[68] The significant cost-reducing effects of PPS have been generated almost entirely as a result of reduced admissions. Occupancy rates fell and length of hospital stay was also reduced. Concerns about cost shifting to third-party payers have not materialized, and there is no evidence to support the fear that Medicare patients are being denied beneficial care.[69]

This optimistic assessment of the impact of PPS has been countered by critics of the system. Critics argue that the system is fraught with problems because of faulty behavioral assumptions and that, instead of pursuing greater efficiency, hospitals will seek ways around the regulation.[70] Because price regulation is a tax on hospital behavior, it not only affects price but also hospital output and quality and quantity of services. Hospitals respond by attempting to reduce use of affected services or resources by modifying their practices and products.[71] Hospitals modify the cost of regulation by seeking an area unaffected by the regulation (i.e., the "unregulated margin"). Organizations respond to regulation through institutional, managerial, and technical changes.[72] Some studies have found this to be true. As a result of PPS, hospitals altered services, influenced practices, and changed the products offered to decrease the impact of regulation at the expense of Medicare patients. Hospitals changed the mix of services offered in the inpatient Medicare market. They expanded the surgical market because surgical DRGs are more profitable than medical DRGs. Often, services were cut.[73]

While PPS has reduced the growth rate of hospital costs somewhat, national health care expenditures continue to rise. This may partly reflect cost shifting to other sectors of the health care market, such as nursing home facilities or home health services.[74] This cost shifting to other sectors is called the "squeezed balloon" effect. According to Altman and Rodwin, by squeezing spending on inpatient care, the system has created a bulge in spending at the opposite end—outpatient and home care.[75]

Controlling Physician Costs

As we have seen, the Prospective Payment System focused on hospitals, but it did have an indirect effect on doctors. Hospitals are the structure or framework, but doctors decide medical or surgical treatment. The PPS, by creating a ceiling on hospital reimbursements, caused hospitals to pressure doctors so as to limit hospital expenditures. But physicians had independent effects on Medicare expenditures and government budgets.

General revenues comprise a significant portion of Part B expenditures. After the 1972 Social Security Amendments, increases in premiums were limited by increases in Social Security beneficiary payments. Thus, whereas in 1972, beneficiary premiums almost equaled general revenue contributions, by 1990, beneficiary premiums accounted for a little over 23 percent of Part B trust fund income. Federal general revenues accounted for over 73 percent of trust fund income.[76] With hospital expenses easing a bit, attention naturally turned to expenditures on the next biggest item, physicians. Further, Medicare payments for physician services began rising faster than for hospital expenses. By 1989, such expenses accounted for 40 percent of total Medicare spending.[77]

In some ways, though Medicare based payments on usual and customary fees, the process was administratively complex and created inequities in physician income and dissatisfaction among physicians. In 1984, Congress froze Medicare physician reimbursements and then limited balance billing (the amount doctors could charge above Medicare). Further, there were significant increases in Medicare beneficiary cost sharing above increases in Social Security benefits. A final factor leading to change was the passage and implementation of the Prospective Payment System for hospitals. As Oliver points out, PPS "demonstrated that health cost containment was both technically feasible and politically feasible."[78]

Although the Reagan administration did not consider a physician payment schedule program, Congress acted.[79] It froze physician fees in Medicare and ordered the Office of Technology Assessment to evaluate different payment schemes. In 1985, Congress created the Physician Payment Review Commission (PPRC), through an omnibus budget reconciliation act, and ordered it to make recommendations regarding a payment system. It simultaneously ordered the Department of Health and Human Services to develop a fee schedule, based on a resource-based relative value scale (RBRVS). Such a scale was adopted in 1989, again through an omnibus budget reconciliation act. The Health Care Financing Administration began implementing the fee schedule in 1992; by 1996, the program will be fully implemented.[80]

A relative value scale (RVS) compares the complexity and time of services offered.[81] Thus a simple office visit would have a lower RVS than a coronary bypass operation. The fee schedule also contains adjustments for geography, and there is a conversion factor that translates the results into dollar amounts. Additionally, volume standards help in establishing growth rates in physician payments.[82]

The impact of the fee schedule varied, depending on the kind of service. Fees for office and hospital visits were generally increased; fees for surgery were significantly reduced. The 1991 average surgeon's payment for a coronary bypass operation was $3,178. The full fee schedule for the same operation was $1,952, a decrease of more than 61 percent.[83] It is no wonder that physicians and their associations were unhappy with the fee schedules. Political pressure by interest groups, Congress, and the Bush administration led HCFA to liberalize the fee schedule.[84] While the fee schedule remains in place, it will have a less drastic effect on Medicare expenditures than originally intended.

At this point, it is too early to detect with any great certainty what effects the physician fee schedule will have. It was originally expected that Medicare might save 6 percent on physician services.[85] Preliminary studies are somewhat contradictory. Some argue that the conversion factors used in the relative value scales are too low, while others say that they are appropriate. The fee schedule, as indicated earlier, was designed in part to redistribute payments toward primary-care physicians and away from specialists. Nevertheless, it may be that surgical procedures will still be generously paid. It is also not clear how physicians will respond to the fee schedule. One such response would be to increase the volume of services, but this is too hard to detect at this point because there have been pre-1992 fee reductions. Access and quality do not appear to have changed with the early implementation of the program. Indeed, there seems to be a declining rate of balance billing.[86]

The Problem of Long-Term Care

> Although the impetus behind the nation's quest for health care reform is public dissatisfaction over glaring deficiencies in America's acute care health system—primarily excessive cost and the inability of millions of Americans to get health insurance—the way the nation provides for the financing and delivery of long-term care may be even more badly in need of reform. Strong considerations, both public policy and moral, argue for addressing health care for the uninsured first, before long-term care. Yet no other part of the health care system generates as much passionate discontent as does long-term care.[87]

As we saw in the discussion of the Medicare Catastrophic Coverage Act, one of the important gaps in Medicare concerns long-term care. We begin this section by looking at some of the data concerning long-term care.

A first point is the significant increase in expenditures on nursing homes. In 1970, about $4.9 billion was spent on nursing homes. By 1993, that figure had risen to $69.6 billion, an increase of 1320 percent. By contrast, overall personal health care expenditures increased by 1090 percent over the same period. For hospital services, the increase was 1066 percent and for physician services, the increase was 1159 percent. By the year 2018, we may be spending $168.2 billion (in 1993 inflation-adjusted dollars) for home health and nursing home care.[88]

Second, Medicare (and most private medical insurance) focuses on short-term or chronic care. It provides limited coverage for skilled nursing care, and then only after a hospital episode on physician orders. The bulk of spending on nursing homes is from Medicaid and out-of-pocket expenditures. Out of $69.6 billion spent on nursing homes nationally, Medicare accounted for only about 3.7 percent.[89] Consider 1993 data. Out of nearly $138 billion on Medicare, long-term care accounted for $15.8 billion. The federal portion of Medicaid paid about $24.7 billion and the states paid about $19 billion. So Medicaid paid about $43.7 billion for long-term care.[90] Further, though the elderly constitute a small portion of Medicaid recipients, about 11.5 percent in 1991, over 28 percent of Medicaid spending is on this group.[91]

Now consider private insurance and government expenditures for nursing homes. For 1993, nursing home expenditures were almost $69.6 billion. Of that, government (Medicare and state and federal Medicaid) paid a bit over $43.6 billion, or about 62.6 percent. Private insurance paid about $1.7 billion, or about 2.5 percent. Out of pocket payments were $23 billion, or about 33 percent.[92]

Having looked at expenditure data, we can look at the population likely to need long-term care.

> Today [1994], approximately 11 million Americans of all ages are chronically disabled and depend on others for assistance in the basic tasks of daily living such as eating, bathing and other activities that most of us take for granted. In this highly diverse population are people with both physical and cognitive disabilities, including the frail elderly, quadriplegics and paraplegics, persons with developmental disabilities, persons with severe mental illness, and children with chronic conditions. Of the 11 million Americans with disabilities, about 3 million are considered to be severely disabled.[93]

Further, some 7.1 million of the elderly need some kind of long-term care and about 1.5 million are in nursing homes.[94] The number of elderly (those sixty-five and over) is growing rapidly, and the segment of the elderly population growing the fastest is eighty-five and older. Thus there are projections that the need for long-term care services, especially nursing homes, will double over the next twenty to thirty years. The projection is that the nursing home population will increase to 3.6 million people in 2018, while those needing home health care will increase to 7.4 million.[95]

> The growth of the elderly population has a particular significance for long-term care. This is because old age is often accompanied by the development of chronic health problems, such as heart disease, arthritis, and other ailments. These problems, important causes of disability among the elderly population, often result in the need for extensive long-term care services. This is especially true for those individuals 85 years of age and over, given that chronic conditions resulting in dependencies increase with age. Over 50 percent of those over 85 years of age are in need of care compared with about 13 percent of those 65 to 69 years of age.[96]

Interestingly, it appears that disabilities among the elderly are declining while they are increasing in the under sixty-five group. One reason is that AIDS has become more of a chronic than an acute disease; thus survival times of those suffering from AIDS have increased.[97] As the baby-boom generation ages, long-term care needs will increase, though estimates of the dimensions of the problem vary.[98]

The nursing home industry was born of two actions by the federal government. One in 1950 was an amendment to the Social Security Act prohibiting payments to residents living in institutional settings such as boardinghouses that did not provide health care. The other major development was the establishment of Medicaid. Though Medicaid does not pick up all the nursing home bill, it does pay for the medically indigent in nursing homes. These two developments created a situation in which long-term care became synonymous with nursing homes.

Long-term care can be delivered outside of nursing homes. Indeed, much care for the elderly is given by relatives. This is free care and does not figure into the estimates of long-term care expenditures ($69.6 billion in 1993). A considerable portion of long-term care is home care and community-based care. Indeed, considerably more is spent on home and community-based care than on nursing homes. In 1993, approximately $7 billion was spent on nursing homes, while about $18 billion was spent on home and community-based care.[99]

Despite the relatively small number of the elderly in nursing homes, the threat of a nursing home stay is that it can wipe out lifetime savings. In 1988, nursing homes cost an average of $25,000 a year. By 1994, that figure rose to $37,000 a year.[100] This can certainly wipe out a family's savings within two years. Eligibility for Medicaid requires spending down one's savings. Many who start out in nursing homes as privately paying patients end up as Medicaid recipients. Further, the middle class has increasingly seen Medicaid has a middle-class entitlement, a way to protect life savings. Thus, families transfer funds from the elderly person to other members of the family so that the elderly person can become eligible for Medicaid. While Congress has tightened the rules (states and HCFA can now look at transfers up to three years prior to placement in a nursing home), the problem remains.[101]

Long-term care thus presents several problems at different levels. At the level of the individual, the problem is financial, being able to afford long-term care, or in some cases being able to arrange it. From the standpoint of government, the problem is the ever-increasing costs of long-term care. From a societal standpoint, the problem is the increasing demand for long-term care in the twenty-first century.

Home and Informal Care

Much care for the elderly is given in the home by relatives, that is, unpaid informal assistance. Some 2 million elderly receive formal assistance at home or in the community. This includes meals, transportation, and home health care. About 1.5 million elderly are so severely disabled that they live in nursing homes. Thus, only a small minority of the elderly at any one time live in a nursing home. At the same time, relatives caring for the elderly need help and understanding as they deal with work and home conflicts.[102]

One way that these informal caregivers, the overwhelming majority of whom are women, can be assisted is by employers (both public and private) in the workplace. They can provide options for their employees that will help them assist their disabled relatives. Some 23 million Americans work in companies that have plans, such as leave policies (both paid and unpaid) or flexible work schedules, to help their employees in these situations. These and similar programs could reduce the chances of institutionalization of the disabled elderly by about a third.[103] Such policies are generally not available through small businesses, and there is considerable variation among employers. Such "elder care" is also available to public-sector employees at all levels of government. While the options are available, however, they are not widely encouraged or promoted.[104] Although it appears that there will be some expansion of elder care in both the public and private sectors, the potential costs of such programs is a limiting factor.

Beginning in 1981, the Health Care Financing Administration granted limited waivers to states to pay for home health care; Oregon is the only state with a comprehensive home health care program.[105] What Oregon has been able to do is fold in Medicaid long-term-care funding with other federal programs aimed at caring for the elderly, creating what is essentially a block grant.[106] It has then been able to reallocate the funds to noninstitutional care.[107] Oregon has simultaneously developed policies to ensure that only those who truly need the care get it. It does this by using case managers to investigate new claims for home assistance. At the same time, it has been aggressive in closing down nursing homes. So while Oregon's elderly population has grown by 40 percent since 1984, it has almost 8 percent fewer beds. As a result, nursing home expenditures in Oregon as a percentage of long-term care expenditures is considerably below the national average of 62.3 percent. Oregon's percentage is 38.5; Utah is the only other state whose nursing home percentage is under 50 percent.[108] Because community-based services are less than one-third of nursing home expenses, Oregon's program has the potential for alleviating cost pressures on the states and the federal governments as well as on individuals and families.[109]

Long-Term-Care Policy Alternatives

One policy alternative increasingly investigated is long-term-care (LTC) insurance. This would be similar to health insurance. Insurance could be sold to the elderly, say when they become sixty-five years old, or to younger people where they work so that a reserve fund could be established.

The long-term-care insurance market is relatively new and still small. The product was almost nonexistent before 1986; by June 1990, some 1.6 million policies had been sold.[110] The policies are generally indemnity policies; that is, they pay a specified amount per day to the beneficiary. Janet Shikles, of the General Accounting Office, testified before Congress that the long-term-care insurance market looked like the "medigap" insurance market prior to congressional reforms. "Early Medigap policies varied greatly in value and coverage. State regulation was inconsistent, with sales and market abuses a recurring problem."[111]

The problem Shikles identified is that policies vary as to what is covered, whether prior hospitalization is necessary, inflation adjustments for coverage, amount of premiums, increases in premiums, and length of time the policy is in effect. While the National Association of Insurance Commissioners (NAIC) has adopted standards for long-term policies on almost an annual basis, many states have not followed suit. Indeed, much of the adoption has been by insurers; even so, it is not of the more recently adopted standards.[112] A study by the Brookings Institution found that only wealthier people are likely to buy long-term-care insurance and that such insurance would reduce total nursing home care costs by 7 to 18 percent in the next century.[113]

Thus, while private long-term-care insurance has the potential for alleviating some of the cost problems, the long-term-care issue has not been fully dealt with. It is not yet a mature policy and requires considerable standardization.

Further, long-term-care insurance is expensive. The average premium for a policy at age sixty-five in 1991 was $2,525 a year. At age seventy-nine, that rises to $7,675 a year. There are two reasons for the high premiums. First, unlike regular health insurance, long-term-care insurance is sold to individuals rather than groups, and thus administrative costs are high. The population that buys it is limited generally to those sixty-five and older, the group most likely to need the insurance. Thus the insurance is sold to high-risk individuals.[114] One possible solution to this problem is to combine long-term-care insurance with Medicaid. A small number of states (Connecticut, New York, Indiana, and California) have begun such a partnership program. The program works as follows:

> As a public/private venture, the Partnership teams the state with private insurance companies to offer affordable long-term care coverage. Consumers who buy Partnership-approved policies are covered by private insurance until the policy runs out, at which point Medicaid pays for their care without forcing them to spend down or transfer assets.[115]

The policies are more affordable than solely private LTC insurance policies. Medicaid saves as well because it does not have to pay for long-term care until the private insurance runs out.[116]

Long-Term Care and Health Care Reform

Given the problems of long-term care, to what extent was it considered in the debate over health care? Two of the plans, the Clinton administration's Health Security Act (based on managed competition and caps on insurance premiums) and the Wellstone-McDermott American Health Security Act (a single-payer plan), had detailed provisions concerning long-term care.[117]

The Health Security Act maintained the traditional distinction between long-term care and acute care. The program would have been state administered and available to all (not means tested). The Health Security Act provided for both institutional and home and community-based care. It would have built on the Medicare program and extended coverage to the medically needy. It would have provided national standards for long-term insurance and increased tax deductions. Finally, there would have been increased federal funding for the new provisions.[118]

The American Health Security Act (single-payer bill) folded long-term-care services (institutional, community-based, and home) into an overall package of national health insurance. It would phase out Medicaid and provide for copayments for long-term-care services and subsidization for low-income people.[119]

Because no health care reform bill passed in 1993–94, the long-term-care issue remains unresolved. The Republican plan, under the Contract with America, contains provisions that would help some of the elderly (largely upper-income people). The plan would allow drawing from pension plans to pay for long-term insurance. It would also provide tax credits for such insurance. The plan would also allow those needing long-term care to draw death benefits from life insurance to pay for the care.[120]

Other proposals include expanding Medicaid and allowing recipients to keep more of their assets and using the social insurance approach of Medicare that would cover everybody.[121] The latter has the advantage of providing a universal benefit and avoiding the stigma of the means-tested Medicaid program. The Medicaid option would be cheaper, however. In either case, the creation of a new entitlement program runs up against the fiscal constraint of the large budget deficits. Further, the costs of such a new program are uncertain.[122] Finally, the new Republican congressional majority promises to end the open-ended nature of entitlement funding, thus limiting any new such programs.

There is one last perspective on long-term care. Except for the single-payer proposal mentioned earlier, most discussions of long-term care consider such care separate from the more familiar acute care. But it may be that integrating the two, say within Medicare, might prove in the long run to provide better care and control costs. One such model of how such integration might work is provided by the social health maintenance organizations (S/HMOs). Though there are only four S/HMOs in existence, there is evidence that such an approach works. Further, such a policy would focus not just on nursing homes but also on home and community-based care.[123]

Conclusion

Medicare faces a number of problems. One problem is that the Medicare hospital trust fund is expected to become insolvent by the year 2001.[124] To resolve that problem, several steps might be taken. General revenue funds from the federal government could be put into the program. Hospital insurance premiums could be raised beyond expected projections (adjustments for inflation). In general, cost sharing on the part of Medicare recipients might be increased.[125] Or some steps could be taken to reduce the demand for services or the pressure on revenues.

One such program was to move more Medicare patients into health maintenance organizations. But as explained earlier in the chapter, this has not saved Medicare money.[126] Another possibility would be to raise the age at which time people become eligible for Social Security and Medicare. A third target is provider reimbursement, especially through the hospital Prospective Payment System and the physician fee schedule.

Indeed, Medicare faces another sort of pressure: the need to reduce the federal deficit. One of the assumptions behind the Health Security Act was that Medicare (and Medicaid) payments would significantly increase the federal deficit during the latter 1990s. The Republican Contract with America promised significant tax cuts, increased defense spending, and a balanced budget by the year 2002. Spending cuts have to come from someplace, and one of the major targets will be federal health care programs.

Thus Medicare enters the latter 1990s facing almost unsolvable problems. On the one hand, the elderly population will be getting bigger and thus will put pressure on Medicare for more services. This is a demographic inevitability. And as the over eighty-five population increases, the need for long-term care will also increase. At the same time, there are pressures for cutting Medicare spending, most notably based on the presence of the large federal deficit.

These pressures on Medicare became evident in 1995. The trustees of the

Medicare Hospital Insurance Trust Fund predicted that the fund would run out of money by the year 2002.[127] To help keep the trust fund solvent and to balance the federal budget by the year 2002, the Republican-controlled Congress proposed to reduce Medicare spending by about $250 billion. The Clinton administration proposed reductions of $124 billion for Medicare.[128] One way this might be accomplished would be to move more Medicare recipients into HMOs.[129] Obviously, the pressures of demography and federal deficits remain the major policy issues facing Medicare.

5

Health Care and the Disadvantaged: Falling through the Cracks

By 1970, health care policy in the United States had reached its maturity. Medicare and Medicaid were passed in 1965; private insurance covered most of working America. But health care costs went up dramatically beginning in the mid-1960s, and portions of the population were left out of the system. Two of the major problems of the health care system are cost increases and access. We consider the problem of cost increases in the next chapter. This chapter focuses on the problem of access and the disadvantaged.

We concentrate on issues of access to the health care system, the problem of the uninsured and the underinsured, low-income groups, and minorities and women. To some extent, these problems overlap. While a good portion of the uninsured are low-income people, some are not. While minorities in general have lower incomes than whites, not all the problems of minorities and health care result from lower incomes. Rural areas have access problems to health care in the same way that inner cities do: lack of providers. We spell out these interrelationships as we go along.

Perhaps the underlying issue in looking at the disadvantaged and health care is equality and equity. We begin this chapter by considering this issue.

Equality and Equity

Equality and equity do not mean the same things. *Equality* means that we should treat people who are in the same situation the same way or treat people who are in different situations differently. That is, we should not discriminate against someone on account of race, religion, age, sex, ethnic group, and so forth. One reality of the health care system, to be discussed later in the chapter, is that there is discrimination based on income or at least based on health insurance. Those with private insurance plans, especially very generous ones, tend to get better service than those on public plans (such as Medicaid); those without health insurance tend to get the worst care. Some have argued that the United States has a two-tiered health care system, one for most of us and another for the poor. In Krause's words,

> we have, combining the doctors and the office and hospital settings, a two-class medical care system. On the one hand, few practitioners and a few public settings for the poor in either the ghetto or rural areas; on the other hand, many practitioners and voluntary nonprofit hospitals for the middle class and the upper class in the suburbs.[1]

This leads us to the notion of *equity,* an extension of the concept of equality. Equity is related to another concept, *social justice.* Both ideas suggest that, given that some are disadvantaged in the health care system, there should be an extra effort made to help overcome those disadvantages. This is, in a sense, the idea behind Medicaid (and to a lesser extent, Medicare). Medicaid recipients do not have to pay for their health care. Instead, their health care is subsidized by the larger community (taxpayers) and to some extent by providers and their patients (in the sense that Medicaid reimbursements are lower than for privately insured patients and costs are shifted to privately insured patients). Compensatory education programs such as Head Start, where we devote more resources to children from impoverished backgrounds, are another example.

One aspect of this underlying issue is whether health care is a right, in the same way that there is a right to education (a state mandate). In most industrialized countries, health care is indeed considered a right. The United States and South Africa are the only industrialized countries without a national health care system.[2] And as we shall see, one of the problems to be discussed is the increasing number of people without health insurance.

Aday argues that we should not base our health care system on a right to health care, which is within the individualistic, liberal tradition of American politics (see chapter 1). Instead, we should employ the notion of the common good, that it is in the best interest of the community, of society, not just the individual, that all its members have access to health care.[3]

In a similar vein, Stone contends that in recent years, and for good financial reasons, the private insurance market has moved away from notions of community. Insurance was originally intended as a means to spread the risk of individual misfortune among the larger community. Private insurers have increasingly sought to fragment the market, however, searching for those who are good health risks and placing more of the burden of financing care on those who are poor risks. This undermines the idea of community.[4]

The debates over national health insurance, Medicare, and health care reform are, in a sense, marked by notions of community. Do we help those who are vulnerable or disadvantaged, or is everyone on his or her own? The implications of the two choices are not trivial.

Jecker, likewise, suggests that the link between employment and health insurance itself creates injustices. She argues that there is discrimination in the distribution of jobs, focusing on gender-based discrimination, and that this creates discrepancies in the availability of health insurance. We consider the problems of women and the health care system in this chapter. As one example, consider that women are less likely to be employed in jobs that offer health insurance than men are.[5]

Thus, access to health care raises important ethical issues. What we must do now is document that the problems indeed do exist.

Uninsured and Underinsured

As noted, most people in the United States who have health insurance have it through their jobs. In 1991, about 84.1 percent of the population were covered by health insurance (see Table 5.1). Of that 84.1 percent, about 13 percent were insured only by public programs. This includes Medicaid recipients and Medicare recipients who do not take out medigap policies.[6] About 10.8 percent of those who had insurance had both public and private coverage. Comparing the 1991 numbers to 1980, we see that dependence on private insurance has gone down. In 1980, about 12.5 percent of those insured were covered by public programs only and another 8.5 percent were covered by both. In 1990, of those covered by private health insurance, about 80.8 percent were linked to employment.[7]

Table 5.2 presents data about the number and percentage of uninsured persons. Note that the percentage of persons without insurance increased from 1980 to 1991 by about 16 percent. The number of uninsured persons increased by about 21 percent over the same period. The country's population increased by about 11 percent over the same time period; therefore, the increase in the uninsured population over and above general population increases was about 10 percent.[8] The comparable figures for 1992 are 38.9 million uninsured people, about 17.4 percent of the population.[9]

These numbers give an incomplete picture of the uninsurance problem. The data are, in a sense, a snapshot, a picture of those without insurance. A number of people experience spells of uninsurance during the year. One

Table 5.1

Sources of Health Insurance Coverage, 1980–91

Survey year	Total[a] insured by all sources (percent)	Total[a] insured by private health insurance (percent)	Total[a] insured by public programs (percent)	Total[a] insured by private insurance and public programs[b] (percent)
1980	86.3	65.3	12.5	8.5
1981	N/A	N/A	N/A	N/A
1982	86.4	63.5	13.3	9.6
1983	85.6	63.1	13.3	9.3
1984	84.8	62.3	13.1	9.3
1985	84.2	61.5	13.2	9.4
1986	84.3	61.4	13.1	9.7
1987	84.4	61.5	13.0	9.9
1988	85.6	62.7	11.9	11.0
1989	84.9	62.1	12.2	10.6
1990	84.5	61.9	12.1	10.6
1991	84.1	60.3	13.0	10.8

Source: Katharine R. Levit, Gary L. Olin, and Suzanne W. Letsch, *Health Care Financing Review* 14, no. 1 (Fall 1992): 33.

[a]In the 1988–91 surveys, additional questions concerning health insurance status of children were asked. This set of questions is referred to as "cover sheet" questions. Responses to these questions resulted in additional children being assigned health insurance coverage. Percentages reported exclude cover-sheet children.

[b]Public programs indicate coverage by Medicare, Medicaid, and/or the Civilian Health and Medical Program of the Uniformed Services (CHAMPUS).

estimate is that about 25 percent of the population was without health insurance at some point during 1990–92.[10] Another estimate was that some 51.3 million Americans were without health insurance for some time in 1993, most of them over four months.[11] Six percent of workers work in firms that offer health insurance but were not eligible for insurance. Fifty-four percent of these workers worked part time; 14 percent had not been in the job long enough (usually three to six months) to qualify for health insurance.[12]

The question to be raised is, why has health insurance coverage decreased? This is an important question, given two facts. One is that much health insurance coverage, as stated earlier, is linked to jobs. Second, such coverage has continued to decrease in the 1990s, even as job expansion has been impressive (7.4 percent increase between 1985 and 1992).[13] One way of looking at this is to consider employment-based insurance for children. In 1987, 64.1 percent of all children were covered under employment-based

Table 5.2

Number and Percentage of Uninsured Persons, 1980–91

Survey year	Total uninsured[a] (millions)	Total uninsured[a] (percent)
1980	30.5	13.7
1981	N/A	N/A
1982	31.0	13.6
1983	33.0	14.4
1984	35.3	15.2
1985	37.0	15.8
1986	37.2	15.7
1987	37.4	15.6
1988	34.8	14.4
1989	36.8	15.1
1990	38.0	15.5
1991	36.9	15.9

Source: Katharine R. Levit, Gary L. Olin, and Suzanne W. Letsch, *Health Care Financing Review* 14, no. 1 (Fall 1992): 33.

[a]In the 1988–91 surveys, additional questions concerning the health insurance status of children were asked. This set of questions is referred to as "cover sheet" questions. Responses to these questions resulted in additional children being assigned health insurance coverage. Percentages reported exclude cover-sheet children.

insurance. By 1992, that number had decreased to 59.6 percent. One projection suggests that by the year 2000, the number of children covered through jobs will decline to 52.4 percent. It should be noted that the number of children without any coverage has remained stable because of expansions in Medicaid. Nevertheless, the numbers show that the unique basis of medical insurance in the United States is declining.[14] Why?

The answer lies partly in the restructuring of the American economy. Insurance coverage is linked to size and type of firm. Larger firms are much more likely to offer health insurance than smaller firms. Ninety-five percent of firms with 100 or more employees offer health insurance, while only 32 percent of firms with 25 or fewer employees offer insurance.[15] Much of the growth in jobs has been in smaller businesses, exactly those that are least likely to offer health insurance.

Why is there so much more insurance coverage in larger as opposed to smaller firms? While there is probably more turnover in smaller firms, the size factor is most important. The idea behind insurance is to spread or pool the risk over a large population. Insurance companies view each individual firm or individual buyer as a self-contained unit, instead of pooling all those covered under the insurance company's policies. Therefore, smaller firms have more difficulty in negotiating favorable rates for their employees than do larger companies. Their costs per employee are higher than in larger firms.[16]

Another reason why there has been erosion in employer-based health insurance has to do with the sectors of the economy that are growing and shrinking. Manufacturing firms and unionized firms (with much overlapping) are more likely to offer insurance than service-based or agricultural firms. The service sector has experienced considerable growth, while the manufacturing sector has shrunk.[17]

Consider the following numbers. In 1970, some 20.7 million workers were in the manufacturing sector; by 1991, that number had declined to 20.4 million, a decrease of about 1.5 percent. By contrast, 20.4 million workers were in the service sector in 1970; by 1991, that number had increased to 39.7 million workers, an increase of almost 95 percent. Another way of looking at this is to compare the relative shares of manufacturing and service workers. In 1970, the share of workers in manufacturing was 26.4 percent; in 1991, that share had declined to 17.5 percent. The share of workers in the service sector in 1970 was 25.9 percent, a little less than the manufacturing share. But by 1991, the service-sector share of jobs had increased to almost 34 percent.[18] Thus, if there is less likelihood that the service sector will offer health insurance than the manufacturing sector, it is understandable why fewer workers have health insurance.[19]

One other element to this picture needs to be addressed. In the 1990s, the manufacturing sector began an impressive recovery, both from the recession of 1990–91 and the impact of foreign competition. But the recovery did not translate into new jobs because corporations engaged in restructuring themselves, captured in terms such as "reengineering" and especially "downsizing." Again, industrial recovery did not translate into more new jobs of the type that usually come with health insurance. As a result of all this, fewer firms are offering health insurance as a benefit. Forty-four percent of firms offered insurance in 1989, but only 40 percent did two years later.[20]

A related problem concerns younger retirees, those between fifty-five and sixty-five. Many such retirees once maintained their health care plans with their former companies. But the same trends can be seen: companies are increasingly withdrawing such coverage. Over half of the early retirees are in danger of losing their benefits.[21]

There are three other components to our understanding of the growth of the uninsured population. First is the growth in part-time or temporary workers. These are also unlikely to have health insurance, even if they work in firms that offer it to their full-time employees.[22] Second, a number of uninsured workers are covered as dependents under their spouses' health insurance. To the extent that this is the case, then the fact that not all firms offer health insurance is not quite as much of a problem. In 1991, some 89 million workers had health insurance and another 21 million workers had insurance as dependents of other workers.[23] Some of these 21 million are workers in jobs that offer health insurance, about 11 percent of workers in such jobs.[24] On the other hand, this amounts to a subsidy from firms that offer health insurance to firms that do not. Additionally, because of the changing job structure situation, sectors that provide dependent coverage are also shrinking, so it is not just those with insurance-covered jobs but the dependents in non-insurance-covered jobs that are losing coverage.[25]

Another part of the explanation for the uninsurance problem is that Medicaid, the health care program for the poor, covers only about 42 percent of those with incomes under the poverty line.[26] The federal poverty line is just an indicator, a measure (and a somewhat controversial one) of the number of people living in poverty.[27] Medicaid eligibility is set by states, and Medicaid is a costly program for them, even though the federal government picks up over half the costs. From 1988 to 1992, Medicaid as a percentage of state spending increased by over 58 percent.[28] Medicaid increases combined with other budget pressures, including spending on crime and education, and resistance to tax increases led to ways to reduce spending. Medicaid is one target.

But there is a more fundamental reason for people being uninsured: health insurance is expensive. This is one of the reasons, discussed earlier, why smaller firms are less likely to offer health insurance than larger firms. If it is difficult for small firms to afford insurance because of the small pool of workers, than it is even more difficult for individuals to afford it.[29] Such plans are not only costly in terms of premiums but are likely to have significant cost-sharing provisions.

One last aspect remains. The section heading refers to the uninsured and the underinsured. The underinsured are those with health insurance but whose insurance is inadequate for their present or future needs. This refers especially to those who may have illnesses such as AIDS or multiple sclerosis, chronic diseases that are potentially expensive to cover. There are cases where an insured person was denied coverage after contracting HIV, the virus that leads to AIDS.[30]

Profiling the Uninsured

The obvious picture of the uninsured is that they should be poor. Yet, the above description of the relationship between jobs and health insurance suggests that a sizable number of people without health insurance work. In terms of income, using 1993 data, about 30 percent of the uninsured had incomes below the poverty line and 60 percent had incomes below 200 percent of the poverty line. About 40 percent were middle or upper income. Much of the uninsured have a regional face. Forty-three percent of the uninsured live in the South and another 24 percent in the West.[31] This is consistent with an earlier argument; those are the regions that have experienced the fastest job growth and have the lowest percentage of unionized workers. Some 53 percent of the uninsured work in small firms or are self-employed. "The profile of the uninsured is predominantly a picture of working people and their families. Most uninsured people—84 percent— are workers or the dependents of workers who do not receive health insurance through their jobs."[32] Younger workers and low-wage workers also tend to be uninsured.

Consequences of Uninsurance or Underinsurance

There is a simple and easy, though not pleasant, answer to the question of what the consequences are of inadequate or no insurance. That answer is that such people are at higher risk of disease and death and are less likely to attain the services they need than those who have insurance. This section documents that claim.

Uninsured people suffering from acute diseases are less likely, about a third less likely, to see a physician than those with acute illnesses who have health insurance.[33] For example, uninsured and Medicaid patients suffering from appendicitis are more likely to experience a ruptured appendix than privately insured patients.[34]

One common finding is that those lacking insurance also do not have a regular private physician. Therefore, they often use emergency rooms, particularly in public hospitals, as their primary source of care.[35] One result of delaying needed physician visits is that Medicaid patients and those without insurance are more likely to be hospitalized for conditions that could be avoided or treated outside of hospitals than those with private insurance.[36] Uninsured hospital patients are more likely to enter hospitals sicker and have shorter stays and fewer procedures performed on them than privately insured patients. They also have a higher death rate than insured patients.[37]

Perhaps the most important impact is on children. Children whose families lack health insurance are less likely to see a physician than children in families with insurance. Typical and treatable maladies of childhood, such as ear and throat infections, may go untreated and worsen. Further, barriers other than lack of insurance may hinder needed physician visits. These include cost-sharing provisions, lack of transportation, and lack of child care.[38]

Lack of insurance may affect the most helpless of people, newly born babies. Uninsured women are less likely to receive prenatal care than are privately insured women.[39] Uninsured (and Medicaid-insured) babies are likely to be discharged from hospitals sooner than privately insured babies. This is the case even though uninsured or Medicaid-insured babies experience more serious health problems than privately insured babies.[40]

The presence of health insurance also has an impact on the diagnosis of breast cancer. Women with no health insurance or covered by Medicaid are more likely to have breast cancer diagnosed later in the progression of the disease and are more likely to die as a result than women with breast cancer who have private health insurance.[41]

Quality of care for uninsured people is often lower than for those with insurance, particularly private insurance. Injuries resulting from negligence or substandard care appeared to be higher, according to a 1984 study in New York State, than for those with insurance.[42]

Those without health insurance also perceive themselves as less healthy than those with insurance.[43] Death rates may be higher for those lacking health insurance than for those with it. This may be both because of lack of access to medical care and lower quality of care when it is received.[44]

Uninsurance and underinsurance have impacts beyond those of the individual. Because uninsured people are more likely to use expensive emergency rooms than use a regular physician, the cost of that care is shifted to others. Indeed, hospitals in particular engage in considerable cost shifting, given service to the uninsured and the low reimbursement rates for Medicaid patients. Those with private insurance are charged more (and pay higher premiums) because of such cost shifting. Because of the Medicare hospital Prospective Payment System, discussed in chapter 4, shifting costs to Medicare patients is virtually impossible. Given this cost shifting, portions of the community pay for uninsured care, but not on an explicit basis. Further, the use of underwriting creates a situation where those who most need the help are least likely to get it. The subtitle of one article on this subject sums up this problem very well: "Only Healthy Need Apply."[45] That runs against the grain of the purpose of insurance.

Further, use of emergency rooms and trauma centers by uninsured patients places a heavy demand on those facilities.[46] Because of uncompensated care, hospitals and trauma centers face financial problems.[47] A further insight into the problem is that about a fifth of the uninsured people using emergency rooms are pregnancy- and childbirth-related cases and often do not get needed prenatal care.[48]

What do underinsured people do to compensate for their potential financial risk? They face high premiums, coinsurance and deductibles, stringent screening for preexisting conditions, exclusions of specific conditions, and limitations on maximum insurance benefits. Kinney and Steinmetz say that they form essentially an "insurance underground." These authors studied people who suffered from multiple sclerosis in Indiana and found various coping strategies. These included staying in jobs so as not to lose insurance coverage (job lock) and avoiding filing claims that would call attention to their condition. The result is even more inadequate insurance coverage and access to care and aggravation of the chronic health problem.[49]

Insurance and the Idea of Community

This brings us back to the issue of equity. Most health insurance provisions are put in place regardless of income. Consider a company that offers a health insurance plan covering dependents. The premiums are $200 a month and there are cost-sharing provisions. All employees are offered the same plan. The general manager of the company makes $100,000 a year and the janitor makes $15,000. Both have to pay the $200 monthly premium. The premium is only 2.4 percent of the general manager's income, but 16 percent of the janitor's income. Now extend this example to those who try to buy health insurance as individuals rather than as part of a group. The premiums might be four times as high as in a group plan and the cost-sharing provisions less generous. The result is that "individuals and families with lower incomes who do seek medical care will spend a greater proportion of their income just to meet the cost-sharing requirements."[50]

There is another way in which ethical issues play a role in the uninsurance and underinsurance problem. This is the problem, briefly mentioned at the beginning of this chapter, of changes in insurance company policy. To simplify, health insurance policies can take two forms. On the one hand is *community rating*. This exists when everybody in the insurance pool pays the same premiums (though there may be differences based on age and other such factors, a practice known as risk adjustment). That way, the risk of using the insurance (needing health care) is spread over a larger population. Larger firms are more likely to have community rating than smaller firms. Because the pool of employees is larger, there is a larger group of workers over which to spread the risk. Smaller firms, with fewer workers, have a smaller group over which to spread the risk. Insurance companies could handle the problem by treating all those it insures as the community, so it would not matter whether the firm was large or small, or the policy was for an individual or a group. Note that pooling risk for individual policies by definition cannot be done.

There has been an increasing tendency for insurance companies to write policies based on *experience rating*. Under experience rating, the premiums are adjusted based on the likely risk of needing health care. A person with a chronic heart problem, for example, is more likely to need health care than one in good health with no chronic problems. Automobile insurance is written on this basis. Premiums are higher for those in the highest-risk groups. This includes those who have been in accidents and those in groups most likely to have accidents. For example, young single males have the highest auto insurance premiums of any group.

Such a practice makes sense from the standpoint of the insurance company, as well as policyholders in low-risk groups. Those more likely to need the service should pay more. Having community rating in auto insurance would mean higher rates for those in the low-risk groups and lower rates for those in the high-risk groups.

But health care and health insurance are not automobile insurance. People in good health can do more, can realize more of their potential, than those in poor health. Health care is instrumental in the sense that it enables one to do other things. If there is a systematic bias through community rating, then it carries over into other areas.

Stone brings the debate of community versus experience rating out into the open, looking at its philosophical underpinnings.

> Actuarial fairness—each person paying for his own risk—is more than an idea about distributive justice. It is a method of organizing mutual aid by fragmenting communities into ever-smaller, more homogeneous groups and a method that leads ultimately to the destruction of mutual aid. This fragmentation must be accomplished by fostering in people a sense of their differences, rather than their commonalities, and their responsibility for themselves only, rather than their interdependence. Moreover, insurance necessarily operates on the logic of actuarial fairness when it, in turn, is organized as a competitive market.[51]

Others have also noted the impact of the trend toward experience rating.[52]

The important idea here is that the insurance practice of experience rating breaks down the idea of community. This argument would support at a minimum insurance reform and at a maximum national health insurance. In-between policies might include tax subsidies and employer mandates.

There is another insurance practice, very much related to experience rating, that leads to some people being uninsured and others being underinsured. This is the practice of insurance *underwriting*. Underwriting occurs when an insurance company refuses to insure workers in an entire firm (a practice known as *redlining*) or individuals with preexisting conditions. About 15 percent of all firms are redlined.[53] Examples of redlined firms include "those characterized by an older work force (over age fifty-five) or high employee turnover, those engaged in seasonal work or exposed to hazardous working conditions, those lacking an employer/employee relationship, and those 'known to present frequent claims submissions.'"[54] Those with preexisting conditions, such as cancer or AIDS, or those with conditions that are likely to result in costly claims in the future, may be denied insurance either permanently or during a specified time. In addition, limits may be placed on payments to such individuals. An alternative practice is to raise all the premiums for the groups significantly, sometimes to prohibitive levels.[55] It is not just insurance companies that engage in this practice. Employers who self-insure, and thus do not come under state regulation as do insurance companies, can also deny claims.

Apart from causing some people to be without insurance, others may be underinsured. Kinney and Steinmetz provide a definition and estimate of underinsurance, based on the 1990 Pepper Commission report: "those at risk of spending more than 10 percent of their annual income for health care in the event of serious illness."[56] Their estimate is that 20 million Americans are thus underinsured.

Solutions to the Problem of Uninsurance and Underinsurance

One possible solution to the problem of those without health insurance or those who are underinsured is to expand Medicaid. This was mentioned by George Bush in 1988. There are some advantages to such a proposal, variations of which have been offered by the American Medical Association, the Health Insurance Association of America, the American Public Welfare Association and the Health Policy Agenda for the American People.[57]

Such a proposal is attractive on several grounds. The administrative structure is already in place, the program's focus is the poor, and states already participate in it.[58] Thus the transition to such a program would not be especially difficult. The proposals would expand the program to the medically indigent. This would include those whose incomes are below the federal poverty line but not below state eligibility levels and those who are medically needy, that is, those whose medical expenses would move them below the federal poverty line. The latter group might "buy in" to Medicaid.[59]

There are considerable problems with such proposals, though none that could not be addressed. The most obvious problem is that of cost. Under Medicaid, the states determine the benefits package (above a specified minimum). Requiring states to provide the benefits of the middle range of packages and expanding coverage to the uninsured could increase Medicaid costs by $16 billion to $22 billion. Implementing the "buy-in" would cost another $18 billion.[60]

Further, the cost of Medicaid, as explained in chapter 3, is shared by the states and the federal government. Medicaid is already a fiscal burden to states. Expansion of Medicaid would exacerbate that burden. And because of eligibility differences between states, states with restrictive Medicaid and Aid to Families with Dependent Children programs (and usually fairly high poverty levels) would have to make considerably more effort than they currently do.[61]

Medicaid also offers a richer package of benefits (though lower provider-reimbursement rates) than private plans. This, combined with limitations on patient cost sharing, could encourage people to move from private insurance to Medicaid.[62] But there is another danger of expanding Medicaid. There is evidence, mentioned later in this chapter and in chapter 3, that Medicaid patients do not have the same access to services as do either privately insured patients or Medicare recipients. This is because low Medicaid reimbursement rates lead to low physician participation in the program. Thus expansion of Medicaid might help the newly covered be insured but not necessarily provide more access.

A companion proposal would expand Medicare, essentially creating a "Part C" that would cover those not insured. It would have the same advantage as mentioned above concerning Medicaid: the structure is already in place. It would add two further advantages. First, Medicare is entirely a federal government program, so the fiscal impact on and program differences between states would not be a problem. Second, provider reimbursement is higher for Medicare than for Medicaid. Thus access to services would be greater. But given pressures to reduce the federal budget deficit, which may result in trimming Medicare, the likelihood of this proposal being adopted is small.

Another proposal, part of a package of health care reform proposed by President Bush in 1992, would use tax credits and tax deductions to the uninsured to help them afford health insurance. Tax credits would be available to the poor, and deductions to middle-income families (including the self-employed).[63] Such tax incentives would be provided to both individuals and to employers.[64] The Bush plan would offer tax credits of up to $3,750 a year for a family and $1,250 for individuals, including a voucher for those whose income was so low that they did not pay taxes (i.e., refundable tax credit). This would cover families with incomes up to $80,000 a year.[65] The estimated cost of the plan would be $55 billion to $110 billion over a five-year period.[66]

One problem that would have to be faced with the tax deduction approach is that health care and, concomitantly, insurance premiums would rise faster than the deduction, even if the deduction were indexed to cost-of-living changes.[67] Another problem with the proposal is that it does not guarantee coverage. Insurance premiums in 1992 were higher than the tax deductions. Further, the deductions would be phased in over a five-year period. While the cost-of-living adjustment would increase the deductions by 2–4 percent a year, insurance premiums have been rising much more rapidly. Over that five-year period, the gap between the value of the deduction and the cost of insurance would increase.[68]

An intriguing 1991 plan offered by the conservative Heritage Foundation meets many of these objections. Butler argues that the major problem of the health care system, at least as concerns the problem of the uninsured, is the tax code.[69] The tax code allows employers to treat health insurance as a business expense eligible for a tax deduction. This leads to three major problems, two of which are relevant to the uninsurance problem.

The first problem is that the system is inequitable. Assume that health insurance as a fringe benefit is part of the total employee compensation package. If this is so, then the cost of the health insurance if given as salary would be taxed at the highest marginal tax rate. Because high-wage workers are at higher marginal tax rates than low-wage workers, the benefit would be highest for the high-wage workers. For those who must pay their own health insurance, the inequity is greater because they have only a limited tax deduction and thus must pay more from after-tax dollars.[70]

The second problem mentioned by Butler is job lock, people who keep their job for fear of losing health insurance coverage. By tying health insurance to employment, the tax code creates strong bonds between worker and job. The final problem created by the tax code, though not directly related to the uninsurance problem, is that it creates inflationary pressures by severing the link between paying for the service and receiving it.[71]

The Heritage Foundation plan would eliminate the employer tax deduction for health care and replace it with a refundable tax credit for individuals. The tax credit would be available even to those who do not itemize their tax returns. If the health care tax credit were greater than the individual's tax obligation, the difference would be refunded to that individual. The credit would be geared toward the portion of family income spent on health care (insurance and out-of-pocket costs). If a family spent 10 percent of its income on health care, it would be eligible for a 20 percent tax credit.[72]

One interesting part of the proposal is the "health care social contract." Under the contract, all families would be required to join a health plan with a minimum package of benefits. Though Butler does not use the term, this plan is thus an individual mandate, rather than an employee mandate. The federal government would be part of the contract by guaranteeing the fiscal viability of the individual mandate, either through tax credits or through access to Medicaid and/or Medicare.[73]

The plan has important advantages. It severs the tie between work and health insurance. Employers would no longer have to worry about the increasing costs of health care and workers would not be tied to a job just because of the health insurance benefit. A second advantage is that it is equitable because it focuses on percentage of income regardless of size of income and would provide more help for those who need it more, such as low-income workers and those with chronic health problems. A third advantage is that the program not only would reduce the costs to both the federal and state governments of welfare and Medicaid but might also provide a net gain to the federal budget, thus reducing the federal budget deficit or enabling the provision of a somewhat more generous program.[74]

Like all policy proposals, this one has its disadvantages as well. One is the equity consideration. The argument that Butler makes that the current tax deduction system is inequitable because those with higher incomes would pay at a higher tax rate than those with lower incomes is an assumption. The numbers, on the face of it, are correct. Consider the following:

Let us assume two families, one with a taxable income of $30,000 a year and the other with a taxable income of $90,000 a year. The families are the same size, the primary worker for each family works for the same company and gets the same health insurance package from the employer. The employer contribution to both families' health insurance is the same, say $3,000 a year. If the tax deduction were removed and the employer kept the total compensation package the same, the workers would each receive an additional $3,000 in salary. This would increase their taxable incomes to $33,000 and $93,000 respectively. The tax for the lower-income family would increase by $450, an increase of about 10 percent (using 1994 tax rates) in tax obligations and a marginal tax rate of 15 percent ($450/$3,000 = 15%). The tax for the higher-income family would increase by $875, an increase of about 4.3 percent in tax obligations and a marginal tax rate of about 29 percent ($875/$3,000 = 29.2%). Thus the equity consideration, if it is a consideration at all, would apply only to those whose income was too low to pay federal income taxes. Otherwise, the current system, as Butler explains it, actually favors lower-income families as long as they pay taxes if one looks at the actual increase in tax obligations versus marginal tax rates. So, in that sense, Butler is partially correct.

But he is incorrect in two other senses. First, workers get the health insurance but not the money. This is a "let-us-assume" proposition rather than the real world. Second, consider how the tax credit system would work. Let us take our families from the above example, the $30,000 income family and the $90,000 income family. Under the new system, both pay the same percentage of their income on health care. For the first family that amounts to $3,000, for the second family it amounts to $9,000. These are the same in percentage terms, but the impact on the two families is much different, given the original size of their income. Both would be eligible for a 20 percent tax credit, but that would amount to $600 for the lower income family (a cut of 13.3 percent in tax obligation). For the upper income family, the 20 percent tax credit would amount to $1,800 (a tax cut of 8.9 percent in tax obligation). While the percentage decrease of tax obligation would be lower for the higher-income family, thus seeming to be equitable, the tax credit would be three times as large as for the low-income family. It would be proportional at best.

A final problem with the tax credit plan is that while it may guarantee insurance coverage, it does not deal with the other problems discussed: risk rating and so forth. It also does not guarantee access to health care in inner cities and rural areas, a topic to be discussed below. The proposal is worth considering as perhaps one component of health reform.

A fourth alternative would be to expand the community health center program. Community health centers (originally called neighborhood health centers) were created during the 1960s as part of President Johnson's War on Poverty. These centers offer comprehensive health services to those in impoverished inner-city neighborhoods and rural areas at minimal or no cost to clients.[75] By 1991, there were some 550 such centers. Evaluations of community health centers have been very positive.[76] In 1991, the Advisory Council on Social Security recommended the addition of 250 more community health centers.[77]

There are two problems with such proposals. One is that providing the additional care would cost money from a federal budget that is already tight and constrained by large budget deficits. A second, and probably more important issue, is ideological. Community health centers would put government in the business of more directly providing health services than Medicare or Medicaid.[78] Tax credits and deductions, as proposed by President Bush, would have a very small role for government provision of services. The Advisory Council's proposal was not included in President Bush's plan.

Another approach to expanding health insurance coverage would focus on employers. Such an approach would involve a combination of employer mandates, requiring employers to provide and help pay for health insurance for their employees, and subsidies to employers (especially smaller firms) either directly or through tax deductions, to enable them to afford such policies. A variation on this is the "play-or-pay" proposal, where the employer would either provide health insurance for employees (the "play" option) or contribute to a statewide or nationwide pool to help the uninsured (the "pay" option).

One advantage of focusing on the employer is that it builds on the present system. A second advantage is that it minimizes costs to government. Mandates do not require additional government expenditures of a sizable amount (the exception of course is subsidies, and these would be targeted and certainly less than the costs of a full national health care system).[79] A typical employer mandate proposal might require employers to pay for 80 percent of insurance premiums. Such a mandate would promote equity and be relatively easy to enforce through Social Security, though administration would be complex.[80] Of course, small businesses in particular have argued that they cannot afford the additional costs. Their opposition to the employer mandate portion of President Clinton's Health Security Act, discussed in chapter 8, was one of the reasons for its failure. A disadvantage of "play-or-pay" is that it might encourage employers to contribute to the uninsurance fund, effectively creating a national system. If that is the desire, a direct approach would be more useful.[81]

Another proposal would combine employer-based insurance with Medicare.[82] This proposal would establish

> a common basic benefit package under both Medicare and employer plans, and [establish] common provider payment methods applicable to both Medicare and employer plans. It would be financed through a combination of employer and individual premium contributions, payroll taxes, personal income taxes, and other general tax revenues.[83]

A final approach is insurance reform. One such reform would be to place a cap or ceiling on insurance premiums. This was part of the Clinton health care plan. States would have the most important role here, as in other insurance reforms, because of their regulatory authority over the insurance industry. Three other insurance reforms might increase coverage of the uninsured. One would be to move back to community rating and away from experience rating. This would lower premiums, particularly for those in higher-risk groups (of course, it would raise premiums for those who are healthy). A related reform would restrict or eliminate underwriting, the practice of excluding or restricting those with preexisting conditions. Essentially this would guarantee that all who wanted insurance could get it at a reasonable price. Of course, insurance companies would raise overall premium rates to make up for the additional costs due to underwriting. The final insurance reform that might be considered is portability. This means that someone who changes jobs (or whose employer changes insurance companies) would still be covered in the new job. Obviously insurance companies oppose restrictions on their business practices.

The experience in Rochester, New York, long a leader in health care reform, is that requiring community rating, which the state of New York has done for several years, does increase access to insurance. Community rating is very high in Rochester; and only 6 percent of residents are uninsured, and job lock does not appear to be an issue.[84] One drawback to the New York State requirement that insurers accept all applicants and use community rating is that it may encourage people to go without health insurance until they know it is needed and cannot be refused. Thus one paradoxical result of the New York plan is that the percentage of insured people in the state has decreased since the law was passed in 1992.

The Disadvantaged

In this section, we consider the health care problems of the disadvantaged, focusing on the poor, minorities, and women. To some extent, the material in this section overlaps with that in the previous section on the uninsured and the underinsured. But as we have noted, a sizable portion of the uninsured are not poor and do work. There are thus other problems that need to be addressed.

Minorities and Low-Income Groups

In general, minorities and low-income groups do not have the same access to health care, or compare on the same level on health statistics as those who are white and/or wealthier. In drawing this portrait of low-income and minority groups, we should point out that this is a statistical portrait. It applies in general to the groups discussed.

In looking at the health status of minority and low-income groups, we should note several important features. First, minority groups tend to have lower educational achievement, higher unemployment rates, higher crime rates, lower incomes and therefore higher poverty rates, higher proportions of female-headed families, and higher proportions of out-of-wedlock births. All of this seems to be correlated with health status. One of the confusing aspects of these data is that they are very much related to income. That is, many of these characteristics may be a result of poverty (socioeconomic class) rather than ethnicity (race).[85]

McBride argues that health care policy toward blacks went through three stages. The first stage was *engagement* (mid-1960s to late 1970s), where health care services and financing were increased to the black community and discrimination was lessened. The second phase, *submersion,* from the late 1970s to mid-1980s, saw a cutback in social programs. For example, as a result of the 1981 Omnibus Budget and Reconciliation Act, the working poor were taken off AFDC and Medicaid rolls. The third phase, *crisis recognition,* began in the mid-1980s. This is a recognition that there is a problem, particularly in the large urban cities. But McBride points out that this last phase has not yet resulted in changed policies. Thus the health care problems of minorities and low-income groups remain.[86] Indeed, a study of Chicago, Houston, and Los Angeles noted "the progressive deterioration in the delivery of health care to the poor and the indigent since the beginnings of the 1980s."[87]

Age-adjusted death rates are higher for minorities than for whites. Minorities tend to have less access to prenatal care and to give birth at earlier ages. This tends to result in higher rates of premature births and low-weight births. These in turn are associated with other problems (not just health) in later years. Infant mortality is higher among minorities. Indeed, the infant mortality rate among African Americans was comparable to the infant mortality rate in Costa Rica.[88]

Why do disadvantaged women not get full prenatal care? One reason is financial barriers. Minority and low-income women are less likely to have health insurance than the general population. Even though Medicaid has been expanded in recent years (since 1986) to cover more prenatal care, many states have not taken the appropriate action. Further, even if all the states covered the entire poverty population of expectant mothers (100 percent of those under the poverty line), those just over the poverty line would still be excluded. It should be noted again that even with recent expansions, Medicaid covers less than half of those under the federal poverty line.[89]

Even if financial barriers did not exist, there are not enough doctors willing to work in low-income areas or with high-risk mothers. According to one report, less than one-third of the nation's doctors participate fully in Medicaid.[90] The Medicaid participation problem is most serious in the case of pediatricians and obstetricians.[91] Thus the services, even if affordable, might not be available.

Minorities also fare worse than the overall population in terms of chronic illnesses.

> In general, Blacks are diagnosed and/or seek treatment later than Whites for many chronic diseases, and this may have significant implications for the efficacy of treatment and for survivorship for many chronic diseases. What is more, once under medical management or therapy, the treatment received by Blacks may be less aggressive than that received by Whites.[92]

For example, studies show that African American women with breast cancer are less likely to receive surgery and more likely to receive no treatment than whites. A study of bladder cancer victims showed that African Americans were less likely to receive treatment than whites at similar stages of disease.[93]

Another health problem of minorities, though it may not appear that way, is homicide rates. Homicide rates of African American males are 544 percent higher than for whites. They are also higher for Hispanics, though the difference is not as great.[94]

AIDS is another health problem that affects ethnicity differently. While a majority of AIDS victims are whites, the relative proportion of AIDS victims is twice as high among African Americans and Hispanics as among whites.[95] The major transmission categories for AIDS are drug related (i.e., IV drug users). For minority women, having sex with someone who uses drugs is a major source of the disease.[96] Further, African Americans are less likely to have health insurance at the same time that they are at greater risk of getting AIDS.[97]

The use of health services for minorities increased beginning in the 1960s with the advent of Medicaid. Nevertheless, such utilization remains below that of whites. Further, minorities are less likely to have a private physician and more likely to seek primary care in hospital emergency rooms.[98] Cutbacks in Medicaid during the 1980s led to a decreased use of services among minorities.[99] Estimates are that just 41 percent of the population below the poverty line were covered by Medicaid and only about half of children in families below the poverty line.[100] Miller and Curtis note that even programs such as Medicare, where essentially all who are sixty-five or older have insurance coverage, have not reduced disparities between blacks and whites in the use of health services.[101]

Ginzberg argues that much of the problem of access to health care is the result not just of lack of insurance but has a supply dimension: the expansiveness of the state Medicaid program and the availability of institutions, largely public, that would treat charity cases. New York City saw less deterioration in services for the poor because of the generous New York State Medicaid program, a large public hospital system, and voluntary hospitals that regularly treat uninsured patients. In contrast, Chicago saw the closing of eleven hospitals in the inner city, while Houston had both a restrictive Medicaid program (the Texas program is limited only to recipients of AFDC) combined with the lack of a tradition of charity cases being treated by voluntary hospitals.[102]

Ginzberg also notes that the number of physicians in impoverished neighborhoods is much lower than in wealthier areas. In the four cities studied, the physician-to-population ratio varied from one physician for every 10,000 residents to one per 15,000 residents. In the wealthier areas, the ratio was about one per 300 residents.[103] Thus, wealthier areas had thirty-three to fifty times more private physicians than poorer areas. Part of this reflects low Medicaid reimbursement rates. Further, "the majority of practitioners serving the poor consisted of foreign medical graduates, many with indifferent professional competence and language problems that impeded effective patient-physician communication."[104]

The strongest perspective suggests that the American health care system shares characteristics with the South African health care system under apartheid. While the South African system was based on explicit racial segregation, the American system is based on socioeconomic differences. But again because of higher percentages of minorities in the lower socioeconomic classes, the effect is the same. Further, the fragmentation of the American health care system furthers the comparison. "Well babies may be seen at one location, but immunizations must be obtained at a different site, while ill children must travel to different clinics or county hospitals."[105] Most striking about the comparisons are health indicators. Both blacks in South Africa and in the United States have high infant mortality rates and high rates of preventable diseases.[106]

Americans of Latino descent appear to have the lowest level of health insurance coverage of any ethnic group, including blacks. Further, there are differences in health insurance coverage within the Latino population, with Puerto Ricans and Cubans having considerably higher levels of coverage than other Latinos.[107] Hispanics also suffer from high rates of chronic diseases, such as cancer, diabetes, and AIDS.[108]

One important and careful study of the quality of care shows that neither race, gender, nor income status was associated with poor quality, defined as adverse events and negligence leading to adverse events. What was important was insurance status: those with no insurance suffered poorer-quality care. To the extent that minorities and low-income groups have high rates of uninsurance, then they are affected by quality of care.[109]

It should be obvious by this time that the problem of the poor and the disadvantaged transcends the problem of lack of insurance. Privately insured expectant mothers begin prenatal care earlier than Medicaid-insured expectant mothers. "Thus, even when prenatal visits are provided free of charge, barriers such as transportation costs, lack of understanding of the importance of prenatal care, unfriendly or poorly organized clinics, poor scheduling, long waiting times, and inadequate social support inhibit access to care."[110]

One way to improve access to doctors, particularly for Medicaid patients, is to increase Medicaid reimbursements at least up to the level of Medicare reimbursements. Rowland and Salganicoff note that Medicaid reimbursements are 66 percent of Medicare reimbursements, and for pediatricians and obstetricians are about 55 percent of what private patients pay.[111] Such a policy would increase participation in Medicaid. But the cost of increasing physician reimbursements ($1.12 billion to $3.23 billion) makes such a policy difficult to adopt in times of budget deficit reductions.[112] Because of the low percentages of physicians located in underserved areas, however, the problem of access will remain unless steps are taken to increase the number of doctors in those areas.[113]

Women and Health Care

To a degree, women's health issues overlap those of minorities (ethnicity) and low-income groups (class). To the extent that women's income, especially in families headed by women, is low, then all the health problems associated with low income show up here. For example, issues surrounding prenatal care, briefly discussed above, while obviously a concern for women, are generally associated with low income. If programs aimed at low-income are cut, as was the case in the early 1980s and may again be in the late 1990s, then women will be affected.

On the other hand, there are certain issues that are unique to women, though of concern to men as well. Reproductive issues, such as abortion and family planning, are among the most controversial issues in health care or any policy field. In general, the availability of abortion, while not completely eliminated, has been reduced beginning in the late 1970s. Some of this has come about because of legislative changes, such as the Hyde amendment forbidding the use of federal Medicaid funds for abortion and similar action by some states. Some is a result of court decisions that have allowed restrictions, such as waiting periods. Another element has been the strong right-to-life movement, which has picketed abortion clinics. Medical schools are less frequently teaching abortion procedures.

Women are also less well protected by health insurance, both public and private. Fewer working women (37 percent) have employer-based health insurance than men (56 percent).[114] Women's employment careers tend to be intermittent (i.e., time off for childbearing or job changes because husband moved), and to be in lower-paying jobs less likely to offer health insurance.[115] Medicaid coverage is sporadic. Fewer than half those eligible are covered; doctors do not have to accept Medicaid patients. Women are less likely than men to have supplemental Medicare health insurance and are less likely to have their illnesses covered under Medicare.[116] Further, because women, on the average, live longer than men, issues of long-term care and chronic illnesses are critical.[117]

The above paragraph probably understates the problem. First, the percentage of workers covered by employer-based health insurance has declined. The recovery from the 1990–91 recession started slowly (though it picked up in 1993), and employers have been making productivity improvements resulting in the need for fewer workers. Further, there is a growing trend toward using part-time or temporary workers, also unlikely to have health insurance benefits.

There have been changes in the workforce participation of women and in the family structure, where there are two-worker families or where the family is headed by a female. Adjustments to these changes have been slow (the Family Leave Act is one recent adjustment). Muller states:

> Independent coverage, benefit content and duplication, and cost sharing are issues that affect women differently in different family situations. Employers have expanded their use of peripheral or contingent workers who have few or no benefit entitlements, drawing on a largely female labor supply. It is not feasible to count on workplace arrangements as the social instrument for protecting individuals against health care costs.[118]

The health care system treats women differently from men. Medicare tends to cover the kinds of diseases more predominant among men (i.e., heart attacks) better than the chronic diseases more prevalent among women. Men receive more preventive services than women. Women also tend to see a number of specialists, and so their care is often fragmented. Two observers label women's health care as a "patchwork quilt with gaps."[119]

Further, as Hafner-Eaton points out, women are likely to have unnecessary surgeries, such as caesarean births, radical mastectomies, and hysterectomies.[120] Despite this, much of the health research carried on in the United States uses the male as the model. Hafner-Eaton writes:

> Government notwithstanding, the National Institutes of Health, as recently as 1990, allocated a mere 13.5% of biomedical research funds to women's health. The remainder of funds went to research on men's health or research affecting both ... Women's different hormonal balance from men's means that pharmaceuticals used to treat jointly shared conditions might not work, or, worse yet, could be seriously injurious if used as tested safely on men. The use of the male body and its reactions as the norm has detrimental consequences for women and many times for their children as well.[121]

This bias in research has been somewhat alleviated. In 1991, the U.S. Public Health Service and other federal agencies began to devote more resources to research on women.[122] But the National Institutes of Health (NIH) research plan has been criticized for focusing too much on the trivial.[123]

There is also some evidence to suggest that women are not nearly as disadvantaged by the health care system and in research as suggested above.[124] Women seek care more frequently than men. The care received by women is at least as good as men's, and there is some tendency for women to receive more diagnostic tests than men. There is a gender difference in cardiac bypass procedures, largely because men who need the procedure tend to be younger (and thus have fewer additional medical problems) and have larger arteries (making the operation easier) than women.

Kadar further points out that much innovative medical technology, such as ultrasound, was originally developed for women. He notes that women have a branch of medicine devoted strictly to them (gynecology) whereas men do not (urology probably being the closest).[125]

It was mentioned earlier that only a small fraction of NIH medical research was conducted on women. Kadar observes that much of medical research uses both men and women as subjects; only about 6.5 percent of NIH research is devoted solely to men. As an example, the highest level of research funded by the National Cancer Institute is on breast cancer. By comparison, research on prostate cancer received only about a fourth as much funding as breast cancer research.[126]

Finally, Kadar mentions that at the beginning of the twentieth century, men had a slightly longer life expectancy than women. By the second half of the twentieth century, the life expectancy of women was about ten percent higher then for men. One of the reasons for the change is that childbirth has become safer. A second reason is that many infectious diseases have been virtually eliminated, and those that remain affect men more than women.[127]

Granting Kadar's argument would mean that specific gender problems in health care are drastically overstated. To the extent that women are subject to the forces of ethnicity and class, however, the health of women remains an important concern.

Conclusion

In this chapter we have considered one of the major problems of the U.S. health care system, that of the disadvantaged. The uniquely American mix of public and private insurance programs, a post–World War II development, covers about 85 percent of the population. But it leaves over 30 million people without any insurance at all. And especially in the case of private insurance, it leaves a portion of the population underinsured and vulnerable to catastrophic medical expenses.

Incremental reforms, the kind that generally characterize public policy in the United States, could begin to address some of these problems. Medicaid, Medicare, or both, could be expanded to cover those without insurance, many of whom work. The tax system, either through subsidies to employers or tax credits for individuals or families, would also help. Insurance reforms, such as mandating community rating and providing for portability for insurance, would also be useful, though there are dangers in doing some of these things individually. A federal or state program of universal coverage, involving either employer or individual mandates, would likely be the simplest, though not necessarily the most politically feasible, way to deal with the problem.

Even were some or all of these policies undertaken, and they have been in some states, the problems of the disadvantaged would remain. Having insurance coverage is important. We know from a considerable body of evidence that those without health insurance have more health problems and receive less and poorer-quality service than those with health insurance. But if the providers are not in the geographical area, such as inner cities or rural areas, having insurance by itself is insufficient.

We also know that poverty and ethnicity plays an important and intermixing role in health outcomes. We know that blacks and Hispanics on the average have poorer health outcomes than whites. We know that minority women and their babies have poorer health outcomes: more troubling pregnancies, low birthweights, and so forth.

These issues, which involve equality and equity, do not lend themselves to easy solutions. Perhaps the most viable solution is the community health center program, where providers are located in underserved areas. But in the mid-1990s, when there is a movement away from social programs and budgets are being cut, the likelihood of the expansion of such programs is minimal. In the absence of a comprehensive transformation of the American health care system, it is likely that the problems of the disadvantaged will remain.

6
Health Care Cost Containment

The 1960s saw a dramatic expansion in social programs. Civil rights, women's rights, educational opportunities, and improved housing and health care for citizens were the battle cries of a social revolution as the federal government attempted to expand individual opportunities. In the health field, health care came to be viewed as a right, rather than a privilege. Providing access to decent health care became the primary goal of the federal government.

Medicare and Medicaid were established by the federal government in 1965 to provide increased access to health care for the elderly and the poor. These programs were successful in increasing access to health care for large numbers of people.[1] The creation and implementation of such programs was made possible by a healthy economy. Additionally, the Comprehensive Health Planning Act and Public Health Services Amendments of 1966 (PL 89-749) established the goal of providing the highest level of health care attainable to every person.

By the late 1960s and early 1970s, the focus began to shift from providing access to concern about rising health care costs. The cost of health care in the United States had been rising faster than the general growth rate of the economy. Health care expenditures accounted for an increased share of the national income.[2] As shown in Table 6.1, national health care expenditures increased from $27.1 billion in 1960 to $74.3 billion in 1970 and to $251.1 billion in 1980. By 1993, national health care expenditures had jumped to $884.2 billion.[3] Spending for health care amounted to 13.9 percent of the gross domestic product (GDP) in 1993, more than double the figure of 5.3 percent in 1960. Another way of looking at the explosion in health care costs is to examine the third line in Table 6.1, which line shows the percentage increase in health care expenditures from the previous period. While there

Table 6.1

National Health Care Expenditures, 1960–93

	1960	1970	1980	1990	1993
National health care expenditures ($ billion)	27.1	74.3	251.1	696.6	884.2
As percentage of GNP	5.3	7.4	9.3	12.6	13.9[a]
Percentage increase in expenditures from previous period[a]		174	238	177	27

Source: Katharine R. Levit, "National Health Expenditures, 1993," *Health Care Financing Review* 16, no. 1 (Fall 1994): 280.

[a]Calculated from first row.

was a slowdown in the increase during the 1980s, it is still impressive. And in the three years of the 1990s shown in the table, health care expenditures increased by about 27 percent.

Hospital and physician care accounted for more than half of all health care expenditures in 1993. Private sources accounted for about 51.3 percent of health expenditures. Federal health spending of $280.6 billion in 1993 accounted for 32.7 percent of all national health care expenditures (see Table 6.2).[4]

There are many causes for such dramatic increases in health care costs. To some, increased costs are the result of increased public expectations about the health care system, advances in health care technology and their success, and the prevailing sentiment that health care is a right.[5] Others see health care cost increases in fee for service, a medical arms race among hospitals, insurance companies and third-party payers, and the purchasers of health care, such as the federal government and industries that, for a long time, ignored the cost problem.[6] Still others argue that virtually all of the medical care price inflation of recent years can be accounted for by general inflation, the labor intensity of health industries, the behavior of wage rates during inflation, and the pattern of labor-productivity changes.[7]

If there is any agreement among policymakers, health care practitioners, researchers, and health care consumers and purchasers, it is that health care costs too much. The federal government is one of the largest purchasers of health care. Federal health care expenditures constitute a significant portion of the federal budget, and the tax burden is large. Accordingly, federal policymakers and bureaucrats face great pressure to contain health care costs.[8] The question for policymakers has become one of how to contain costs and still maintain quality medical service.[9] The focus in the health

Table 6.2

National Health Care Expenditures for 1993, by Sources of Funds and Types of Expenditures (in billions of dollars)

	Total	Out-of-pocket	Private insurance	Federal	State/local
Total national health expenditures	884.2	157.5 (17.8%)	296.1 (33.5%)	280.6 (32.7%)	107.3 (12.1%)
Hospital Care	326.6	9.1 (2.8%)	117.8 (36.0%)	149.2 (45.7%)	33.7 (10.3%)
Physician Services	171.2	26.2 (15.3%)	84.1 (49.1%)	45.0 (26.3%)	13.1 (7.7%)
Dental Services	37.4	18.7 (50.0%)	16.8 (44.9%)	1.0 (2.7%)	0.8 (2.1%)
Home Health Care	20.8	4.3 (20.7%)	2.5 (12.0%)	9.8 (47.1%)	1.5 (7.2%)
Drugs and other medical nondurables	75.0	47.4 (63.2%)	18.4 (24.5%)	4.7 (6.3%)	4.4 (5.9%)
Nursing Homes	69.6	23.0 (33.0%)	1.7 (2.4%)	28.3 (40.7%)	15.3 (22.0%)

Source: Katharine R. Levit, "National Health Expenditures, 1993," *Health Care Financing Review* 16, no. 1 (Fall 1994): 284.

care policy debate has shifted from "should we contain costs?" to "how should we contain costs?"[10] This is not just a problem of public expenditures; the business sector also faces considerable health cost problems.

The debate over how to contain rising health care costs centers, perhaps oversimplistically, on two broad approaches or strategies.[11] One strategy relies on government regulation, while the other relies on increasing competition in the health care market. During the 1970s and 1980s, the federal government tried both regulatory and competitive strategies to contain health costs. In recent years, state governments and the private sector have established new initiatives for the same purpose.

This chapter has three purposes. First, it provides a brief theoretical rationale of regulatory and market strategies. Second, it examines the regulatory and market strategies used by the federal government to contain rising health care costs. Third, it analyzes recent state government and private-sector innovations and initiatives to contain health care costs.

Theoretical Framework: Government Regulation and Market Competition

The Regulatory Strategy

One of the most important assumptions of the *regulatory strategy* is that the health care market suffers from too many shortcomings. Government regulation can therefore help improve the performance of the market. Thus, one motivation for economic regulation of the system is the premise that the system suffers from serious market failures including information disparities between providers and consumers of health services and an insurance system (third-party financing) that masks the costs of health services. This in turn produces excessive expenditures, inefficiency, and maldistribution of labor power and resources. A related market failure is that the health care system has a severe equity problem (differential access to services and financing). Thus the government must play a role, under this assumption, in providing greater access to the health care market for those who cannot afford it.[12] The second assumption of the regulatory strategy is that the health care market is different from other economic markets. In health care, physicians control both supply and demand because the physician is both the patient's consultant on what services are needed and the provider of these services. Physicians are not trained to think in terms of aggregate costs. Physicians not only influence cost decisions regarding individual patients but also influence the growth and expansion of health care institutions, thus affecting hospital costs. In addition, the third-party payment system, based on private health insurance and government payment, tends to remove the patient from the effects of health care costs.[13]

Another important potential difference between medical care and other goods and services is the absence of consumer information about appropriate price-quality levels.[14] The role of information in facilitating choices about health care goods and services is crucial.[15] Some have argued that the medical market is on the verge of remedying the information deficit and that the determination of whether medical care is really different from other goods and services is ultimately a political question.[16]

The third assumption of the regulatory strategy is that public regulation promotes important values of political accountability, public access to information, and public participation.[17] The regulatory process is characterized by a high degree of formal due process. The requirements of public notices, public meetings, adversary procedures, formal recordkeeping, and limits on appeals help inform consumers by providing access to information and extending to them an opportunity to participate in the policymaking process.

Thus, government regulation of the health care system is justified on many grounds: as a way of improving the workings of the health care market, providing equity, and promoting crucial public values with the hope that it will help contain health care costs. Some advocates of a regulatory strategy argue that a pure market in health care is unattainable and thus regulation is the second-best choice.[18] Others argue for a more tightly regulated health care system as the best policy.[19]

Critics of the regulatory strategy charge that examples of past regulatory failures suggest that government regulation does not work.[20] These critics argue that too many fundamental structural and incentive problems are stacked against good regulatory performance[21] and that comprehensive regulation will raise, not lower, the true cost of medical care,[22] thus contributing to health care cost inflation.[23] Regulation is not cost effective; it produces inefficiency and prevents technological innovations. Regulation often produces a cartel-like situation resulting in a monopoly on prices because regulatory agencies become captured by the regulated industry.[24] To the critics of a regulatory strategy the answer is competitive market strategy. Competition is the latest buzzword among many health policymakers and health care providers.

The Market Strategy

One of the major assumptions of the *market strategy* is that the principal source of rising health care costs is an attempt by the government to base the distribution of health care on the egalitarian principle of need, which does not allocate health care resources in an efficient manner.[25] The advocates of this strategy argue for creating incentives and mechanisms to increase competition and relying on the health care market for better and more efficient allocation of health care resources.[26] Some market reformers argue that health insurance creates a "moral hazard," masking the true costs of health care from both consumers and providers. From this it would follow that consumers must be presented with options that have genuine cost consequences.

New alternative mechanisms of health care delivery must be found that provide health care consumers with multiple choices with cost consequences in health plans. Creating conditions for fair market competition will produce competition in the market, which will help contain health care costs.[27] New incentives should be created. To make businesses more conscious of health care costs, tax laws should be altered to place a ceiling on the total amount of health insurance premiums that employers can deduct as a business expense. To make consumers more conscious of health care costs, insurance plans should rely on coinsurance and deductibles.[28] What is needed, some have argued, is to combine markets with a minimal but necessary amount of government regulation. This combination is known as *managed competition.*[29]

Some procompetition advocates, such as Clark Havighurst, have argued that one of the most effective and least intrusive methods for assuring fair competition is enforcement of antitrust laws. Antitrust principles are based on the assumptions that competition promotes efficiency and innovation and encourages diversity through decentralization, and that competitive markets are more stable than noncompetitive markets because the former adjust continuously to market conditions. These assumptions, in turn, are based on social values of individual initiative, individual freedom of choice, and the dangers of big business and big government.[30] This does not mean that a competitive market would be unregulated; any competitive market requires monitoring and intervention from time to time to assure that competition is fair and open. According to antitrust enforcement advocates, given the potential for exercise of monopoly power by physicians, hospitals, and other health care providers, policing health care markets must be an integral part of reforms designed to enhance competition.[31]

In summary, advocates of the competitive strategy argue that improving structural mechanisms and changing incentives through introduction of competition in the health care market will result in better economic performance and reduced health care costs.

Critics of the competitive strategy are skeptical of the results of market competition. To some, the prospects of a competitive strategy are promising but uncertain technically and politically.[32] Others argue that markets in health care are usually pseudo markets dominated by one side of the transaction,[33] and that the supporters of competition may be grossly overemphasizing the beneficial results.[34] It would take more than the stimulus from increased consumer cost sharing or reduced tax subsidies to produce competitive behavior on the part of health care providers.[35] Opponents of an antitrust enforcement strategy argue that professional autonomy and self-regulation produce significant social benefits. In addition, physicians are likely to oppose antitrust enforcement because a free market could be worse for physicians' economic well-being than government regulation. Physicians often reap substantial economic benefits from regulations they control and the government programs that pay the bills.[36]

The Role of the Federal Government in Cost Containment

Over the years, the federal government has followed a middle road between the harsh realities of a private health care marketplace and a nationally planned and regulated health care system through a comprehensive national health insurance system. Thus, while the federal government has used both regulatory and competitive strategies in an effort to contain health care costs, the major efforts have been in the regulatory field. One of the regulatory strategies used by the federal government has been health care planning.

Health Care Planning and Cost Containment

During the late 1960s and early 1970s, the federal government responded to the concerns of rising health care costs by adopting various regulatory mechanisms. Health planning emerged as one of the major methods for controlling health care costs. While the federal government had always engaged in some planning, not until the late 1960s and early 1970s did health care planning became a dominant theme. Planning relies on a regulatory strategy and uses centralized decision making to guide the allocation of resources and ensure access to services.

The rationale for health care planning is based on the argument of excess capacity in the health care system in general, and in the hospital industry in particular, as a significant contributor to rising health care costs. The argument is that there are too many hospitals, beds, and medical equipment. This not only creates unnecessary expansion and duplication of expensive resources but it also leads to overutilization of medical facilities.[37] Supply creates its own demand following Roemer's argument that "a bed built is a bed filled is a bed billed."[38] This excess capacity, expansion, and duplication are encouraged by factors such as the third-party payment system, the inability of the market to induce inefficient hospitals to reduce the number of beds or go out of business altogether, and competition among hospitals for prestige and physicians.[39]

While early approaches to planning were aimed at ensuring high-quality health care to everyone,[40] health planning in the 1960s and 1970s focused explicitly on the problem of rising costs. One of the significant regulatory developments in the area of health care planning were *certificate-of-need (CON)* laws.[41] By 1973, twenty-three states had adopted such laws. The federal government got into the act with the passage of the 1972 amendments to the Social Security Act of 1935. This created the section 1122 program, which called for review of hospital expansion proposals when Medicare funding might be involved.

Two years later, the federal government assumed control of the entire certificate-of-need process. The *National Health Planning and Resource Development Act of 1974 (PL 93-641)* provided an institutional framework for health care planning. It replaced three previous federal programs: Comprehensive Health Planning, the Regional Medical Program and the Hill-Burton Hospital Construction Program.[42] The law required all states to adopt certificate-of-need laws by 1980. The law also established a network of state and local health planning agencies to shape local health systems based on national priorities. More than 200 local *health systems agencies (HSAs)* were established, each responsible for governing a specific area, to administer the certificate-of-need laws. State health planning development agencies roughly paralleled the roles and responsibilities of local HSAs. The law provided for the representation of consumer and provider interests in the HSAs.

Certificate-of-need laws require hospitals to document "community need" to obtain approval for major capital expenditures for expansion of physical plants, equipment, and services. The primary purpose of these laws was to prevent unnecessary investment in facilities and services. The laws were also designed to prevent the entry of new providers in the health care market unless a clear need was demonstrated.

Did the certificate-of-need laws and the HSAs help contain overall growth in hospital costs in particular and health care costs in general? The available empirical evidence overwhelmingly points to the failure of health care planning to control health care costs. Research findings show little evidence that CON constrained investment or had any significant effect on the total level of investment.[43] CON laws may have changed the composition of investment, but they may, in fact, have led to increased overall hospital costs.[44] There was some evidence that programs that focused on hospital beds alone may have had more success than those dealing with review of expansion of facilities, equipment, and services. Nevertheless, the effects of these narrowly focused programs were very weak. Some initial decline in investment after adoption of the CON programs is explained more by the investment in anticipation of regulation, rather than the effect of the CON laws.

What accounts for the failure of CON laws and HSAs? There are many explanations. One possible explanation is the *capture theory* of regulation. This occurs when a regulated industry subverts or captures the regulatory agency through politically inspired appointments, lucrative employment prospects in the industry for cooperative regulators, regulated industry's ability to outspend the regulatory agency, and industry's influence with the elected officials who control a regulatory agency's appropriations. Thus, regulatory agencies adopt policies similar to the ones desired by the regulated industry, resulting in a cartel or monopoly situation. The fact that the American Hospital Association supported CON laws—and a fairly close correlation exists between the attitudes of the hospital industry and the regulators—may lend some legitimacy to this argument, even though it would be difficult to prove.[45]

A second explanation is that despite consumer representation in the HSAs, provider interests have many more advantages in terms of information, expertise, and legal counsel.[46] In addition, consistent political participation by consumers in the form of attending public hearings was difficult to achieve because it required time, effort, and money.[47] Most public meetings were dominated by representatives of the health care providers.[48] It has also been argued that pluralist interest-group representation, as was the case with HSAs, leads to bargaining, log-rolling, and collusive competition among narrowly defined special interests in which the interest of the general public is not well served.[49]

A third explanation for the failure of the CON laws and HSAs lies in the lack of public support. A nationwide public opinion poll in 1978 revealed that the public had very little confidence in, and recognition of, HSAs and had little support for hospital cost-containment strategies and their consequences. There was also little support for the goals and consequences of cost-containment strategies among groups traditionally underrepresented in health planning activities.[50]

Within less than a decade, health planning, as established under the National Health Planning and Resource Development Act of 1974, was dismantled by the Reagan administration. Congress reduced health planning funding from $167 million in 1980 to $58 million in 1983.[51] Most of the states eliminated local HSAs. This is not to suggest that the concept of national health planning is dead. It is in a period of unsettlement and retrenchment. There is a danger that the total absence of hospital planning would lead to unnecessary duplication of facilities and equipment as strong hospitals attempt to increase their market share. Critics argue that a move toward free competition must embody an interim phase that eases regulation but does not do away with it entirely.[52]

Professional Standards Review and Cost Containment

One of the factors often cited as responsible for rising health care costs is overutilization of health care resources. The rise in health care costs since the enactment of Medicare and Medicaid programs in the mid-1960s created concern in Congress about the cost and quality of these programs. The Social Security Amendments of 1972 established the *Professional Standards Review Organization (PSRO) program.* The PSRO program was designed as a peer review mechanism to promote effective yet efficient and economical delivery of health care services for government-financed programs such as Medicare and Medicaid. Under the law, more than 200 local PSROs were created and staffed by local physicians to review and monitor care provided to Medicare and Medicaid patients by hospitals, extended-care facilities, and skilled nursing homes. The PSROs were responsible for determining whether the care provided was medically necessary, of professional quality, and delivered in an appropriate health care facility. They also had the authority to deny approval of payment for services to physicians who provide care to Medicaid and Medicare patients. Two of the stated goals of the program were to eliminate unnecessary medical treatment and unnecessary institutionalization. Thus, the PSRO program was created as a regulatory mechanism for reducing the cost of federal health care programs.

Did the PSRO program succeed in achieving cost reductions? The majority of evidence suggests that it did not. A 1981 study by the Congressional Budget Office concluded that the cost of the program exceeded its benefits. Although the program slightly reduced Medicare utilization overall, it consumed more resources than it saved. It had very little impact on the federal budget.[53]

Many explanations are offered for this. One is that PSROs controlled by local physicians have no incentives to reduce utilization because it leads to reduced federal payments to the locality. Second, the program suffered from potential conflict between quality-enhancing and cost-reducing goals, a persistent problem. Third, the PSRO program could be used to advance the cartel objectives of health care providers.[54] Doctor-policing laws such as PSRO or hospital peer review committees aimed at self-policing are generally ineffective because of a reluctance to speak out against colleagues, concern over libel lawsuits, and problems of due process safeguards.[55]

The Reagan administration came to office in 1981 strongly supporting the elimination of federal regulatory programs. The PSRO program was on its target list, but it failed to eliminate the program because of opposition in Congress. Federal funding for the PSRO program was cut from $58 million in 1980 to $15 million in 1983.[56] Congress, through the Tax Equity and Fiscal Responsibility Act of 1982 (PL 97-248), renamed the program *Peer Review Organizations (PROs)*. Today, PROs are responsible for reviewing the appropriateness and quality of health care provided to Medicare beneficiaries. The Medicare program has relied on the PROs to safeguard against inadequate medical treatment for individual patients. In 1987 the scope of the program was expanded beyond hospital-based care to include review of outpatient care. Hospitals, in general, view PROs as a nuisance causing financial and administrative headaches or hassles. Hospitals in many states report numerous problems with PROs, such as a lack of communication regarding review methods, lack of clear criteria on procedures to be reviewed, and backlogs.[57] A telephone poll revealed that 70 percent of hospital chief executive officers believe that the high cost of administering Medicare, including the utilization review requirements, is responsible for a significant portion of the increases in health care costs.[58] Medicare PROs also suffer from extreme variations in organizational structure and activities.[59]

While utilization review from a public standpoint remains weak, the private sector has moved in this direction. Indeed, one of the newer health care reform concepts, to be discussed in chapter 8, is *managed care*. Though the term was not used originally, managed care is a fundamental part of the health maintenance strategy.

Health Maintenance Organizations and Cost Containment

The CON, HSA, and PSRO programs were examples of behavioral regulations. These programs were designed to scrutinize decisions about utilization, expansion, and acquisition of health care resources by providers. They were based on the assumption that by changing behavior and cutting waste, health care costs could be contained.[60] They were not very successful.

During the early 1970s, the federal government also tried a competitive market strategy to contain health care costs through *prepaid group plans (PGPs),* commonly known as *health maintenance organizations (HMOs).* The concept of PGPs was not new. Such plans had existed in the health care system without any federal assistance since the 1920s. During the early 1970s, the number of HMOs grew as a result of favorable market conditions and the rhetorical support provided by the Nixon administration. According to one estimate, the number of HMOs increased from 41 in 1970 to 133 in 1973.[61]

Dr. Paul M. Ellwood, Jr., a key health adviser to President Nixon, is credited with bringing the competitive market strategy in the form of HMOs to the attention of national health policymakers.[62] In 1970 the Nixon administration asked Congress to create a new HMO option for Medicare recipients. In 1971 the administration began to use discretionary funds to plan the development of about a hundred HMOs around the country and asked Congress to create a special HMO development plan. The Department of Health, Education, and Welfare (now the Department of Health and Human Services) argued that there could be as many as 1,700 HMOs within a few years with perhaps as many as 40 million people enrolled.[63] After long debate, Congress passed the *Health Maintenance Organization Act (PL 93-222)* of 1973.

The federal government assumed the role of venture capitalist.[64] It encouraged the development of HMOs in an attempt to induce competition in the health care market with the hope of containing health costs. This market strategy was designed to eliminate, or at least reduce, centralized health care bureaucracy and replace it with decentralized market building. This was to be accomplished through the use of federal funds to support efforts in developing new health care organizations and alternative means of health care delivery. It promised pluralism, choice, efficiency, and reorganization through competition, markets, and incentives.[65] The expectation was that HMOs would contain costs by (1) creating incentives for channeling health service utilization from costly inpatient settings (hospitals, skilled nursing homes, etc.) to less costly outpatient settings (visits to doctor's office), (2) promoting competition with traditional health care delivery systems, and (3) exercising market power by obtaining preferential prices from various health care providers.[66]

An HMO is a prepaid medical practice delivering a comprehensive set of health care services to enrollees for a fixed fee (capitation) paid in advance. The Health Maintenance Organization Act of 1973 provided for an expenditure of $375 million over five years. Most of these funds were used to encourage development of HMOs by providing start-up costs. The law offered federally qualified HMOs three basic benefits: (1) money for development of HMOs; (2) overriding of certain restrictive state laws; and (3) a mandate to employers, covered by the Fair Labor Standards Act of 1938, that employ twenty-five or more employees to offer HMO coverage as an alternative to whatever other health plans they provide. This was designed to provide health care consumers with at least a dual choice in health plans. In return, to qualify for federal funds HMOs were to deliver a *comprehensive package of benefits* to a *broadly representative population* on an *equitable basis* with *consumer participation*. This was to be done at the same price or lower than traditional forms of health insurance.[67]

The original legislation so heavily burdened HMOs with special services (comprehensive benefits, open enrollment, dual choice, and limits on copayments) and pricing requirements (same premiums to be charged to all enrollees, that is, "community" rate" as opposed to "experience rate")[68] that very few developers applied for federal support. By 1975, only five HMOs had qualified for federal support. Between 1974 and 1976, the growth in the number of federally supported HMOs was very slow.

To remedy this problem the HMO amendments of 1976 and 1978 deregulated service and pricing requirements, including a reduction in service requirements and the elimination of open enrollment with the exception of large and established programs. In 1981 the federal government stopped providing new grants to HMOs. Since then, the federal government has focused its attention on the promotion of competition in general, incentives designed to increase private-sector involvement in HMO development, and risk contracts to HMOs that agree to enroll Medicare beneficiaries. The federal government continues to designate HMOs that meet certain standards as federally qualified.[69]

In the past five years the HMO market has gone through significant changes. A market previously dominated by traditional HMOs and traditional fee-for-service plans has been transformed into a variety of plans competing on the dimensions of premiums, provider choice, and coverage. The HMO programs have changed to such an extent that it is becoming increasingly difficult to distinguish them from other health plans.[70] Current HMOs can be divided into four different models—staff, group, network, and independent practice associations (IPAs)—based on organization of physician services and the method of payment to physicians. All four HMO models may use one or a combination of three methods of payment. Under the capitation method, a physician is paid a fixed fee for each patient served. In the fee-for-service method, a physician is paid an agreed-upon fee for each service delivered. Under the salary method, a physician is paid a fixed salary regardless of the number of patients he or she serves.[71]

In the *staff model*, physicians are employed on a full-time basis. Neither the physicians nor the personnel employed by the staff model are at risk financially. A salary system with bonuses is utilized to pay physicians. In the *group model*, the HMO provides the facility, administrative support, and nonphysician staff. Physician services are obtained by contracts with one large, multispecialty medical group practice. The physician group is paid a fixed capitation fee for caring for each HMO member per month. Physicians are free to enter into various profit-sharing arrangements that generally are not available in the staff model. Many of the large group-model HMOs own and operate their own hospitals. The *network model* HMO contracts with more than one physician group. In this model, facilities and support personnel are provided by physician groups. Each physician receives a capitation payment. Most groups continue to see non-HMO patients in addition to HMO enrollees. In the *IPA model*, the HMO uses a percentage of practitioners' time to provide care for prepaid clients. They typically contract with a large number of solo practitioners as well as single or multispecialty group practices. Most IPA-model HMOs reimburse their physicians based on agreed-upon fee schedules or payment limits drawn from a collective account. The staff, group, and network model HMOs are commonly known as prepaid group practice plans (PGPs). The key point here is that prepayments, the premiums from subscribers, provide the vast bulk of revenues for the HMO. Thus the HMO, whatever the model, has an incentive not to overprovide services. HMOs do this by emphasizing primary care and reviewing the need for more specialized services as well as hospital services. In this sense, HMOs employ the concept of managed care.

The Impact of HMOs on Costs

Has HMO development helped contain health care costs? The success of a competitive health strategy depends on the creation of health care delivery systems that are more efficient than the traditional system and are able to compete on price, benefits, access, style of medical care, and the existence of sufficient numbers of such systems throughout the country.[72] Available empirical evidence suggests that HMOs, especially PGPs, are more economical and efficient than traditional health care plans. Studies indicate that total costs (premiums and out-of-pocket expenses) for HMO enrollees are 10 to 40 percent lower than those of comparable people with traditional health insurance.[73] Studies have also shown that HMO enrollees have a 20 percent to 40 percent lower hospitalization rate compared to traditional fee-for-service plans because of incentives to reduce utilization (fixed payments), which in turn helps lower cost to HMO enrollees.[74] Nevertheless, critics have argued that reduction in hospital use cannot be easily attributed to HMO-induced competition but to factors such as biases in data, long-term trends predating HMOs, indirect effects of other policy changes, and other forms of competition.[75]

Some have argued that the lower cost and lower inpatient utilization rates reflect "creaming," or biased self-selection. Creaming is done when an HMO enrolls only younger or healthier persons, who use less medical care, and avoids enrolling elderly or high-risk groups and poor people.[76] Some HMOs use marketing strategies that encourage a favorable selection of patients by offering services such as sports medicine that are more likely to attract younger and healthier people, and by locating themselves in middle-class neighborhoods.[77] The practice of healthier people enrolling in HMOs is referred to as biased self-selection. HMO costs and utilization rates are lower because HMO enrollees are healthier and use fewer medical services.[78] Other studies have disputed such claims.[79]

While there is some evidence to suggest that HMOs reduce health care costs and utilization rates, does this translate into an overall reduction in hospital costs? The research in this area suggests that HMOs have not succeeded in reducing overall hospital costs or health care costs in general. A study of the impact of HMOs on total hospital costs and utilization rates in twenty-five cities from 1971 to 1981 concluded that the extent of HMO penetration in a community did not have any spillover effect on reducing overall hospital costs.[80] Studies of Minneapolis–St. Paul hospitals from 1979 to 1981 revealed that HMO-induced competition did not restrain hospital costs per admission. Hospitals with a large share of HMO patients did not have lower costs per admission compared to other hospitals. In addition, hospital profits demonstrated an upward trend.[81] Similarly, an analysis of hospital expenses in forty-three metropolitan areas revealed that while the nationwide HMO enrollment increased from 4 percent in 1980 to 7.1 percent in 1984, total hospital costs were reduced by only 0.9 percent.[82]

Though HMOs may offer lower costs, they have not been able substantially to alter the national pattern of medical care inflation and increasing resource use.[83] This may be because while the number of HMOs have grown over the years, the overall growth in HMOs and enrollment in them is not large enough to have a significant impact on national health care costs.

By 1987, there were only about 650 HMOs, with a nationwide enrollment of 12.1 percent. Of the 650 HMOs, 411 were IPAs, which do not operate from a group setting and generally use a fee-for-service payment method. HMO enrollees may constitute a very small percentage of any IPA physician's practice. Thus, IPAs may be less able to reduce costs as effectively as other models of HMOs.[84] IPAs are growing three times faster than PGPs and are likely to dominate the HMO industry in the near future. Purists in the PGP movement fear that the industry may be taken over by insurance interests using HMOs for their own ends. Other concerns are that, under IPAs, physicians may give their patients second-class care and save very little and that IPAs allow local medical societies to preempt real competition with real HMOs. There is some evidence that in recent years IPA physicians are given financial incentives to control costs.[85] What impact this has had on overall health care costs remains to be seen.

Lawrence Brown has argued that a competitive strategy such as HMOs cannot have a significant impact on health care costs because it is based on an uncritical application of the concept of incentives. HMOs fail to influence all five of the crucial variables related to health care costs: consumers, medical technology, physicians, hospitals, and third-party payers.[86] The major sponsors of HMOs are laypersons, consumer groups, foundations, hospitals, and insurance companies. Since HMOs are an alternative to traditional insurance, one would not expect insurance companies to become involved in HMO development; however, insurance companies have entered the HMO market as a way of protecting their market share.[87] The HMO-insurer alliance has very little incentive to cut costs.[88] Hospital-sponsored HMOs are difficult to maintain because both are trying to pursue separate ends. Hospitals want to increase utilization, while HMOs want to reduce hospital utilization.[89] Thus, the hospital-HMO relationship is difficult to maintain. Overall, HMO competition to date has failed to provide a powerful federal strategy of cost containment.[90]

Prospective Payment System and Cost Containment

With the enactment of Medicaid and Medicare in the mid-1960s, the federal government became a major purchaser of health services in the health care market. Part of the increase in overall health care costs is attributed to dramatic increases in the cost of these programs. Federal spending for these programs has almost doubled every five years. By 1980, spending had reached about $61.2 billion, and it constituted about 27.8 percent of total national health spending—financing health care for about 50 million people.[91] At the same time, hospital costs were also rising dramatically. The cost of hospital care had increased from $28 billion in 1970 to $102.7 billion in 1980.[92] From 1977 to 1982, Medicare hospital expenditures grew at an average annual rate of 18 percent compared to a 14.6 percent increase in overall hospital spending.[93]

The burden on the federal health budget created the political environment for federal regulation of hospital costs.[94] Advocates of regulation argued that cost controls on hospitals would limit waste and inefficiency without sacrificing quality of care.[95]

President Carter, in response to rising hospital costs, proposed hospital cost containment legislation (HR 6575) designed to constrain the rate of increase in hospital costs and to limit the rate of increase in hospital revenues. The hospital industry strongly opposed such a measure and proposed a voluntary plan to control costs on its own. The controversy surrounding both plans lead to their demise in 1979.

As mentioned earlier, President Reagan came to office in 1981 with the expressed intention of eliminating federal regulatory health care programs in favor of a market-oriented, competitive strategy to contain health care costs. Federal funding was cut for health planning programs, and the PSRO program was renamed PRO and given reduced funding. Budget cuts were made in Medicaid and Medicare, and new federal grants for HMO start-up were eliminated.

Minor changes were made in Medicare by the Omnibus Budget Reconciliation Act of 1981. This included tightening Medicare reimbursement payments. The 1982 Tax Equity and Fiscal Responsibility Act (TEFRA) limited the increase in Medicare hospital payment rates, created an early basis for prospective payment based on a case-mix index, and called for incentive payments to hospitals defined as efficient. TEFRA required that the Department of Health and Human Services (HHS) design a prospective payment plan for the Medicare program. That new system, implemented in 1983, was the *Prospective Payment System (PPS)* for Medicare reimbursement to hospitals. The PPS for Medicare reimbursement was based on the New Jersey program.[96] This is an example of the federal government embracing a program originally implemented at the state level.[97]

Under PPS, hospitals are paid according to a schedule of preestablished rates linked to 468 DRGs. All major diagnoses are classified into 468 categories, with each category assigned a treatment rate. Hospitals are reimbursed according to these rates. There are economic incentives in the form of rewards and punishments built into the system. If a hospital spends more money than the preestablished rate for a particular diagnostic treatment, the hospital must absorb the additional cost. If the hospital spends less money than the preestablished rate, it is still paid the preestablished rate and can keep the overpayment as profit. The Health Care Financing Administration within HHS was assigned the responsibility of establishing the DRG payment schedule. To safeguard against reduction in quality of care as a result of PPS, Congress assigned PROs the responsibility of monitoring the quality and appropriateness of care for Medicare patients. If a PRO finds inappropriate or substandard care, the hospital may be denied Medicare payment. If a pattern of inappropriate or substandard care is discovered, the hospital Medicare provider agreement may be terminated.

The shift in the Medicare payment method to hospitals from a retrospective reimbursement system to a PPS based on DRGs is the most far-reaching change in Medicare since its inception.[98] The changeover to PPS was expected to revolutionize the economics of American health care.[99]

There are three major kinds of hospital regulations: facilities and service regulation, utilization review, and rate and revenue regulations.[100] The first two were used by the federal government in programs such as CON, HSAs, and PSROs. The DRGs, under the PPS, involved rate and revenue regulations, commonly referred to as *price regulation*. Price regulation typically involves a regulatory agency that establishes a minimum, maximum, or range of prices an individual or an institution can charge for particular goods or services.[101] The rationale behind replacing the retrospective payment system was that under that system, hospitals had no incentive to economize in their use of health care resources in treating Medicare patients. If anything, such a system tended to encourage overutilization of health resources, since hospitals were assured that they would be reimbursed for all reasonable costs incurred. PPS was based on the assumption that given built-in incentives, hospitals would be forced to consider cost factors in treatment and would be encouraged to be economically more efficient. Thus, inefficient hospitals would be forced to close. An economically more efficient hospital sector would help contain increases in hospital costs. PPS was viewed as a method of influencing hospital activities, creating cost-containment constraints, and introducing incentives into hospital payments.[102] The cost-control incentive was the primary purpose in establishing the PPS.[103]

Evaluating the Prospective Payment System

How well has the prospective payment system constrained hospital cost increases? Early studies were encouraging, though not decisive. Any assessment of the impact of PPS must be viewed with caution for two reasons. First, PPS was not put into immediate implementation in 1983 but was phased in over a period of time. The complete transition to a PPS system occurred in November 1987. Thus, sufficient time has not elapsed to make any definitive conclusions about the impact of PPS.[104] Second, it is very difficult to assess changes in hospital behavior using aggregate data. It is even more difficult to disentangle the effects of Medicare PPS from other influences on hospital costs, let alone measure the magnitude of any effects.[105]

The initial years of PPS showed some reduction in the growth rate of hospital costs. Hospital expenditures increased more slowly in the first three years of PPS implementation as compared to the three previous years.[106] Cost reductions have largely resulted from reduced admissions. Occupancy rates fell, and length of hospital stay was reduced. There does not appear to have been any cost shifting, nor has the quality of care for Medicare patients declined.[107]

There have been criticisms of the new payment system. Some suggest that hospitals will seek ways to limit the impact of the new hospital regulations.[108] Because price regulation is a tax on hospital behavior, it not only affects price but also hospital output and quality and quantity of services. Hospitals respond by attempting to reduce the use of affected services or resources by modifying their practices and products.[109] Hospitals modify the cost of regulation by seeking an area unaffected by the regulation, that is, the "unregulated margin." Organizations respond to regulation through institutional, managerial, and technical changes.[110] Hospitals altered services, influenced practices, and changed the products offered to decrease the impact of regulation at the expense of Medicare patients. They also changed the mix of services offered in the inpatient Medicare market and expanded the surgical market because surgical DRGs are more profitable than medical DRGs. Often, services were cut.[111]

Despite the impact of PPS, national health care expenditures continue to rise. Providers may have concentrated on other sectors of the health care system.[112] Thus, one response to PPS may be higher costs for outpatient and home care services.[113]

State Governments and Cost Containment

During the 1960s and 1970s, there was rapid growth in state and local governments' public health programs. They took on many new functions in the health care field by expanding their role beyond the traditional public health activities.[114] Their traditional role focused largely on problems of sanitation and communicable disease. During the 1960s and 1970s, state and local governments' role expanded to include a broad range of environmental concerns: air and water pollution, radiation control, hazardous waste, and occupational health and safety, as well as the delivery of medical services, particularly to the poor (as a result of the federal Medicaid program).

This expanded role also led to dramatic increases in health care expenditures of state governments. Their total health care expenditures increased from $9.9 billion in 1970 to $33.2 billion in 1980. Medicaid expenditures accounted for $11.4 billion in 1980.[115]

By the early 1980s, health care cost containment had emerged as a major issue for state and local governments. A number of factors contributed to this. One was the general taxpayer revolt in many states that followed the passage of Proposition 13 in California. The second factor was a national recession, which left state and local governments with reduced resources. Third, and perhaps most important, was the sharp cutback in federal aid that occurred during the first term of the Reagan administration. The consolidation of many categorical health grants into block grants substantially reduced available federal money. The federal Medicaid contribution was reduced 3 percent in 1982, 4 percent in 1983, and 4.5 percent in 1984. The administration showed considerable interest in granting states more discretion when such discretion seemed to promise cost reductions.[116]

Faced with reduced revenues and increased health care costs, state governments have attempted a number of different strategies to contain cost increases. By 1982, seventeen states had legislation requiring the disclosure, review (such as HSAs and CON), or regulation of hospital rates or budgets.

State Rate Setting

One major strategy used by the state governments is *rate setting*. This strategy emerged in the mid-1970s as the regulatory instrument of choice in several eastern industrial states as a response to Medicaid's financial crisis. Today, hospital rate-setting programs are no longer confined to traditionally proregulatory states in the industrial Northeast. Limited prospective payment schemes for Medicaid reimbursement have been adopted in Kentucky, Missouri, Alabama, Georgia, Mississippi, and North Carolina.[117] Some states have mandatory rate-setting programs, while others solicit voluntary compliance with the results of the review process or operate as disclosure programs. There is a considerable amount of diversity in these programs. Some relate to revenues, others to costs. Most programs are revenue based and are concerned with the total financial needs of the hospital. The cost-based programs are used for establishing reasonable payment rates for hospitals.[118]

Proponents of regulation see state rate setting as an approach most likely to win political support and argue that hospital expenditures exceed corresponding benefits. Therefore, society in general and government in particular can no longer afford to finance the excess. In contrast, proponents of medical marketplace competition argue that the imposition of rate setting tends to remove flexibility and interest in innovation from the hospitals affected. State rate regulations involve a complex set of issues such as which providers to regulate, how the rate-setting body should be organized, and how it should set rates.[119] Such programs are likely to continue and increase in number.

State rate-setting programs have produced different results. Proponents have argued that some mandatory prospective rate-setting programs have been successful in reducing hospital expenditures per patient day, per admission, and per capita.[120] Opponents argue that in many states, rate-setting programs have failed to produce the promised results, and the positive impact of state rate-setting programs has been overstated.[121] The failure of some state rate-setting programs is attributed to the fact that regulators often lack the necessary skills in the complex field of financial regulation and have fewer resources than the hospital industry. For example, the State Rate-Setting Commission in Massachusetts has only a few professionally trained people in a bureau that sets rates for 140 acute-care hospitals in the state. The staff of virtually every major hospital is larger than the state's.[122] In sum, state rate-setting programs have not provided a "quick fix" for the rapid rise in spending for hospital care.[123]

The most successful state rate-setting program is in Maryland. It is unique because it operates with the support of the Maryland Hospital Association. The result has been dramatic. Costs per hospital admission from 1980 to 1991 increased by the smallest percentage of any state in the country and were well below the national average. Apart from the support of the

Maryland Hospital Association, another reason for the program's success was that it covers all sources of payment and thus prevents cost shifting. At the same time, the program is flexible enough to account for inflation and to cover losses for charitable or uncompensated care.[124]

Negotiating Prices

Another approach—a competitive strategy—used by the states is to attempt a fundamental reform in their approach to Medicaid. This involves replacing a fee-for-service system with *negotiated or competitively bid fixed-price arrangements* for Medicaid services. For example, California relies on negotiated fixed-price arrangements. The Arizona Health Cost Containment System (AHCCS) relies on provider bidding for the delivery of health care to the indigent. In such a prepaid, capitated system of health care, financial risk bearing is shifted, partially from the consumer and totally from the third-party insurer, to the provider. According to proponents, such a system internalizes economic incentives.[125] Competitive bidding is also becoming increasingly popular for such health care services as clinical laboratory services, home health care, and mental health care.[126] How such approaches work out in practice and what impact they will have on cost containment remains to be seen.

Rationing

Some states have attempted Medicaid cuts by reducing the number of people on the program, reducing benefits for those who are covered, or both.[127] A new theme is being heard in the health care field. It implies that there are limits to what we can expect and afford in the way of health care. It is based on the notion that health care costs are rising disproportionately compared to the small or marginal gains in overall national health. Therefore, we must establish priorities in health services and become more rational in our health care spending.

Advocates of this new school of thought argue that health care costs are out of control and that regulatory controls on spending or competitive approaches based on economic incentives are doomed to fail. Regulatory approaches are, it is asserted, based on the faulty assumption that medical care produces health, and more care produces more health. The only realistic solution, therefore, is the *rationing* of health care resources. If the United States is serious about containing health care costs, society will have to forgo some medical benefits, and patients should not expect to receive all the care they want regardless of the costs.[128] Proponents argue that health care rationing already exists in the actions of insurance companies, legislatures, hospitals, physicians, and individual premium payers, and we need to get on with the public business of determining how health care rationing should be carried out ethically.[129] Observers call the existing de facto rationing "silent rationing," "under-the-table rationing," "rationing by finance," or "rationing by wallet."[130]

In Oregon, health care rationing has moved beyond the talking point to the way in which health care programs might be structured. The state provoked a national debate in 1987 when it decided to stop financing most organ transplants for Medicaid patients and use the money instead for prenatal care for pregnant women. In 1990 it produced a revolutionary Medicaid plan. Rather than offer a minority of the poor a comparatively full package of services, the state proposed to give all of its poor access to health care but with a reduced level of services. The state ranked most medical conditions as least or most economically worthwhile to treat under the plan. If money ran out before all services were covered, the lowest-priority services would not be covered. Faced with intense criticisms of the listed priorities, in 1991 Oregon health officials overhauled the ranking and produced a new list. The Bush administration turned down Oregon's request for a Medicaid waiver, necessary to implement rationing, partly on the grounds that it might conflict with the Americans with Disabilities Act. The Clinton administration, however, did issue the waiver in 1993.[131] Colorado is working to develop a plan modeled after Oregon's.

Critics of rationing are skeptical of the process by which the state would determine what is high- or low-priority care. The state plans to blend public comments about what they value in health care with an elaborate system of medical cost-benefit analysis. Critics are cynical of health care by democracy. The most vehement reaction against the plan is that it targets the poor—mainly women and children, who make up most of the Medicaid population—and the disabled.[132] Another criticism of the plan is that the meat-ax approach of denying payment for treatment of a given condition makes very little sense. While the plan has good intentions, it will, critics assert, inevitably lead to gross misallocation of resources and will provoke legitimate cries of outrage from patients, physicians, the media, and interest groups.[133]

The Private Sector and Cost Containment

The dramatic rise in health care costs also has had significant consequences for the private sector. Today, many corporations spend 25 percent of their gross revenues to provide medical coverage for their employees. According to a national survey of 1,955 employers conducted by Foster Higgins & Company of New York, an average company spent 21.6 percent more in 1990 to provide doctor and hospital care to their employees than in 1989. During the 1989–90 period, the cost to employers of providing employee health care benefits rose 46.3 percent.[134] This has led the business community to search for solutions to contain health care costs. Many businesses participate in freestanding health policy groups or health coalitions. Business reformers have pushed the concept of managed care.[135] The term implies a stepped-up coordination and oversight of employee use of medical care for the purpose of eliminating unnecessary care typically found in insurance plans. In managed care programs, companies limit the medical care of their employees to doctors and hospitals that agree to provide care for a set price.[136] As we saw earlier, health maintenance organizations embody the concept of managed care.

During the late 1970s, the business community was not very concerned about rising health care costs and was not very interested in taking actions to control them.[137] Since the early 1980s, however, faced with a dramatic rise in costs, the private sector began to look for solutions to the problem. As a major purchaser of health care services, businesses have become conscious of their capability and responsibility for controlling health care costs. The private sector has become concerned because soaring costs are having negative effects on their profit margins.[138] The government itself has fostered the emergence of private-sector initiatives through legislative changes that alter incentives by providing technical assistance and/or financial support, and by demonstrating feasible options in its own cost-containment strategy as a major purchaser of health services.[139]

Cost Sharing

The private sector has responded in a variety of ways and has established numerous initiatives to control costs. These initiatives fall into four major categories.[140] One category consists of *greater employee cost sharing* for health services. The patient shares in the direct cost of health care services for his or her own coverage or that of dependents. Cost sharing can include deductibles, coinsurance, or copayments. A *deductible* is the fixed amount that must be paid by the patient before the insurance benefits begin. *Coinsurance* is the percentage contribution patients pay once the deductible is exceeded. *Copayments* are generally a fixed contribution, rather than a percentage contribution, toward each unit of service. This strategy helps reduce the cost to the employers by shifting part of the cost to the patient. It is based on the belief that when patients are made to share a higher cost for treatment (negative incentive), they will reduce health service utilization. Some studies have demonstrated that cost sharing in the form of deductibles or coinsurance reduces the use of health care services.[141] Others have argued that increased cost shifting is not in the best interest of the workers, that some of the cost savings are illusory, and that other savings are likely to be one-time savings.[142] Whatever the case, more and more employers are seeking to reduce costs through cost-sharing.

Perhaps the ultimate in cost sharing is a disturbing new trend. Companies have begun to eliminate certain coverage. This has taken two forms. In one, companies that self-insure, rather than use a third-party health insurer, have cut or drastically reduced benefits for employees with diseases that are very expensive. These diseases include cancer and AIDS.[143] In the other case, companies have reduced or eliminated medical coverage for their retired employees.[144] In both instances, the worker or former worker is left to use his or her own resources or rely on public-sector programs.

Direct Action

A second category of initiatives is designed to reduce health service utilization, especially the use of hospital services, through *direct action*. Here, initiatives include requiring employees to get a second opinion for surgery, preadmission review (often prospective) of all nonemergency hospital admissions, more careful review of medical claims, coverage of certain services and procedures on an outpatient basis only, and providing incentives to shift care to an outpatient setting.

HMOs and PPOs

The third set of initiatives consists of encouraging or requiring employees to use HMOs or Preferred Provider Organizations (PPOs) for health care services. A PPO either restricts beneficiaries to a list of providers such as hospitals and physicians or provides financial incentives for beneficiaries to obtain their care from the list of preferred providers. Providers are generally selected on the basis of lower price or lower expected utilization. PPOs differ from traditional health insurance plans in two ways. In PPOs, the insurer takes an active role in negotiating payment rates or selecting providers, and the providers are on notice to comply with aggressive utilization review procedures.

PPOs also differ from HMOs. PPO providers are paid on a fee-for-service basis and thus are not at financial risk for services they provide, nor do they have incentives to reduce utilization. Under PPOs, beneficiaries can use providers outside the PPO plan, which is not the case with HMOs. Unlike HMOs, PPOs do not generally practice in a common location or in group practices.[145] PPOs are mainly sponsored by health care providers such as hospitals and physicians and by insurance companies.

Wellness Programs

The fourth set of initiatives consists of employee *wellness programs*. Larger employers are increasingly promoting programs designed to encourage healthier lifestyles and behavior. The emphasis is on preventive care to reduce the need for health care services. The assumption here is that prevention will lead to healthier workers and therefore reduced health care costs. Such employee wellness programs tend to penalize workers with unhealthy lifestyles by reducing their health care benefits. Some health care experts express concern over such meddling by employers because some of the health care problems of workers may be related to hereditary, environmental, or socioeconomic factors over which they have very little control. Some firms have also begun to take lifestyles into account in hiring and firing decisions. This has led the American Civil Liberties Union to charge that some employers are overstepping their bounds. It argues that if employers are allowed to refuse to hire or to fire workers because of something they do in their private lives, workers will not have any private life left.[146]

Other Private Sector Initiatives

In addition to the four major strategies discussed above, industries and firms are beginning to rely on other initiatives to contain rising health care costs. A number of organizations have moved toward self-insurance. Rather than contract out with private insurance companies, these companies try to reduce their health costs through administrative savings. One important feature of self-insurance is that such plans are not covered under the federal Employment Retirement Income Security Act (ERISA). This allows employer flexibility in maintaining or cutting coverage.[147] Some large businesses have begun to offer general medical services at in-house medical clinics, staffed by their own doctors or provided by contract medical firms as a cheaper alternative to constantly rising insurance rates. The Goodyear Tire and Rubber Co., for example, runs its own drugstore for workers and their families. The Gillette Co. provides its own X-ray services at the company's medical centers. Besides saving on drugs and tests, companies can save money by avoiding unnecessary hospitalization through careful monitoring of individual workers' health. A large company can also negotiate low fees with contracted medical firms. In addition to the cost savings, one of the most attractive features of such initiatives is the convenience it offers.[148]

Private-sector officials widely believe that these cost measures have been effective. Increased cost sharing by employees is perceived as the most effective. Others are more skeptical, arguing that cost shifting does not necessarily translate into cost containment. They express concern that cost shifting may have adverse effects on low-income patients or patients with serious health problems.[149] Because many of these initiatives have been in existence for only a short time, available empirical evidence is very limited. It is impossible to make any meaningful judgment about the impact of these initiatives on health care cost containment.

Private Insurers

Private insurers are also undertaking new initiatives. Some of them are moving away from spreading the cost of health insurance equally across all groups and are increasingly charging different rates for different people. Young and healthy employees are charged less at the expense of older and less healthy workers. Some experts on health care economics are troubled by such practices. Blue Cross and Blue Shield of Minnesota (BCBSM) has become the first national insurer directly to link health care reimbursement to patient outcomes. The plan, which went into effect in January 1991, uses a new system of risk classification called *illness outcome groups* (IOGs) to classify illnesses by their expected rate of adverse outcomes. In a major departure from past patient-assessment methodologies, this new system takes into consideration not only the severity of the patient's condition but also the anticipated risk from medical treatment. The plan is based on the assumption that severity itself is not the strong predictor of patient needs. Severity does not measure the risk of intervention. The new plan is designed to assess two risk dimensions. One is the illness the patient presents when he or she is admitted to the hospital, and the other is associated with the level of care provided by that hospital.

Under this system, four new outcome categories of IOGs will be used to group procedures by anticipated risks and outcomes. IOG-1 indicates a minimum risk, while IOG-4 indicates a high risk. The basic building block of each IOG will be the DRGs. Hospitals whose adverse outcomes exceed the outcome rates predicted by the BCBSM system will not get reimbursed for the extra cost associated with treating those excess adverse outcomes. The precise mechanisms of the programs are still being developed, but many see it as the wave of the future in American health care policy.

Conclusions

This chapter has examined various regulatory and competitive strategies by the federal and state governments and the private sector to contain health care costs. Federal strategies aimed at health planning and peer reviews have proven to be failures. There is some evidence that the competitive strategy of HMOs has lowered costs to enrollees and reduced their hospitalization rates. Nevertheless, the impact of HMOs on containment of overall health care costs has been very limited. The changeover from a retrospective payment to a prospective payment system for Medicare reimbursements to hospitals, through the DRGs, has reduced the average length of hospital stays and has slowed the growth rate in hospital costs for the initial years of PPS. Medicare costs have continued to climb upward, however, and PPS has had limited impact on overall health care costs. There is some evidence that the reduction in inpatient service utilization has led to significant increases in costs for outpatient services.

State efforts in cost containment thus far have had a limited impact on overall health care costs. State rate-setting programs have shown mixed results. States' attempts to replace the fee-for-service system with a negotiated or competitively bid fixed-price arrangement for Medicaid services, as in California and Arizona, have shown some success in reducing costs. Thus far, such reforms have been limited to a few states and have been in existence for such a short time that it is impossible to make any definitive conclusions. The same is true with state efforts at health care rationing for Medicaid services.

Private-sector innovations are relatively new and thus are difficult to evaluate. Whether the technique of cost shifting through increased deductibles, coinsurance, and copayments will lead to cost reductions is problematic at best. In addition, cost shifting, utilization reviews, and increased reliance on HMOs and PPOs present a potential concern about access and equity. Wellness programs are increasing but are not widespread among all industries.

Overall, neither regulatory nor competitive strategies have thus far succeeded in containing health care costs. The future prospects for cost containment are also not very bright for a number of reasons. First, government efforts at formulating health policies directed toward cost containment must be made in a political environment. Just as in any other public policy area, the interplay between various interest groups leads to the formulation of policies built on compromises, bargaining, and consensus building, which fail to produce the desired results. Often regulatory policies are built on faulty or mistaken assumptions and are opposed by health care providers.

Health care providers have often found ways to get around regulations.

Second, the value of cost containment inevitably comes into conflict with the cherished values of access and high-quality care in American culture. Almost all government programs aimed at cost containment have also attempted to ensure access and quality of care. Public opposition is likely to be high in any program that attempts to reduce access or lower the quality of services or the number of services provided. A good example of this is Oregon's experiment with restructuring the Medicaid program to contain costs. Even though the program promises increased access in return for funding only high-priority services, public opposition has led state officials to rearrange their list of priorities. Health care democracy, guided by public opinion polls, is likely to make sound medical policymaking more difficult and its consequences more unpredictable. Many health care providers are likely to oppose health care rationing. For example, physicians, who are largely dependent on patient fees, will find it harder to consider only the public interest when their caseloads, and consequently their incomes, are falling. Even if rationing were accepted by physicians and hospital administrators, it would be resisted by most patients, and patients who could afford it would seek care outside the budget-constrained system. Health care rationing has the potential to create a two-tiered health care system—one for the rich and another for the poor.

Third, demographic changes are likely to create further pressures for more, not less spending. When the baby boom generation reaches retirement age between the years 2010 and 2015, there is going to be a dramatic increase in the number of elderly people in our society. This is going to accelerate demand for health care resources.

Finally, technological advances in medicine are likely to continue at a rapid pace. Medical technology is very expensive, and it is one of the major contributors to increases in health care costs. We, as a society, have come to value medical technology regardless of the cost and regardless of the benefits it brings. Many of the advances in medical technology have helped prolong life, and in some instances have eased pain and suffering, but they cannot cure many major illnesses. Nevertheless, the general public clings to the glimmer of hope offered by medical technology, and, in the process, society's notions of health, life span, and life itself have changed. Until we as a society learn to resolve these value conflicts, future prospects for health care cost containment remain tenuous.

7

Health Care Technology

In the previous chapter health care technology was mentioned as one of several factors that have contributed to spiraling health care costs. This chapter focuses on the role of technology in the U.S. health care system. Technological developments in the past twenty years have dramatically changed the methods for diagnosing illnesses and the delivery of health care services in the United States. In the next ten to fifteen years the rate of technological change and the magnitude of the impact of technology on the health care delivery process is expected to be of quantum proportions compared to what it has been in the past.[1] These medical technologies have created high levels of expectations on the part of health care providers as well as consumers and have opened diagnostic and treatment avenues once unimaginable. These technological advancements encompass not just diagnoses and treatment abilities but also patient-monitoring. For example, patient-monitoring systems are making increased use of computer technology for data display and retrieval.

The past twenty-five years have seen significant developments in physics, electronics, computer science, and biotechnology, which is increasingly felt in the field of health care.[2] This in turn has raised questions about the factors that have contributed to the growth of medical technologies, the cost and effectiveness of such technologies, and the ethical dilemmas they raise. If technology is to be used effectively and efficiently, we must understand not only the technological tools used by modern medicine but ethical dilemmas involved and learn to make decisions that are individually and socially correct.[3] In this chapter we address these issues. First, we examine the growth of medical technology and the factors that have contributed to this growth. Second, we analyze the cost of the medical technology and its relation to overall health care costs. Third, we address the issue of the assessment of medical technology. Finally, we examine the ethical concerns and dilemmas raised by medical technology by analyzing some specific cases.

The Growth and Diffusion of Medical Technology

Before we discuss the growth of medical technology and the factors that have contributed to its growth, it will be helpful to define medical technology. Medical technology can be defined simply as drugs, devices, and medical or surgical procedures used in medical care.[4] More recent medical technology has been defined by some to include medical techniques, equipment, and pharmaceuticals.[5] Examples of medical technology under these definitions include pharmaceutical drugs such as AZT, medical devices such as CT scanners, and organ transplants.[6] High-tech medicine is the term often used to refer to developments in the field of medical technology in the past twenty or so years. High-tech medicine has been defined as the "sum of all the advances in medical knowledge and techniques that have been translated into improved diagnostic, therapeutic, and rehabilitative procedures during the last several decades."[7]

The transformation of medicine is associated with the Renaissance, when different applications of scientific methods were introduced. Disciplined observation of the empirical symptoms of illness was brought about by the influence of Francis Bacon (1561–1626) and Thomas Sydenham (1624–89). During the seventeenth century, there was a significant increase not only in the ability to understand illnesses but also to classify them. By the nineteenth and twentieth centuries, medicine had progressed to the point where it was capable of healing illnesses and preventing illnesses from starting.[8]

The practice of medical technology emerged in the late 1800s as an outgrowth of scientific advances that created a need for clinical pathology laboratories. Before the 1890s, physicians were expected to perform and interpret almost all laboratory tests themselves. By the early 1900s, interns in larger hospitals had begun to perform laboratory tests as part of their responsibilities. The years 1890 to 1928 marked the emergence of clinical laboratory practice as an occupation separate from medicine and nursing. Pathology became established as a recognized specialty after World War I. Laboratory testing and interpretation of results became the responsibility of the pathologist.[9]

The professionalization of medical technology occurred between the 1920s and 1930s. In 1928 the American Society of Clinical Pathologists set up the national Board of Registry for clinical laboratory technicians. For the first time, educational and training standards for students were established. The Board of Registry also assumed responsibility for accreditation of schools of medical technology and for certification of clinical laboratory technicians. The professionalization of medical technology was also reflected in the establishment and publication of professional journals: the *Bulletin of the American Society of Clinical Laboratory Technicians* in 1933 and the *American Journal of Medical Technology* in 1935. The latter journal was renamed the *Journal of Medical Technology* in 1984, and in 1988 it came to be called *Clinical Laboratory Science.*[10]

Some of the major advances in medical technology during the first fifty years of the twentieth century included X-rays for diagnoses (1901); insulin (1921); the first sulfa drug (1937); penicillin (1943); DDT (1944); renal dialysis (1945); streptomycin, the first anti-TB drug (1948); and tetracycline, the first broad-spectrum antibiotic (1949).[11] These early developments, particularly antisepsis techniques and anesthesiology, made a critical contribution to the advancement of medicine and the health of human beings.

In the fifty years since the end of World War II, dramatic developments in medical technology have revolutionized the American health care system. Almost all of today's disease diagnosis and treatment devices and techniques were unknown forty to fifty years ago. The role of the physician was mainly that of diagnostician, limited to identification of illness, prediction of likely outcome, and the provision of guidance to the patient and his or her family while the illness ran its course. All this has changed dramatically. Today the scope of medical intervention includes kidney dialysis, organ transplants, laser surgery, arthroscopic surgical techniques, computed tomography scanners, nuclear magnetic resonators, and much more. New miracle drugs are being marketed each year. Of the prescription drugs, about 10 percent of the 200 top-selling drugs are new each year, while only 25 percent of the 200 top-selling drugs in 1972 remained in the group fifteen years later.[12]

Not too long ago, except for X-rays, the only way a doctor could see inside a patient's body was through exploratory surgery. Today a wide variety of medical technologies are available that are nonintrusive to the patient. One such technique is the CT scan, or computerized tomography. A CT scan provides a detailed X-ray of the entire body and converts a two-dimensional picture into three-dimensional images. Magnetic resonance imaging (MRI) uses a combination of radio waves, a computer, and a magnetic coil that allows a doctor to see tissues hidden or surrounded by bone. This is not possible to do with a simple X-ray. MRI scans are increasingly used by doctors to diagnose tumors, arthritis, and problems associated with tissues and organs. Magnetic resonance spectroscopy uses a similar technology to gather information about body chemistry, while magnetoencephalography (MEG) allows the doctor to measure brain activity. Another imaging technique—PET scan, or position emission tomography—uses a low-level radioactive chemical that travels through the body. PET scans are used to diagnose strokes, epilepsy, schizophrenia, and Parkinson's disease.[13]

As diagnostic abilities have improved, so have the treatment options available to doctors. For example, surgeons have been using lasers since the 1970s instead of scalpels to cut skin, remove growths, and unclog blood vessels. The new free-electron laser has made possible photodynamic therapy that makes it possible to kill viruses in the blood.[14] Surgical techniques have also undergone dramatic changes in the past thirty to forty years. Organ transplants have become increasingly common, especially with respect to heart, liver, and kidney. Replacement of human body parts with artificial parts is also becoming a reality. Today it is possible to replace human arms or hands with a realistic artificial arm or hand that can perform almost the same functions. Soon it may be possible to replace eyes, ears, bones, and other vital organs.

Most of the developments in the field of medical technology can be classified as of two types.[15] One is replacement technology, which replaces an old procedure with a new one. Replacement technology enables doctors to do more efficiently and effectively what they have already been doing. One example includes diagnostic tests such as the CT scanner, which replaces intrusive exploratory surgery. A second development is what might be called "new technologies." These allow doctors to do things that were not being done or that were not possible to do before. Some examples include organ transplants, reproductive technologies, and life-extending and life-sustaining technologies. Both types of technology are developing rapidly.

Lewis Thomas provides another useful way of classifying three levels of technology in medicine.[16] "Nontechnology" tides patients over diseases that are not well understood. This mainly involves reassuring patients and providing nursing and hospital care, but offers little hope for recovery. Nontechnology is applied in cases including intractable cancer, multiple sclerosis, and stroke. The second level of technology is called "halfway technology." This represents the "kinds of things that must be done after the fact, as efforts to compensate for the incapacitating effects of certain diseases whose course one is unable to do very much about. It is a technology designed to make up for disease, or to postpone death."[17] Examples include organ transplants and the use of artificial organs, among others. Halfway technology for chronic kidney failure means dialysis or kidney transplant. For heart disease, the halfway technology can mean open heart surgery, a pacemaker, a transplant, or an artificial heart. Such halfway technologies are generally very expensive.[18] John Cooper, president of the American Association of Medical Colleges, in 1973 congressional testimony, described halfway technology as not "really evidence of success in dealing with disease," but rather "confessions of failure, of a lack of understanding to prevent disease before clinical signs and symptoms appear. They are the consequence of partial understanding."[19] The final level of technology, "high technology" is exemplified by immunization, antibiotics for bacterial infections, and prevention of nutritional disorders. High technology "comes as a result of genuine understanding of disease mechanisms, and when it becomes available it is relatively inexpensive . . . to deliver."[20]

In recent years, most of the growth in medical technology has been in the area of halfway technologies, which is the most expensive.[21] What accounts for the growth of medical technology in general and halfway technologies in particular?

Factors Responsible for the Growth of Medical Technologies

Many factors have influenced the dramatic growth in medical technologies in the United States. In this section we discuss some of the major influences on the growth of medical technologies. These factors are not discussed in any particular order. Thus we do not suggest the relative contribution of each factor to the overall growth in medical technologies.

The Public and Private Sectors

Vannevar Bush, science adviser to President Franklin Roosevelt, in his 1945 report *Science: the Endless Frontier* recommended a significantly enlarged federal government role in support of science. The federal government not only dramatically increased its funding for biomedical research but it made large amounts of federal funds available to outlying communities for construction of hospitals. During the 1960s, the federal government played a role in expanding physician supply (heavily weighted toward specialists) through funding of medical schools and medical students. It also created Medicare and Medicaid, enlarging federal funding. One of the results of the massive flow of federal dollars into the health care system was the rapid development of academic health centers. Given the availability of a large amount of federal dollars, leading medical schools changed their focal interest from the training of medical students to biomedical research. This, combined with the increasing supply of medical specialists, set the stage for rapid growth in medical technologies.[22] Modern hospitals became repositories of high-tech medical equipment. Similarly, private-sector spending in research and development (R&D) has exploded. At present, the industry invests 7 to 13 percent of its annual gross profit in R&D.

All parties in health care—hospitals, clinics, physicians, consumers, manufacturers of medical devices—have a stake in the development and diffusion of medical technology.[23] From World War II to the early 1970s, health care financing in most countries was very generous, based on retrospective pricing. The result was the emergence of very expensive halfway technologies such as organ transplants, MRI, and high-priced drugs with marginal value. Such financing also contributed to the development of such "high-technology" items as new antibiotics and vaccines that were cost effective.[24]

The Health Insurance/Finance System

The usual method for limiting demand in the marketplace is to raise prices. The third-party payment system has made such a mechanism largely irrelevant in the health care market. The third-party payment system insulates the consumer from the high cost of the treatment. Consumers have little incentive to question expensive care since the third party (the insurance company) is going to pay most or all of the bill.[25] The reimbursement system used by the insurance companies—retrospective payment, which pays a provider on the basis of costs incurred—has stimulated demand for medical technology by encouraging any innovation that promises some benefit, regardless of the cost. Victor Fuchs has claimed that hospitals operate under a technological imperative that drives them to adopt the latest technology, regardless of the cost. The incentive system helps explain the rapid and indiscriminate adoption of medical innovations.[26] The retrospective payment mechanism also sends a clear message to research and development. The message is to develop new technologies that enhance the quality of care, regardless of the cost. Examples of high-cost medical innovations made possible by a retrospective payment system might include natural organ transplants and artificial organs.[27]

The new prospective payment finance mechanism, which pays health care providers sums that are independent of the costs incurred, sends a different signal to the R&D sector. The message here is to develop new technologies that reduce costs as long as quality does not suffer too much. The shift to this new system under Medicare, while not resulting in decreased use of intensive-care units, does seem to have helped decrease the use of diagnostic procedures such as chest X-rays.[28] But the long-term effect of the Prospective Payment System (PPS) on Medicare is far from conclusive.

In most industries, before a new cost-increasing technology is adopted it must satisfy two criteria: it must represent an advancement to what we currently have, and there must be a market for it. Unfortunately, in the health care market, whether a technological change occurs or not is largely determined by the first criterion. The presence of a third-party-payer system makes the second criterion irrelevant. Insurance leads to technological change, and more costly technological change increases demand for insurance, since most patients cannot pay for costly technology out of their own pocket.[29] Some of the evidence gathered thus far suggests that insurance coverage, to a great extent, determines whether or not a new technology is developed, manufactured, and used.[30]

The Hospitals

Aside from the influence of a retrospective insurance payment system, hospitals have other reasons for the acquisition of the latest medical technology.[31] By stocking hospitals with the latest medical technologies, hospitals hope to recruit physicians and attract patients. From the physician's perspective, a hospital with the latest technology and empty beds promises little delay in admitting and treating his or her patients. Hospitals also hope to attract patients by portraying themselves as state-of-the-art facilities. The result is a medical arms race between hospitals as each hospital tries to maximize its own status, prestige, and profits. The result often is a tremendous duplication of very expensive medical technologies among many hospitals within the same community. This is helped by the fact that there is a lack of incentives for hospitals to cooperate and coordinate efficient use of medical technology.[32] The acquisition of diagnostic imaging technologies (CT scan, MRI, etc.) by hospitals requires a significant initial capital investment and a high level of operating costs. To avoid the financial risks involved and generate profit requires a high volume of use of such technologies. Thus, once a hospital buys an expensive new technology, there is pressure to use it more frequently to produce sufficient demand to cover the operating costs and increase profit margins.[33] This has often led to excesses and overuse of medical technology in the United States.

Physicians

According to Eric Cassell, five human characteristics help explain physicians' enchantment with medical technology. One is wonderment with something new that can do fantastic or inexplicable things. It causes physicians to use and overuse medical technology. It also helps solve the problem of boredom and loss of motivation. A second reason for physicians' attraction to technology is that technology tells them directly what it means in immediate terms. For example, computer-generated EKG interpretations provide immediate information and answers. The third reason for technology's hold on physicians is that virtually all technology is characterized by unambiguous values. Lack of ambiguity is generally considered essential for good science of medicine. Thus, technological values and medical values reinforce each other because both are intolerant of ambiguities. A fourth and related factor has to do with the fact that one of the main problems physicians confront is uncertainty. This is caused by shortcomings in the individual physician's knowledge and/or the inadequacies of the profession's knowledge. Technology helps physicians reduce some of the uncertainty. A medical problem is often redefined in terms of a technological answer. The final reason technology lures physicians is the power it confers on them. Every therapeutic and diagnostic test is a demonstration of a physicians's efficacy and thus of his or her power.[34]

According to David Freed, physicians have capitulated to the growth of medical technology at both the structural and applied level. At a structural level, medical education has emphasized the scientific basis of medicine and downplayed its role as a healing "art." Physicians and the science community's compulsion about avoiding uncertainty has stimulated excessive dependence on clinical tests and treatment of marginal value in pursuit of certainty. Another structural factor is a strong tradition of professional autonomy in the medical profession. Physicians are the key decision makers with respect to the use of medical technology, and as long as physicians believe that a new technology might benefit a patient, they are likely to use it. At an applied level, physicians are trained to be advocates for their patients. They are also comfortable doing what they learned to do in their training. There are no general decision-making models that all physicians can apply with respect to the use of technology, and thus decisions are made at an individual level, resulting in a wide variance in physician practice. Finally, the fear of malpractice lawsuits and medical liability risks has also encouraged tremendous growth of expensive diagnostic imaging technologies.[35] How physicians will respond to the new era of economic constraints and the changing health policy environment and market forces—managed care, managed competition, HMOs—remains to be seen.[36]

The Health Policymaking Environment

The diffusion of medical technology has taken place in the United States in an environment of both regulation and free enterprise. Attempts at regulating the diffusion of CT scanners through certificate-of-need (CON) programs were not very successful. By the 1980s, the use of CT scanners had become widespread, and CON agencies were either abandoned in some states or had become liberal in their requirements. Supporters of the marketplace model (i.e., free enterprise system) argue that the health care delivery system should operate according to the principle of supply and demand. Thus the diffusion of medical technology in the United States has taken place between the two competing models—the regulation model and the free enterprise, marketplace model. Each, to some extent, has been manipulated by health care providers. Overall, the market model has continued to operate in the medical technology area, despite some attempts at regulation.[37]

Societal Culture and Values

American society places a great deal of emphasis on individual autonomy, self-determination, personal privacy, and shared belief in justice and equality. This is reflected in the health care field by a belief held by many that health care is a right to which everyone is entitled. Access to the latest medical technology is also viewed as a right, and demand for it has increased because of greater public awareness of the latest technological innovation. Compared to many other countries, the American public is more aware of the latest technological advances in medicine because of considerable coverage in the mass media. The public demands the newest and the best in medical technology, even though it continues to express dissatisfaction with high cost and low efficacy.[38]

In addition to significant emphasis on individual autonomy, rights, and self-determination, American culture is heavily predisposed toward progress through technological means and faith in scientific progress. Our culture equates reduction of uncertainty and gaining control over ambiguities with progress. This has often led to an unrealistic dependence on technology to fix problems of the health care system and exclusion of nontechnological solutions. We have come to equate sophisticated medical procedures with better health care.[39]

We are a culture that believes that "we can have it all." We want the latest and the most sophisticated medical technology, and we want to apply it indiscriminately to the very young, the very old, and the hopelessly ill. We want the physician to do everything possible for the patient even when there is little or no hope for survival. We want the best, yet we want to pay the least. We admire countries that place limits and global budgets on health care and want to adopt their health care system, but we do not want to accept any limits.[40]

In view of the above discussion, it is not too surprising that we have witnessed a rampant growth in medical technology in the United States, and such a growth is likely to continue in the future. The biotechnology industry is expected to grow from an $8 billion (revenue) industry in 1992 to a $50 billion industry by the year 2000.[41] The availability of large-scale technology has been much greater in the United States than in Western European countries. The concentration of medical equipment in the United States is far greater than in other countries that have good-quality health care systems.[42] For example, the United States has 11.2 MRI units per million population compared to 1.1 units per million in Canada and 3.7 units per million in Germany. Similarly, in 1992, the United States had 3.7 installed open-heart surgery units per million population compared to 1.3 units per million in Canada and 0.8 units per million in Germany.[43]

The rapid proliferation of health care technology has raised concerns in many quarters about the cost of such technologies and the strain they put on the nation's resources. It also raises issues about the cost-effectiveness of such technologies.

Health Care Technology and Costs

A great deal of modern technology—medical equipment, medical techniques and pharmaceuticals—is very expensive. One of the most significant advances in medical technology, and one of the most costly, is the spread and increased use of such diagnostic tools as MRI and CT scans. Since such new diagnostic therapies are simpler and safer than exploratory surgery, they are used at a much higher rate, adding to health care costs. MRI equipment costs between $2 million and $3 million, and the cost of one MRI scan ranges from $600 to $800. In fact, MRI equipment has proved to be so popular that today it is available not only in hospitals and doctors' offices but in roadside facilities and shopping centers.[44]

Another device, a free-electron, laser equipment, is likely to cost about $2 million and portable laser equipment about $70,000.[45] Many technological advances such as coronary bypass surgery and hip-replacement operations are also very expensive and contribute to overall health care costs. Liver transplants cost about $200,000 per transplant on the average. The discovery in the early 1980s of the drug cyclosporine, which prevents the body's immune system from rejecting organ transplants, has been instrumental in increasing the number of liver transplants from 15 in 1980 to 3,056 in 1992.[46]

The field of neonatology is another example of how technology has allowed us to save lives at increased cost. Numerous medical breakthroughs —incubators, intravenous feeding, advances in cesarean section, controls for infection—during the 1950s and 1960s have succeeded in saving the lives of babies with increasingly lower birthweights. But the cost has been very high. In 1984 constant dollars, cost per survival of an infant born weighing between 750 and 1,000 grams is estimated to be about $125,000, while cost for an infant born weighing less than 750 grams is about $175,000.[47] Many economists argue that we would be better off providing intensive care for babies over 1,000 grams than spending resources on children with birthweights of less than 800 grams. They justify such arguments on the ground that we can actually reduce suffering by targeting only those newborns who are most likely to benefit from medical intervention.[48] This example demonstrates the complexity as well as the difficult nature of the problems created by medical technology.

Many economists argue that new health care technology is the largest factor driving up health care costs in the United States. They believe that technology accounts for as much as 50 percent of the growth in health care cost beyond overall inflation.[49] Most analysts believe that advances in medical technology have been largely responsible for a 4 to 5 percent annual rate of growth in the industrialized nations' health care costs.[50] According to Henry Aaron, medical technologies that did not exist twenty to thirty years ago account for most of the rise in health care spending in the United States.[51] He argues that developments in medical technology affect outlays in two ways: new technology adds new treatments, and because of its less intrusive nature, many more patients benefit from it, resulting in increased use and costs.[52]

The hospital is the major center of high-tech medicine, and hospital care constitutes the single largest component of our health care spending, about 40 percent. The most important factor stimulating hospital cost increases is the rapid adoption of new medical technology, according to a report by the General Accounting Office. Competition among hospitals combined with a third-party reimbursement system provides incentives for rapid advancement of medical technologies in hospitals. Since hospitals do not compete for patients on the basis of price, hospitals try to gain market advantage by offering the most up-to-date services, and the cost of these technologies is passed on to the third-party payers—insurance companies.[53]

Attempts at controlling costs associated with medical technology immediately produce confrontation between two powerful interests in the health care system, insurance companies and manufacturers of medical devices. Medical device manufacturers argue that they are unfairly singled out and that many new inventions provide less costly alternatives for diagnosis and treatment. Today, many surgeries require shorter hospital stays and significantly reduced recovery time.[54] Needless to say, any technology that allows us to produce existing goods or services at a lower cost, while maintaining or increasing quality, is to be welcomed. Nevertheless, rapid cost escalation related to wasteful technologies deserves close scrutiny.

Insurance companies generally try to limit coverage to care that is "reasonably necessary" or "medically necessary." These terms are generally interpreted broadly to cover any nonexperimental technology accepted by the medical community that is not considered unsafe or ineffective. Courts have often expanded the scope of insurance coverage by relying on the notion that all ambiguities should be interpreted against the insurer and in favor of the beneficiary. Courts have often forced insurance companies to cover technologies and treatments still considered to be in an experimental stage. Extra insurance rights established through the courts are often called "judge-made insurance."[55]

The relationship between health care technology and health care costs is a complex one because technology affects costs in many different ways. Not all technology is good or bad. On the positive side, technology can play a significant role in supporting the provision of adequate care in the areas of prevention and rehabilitation. Mobile health care units can help overcome the challenge of geographic maldistribution by helping extend service areas and helping make medical service distribution more equitable.[56] On the negative side, technology can be unsafe, ineffective, and inefficient.

Some technologies can increase costs considerably through introduction of new diagnostic or treatment therapy and improve health. In other words, some technologies are both high cost and high benefit. Some technologies may decrease costs by allowing care to be given in a lower-cost setting, by replacing expensive procedures, keeping people healthier, reducing hospital stay and recovery time, and returning people to work sooner. Such technologies may be both low cost and high benefit. In contrast, some technologies may be very costly but produce only marginal benefits. It is these technologies —high cost and low benefit—that raise serious concerns on the part of critics of the U.S. health care system. Some technologies are unsafe, while others are ineffective. Some technologies are medically effective, but they are not cost effective. Technologies that are unsafe, ineffective, or not cost effective are called "wasteful technologies."[57]

Examples of wasteful technologies abound. An estimated 50 percent of all U.S. births are electronically monitored. Eight controlled studies have found that electronic monitoring has no advantage over a stethoscope placed on the mother's stomach, even in high-risk pregnancies. Yet electronic monitoring is growing at a cost of $1 billion a year.[58] U.S. doctors perform about 600,000 hysterectomies a year at a cost of $5 billion. Almost a third of women undergo the operation by the time they are sixty. Yet it is not clear how many of these women gain anything from it.[59] In recent years, late-stage breast cancer victims have turned to a treatment known as autologous bone marrow transplant. The procedure is considered risky and costly, costing about $100,000 a patient; however, there is no solid evidence at the present time that it works better than less expensive treatments.[60] Every year, about 400,000 patients undergo heart bypass surgery at a cost of about $12 billion. Studies show that it is no better than drug treatment for less dire conditions. About 300,000 Americans receive angioplasties a year at a cost of $10,000 a procedure. Drug treatment generally yields similar benefits at a fraction of the cost. The procedure has not been shown to prevent heart attacks.[61]

Attempts at cost control through CON, HSAs, and planning have met with little success, as we discussed in chapter 6. Currently, in the United States most drugs and medical devices are assessed for safety and efficacy only and not for cost effectiveness. Most medical and surgical procedures are not formally evaluated at all. It is clear that what is needed is a systematic assessment of medical technologies that would allow us to weed out wasteful technologies.

Technology Assessment

The rate of diffusion of high-cost technology varies between countries. In mainly public, government funded, and planned nonmarket health care delivery systems, such as those in Great Britain and Scandinavia, there are generally more constraints built in that limit the introduction of new technologies. In the United States, market forces are the most influential with respect to diffusion of high-cost technologies, often resulting in a medical arms race.[62]

The late 1990s might witness even more dramatic developments in health care technology.[63] Currently, biotechnology is the most radical research area. At present, more than 100 biologically derived drugs are in clinical trials. Some of the products now in the developmental stage are likely to cost as much as $5,000 per therapeutic regimen; portable EKG units are already on the market.[64] According to M. Roy Schwartz, senior vice president of medical education and science with the American Medical Association, most of America's economic growth comes from technology, specifically biotechnology, and technological development pays off in the long run.[65]

Nevertheless, the country is facing some tough decisions about access, funding, distribution of health care resources, and cost containment. Today, evaluating health technology is one of the most important challenges facing policymakers and researchers alike. Improving the process of technology diffusion requires continuous monitoring of technological development, identifying technologies for assessment, and conducting early assessment before technology is marketed.[66] With more availability of outcome data, employers, insurers, and researchers are beginning to question the value of certain high-cost technology.[67]

The history of technology assessment in the United States is a very brief one. The dramatic growth in medical technologies in the 1970s raised some concerns about technology. In 1972, the Office of Technology Assessment (OTA), a congressional staff agency that maintains a concern for medical technology assessment, was established. The current Republican majority in Congress is considering eliminating OTA as a cost-saving measure. Another congressional agency, the General Accounting Office (GAO), often analyzes the role of technology in its health reports. In 1978, the National Center for Health Care Technology was established by law and was responsible for examining the cost effectiveness of new technologies. Although the agency was reauthorized in 1981, at the urging of the medical device industry, the Reagan administration did not seek any funding for the agency in its 1982 budget. No funds were appropriated, and the agency went out of existence in 1982. At the urging of the Reagan administration, Congress also cut off funds for state health planning agencies that required hospitals to seek approval of large capital investment in technology.

Skyrocketing health care costs and evidence of inappropriate use of technological devices and procedures led both Congress and President Bush to revisit the issue of health care technology assessment in the late 1980s. The result was the establishment in 1989 of the Office of Health Technology Assessment (OHTA) in the National Center for Health Services Research (NCHSR). OHTA is responsible for advising the Health Care Financing Administration (HCFA) about technology as it is applied to Medicaid and Medicare, but the influence of OHTA is indirect and limited.[68] In 1989, the Agency for Health Care Policy and Research (AHCPR) was also created within the National Center for Health Services Research to develop guidelines on the appropriate treatment of common illnesses. The agency also evaluates the effectiveness and cost of specific technologies related to federal health programs.

Another agency, the Food and Drug Administration (FDA), is responsible for regulating the safety and efficacy of drugs and medical devices, but not their cost effectiveness. The FDA's role in the regulation of drugs has been shaped by the 1906 Food and Drug Act, the 1938 Federal Food, Drug and Cosmetic Act, and 1962 amendments. The drug companies are required to get advance permission from the FDA for every important step in testing, production, and marketing new drugs. The 1938 Federal Food, Drug and Cosmetic Act gave the FDA jurisdiction over medical devices for the first time. The 1976 Medical Device amendments to the act strengthened the FDA's hand in regulating medical devices. The 1990 Safe Medical Devices

Act also strengthened the FDA by controlling the entry of new products and monitoring the use of marketed products.[69] Nevertheless, it is important to emphasize again that the FDA is mainly concerned with the safety and efficacy of drugs and medical devices, and it is not heavily involved in assessing cost effectiveness. Furthermore, as mentioned earlier, most medical and surgical procedures are not evaluated at all in the United States.

The private sector's record in technology assessment has been uneven. The Council on Health Care Technology of the Institute of Medicine, created in 1986, operated for four years and became defunct in 1990. Other organizations in the private sector that continue to engage in some technology assessment are Blue Cross and Blue Shield, the American Medical Association, and the American Hospital Association.[70]

What is clear is that the efforts at technology assessment in the United States have been sporadic, uncoordinated, and limited. According to the Office of Technology Assessment, fewer than 20 percent of all existing medical technology has been subjected to systematic study via controlled clinical trials.[71] Spiraling health care costs in the 1980s have again revived interest in technology assessment. Technology assessment raises a number of questions: What is technology assessment? How is it conducted? Who should conduct technology assessment?

Traditionally, technology assessment concerned itself with evaluating the safety and efficacy of drugs and medical devices. In recent years, there has been a broadening of perspective in defining technology assessment. Proponents of technology assessment argue that technology assessment should go beyond the traditional concerns of safety and efficacy to include evaluation of the cost effectiveness of various technologies, including therapeutic and surgical procedures. Some go even further.

David Banta and Stephen Thacker have argued that "technology assessment is a comprehensive form of policy research that examines short and long-term social (e.g., clinical, societal, economic, ethical, and legal) consequences of the applications of technology."[72] As the perspective on technology assessment has changed, so has the nature of researchers who engage in that assessment and the methods of assessment. In the past, technology assessments were mainly carried out by scientists and physicians. Today, with its emphasis on cost and quality-of-life concerns, among others, the approach to technology assessment has become more interdisciplinary, requiring more collaborative effort on the part of researchers trained in economics, epidemiology, operations research, ethics, and other social sciences.[73] Americans, on the one hand, demand more and more technology. On the other hand, they are reluctant to pay for it and believe they are not getting good return (benefits) for their money. Given this, one of the tasks of technology assessment is to connect the costs of medical service to the value attached to it.[74]

In traditional technology assessment, where safety and efficacy were the two main concerns, the most important methodological tool was clinical testing or randomized clinical trials. The new perspective on technology assessment, with its emphasis on cost effectiveness and medical, social, and ethical end results, requires the use of many different methodological tools. Today, technology assessment relies on epidemiologic tools, biological/medical models, laboratory tests, clinical trials, the use of samples, control groups, replications, and cost-benefit analysis. A highly developed set of rules and conventions governs sampling, random selection, reliability, and validity. Statistical analysis has made a contribution to technology assessment with techniques of sample designs, proper testing methods, and the use of confidence intervals. In short, methodologies for technology assessment have become more varied and more sophisticated. But it is important to remember that despite better and more sophisticated methodologies, technology assessment is still not a perfect science and subjective factors may influence the assessment itself or the interpretation of results.[76]

Another relevant question about technology assessment is who should do the assessment. Medical device manufacturers and professionals who perform high-tech procedures have fought government efforts to assess health care technology on the ground that it would lead to a small number of people deciding whether Americans have access to new technologies. They also argue that government involvement would lead to cost controls and national spending limits, which would have a detrimental effect on technological innovations. Critics of the medical device industry argue that the industry opposes the government's role in technology assessment for purely selfish reasons—out of the fear that technology assessment by the government will lead to useless products and procedures being weeded out of the marketplace, cutting into industry's profit. Given the huge economic self-interest involved on the part of the medical device industry, we cannot leave the task of technology assessment to the manufacturers and marketers of new medical products and procedures.[77]

Insurers and different health plans argue that they are not in a position to assess new technologies because of the scarcity of information about new products and lack of resources to develop the information base. When individual health or insurance plans do engage in assessment, the results are kept in-house for competitive reasons. Even if individual insurers or health plans conduct their own assessment, they may reach different conclusions about the value of various technologies because of differences in methodologies used or differences in interpretations.[78]

Governments in many Western European countries play a more prominent role in health care technology assessment than is the case in the United States. Given the fragmented nature of technology assessment in the private sector and the economic and profit motives at work, it seems to us that the federal government needs to play a more active role in technology assessment. The federal government can influence the diffusion of technology in two ways. First, the government could issue regulations or directives. These could include premarket controls, pricing decisions, reimbursement methods, licensing of advanced medical facilities, and generating and distributing information about the cost effectiveness of medical devices and procedures. Second, the government could use economic incentives. These could include changing the financing or fee system, cost sharing, or inducing competition in the marketplace. At the present time, this second approach seems to be gaining momentum.[79]

Technology assessment can add a great deal of information that can help policymakers make decisions about the allocation of scarce resources. It can inject rationality and scientific knowledge into the policymaking process. Nevertheless, it is important to remember that technology assessment is not a miracle cure that will solve all problems. There is a limit to how much policymaking can be guided strictly by scientific knowledge and rational processes. Policymaking is a very complex process that attempts to integrate a variety of economic, social, political, and ideological values and belief systems.[80] Policymaking often involves the "science of muddling through."[81] Even good cost-effectiveness analysis may have only a limited impact on policymaking.[82] Technology assessment may tell us something about cost effectiveness; however, it cannot tell us how much we should be willing to pay for a given health effect. This involves making explicit value judgments, something that both the old and the new technology assessment abhors.[83]

Despite these weaknesses, health care technology assessment can play an important role in societal decision making about the allocation of scarce resources and the acceptance or rejection of new technologies. Technology assessment raises two issues. One has to do with the value of economic efficiency, that is, whether the new technology is cost effective. This involves making societal judgments about whether to accept or reject new technology. The other issue has to do with the value of equity. This involves making societal judgments about relationships between needs and demands, distribution of health care spending, and access to high-cost technology for different groups in society. These issues have ethical implications. Ethical issues become more prominent when values of efficiency and equity come in conflict.[84] The ethical implications of and concerns raised by biomedical technology have created a new field of bioethics.[85]

Health Care Costs, Technology, and Ethics

Technology assessment has been highly fragmented and sporadic in the United States. As a society, we have failed to make systematic decisions about research and development of medical technologies, such as who should determine whether a particular technology should be developed and funded, on what basis individuals should be provided access once a technology is available in the marketplace, what level of technological intervention is appropriate for a specific medical problem, and what the total impact is of the rapid spread of high-cost medical technologies on society in general and the U.S. health care system in particular.[86]

The rapid proliferation of halfway technologies and spiraling health care costs also raise many ethical concerns and dilemmas that we as a society must confront and address through public policies related to health care. The term "dilemma" in a popular sense is understood to mean a difficult choice between two or more alternatives. An ethical dilemma refers to a situation in which all the alternatives are morally problematic, that is, each alternative seems to involve a wrong act or action.[87]

In the following pages, we discuss some of the ethical dilemmas raised by medical technology at two levels. First, at a broad level, we discuss the issue of health care rationing and the ethical concerns it raises. Second, we discuss the ethical dilemmas raised by specific medical technologies such as life-sustaining technologies, organ transplants, and reproductive technologies.

Health Care Rationing

The state of Oregon adopted a rationing plan for Medicaid to contain rising health care costs. The Oregon plan has been praised by some and criticized by others.[88] We discussed the plan in our chapters on Medicaid and on cost containment. Here, our discussion focuses on health care rationing in general.

As past efforts at cost containment have failed, and as health care costs have continued to escalate, the debate over health care rationing has intensified. How much can we afford, and for how many people? Should everyone or every group have equal access to high-cost technology? If not, what criteria do we use to allow access to some and deny access to others? Do patients have a right to receive the best technology available, regardless of their ability to pay? Should patients be denied medical treatments when social costs outweigh individual benefits? Should patients' medical needs or economic status (i.e., ability to pay) determine the treatment they receive? Given limited resources, what is the best and the most efficient way of allocating scarce resources? How do we limit access and allocate resources in a way that is acceptable to society?[89]

The term "rationing" can be used in two different ways. One way in which rationing occurs is when market economies deny goods or services to those who cannot afford them. Just like many others goods, health care is certainly rationed in this manner, especially for the poor and the uninsured, who cannot afford a variety of expensive health care services (see chapter 6). This type of rationing affects only about 15 percent of the population.

The current debate about health care rationing focuses on the second type of rationing. The question is whether certain health care goods and services (e.g., halfway technologies) should be denied or their availability limited even to those who can afford to pay? Needless to say, this rationing raises intense debate, since it would cover about 85 percent of the population—those who have access to health insurance.[90] Such rationing is not common in the United States, but it has been practiced in other countries, such as Great Britain, for a long time. For example, virtually every patient suffering from chronic kidney failure is treated in the United States; in Britain, most are not treated. The British society is much more willing to deny treatment for chronic kidney failure to older patients. Similarly, in Britain, patients over the age of sixty are generally not considered suitable for kidney transplants. Limited resources and age are two factors that act as a basis for a great deal of rationing in Britain. Consequently, the rate and the cost of treatment for certain health services is much lower in Britain than in the United States.[91]

In the United States, Medicare provides major funding for acute health care of persons over sixty-five and for the permanently disabled between the ages of fifty-five and sixty-five. But there is no comparable source of funding for the young, except through Medicaid, which provides limited support. Some people feel that it is unethical for a society to devote so much of its resources to the care of the elderly and to spend so little on the young. They argue that this imbalance is more the result of the political clout of the elderly, who are organized and vote in large numbers, than the rational allocation of resources.[92] Some find the use of age as a criterion in allocating resources unjustifiable.[93] Still others express concern over keeping extremely low-weight babies alive even when there is a high probability that they will be confined to a life of severe and permanent disability, and many of them will require continuing institutional or specialized care for the remainder of their lives.

Some observers have argued that if the U.S. government is serious about containing health care costs, it needs to consider rationing seriously. One of the prominent proponents of health care rationing is Daniel Callahan, a philosopher who is the director of the Hastings Center.[94] Callahan argues that in the United States, from the beginning, bioethics has gravitated toward an emphasis on individual autonomy and integrity because it fits very well with the dominant ideology and values of American society. According to Callahan, this has led to ignoring the value of the common good or public interest. What is needed, he argues, is a communitarian ethic—a blending of cultural judgment and personal judgment.[95] In his book *Setting Limits: Medical Goals in an Aging Society,* Callahan addresses the question of how much health care the aged should have.[96] In a more recent book, he addresses the question of how much health care Americans are entitled to have. Callahan argues that individual demand for health care is limitless, and he blames the "liberal society" for not curbing individual desires and needs.[97] John Kilner challenges the popular myth that Americans have enough resources to treat every terminal disease and argues for rationing.[98] Others have also argued for rationing health care in the United States.[99] Critics of health care rationing argue that any attempt to justify rationing using principles such as social worth, ability to pay, or age leaves enormous potential for mischief. Furthermore, arriving at any societal consensus about these principles would be very complex and problematic at best.

Life-Sustaining Technologies and the Right to Die

Today's life-support technologies are capable of keeping patients alive for a long time, even when they have no chance of regaining consciousness. Mechanical ventilators can keep patients breathing, and artificial nutrition and hydration can sustain severely debilitated and dying individuals for many years. This raises the specter of individuals being kept alive in a vegetative, helpless states, sustained by a host of tubes and machines.[100] The question of life and death, the question of who shall live and who shall die and who shall decide raises difficult ethical and legal issues.[101] Some well-publicized court cases help illustrate the complexities involved in such situations.

One of the early cases to highlight the ethical and legal dilemma involved a New Jersey woman named Karen Quinlan. At the age of twenty-one she slipped into a deep coma. She was hooked up to a respirator in a hospital. Her doctor informed the parents that their daughter was never going to come out of her coma because her brain was severely damaged. She might not necessarily die and, kept on a life-support system, might live for many years. Quinlan's parents asked the doctor to turn off the respirator. The doctor refused, and they went to court. The judge in the lower court disagreed with the parents. They then appealed the decision to the New Jersey Supreme Court, and on 31 March 1976 the parents won the right to have the respirator turned off. Ironically, Karen Quinlan was able to breathe on her own. She was moved from a hospital to a nursing home, where she died in June 1985. The state supreme court ruled that Karen had a constitutional right of privacy, which her guardian could assert on her behalf.[102]

A different dilemma was presented in the case of twenty-six-year-old Elizabeth Bouvia, who in September 1983 admitted herself to the psychiatric unit of California's Riverside General Hospital. She had had a very difficult life and was almost totally paralyzed from cerebral palsy. Once admitted, she asked for assistance in starving herself to death. She wanted the hospital staff to provide her with pain-killing drugs and hygienic care while she waited to die. The hospital refused. Elizabeth Bouvia went to court and she lost; the court ordered her to be force fed. On 7 April 1984, she left the hospital. The hospital bill for the 217 days, excluding physicians' fees, was more than $56,000 and was paid by the hospital and the state of California. After repeated court appeals, the California Court of Appeals found in her favor. The court said that she could refuse life-sustaining medical treatment. The court ruled that the right of a competent adult patient to refuse treatment is a constitutionally guaranteed right. After her victory, Ms. Bouvia changed her mind and did not kill herself.[103] What was unique about this case is that Ms. Bouvia was not terminally ill, and she was asking for the help of the medical staff to starve herself to death.

A more recent case involved thirty-two-year-old Nancy Cruzan of Missouri. She had been in a persistent vegetative state for seven years since a car accident. Her prognosis was hopeless. Her cerebral cortex had atrophied, but she was not dead, and she could have lived in such a vegetative state for many more years. The cost of her medical treatment was about $130,000 a year, paid by the state. In 1987 her parents requested that Nancy's feeding tube be removed so she could die. A lower court granted the request in July 1988, but the state supreme court in November 1988 reversed the decision, agreeing with the state's argument that the state of Missouri had an "unqualified" interest in preserving life. According to the court, the state's interest was not in the "quality" of life; the state's interest was in "life."[104] Nancy's parents appealed the decision to the U.S. Supreme Court. In June 1990, the Court, in a 5–4 decision, agreed with the decision of the Missouri Supreme Court. The Court found that a competent person has a constitutionally protected right to refuse life-saving hydration and nutrition. If the person is incompetent, the Court ruled, the state is entitled to require rigorous proof that this person, when competent, would have requested removal of a feeding tube in the event of his or her future incompetence. According to the Court, the state of Missouri was entitled to require clear and convincing proof that a surrogate decision maker was choosing what Ms. Cruzan herself, when competent, desired.[105] It is interesting to note that the Court based its ruling, not on the ground of a fundamental privacy right, as was the case with Quinlan, but on the ground of the liberty interest. The Court argued that the state's interest must be balanced against those of the patient.[106] On 14 December 1990, the Circuit Court of Jasper County, Missouri, declared that there was clear and convincing evidence that if Nancy Cruzan was mentally able, she would want to terminate her nutrition and hydration, she would not want to continue her present existence, and her parents were authorized to remove the nutrition and hydration. After the removal of the feeding tube, Nancy Cruzan died on 26 December 1990.

On the other side of the ledger was a case in Minnesota where a public hospital sought permission to remove a respirator from an eighty-seven-year-old woman. The woman was in a persistent vegetative state. The hospital argued that continuing treatment was not in the woman's best medical or personal interest; however, the family of the woman opposed the request. The family won, and the woman died a year later.[107]

These cases illustrate the legal and ethical complexities created by today's life-sustaining technologies. Who should live and who should die? Who decides? When is life worth preserving? Who determines what is quality of life? How does one measure a person's quality of life? Should the courts be involved in making such decisions? Can euthanasia ethically be justified? What should be the ethical role of the physician and other caregivers? Does a patient have a right to demand unending medical treatment in a hopeless case?

Today, approximately 10,000 patients live in a vegetative state in the United States. The complexities created by the life-sustaining technologies have given rise to the "right-to-die" movement across the country. Proponents of the right to die argue that individuals have a right to die with dignity and to determine when to end their lives. Proponents of the right argue that passive as well as active euthanasia is justified. Passive euthanasia refers to a situation in which death results from omitting or terminating treatment. Active euthanasia, that is, actively assisted suicide, refers to a situation where the health care provider gives the patient a means to kill himself or herself or assists in the administration of the means. The publicity surrounding pathologist Jack Kevorkian of Michigan, who has assisted numerous terminally ill patients to kill themselves, has heightened the debate over the issue of the right to die. In fact, it has led the state legislature to pass a law making it a crime to assist someone in euthanasia.

Opposition to the right-to-die movement has come from many sources, including the right-to-life movement. Opponents argue that suicide is wrong on religious and theological grounds, as well as being harmful to the community and the common good, and that it produces harmful consequences for other individuals in society.[108] Others have argued that no human being has a right to decide, for themselves or for others, when life is no longer worth living. Opponents argue that there is a danger that such decisions may be made on wrong or ulterior motives. Thus, for example, one might agree to end the life of a patient whose continual stay in the hospital is a financial burden to his or her family or when members of the family stand to benefit financially by inheritance. Others argue that once a society agrees that at some stage a life is not worth sustaining, that society is on a "slippery slope." Once passive euthanasia becomes acceptable, the next step will be active euthanasia, which in turn can easily lead to forced or involuntary euthanasia. Others worry that if active euthanasia becomes a common practice, it could undermine the role of doctors as healers and caregivers.[109]

Public sentiment seems to favor the right-to-die movement. A poll conducted in 1990 for Time/CNN by Yankelovich Clancy Shulman revealed that 80 percent of those surveyed said that decisions about ending the lives of terminally ill patients should be made by their families and doctors and not by lawmakers. Eighty-one percent believed that if a patient is terminally ill and unconscious but has left instructions in a living will, the doctor should be allowed to withdraw life-sustaining treatment—passive euthanasia. Fifty-seven percent went even further and said that in such cases it is all right for a doctor to administer a lethal injection or provide a lethal pill—active euthanasia.[110]

Washington State's "death with dignity" initiative, also known as Initiative 119 on the state ballot in a 1991 election, failed to garner a majority vote and lost by a margin of 54 to 46 percent. The initiative was supported by a large majority of voters for much of the campaign, but it lost support in the last few weeks before the election. A similar initiative in California in 1992 was defeated by the same margin as in Washington State.[111] On 8 November 1994, Oregon voters approved the "Death With Dignity Act" by a margin of 52 to 48 percent. Known as Ballot Measure 16, the act allows physicians in the state to write lethal drug prescriptions for terminally ill patients who are expected to die within six months. At present the measure is tied up in the courts because it is being challenged by its opponents. In the first six weeks of their 1995 legislative sessions, eight states—Colorado, Connecticut, Hawaii, Maine, Maryland, Massachusetts, New Hampshire, and Wisconsin—proposed bills patterned after Measure 16 in Oregon.[112] It is clear that such measures, even if they pass, are likely to end up in the courts for resolution.

There are a variety of ways that individual health care providers and society have tried to address some of the problems arising out of life-sustaining technologies. Many hospitals have established ethics committees to help with ethical and related issues arising out of treatment of terminally ill patients. They often perform the functions of educating the hospital staff, developing policies in problem areas, and acting as advisory consultants to health care providers and occasionally to family members. Some have expressed concerns that the committee's decisions, instead of being advisory, may turn into de facto binding decisions, diminishing the role and rights of patient, family members, and health care providers.[113]

There has also been a significant interest in "living wills" and "durable power of attorney." A living will is signed by a competent person in good health and gives permission to his or her doctor to turn off life-support systems in the case of terminal illness or a permanent coma. Thus the living will gives the person some control over his or her last few days or weeks of life. Because both the National Conference of Commissioners of Uniform State Laws and the American Bar Association have given their stamp of approval to the Uniform Rights of the Terminally Ill Act, the number of persons signing living wills is expected to increase. To prevent abuse, state laws in the area of living wills often specify specific conditions that must be met. For example, some states require that at least two physicians certify that the patient's illness is terminal. Some states require that the living will must be witnessed by people who are not health care providers or beneficiaries of the person's last will.

An option to a living will is for an individual to assign a permanent power of attorney to another person. In this scheme, another person, for example a spouse, a family member, or a friend, is designated as a surrogate health care decision maker in case a person is unable or incompetent to make decisions for herself or himself due to serious illness.

Conclusion: Medical Technology, Ethics, and Public Policy

The discussion on life-sustaining technology exemplifies the complexities of legal and ethical issues raised by modern medical technology. Similar complex issues are raised by health care technology in areas such as organ transplants[114] and reproductive technologies,[115] to name two. Organ transplants raise many ethical issues for donors, recipients, health care providers, and society as a whole. When is it ethical to donate organs? What criteria should be used in deciding who gets an organ transplant and who does not? Is it ethical to sell organs? Since it is reasonable to assume that there will always be more demand than supply of available organs, would it produce an economic market for organs where organs would be bought and sold like others goods and services? What are the ethical issues related to living donors versus the living but terminal donor? Is it ethical to end the life of a terminal patient in order to make an organ available?

Health care technology has also produced a revolution in reproductive processes that raises many difficult ethical problems. Ethical objections to artificial insemination are often raised on religious or theological grounds. Objections are also raised on the ground that artificial insemination produces harmful consequences for society when the woman is not married, when the donor is not screened, or when the identity of the donor is concealed. Similar ethical concerns are raised with *in vitro* fertilization (i.e., test-tube fertilization), surrogate parenthood, embryo transfers, and the use of frozen embryos and sperm banks.

Health care technology is developing at a rapid pace, while our capacity and ability to comprehend and deal with the legal and ethical issues raised by medical technology is lagging behind. As we approach the twenty-first century, policymakers will be increasingly confronted with the challenge of formulating public policies that require an understanding of legal and ethical implications of rapidly emerging new technologies. Despite this, at present no formal mechanism or forum is available at the national level in the United States that can allow for systematic examination of and debate over the legal and ethical issues dealing with health care technology. This is in sharp contrast to many other countries, where government-sponsored or encouraged bioethics forums have flourished. For example, governments of at least twenty-seven countries have established a national commission of some kind or have legislation pending to do so.[116]

Australia was one of the first countries to adopt legislation in 1984 regulating *in vitro* fertilization. In general, efforts at regulations in Australia have met with success at both the state and federal levels. At both levels of government, formal bodies exist that reflect on bioethical issues and have the authority to recommend regulatory responses.[117] Canada has also developed a national ethics forum with specific mandates to address ethical issues. This include groups such as the Advisory Committee on Medical, Ethical, Legal and Social Issues, the Royal Commission on New Reproductive Technologies, and the National Council on Bioethics in Human Research.[118]

Developments in the United States can be best characterized as a patchwork approach to bioethics. Most initiatives have tended to be private initiatives rather than government-sponsored initiatives. This has the advantage of producing multiple or pluralistic approaches which foster diversity. Private bodies also are under less political pressure.[119] But such approaches often lack the necessary authority to produce meaningful and timely responses. Kathi E. Hanna, Robert M. Cook-Deegan, and Robyn Y. Nishimi have advocated a new approach for the way in which the United States addresses issues arising out of bioethics. They have called for the establishment of a centralized national forum, a body along the lines of a presidential commission, which would conduct research, hold hearings, and address issues of broad public interest dealing with, for example, assisted suicide and life-sustaining and reproductive technologies. The same advocates have also recommended creation of an entity within the Department of Health and Human Services to establish protocols for federally funded biomedical experiments and research.[120] Such proposals have come under criticism from some quarters. For example, Ira H. Carmen argues that defining "good" biomedicine or "ethical" biomedicine cannot be done in the abstract. According to Carmen, our constitutional and political order requires a delicate weighing and balancing of competing interests by the policymakers. The Madisonian model that underlies our political system requires that the people's representatives working through the political branches formulate national policies and not some presidential commission.[121] Whether the Congress of the United States is up to the task remains to be seen.

8

Reforming the System

*Politics is how society manages conflicts about values and inter-
ests. The United States, a large, heterogeneous society with
complex cross-cutting divisions by race, ethnicity, class, region,
and more, naturally presents many such conflicts to manage.
Health care, an arena of high popular expectations, settled professional prerogative, and expenses that now total nearly $1 tril-
lion per year, piles on further problems of its own. The conflict
management that is politics, therefore, is not some nonrational
and inefficient sideshow that threatens the reformist visions of
the best and the brightest but rather a challenge central to making health reform come out for the better—indeed, come out at
all. And no issues trigger battles over values and interests more
quickly and acutely than do the source and use of money in
health reform proposals.*

—Lawrence D. Brown

As Brown states, reforming the health care system presents a huge
challenge.[1] Previous chapters have concentrated on specific aspects of health
care. Chapter 3 looked at Medicaid and chapter 4 examined Medicare. Chapter 5 examined the problems of the disadvantaged. Chapter 6 focused on cost
control and chapter 7 on technology. Chapters 1 and 2 presented some background material for understanding the context of health care policymaking in
the United States. Chapter 1 discussed the politics of health care and chapter
2 presented a history of health policy in the United States. But none of these
chapters provided a systematic examination of the health care system as a
whole. That is the purpose of this chapter.

We begin by looking at some of the problems of the health care system,
in a sense bringing together much of the material of the previous chapters.
We then look at economic critiques of the health care system, which sug-

gest major reform. Following that, we present some policy history of attempts at injecting competitive reforms into the health care system. In particular, we examine the development of ideas that eventually became known as managed care and managed competition. Using this as a focus, we look at the attempt to reform health care in the early 1990s and why that attempt failed. We also examine the role of the states and the private sector in the transformation of the American health care system. Finally, we make some predictions about the future of health care reform.

Systematic Problems

The problems of the health care system have been dealt with at length in this book. The overarching problem is one of finance. From an individual perspective, medical care is expensive. For those with adequate and secure sources of health insurance, medical costs are ameliorated. Even then, premiums for health insurance continue to rise. For those with no health insurance, public or private, cost is a key barrier (though not the only one) to obtaining care. Medicaid covers less than half the people whose income is below the poverty line. A growing number of people find that their health insurance is either inadequate or insecure.

Cost is also a problem for the business sector. Smaller firms are less likely to provide health insurance for their employees than larger firms, again primarily because of cost. Larger firms do provide health insurance, but the cost of providing that insurance has risen markedly. They have sought to manage those costs by cutting back, shifting more costs to employees, or moving their employees toward managed care plans.

For governments, health care costs are barely controllable. On the state level, Medicaid is one of the fastest-growing budgetary items. At the federal level, Medicare costs have grown faster than either the growth of the overall economy or government budgets. Governments have sought to control costs through reimbursement policies in both Medicaid and Medicare (DRGs, physician fee schedules), with some success. But the result has been either some cost shifting or fewer physicians participating in the programs (especially Medicaid).

Other problems exist. For those in inner cities or rural areas, there is an insufficient supply of providers. Medicaid eligibility does not guarantee service if few doctors are willing to accept Medicaid patients. Certain sectors of society, the poor and minorities, have less access to care and thus higher rates of health problems than the population at large. And some 14 percent of the population is not covered by health insurance.

From the systemic perspective, the United States spends more on health

care (absolutely and relatively) than any other country. It is the largest
sector of the American economy. Yet, by many health indicators (such as
infant mortality rates), the population is not necessarily healthier. Medical
technology is most developed in this country, yet that same technology
presents problems. It is one of the reasons for the cost problem. And it
creates ethical problems surrounding the issue of quality of life. Much of
the technology is "halfway" technology, which does not cure "but requires
months or years of extremely expensive life-prolonging therapies."[2]

Furthermore, and paradoxically, the United States has both the most
complex regulatory control over health care and the least control over the
system. Because of numerous decisions that have largely left medical care
in the hands of providers, insurers, and pharmaceutical and medical technology companies, government response has been at best reactive and piecemeal. Medicare and Medicaid (as well as other programs of the 1960s)
reinforced the predominant "interests and values," Lawrence Brown's terms
in the book's epigraph, of health providers and insurers. The federal tax
code aided in the development of private insurance but never challenged the
medical establishment.[3]

We have looked in various chapters at attempts to overhaul the system
through national health insurance. Some six tries have failed, most recently
in 1994. But alongside those attempts at nationalizing health care were
critiques of the system and of government's role based on an economic
analysis of health care, and they led to calls for reform. These critiques
would eventually become married to some form of national health insurance, relying on competition strategies, and peaking in the 1990s.

The Economic Critique

The economic critique begins with a consideration of some classic works in
economics. The "bible" of economics is Adam Smith's *The Wealth of Nations,* published in 1776.[4] Smith argued that unfettered markets, free from
government or monopoly interference, would produce the greatest benefits
for humankind. Such markets were the most efficient, producing precisely
the amounts of a good or service that producers want to sell and that
consumers want to buy through the price mechanism. Anything that impeded the price mechanism would lower efficiency.

Smith's work formed the basis for classical (and neoclassical) economics
and remains an important part of American ideology. The American bias
has always been toward free markets and away from government, though as
we see below, in health care (and in other areas) the viability of free,
competitive markets is questionable.

Frederick Hayek, writing just at the end of World War II, warned the country of moving toward more government control.[5] Most influential was Milton Friedman's *Capitalism and Freedom*. Friedman argued that economic freedom, a capitalist society, was the support for political freedom. He discussed a number of policy issues showing how free markets would work better than government intervention or control.[6]

So what is the economic critique of the health care system that dates back to Adam Smith? The critique is that the incentive structure of health care moves the system toward inefficiencies. It does this in several ways. Consider the traditional fee-for-service, third-party payment system.[7]

There are four parts to the transaction: the patient with health insurance seeks a service; the patient sees a doctor, who provides that service; the doctor's charges depend on the amount of services provided; the more services, the higher the charge (that is why it is called fee for service). The doctor knows that the patient is covered by health insurance provided by the employer through an insurance company. The patient pays the bill and then files a claim with the insurance company for reimbursement. In some instances, the health insurance policy is so generous that the patient does not have to pay anything. In other cases, the doctor's office files the claim and bills the patient for the balance after the claim is paid. Depending on the policy, the patient may have met the deductible for the year and may have limited copayments. The insurance company processes the claim and either pays the doctor or reimburses the patient. The employer pays the premiums on the employee's health insurance and may also (if the policy is especially generous) pay premiums for dependents. If not, then the employee pays the premiums, but at a group rate.

Who is concerned about the cost of care and the quality and efficiency of care (whether a particular test or treatment was really necessary) under such a system? If the doctor and the patient both know that third-party insurance will cover the cost, there is little concern. As long as the premiums cover the reimbursements (plus a profit), the insurer does not care. As long as premium costs are reasonable, and the federal government allows a business tax deduction for premiums (an incentive to cover or continue coverage), the employer does not care. The same situation is true for hospital care.

That is exactly the point that economic reformers seek to make. Under this kind of situation, typical up through most of the 1980s, the cost and price of service is irrelevant. Economists argue that in the absence of paying the true cost of care, consumers will demand more health care than they really need, a problem labeled "moral hazard."[8]

Health care suffers from another problem that impedes the operation of free, competitive markets: imperfect information. Providers have considerable information and expertise (though not complete information) and are in a power position compared to other actors, especially consumers/patients. Thus additional treatments are not the result of consumer demand for them, but of provider requests. In that sense health care is provider driven, rather than consumer driven. Furthermore, consumers do not shop around comparing service and price at critical times (e.g., during a heart attack). Imperfect information, power asymmetries, and lack of a clear price mechanism work together to create market failures in health care. The problem is how to solve those problems.

Market Reforms

The simplest way to reform health care markets focuses on the consumer and insurance. The more generous the insurance policy, the less likely that costs are a consideration. So the obvious solution would be to make health insurance less generous. Insurance may have what is known as "first-dollar coverage," beginning coverage with the smallest illnesses. Rather than cover everything, a catastrophic health insurance policy might be substituted. Such a policy would go into effect after a rather high deductible was met, perhaps as a percentage of family income.

A typical health insurance policy might have a $300 deductible (some have no deductibles). After the first $300 of medical expenses, 80 percent or more of further medical expenses might be covered by insurance. But what if the policy were changed so that the deductible were $2,000 or 10 percent of a family's income? Then the consumer/patient would have to bear the expenses of further care and might not go to the doctor for every cold or sniffle. Only truly needed care would be undertaken. Further, the family would be protected from very high medical expenses (such as a cancer operation and treatment) after the deductible was met. Moreover, as we know with automobile insurance, the higher the deductible, the lower the premium to the worker and/or employer.

There is an element of simplicity to such plans, which were proposed in the late 1970s and early 1980s. But consumers preferred first-dollar coverage, and the plans never went anywhere.

Such catastrophic plans concentrated on what could be called the "demand side" of health care, the consumer. But most reform plans focused on the "supply side" of health care, the provider.[9] To do this would mean changing the incentives built into the traditional system and trying to create more competitive markets.

The first attempt at a supply-side, market-reform solution came in the 1960s and 1970s. This was the "health maintenance strategy" mentioned in chapters 2 and 6. The strategy, the brainchild of Dr. Paul Ellwood, was an elegant idea.[10] Based on already existing prepaid group plans (PGPs), the idea was to limit the money available to providers through a capitation system. The health maintenance organization (HMO) enrolls subscribers, who pay a monthly premium. Those premiums constitute the total budget for the HMO. Providing more services does not produce more revenues. So the incentive was not to overtreat, as market reformers argue exists within the fee-for-service system, but to treat only as necessary. The HMO became the prototype of a managed care organization (in 1990s language), one that would review services and try to eliminate unnecessary care.

There was a further hope behind the HMO strategy: HMOs would create competitive pressures on the fee-for-service system so that all providers and insurers would begin to look at costs. As HMOs penetrated a market, competitive pressures would increase. This idea was embodied in the 1973 Health Maintenance Organization Act to promote with federal assistance the development of HMOs. Into the 1980s, at least, the competitive impact of the strategy was questionable.

The second stage came in the late 1970s and early 1980s. Alain Enthoven took the competitive strategy a step further by suggesting a complete reorganization of the health care system, in essence national health insurance. Originally writing in the 1970s in the *New England Journal of Medicine* (and other journals) and then in his 1980 book *Health Plan*, Enthoven wanted to eliminate the employment-insurance connection.[11]

The Consumer Choice Health Plan (CCHP) was a form of national health insurance that would work as follows:[12] Providers and insurers would organize into competitive health care plans. Each plan would then determine what its premiums would be. The federal government would estimate the average cost of care in various geographical areas and pay a percentage of that average cost through tax credits or 100 percent of the average cost for the poor via vouchers. CCHP featured an open-enrollment period, community rating (see chapter 5), and a limit on out-of-pocket costs. Consumers would then choose among the competing plans, which could include a traditional fee-for-service plan, an HMO, a plan with a very high deductible, and so forth. Each plan would charge a different premium, but the federal government would pay the same amount regardless of plan chosen. Thus, consumers would face the decision of what plan to choose depending on the financial consequences for them. The newly regained place of price signals plus open enrollments would create the competition among the plans and restrain (one hoped) the costs. Thus health care would be consumer driven rather than cost driven.

A somewhat less ambitious version of CCHP built on the employment-based insurance system already in place. For those with work-based insurance, the employer would pay the same premium for each employee regardless of which plan was chosen. Employees would have a choice of plans, with similar features, as mentioned above. For the poor or those without employment-based insurance, vouchers from the federal government could be used.

Competition plans created a great deal of interest in the late 1970s and early 1980s.[13] Congressmen Richard Schweiker (R-Pa.) and David Stockman (R-Mich.) offered bills based on the CCHP. In 1981 Schweiker became the secretary of the Department of Health and Human Services (HHS) and Stockman became director of the Office of Management and Budget in the Reagan administration. A task force within HHS was created to investigate competitive ideas; however, nothing further came of the effort, perhaps because CCHP or a variant was essentially a form of national health insurance at a time when the Reagan administration was seeking to reduce the federal government's role.

In addition, several practical developments began to move toward competitive plans. One was a focus on deregulating the health care industry but engaging in vigorous anticompetitive regulation.[14] For example, the AMA had for a long time opposed the group practice of medicine, arguing that it trespassed on the traditional autonomy of the individual practitioner. Over time, the AMA's opposition lessened, though it still has some problems with managed care organizations.

Two developments among public employers provided some experience with choosing among competitive plans. The Federal Employees Health Benefits Program (FEHBP) allows federal employees to choose among competing plans while the federal government provides level premium contributions. A similar program was established in California, the California Public Employees' Retirement System (CalPERS), which enrolls nearly a million public employees at all levels of government. CalPERS is a purchasing cooperative that negotiates with a number of different plans, such as HMOs, preferred provider organizations (PPOs) and traditional fee-for-service plans.[15]

In the late 1980s and early 1990s, Ellwood, who had moved from Minnesota to Jackson Hole, Wyoming, formed a working group to develop a strategy for change based on the idea of managed competition. The work group and guests "included academics, public officials and leaders of the insurance and health industries."[16]

Enthoven, perhaps the chief theorist of the Jackson Hole group, began advocating managed competition in the late 1980s and continued into the 1990s.[17] Managed competition is an attempt to marry several different ideas—national health insurance, insurance reform, managed care, organization of providers and purchasers, and choice for consumers—while building on the present system.

Managed Competition

The managed competition proposal was designed, according to Enthoven and Kronick, to meet two major goals: "to provide financial protection from health care expenses for all . . . and to promote the development of economical financing and delivery arrangements."[18] This would be done by enabling those not already in Medicare or Medicaid to purchase health insurance either through their employer or through a public sponsor organized by the states. The purpose of aggregating purchasers of insurance, either through employment or through sponsors (health care alliances) would be to allow them to bargain with and contract with provider organizations, such as HMOs, PPOs, or the traditional fee-for-service system (or some other of the many possibilities).

Employers would pay a specific amount for full-time employees and dependents and pay a payroll tax for those not covered.[19] The employer contribution would be 80 percent of an average of the price of plans offered (a defined-contribution regardless of plan chosen); subscribers would pay the difference. The tax laws would be changed to limit contributions by employers beyond the specified amount. Those not covered by an employer plan, such as those who are self-employed, would pay into the public sponsor plans, up to an income ceiling. The program would also include subsidies to pay for the premiums of the poor (not covered by Medicaid) and for small businesses.

Employers and sponsors would then negotiate with qualified health plans, made up of some combination of providers and insurers, who would offer a variety of plans. Subscribers would elect a plan each year. The federal government would collect the funds and make determinations about average costs of plans. The program could be run entirely by the federal government or by both the states and the federal government. Medicaid and Medicare would be left alone, at least at first, though recipients would be encouraged to join HMOs.

Like the earlier CCHP, the intent is to promote efficient organization of health providers and provide competition among that organization. The major difference between the earlier and later plans is that purchasers would also be aggregated and be in a position to bargain with providers, not at the time of the occurrence of an illness but at the point of purchasing coverage.[20] While the plan does not attempt radical surgery on the health care system, the hope is that forces put into place will in fact create significant changes, cover virtually the entire population, and cost less than the present system.

Moving toward Reform

The push for managed competition was one of the forces that led to a renewed focus on health care in the 1990s. The problems of the health care system were also creating a momentum toward change. The increasing costs of heath care to business and government and the associated rise in the cost of premiums were major problems. There were other difficulties as well, many created by cost problems. Fewer workers found themselves covered by employer-based health insurance. The number of uninsured kept rising, with about 14 percent of the population lacking health insurance (see chapter 5). The problem of the uninsured was compounded by growing economic insecurity. Even those with health insurance were fearful that if they or their dependents became sick, their health insurance would be inadequate. Changing jobs might result in losing coverage for a preexisting problem. Medicaid seemed to cover smaller and smaller proportions of families with incomes below the poverty rate. All of this was exacerbated by the recession of 1990–91 and the reengineering of corporations to become more efficient and competitive (i.e., more productive with the same or fewer workers).

One response to the growing problems was the report of the Pepper Commission, originally known as the U.S. Bipartisan Commission on Comprehensive Health Care. Created in 1988, the report called for coverage for long-term care and for universal coverage for those under the age of sixty-five. Medicare would be retained, but Medicaid would be phased out. The report proposed the elimination of experience rating among insurance companies.[21] While there was more consensus on the long-term coverage than on universal coverage, there was no agreement on financing. Nevertheless, the Pepper Commission report was another factor in moving toward consideration of change.

Perhaps the most important factor was political.[22] The political aspect was set off by an unusual off-year senatorial election in Pennsylvania. Republican Senator John Heinz died in a plane crash in 1991, and Democratic Governor Bob Casey appointed Harris Wofford to the seat. Wofford would have to run in a special November 1991 election to see who would fill the remainder of Heinz's term (which was up in 1994). Wofford's Republican opponent was one of the most popular politicians in Pennsylvania, Richard Thornburgh. Thornburgh, at the time attorney general of the

United States in the Bush administration, had previously been governor of the state. He resigned his position and was widely expected to win against the little-known Wofford.

To the surprise of everyone, Wofford won. In his campaign, Wofford played up the economic insecurity issue, focusing on heath care. His memorable campaign sound bite was that if we had the right to a lawyer, we should have the right to health insurance. Wofford's call for national health insurance resonated well among the voters and was widely considered to be one of the major factors in his victory.

The Pennsylvania off-year election demonstrated that health care could be a powerful campaign tool. In December 1991 Democrats began holding "town meetings" to discuss health care. Potential Democratic presidential candidates met on television to discuss health care. A group of touring Democratic senators held hearings and news conferences around the country. A majority of House Democrats held a simultaneous town meeting in January 1992.[23]

In February 1992 President Bush announced a health care initiative that would cost an additional $100 billion over a five-year period, to be paid for by limits on Medicare and Medicaid. The plan was based on tax credits and vouchers. Tax credits up to $3,750 per year would go to families with incomes up to $70,000 (and phased out for higher-income families, with those with incomes higher than $80,000 not having the credit). For poor families, a voucher equal to that amount would be issued. For the self-employed, there would be a tax deduction equal to the size of the premiums. Small business would be given tax inducements to band together and spread risk. There would also be some mild insurance reform.[24] The plan was a limited one and vague in detail, especially concerning cost control. Further, the plan did not address long-term care and was administratively complex. Finally, the value of the tax credits, deductions, and vouchers would erode over time. This was true because their value would be indexed to the consumer price index (CPI), but the cost of insurance premiums generally climbs faster than the CPI. Thus the amount of insurance the voucher or tax incentives could buy would decrease over time. Nevertheless, the Bush plan was an important piece in moving health care reform forward.[25]

But even at this early stage of the health care reform debate the outlook for change was troubling. This reflected the presence of interest groups representing those with the major financial stakes in health care. They included providers, such as the American Medical Association and specialty groups, the American Hospital Association and specialty hospital groups such as those representing the for-profit or proprietary sector, insurance groups such as the Health Insurance Association of America and a group representing the four largest insurers such as Aetna, and business groups of all sizes. While larger employers supported employer mandates, small businesses did not. The American College of Physicians came out in favor of a cap on spending and a managed competition plan.[26]

The lobbyists and lawyers for these groups continued their efforts into 1994, and their impact was largely one of impeding change or, to put it another way, of protecting their interests. According to one observer of the health policy scene:

> On the whole, health-care lobbyists have had the effect of retarding change and blocking it. That's because most of the effort has come from smart, well-financed groups that have a vested interest in the status quo. They do a good job of pointing out the potential risks and costs of change, but there is little information about the broader public interest in the benefits of change.[27]

Meyer's comment is an example of a pervasive problem of American politics and government. As government, especially at the federal level, has sought to do more, more groups with stakes in the outcome of government deliberations have risen. Each program that government undertakes, whether a subsidy, a tax credit, or services, has interest groups to protect it. In 1979 there were about 117 national health care interest groups; by 1992 that number had increased to 741, an increase of over 500 percent.[28]

The more general problem is one that has been labeled *demosclerosis*.[29] As Rauch describes it, demosclerosis is a kind of hardening of the arteries, or arteriosclerosis. As the number of interest groups increase, and their lawyers, lobbyists, and consultants increase, government is less likely to cut unneeded programs or make needed changes that might adversely affect an interest. This early stage of the health care reform debate started ominously.

The initiative for the Bush plan was clearly the coming presidential elections (as well as the 1991 Pennsylvania senatorial elections). Arkansas Governor Bill Clinton promised that he would offer a health care plan. To support Clinton, Democratic leaders in the House of Representatives offered a health plan in June 1992 similar to one that Clinton was discussing. The plan would extend coverage to most, but not all, of the uninsured, and contained provisions to control costs (price controls). The politics of the situation was clear: the Democrats offered a plan knowing that President Bush would veto it, thus giving them a campaign issue.[30] In a preview of the split among congressional Democrats in 1993–94, conservative Democrats in the House offered a plan, sponsored by Jim Cooper (D-Tenn.), based on managed competition but with spending limitations.[31]

By October 1992, both President Bush and Governor Clinton had endorsed managed competition as the centerpiece of their health care plans.

The difference between the two proposals was that the Bush plan relied on tax incentives while the Clinton proposal also had mandates and spending limitations. Both proposals would, at least in the short run, increase health care expenditures.[32] With Clinton's election in November 1992 health care reform would be placed solidly on the governmental agenda.

Health Care Reform on the Front Burner

It appeared that after all the previously failed attempts in this century, health care reform and national health insurance had finally arrived. Most thought that change would take place, and many sought to benefit from it. The insurance industry, long an opponent of federal regulation, began to advocate universal health insurance. The major interest group, the Health Insurance Association of America (HIAA), advocated tax incentives, an individual mandate to purchase insurance (and possibly an employer mandate), and insurance reform. Part of the reasoning behind the insurance industry move was to become a player in reform. The industry also felt that it would benefit substantially from reform because more people would be buying insurance.[33]

Further, early public opinion polls supported President Clinton's efforts. A strong majority of the public, which included supporters of President Bush, felt that the president would be successful in extending health insurance coverage.[34] A poll several months later found that support for change remained, but that support was in some cases shaky. There was backing for change and even for paying additional taxes, under some circumstances. Typically, most Americans expressed dissatisfaction with the health care system as a whole, but satisfaction with their own coverage and their own doctors. But the results of the poll also showed what would eventually become a problem for the Clinton plan: "the political conundrum that some analysts see at the heart of the health-care debate: The public wants the current quality of care, at a lower cost and with the assurance that they will never lose it."[35] Other poll results showed that physicians favored universal health coverage and supported managed competition. This was true even though managed competition would likely reduce physician income.[36]

To develop a health care reform plan, Clinton set up a series of task forces, composed of some 500 people, headed by First Lady Hillary Rodham Clinton and Ira Magaziner. The task force, composed of people in government and the private sector, met in secret over a period of months. Details of the plan leaked out, with the major roadblock being how to finance the plan. The alleged secretness of the task force meetings became a point of controversy. According to one account, Clinton and his aides had decided on the overall health care reform plan prior to the inauguration in January 1993.[37] The outlines of what became the Clinton plan were mentioned during the campaign, "competition within a budget," and a proposal and rationale for such a plan were published in book form in 1992.[38] Some charged that the meetings violated the Federal Advisory Committee Act because private-sector people were involved. Others, especially industry representatives, complained that they were left out of the deliberations, though members of the task force met with outside groups as well as members of Congress and their staffs.[39]

The president's plan was presented to the nation in September 1993 and a bill was sent to Congress the next month. The proposal, entitled the Health Security Act, had several fundamental value premises. One, captured by the title of the bill, was security. The bill provided for universal coverage through an employer mandate and subsidies for poor people and workers without health insurance. The Clinton motto was health care that's always there.[40] There would be a minimum benefits package covering the following services: hospital, emergency, physician, clinical preventive, mental health and substance abuse, family planning, pregnancy related, hospice, home health care, extended care, ambulance, outpatient laboratory and diagnostic, outpatient prescription and biologicals, outpatient rehabilitation, durable medical equipment, vision and hearing, preventive dental services for children, and health education classes.[41] There were of course limitations on the services. For example, the extended-care services were limited to 100 days a year.

The plan was based on the concept of managed competition.[42] All would belong to a health alliance, a purchasing cooperative, that would be set up by the states. Large corporations (5,000 or more workers) could set up their own health alliances. Similarly, insurers and providers would establish plans. The alliances and plans would negotiate and subscribers would be offered a minimum of three plans. One would be a health maintenance organization providing all services to subscribers. A second would be the traditional fee-for-service system, the most expensive plan in terms of premiums and copayments. The third alternative was a hybrid or combination plan. This might be a preferred provider organization, where subscribers would get discounts for providers on the approved list.

The plan also specified how people would pay for health care. For example, self-employed workers would pay their own health premiums up to a point ($1,800 for individuals and $4,200 for families), and all premiums would be fully tax deductible. In the case of employees, employers would pay 80 percent of the premiums and workers the remainder. For small employers (fewer than fifty workers), there would be government subsidies to employers. The unemployed would receive government subsidies for premiums. Medicaid would be eliminated, but the federal and state governments would pay the premiums for the poor (though only for the low-cost plans). Medicare would remain and the federal government would pay the bills. For retired people under the age of sixty-five, the federal government would pay the premiums.

The plan continually referred to employers paying 80 percent of the premiums. The reference was to 80 percent of the average cost of premiums for the alliances (defined contribution). Subscribers would pay the additional amount. This, as mentioned earlier, was an essential component of consumer choice: give the consumer a financial stake in the decision of which plan to choose. The alliances would also work toward insurance reform, so that experience rating would not be allowed, but some premium adjustments based on risk could be granted.

The Clinton proposal also discussed financing. Part of the financing would come from employers and subscribers. While mid-size and large businesses paid for health insurance, small employers were less likely to. Through the employer mandate, they would now be brought into the system. Even those who were uninsured would be contributing. Thus about 75 percent of the financing for health care under the Health Security Act would come from the private sector.[43] A second source of funds was savings from Medicaid and Medicare. Medicaid would be eliminated entirely, and there would be savings in Medicare. The plan was less specific about new sources of financing. After considering a number of options, a tax on tobacco was the most politically feasible one.

The Health Security Act also focused on cost control. Both managed competition and managed care would help restrain cost increases. Analysts believed that a sizable portion of the population would choose the HMO or other managed care option. This would, as explained above and in chapters 2 and 6, change the incentive structure of medical care toward more efficient care and away from cost-increasing, dubious services. The competition-inducing effect, based on experience with the federal employees program, California, and elsewhere, would also lower costs and change the system toward more integrated care. Finally, supporters of the plan argued that the Health Security Act would reduce administrative complexity. All these things, it was hoped, would eventually result in lowered costs.[44] The Clinton administration recognized that in the near future costs would have to go up because more of the population would have health insurance.

But what if managed competition and managed care did not restrain cost increases? The Clinton plan contained a set of backup regulatory provisions. This "second line of defense" was a cap or ceiling on growth of insurance premiums.[45] Starr describes how the premium caps would work:

> Under the Clinton plan, the caps apply not to the premiums of individual health plans but to an alliance's weight-average premium (the average of all premiums weighted according to the share of enrollment in the various plans). Federal legislation would set a growth rate for premiums for covered benefits for the country as a whole, and the National Health Board would adjust that rate for specific alliances depending on demographic changes and other factors. Alliances could meet their targets without any enforcement of caps as competition held down premium increases of individual plans or as consumers switched out of high-cost plans, thereby dragging down the average. If, however, health plans' bids threatened to push an alliance's average over the allowable growth, the federal government would deny full rate increases to the plans seeking the biggest jumps and require the plans to pass on these rate reductions to their providers.[46]

As can be seen from this brief description, the Clinton proposal was a complex one, over 1,300 pages in length. It was a combination of ideas. It contained an employer mandate (and to some extent an individual mandate for the unemployed) combined with subsidies for both businesses and individuals. It promised universal coverage. It allowed for the possibility of a single-payer system, by permitting states to establish such a system if they wished. Most important, it sought to reform the health care system through a set of health care purchasing cooperative alliances and incentives for providers to integrate into more efficient units. It sought to marry competition with regulation.

The Clinton plan was therefore not a pure plan. While it provided for universal coverage, insurance, and administrative reforms, it did not adopt a single-payer system. Such a system is simpler than either the present system or the one envisioned under the Clinton plan. It was not viewed as politically feasible, however, and the Clinton plan sought to build on the present employer-based insurance system. It was also designed to meet the needs of various constituencies.[47]

Insurance companies in general would benefit in two ways. First, a larger proportion of the population would be covered. Second, insurers could be major forces behind the provider plans. This would be more true for large insurance companies such as Aetna and Prudential.

Business would also benefit from the plan in several ways. It was true that there would be an employer mandate. This was good from the standpoint of large businesses, because with everyone covered and more paying, cost shifting would effectively be ended. For small businesses, there were subsidies and limitations on their contributions. Further, the Health Security Act would cover early retirees (those under sixty-five and therefore not yet eligible for Medicare), a growing cost burden for larger employers.

Thus there appeared to be something for everyone. States had an important role, managed competition would be tried, everyone would be covered. The plan, as originally estimated, would reduce the budget deficit in the long run as health care costs were restrained.

The initial reaction to the Clinton plan was positive. Public opinion, at least initially, supported the change, though there was some concern about the complexity of the plan and the additional layers of bureaucracy and government regulation that the plan proposed. In the early stages, both interest groups and Republicans supported the plan to remain part of the action.[48]

It should be further noted that despite the complexity of the plan and the effort that went into the formulation stage, the Clinton administration never saw the plan as one written in stone. They knew the plan would be modified in Congress; this was the opening move.[49] Indeed, some of the provisions, such as a generous benefits package, high employer cost sharing, and strict limitations on the growth of insurance premiums, were designed to allow some negotiating room.[50]

It was also clear that despite the administration's attempt to meet the needs of various constituencies, there would be still be those who won and lost by the Clinton plan. Younger people would be asked to pay more, as would those in rural areas. Working couples would also be losers under the Clinton plan because both would have to pay for health insurance, rather than rely on one job for insurance. Couples with self-employed spouses, who paid nothing, would also be dramatic losers.[51] Similar estimates could be made among providers and insurers. Primary-care physicians would be winners, and specialists would be losers. This is true because under managed care arrangements, especially HMOs, primary-care physicians would act as "gatekeepers," deciding when additional services were necessary. Specialists, therefore, would be more limited in their ability to offer services. Doctors who joined health care plans would be both winners and losers. They would be winners in that they would be guaranteed access to patients and losers in that they would lose some autonomy and perhaps some income. Doctors who did not join plans would likely be losers because they would not be able to hold on to their patients. Large insurers would be able to organize health care plans, whereas small and medium-size insurers would not.[52]

The Legislative Stage

Deliberations over the health care reform plan did not begin until 1994, an election year. One of the key aspects of the legislative process is that a complex plan such as the Health Security Act is generally shared among a number of congressional committees. The bill was divided among six committees in the House and five in the Senate.[53] To pass health care legislation would take strong leadership on the part of the majority Democrats. While health care reform bills did emerge from several House committees, no Senate committee reported a bill.

One problem was financing. A study by Lewin-VHI, a health care consulting firm, found the cost estimates optimistic. The original estimate of the additional costs of the program was $286 billion over a five-year period. The Lewin study estimated that the program would cost about $78 billion more than the administration estimate over the same period. So, rather than reduce the budget deficit by $103 billion, it would decrease it by about $25 billion.[54] During the deliberations of the task force in 1993, economists in the Treasury Department argued that the cost figures were not reliable.[55]

Doubts were also expressed about various aspects of the health plan. For example, an early 1994 report by the Congressional Budget Office said that the regional alliances were being asked to do numerous complex tasks in a very short period of time. The tasks included "the functions of purchasing agents, contract negotiators, welfare agencies, financial intermediaries, collectors of premiums, developers and managers of information systems, and coordinators of the flow of information about themselves and other alliances."[56]

Even those whose support should easily be forthcoming criticized the Clinton plan. The Jackson Hole group opposed the plan on a number of grounds. Enthoven wrote that the plan promised too much (covering everyone, restraining costs) and would likely not result in cuts in Medicare. He opposed the employer mandate. The group also did not like the price controls that were an important part of the plan. More important, Enthoven stated that the Clinton plan had taken the idea of health care cooperatives of a limited size and changed them into monstrous alliances.[57] Enthoven favored a bill by Congressman Cooper (see below). In response, Paul Starr, a member of the Clinton health care reform task force and one of its leading advocates, argued that in some respects the Clinton plan was quite close to what Enthoven had previously written. For example, Starr pointed out that Enthoven had favored an employer mandate but no longer did so. Further, Starr noted that Enthoven took a strong antigovernment position about the Clinton plan, yet the Jackson Hole proposals would require significant government involvement to help structure markets.[58]

The Clinton plan was not the only one put before Congress. Some six alternative plans were proposed, some by Democrats, others by Republicans.[59] The Clinton plan had 100 cosponsors in the House and 31 in the

Senate.[60] The Democratic proposals were divided among two widely disparate proposals. On the left, Senator Paul Wellstone's (D-Minn.) and Congressman Jim McDermott's (D-Wash.) bill called for a single-payer approach to be administered by the states. That bill had ninety-two cosponsors in the House and five in the Senate. On the right, Congressman Jim Cooper (D-Tenn.) and Senator John Breaux (D-La.) sponsored a bill that was sometimes referred to as "Clinton-lite." Their bill would expand access to insurance through voluntary cooperatives, subsidies for low-income people, and insurance reform. The Cooper bill had fifty-seven cosponsors in the House and four in the Senate.

Republicans offered three different plans. One bill, offered by House Minority Leader Robert Michel (R-Ill.) and Senator Trent Lott (R-Miss.), expanded access to insurance but contained no mandate. It was a voluntary program that expanded Medicaid and provided for insurance reforms. Employers had to offer their employees health insurance, though they did not have to pay for it. The bill had 139 cosponsors in the House and 10 in the Senate. A second Republican bill was offered by Congressman Stearns (R-Fla.) and Senator Don Nickles (R-Okla.). The bill was a voluntary program but had penalties for individuals not purchasing catastrophic insurance. There would be tax changes regarding the deductibility of health costs and expansion of Medicaid. The bill had eighteen cosponsors in the House and twenty-five in the Senate. The final bill was the one offered by Congressman William Thomas (R-Calif.) and Senator John Chafee (R-R.I.). The bill was basically an individual mandate to purchase insurance and enroll in a plan (either government, employer, or purchasing cooperative). Employers had to offer coverage but did not have to pay for it. Those not purchasing insurance would be penalized. The bill also called for an individual mandate to purchase long-term care insurance. The Thomas/Chafee bill had four cosponsors in the House and twenty in the Senate.

The abundance of plans did not necessarily translate into support for health care reform. There seemed to be a consensus that some change would take place, given the Democratic majority in Congress and the priority placed on reform by the Clinton administration. But the motives of those proposing and supporting the other plans varied. Some wanted to show that they were involved and wanted to have a say in the final outcome. Others had particular features they wanted included in a health care reform bill. Some wanted to show that they were concerned about the issue.[61]

As the debate over health care reform moved closer to congressional deliberation, however, support for the plan began to diminish. Interest groups began to attack individual portions of the plan. Perhaps the strongest opposition came from the National Federation of Independent Businesses

(NFIB), the association of small businesses. NFIB opposed the employer mandate and lobbied against the Clinton plan from the beginning.

Another major opponent was the Health Insurance Association of America (HIAA). A trade association of most of the nation's insurance companies, it felt that its members were left out of the plan. Unlike the largest insurance companies, they would not be able to sponsor or work with alliances and so would be forced out of business. They, therefore, opposed alliances; they also argued that the Clinton plan reduced patients' choice of doctors. The insurance industry was not of one mind, however. The five largest insurance companies (Aetna, Cigna, Metlife, Prudential, and Travelers) formed the Alliance for Managed Competition and sponsored ads promoting managed competition and managed care. This did not, nevertheless, translate into support for the Clinton plan.

This is not to say that no interest groups supported the Clinton plan. The Democratic National Committee was given a major role in sending out mail to contributors and potential contributors for their campaign in support of health care reform. The liberal group Families USA also engaged in direct-mail campaigns. Conservative groups likewise utilized direct mail.[62] Interest groups (about 650 of them) and lobbyists on both sides showered key congressmen and senators with campaign contributions. For example, from 1 January 1993 to 31 May 1994, the AMA political action committee gave almost $1 million in contributions.[63]

Interest groups on both sides also turned toward the grass roots, trying to mobilize supporters for their positions in the districts. Some of the grass-roots support was genuine, especially on the part of employees of tobacco firms arguing against additional taxes on tobacco products and small business owners arguing against employer mandates.[64] Other support was manufactured (sometimes known as "AstroTurf" lobbying):

> Pharmaceutical companies, for instance, are writing to their shareholders warning them that profits could suffer if price controls impede new drug research. Planned Parenthood is encouraging its members to deluge Congress with a post-card campaign demanding that abortion services, prenatal care and estrogen replacement therapy are covered under a proposed insurance blanket.[65]

A portion of the health care reform debate was fought through advertising, both print and electronic. The most famous of the television ad campaigns were the "Harry and Louise" and "Libby and Louise" ads by the Health Insurance Association of America. HIAA's major problems with the Clinton health care plan were threefold: it opposed the ceiling or cap on insurance premiums, it opposed the requirement that people join the regional cooperatives (because smaller and midsize insurance companies would not be large enough to participate and would be forced out of the business) and it opposed community rating. As an example of the kind of pitch made in the HIAA ads, consider the following:

> *Harry:* I'm glad the President's doing something about health care reform.
> *Louise:* He's right, We need it.
> *Harry:* Some of these details—
> *Louise:* Like a limit on health care?
> *Harry:* Really.
> *Louise:* The Government caps how much the country can spend on health care and says, "That's it!"
> *Harry:* So, what if our health plan runs out of money?
> *Louise:* There's got to be a better way.[66]

A related HIAA ad saw Louise and her business partner, Libby, discussing the Clinton plan:

> *Libby:* I want Congress to pass health care reform . . .
> *Louise:* Make sure everyone is covered.
> *Libby:* . . . but not force us to buy our insurance from these mandatory Government "health alliances."
> *Louise:* So we couldn't choose a plan that's not on their list even if we think it's better for our employees and their families.
> *Libby:* Not according to this. *(Holds up president's health plan.)*
> *Louise:* But Congress can fix that—cover everyone and let us pick the plan we want.
> *Libby:* And they will, if we send them that message.
> *Announcer:* For the facts you need to send a message, call today.[67]

Opponents of the Clinton plan used ads to attack various aspects of the proposal. Some, such as the Project for the Republican Future, argued that the greatest jeopardy to health care security was in fact the Clinton plan. Others, such as HIAA, attacked the plan as bureaucratic and restricting choice. Still others argued that the plan would cost more for people currently with coverage.[68]

The ads were often incorrect or misleading. Some suggested that the Clinton plan would reduce choice of doctors. The reality is that the Clinton plan might in fact have increased choice for certain segments of the population.[69] Other ads attacked health care alliances long after that idea had been dropped by Congress.[70]

Supporters of the program were also active. The Democratic National Committee ran a series of ads that counterattacked and parodied the "Harry and Louise" ads. In the DNC version, the couple get injured, lose their health insurance, and Harry loses his job. Louise turns to Harry and says:

"You said universal coverage was too complicated. You said you'd never lose your job, so we'd always be covered. You said, what would we do when the government runs out of money? Well who's out of money now, Harry?" The ad closed with the tag line, "There is a better way. Tell Congress you want what they already have: the security of affordable, universal health care."[71] A coalition of consumer, labor, civic, professional, and other groups ran a newspaper and radio campaign touting the benefits of health care reform.[72] Pro-choice and pro-life groups ran ads on whether health reform should include or exclude abortion provisions.[73] Another parody of the "Harry and Louise" ads came from those sponsoring a single-payer system, with the tag line delivered by comedienne Anne Meara, "Harry and Louise, there *is* a better way." Of course the money raised by those supporting the single-payer plan was dwarfed by other interests.[74]

The ads may have made a bigger impact on the Clinton administration and the media than on the public. The Clinton administration attacked the ads and, as noted, the Democratic National Committee ran ads parodying them. News media focused on the ads and the attacks on them and attributed to them more power than perhaps they had. A study testing the effectiveness of the "Harry and Louise" ads found little retention of the content of the ads and showed little effect of the ads on attitudes.[75]

Another way that opponents of health care reform had of attacking the plan was to suggest that while the country's health care problems were serious, they were not critical, requiring radical surgery. For example, Senate Minority Leader Robert Dole (R-Kans.) stated in January 1994 that there was no crisis in health care; Senate Finance Committee Chairman Daniel Patrick Moynihan (D-N.Y.) made a similar point.[76] Public opinion polls gave ambiguous signs about whether the public saw a crisis. When asked to name the country's most important problems, only 7 percent listed health care (considerably behind the economy and crime). On the other hand, when asked whether the country faced a health care crisis, a problem, or no crisis, 57 percent said it had a crisis and 42 percent said a problem. Further, most people were satisfied with the quality of health care they received and with their health insurance. At the same time, a sizable majority favored universal health insurance.[77] To some extent, the idea of a crisis in health care in the early 1990s that could fuel an upset victory by Harris Wofford was caused by the economic conditions of that time. The recession of 1990–91, the continued increase in health care costs, and the diminishment of health insurance coverage among workers also contributed to the feeling of a crisis. But as the economy recovered from the recession and began to expand, and health care cost increases moderated, the atmosphere of crisis diminished. Between the lessened crisis atmosphere, heavy lobbying, and advertising on the part of opponents, public support for the Clinton plan dwindled.[78]

Public Opinion and the Health Care Reform Debate

Early public opinion polls showed some support for the Clinton plan, though on a partisan basis. Sixty-one percent in a *New York Times*/CBS News poll said they would be willing to pay higher taxes so that universal coverage could be achieved. Forty-five percent felt that the president would be able to bring about reform, 41 percent said that the plan would being about needed changes, 40 percent said that it would be fair, and 46 percent said that it would make health care better. Republicans and independents expressed greater skepticism and much lower levels of support for change. The poll, like most others, showed the public's dissatisfaction with the system as a whole, though satisfaction with their care. A majority would support a limitation on choice of doctors and increased waiting for noncritical appointments if it meant that more could be covered. Only 36 percent, however, supported rationing (limiting coverage for expensive treatments with limited effectiveness). The poll showed majority support for employer mandates and for several ways to finance universal coverage: increased taxes on alcohol and tobacco and limitations on charges by doctors and hospitals through the Medicare program.[79]

A study of public opinion polls commissioned by the House of Representatives Ways and Means Committee found limited and declining support for increased taxes, though an increase in the number of people who felt that the country was spending too much on health care. The report concluded that "most Americans would rather see the scope of the Clinton reform plan scaled back than pay new taxes. In addition, the public is strongly opposed to increasing the deficit in order to pay for health reform."[80]

By March 1994, public support for the Clinton planned was declining precipitously. While there was support for the goals of the plan, more people disapproved of the proposal than approved it. Part of the problem was that the complex plan was difficult to understand. Another part was the criticisms leveled at the proposal through ad campaigns. There was fear that the quality of care would decline, that rationing would occur, and that the middle class would be hurt by the proposal. A slim majority hoped that either nothing changed or that Congress would make changes in the plan. Nevertheless, the public still supported employer mandates and controls on premiums. Further, the public gave Clinton credit for trying to change the system.[81]

Two findings about public opinion were especially interesting. One was that while the public thought that the government could guarantee security of insurance coverage, there was doubt that the government could control costs. This was one reason why the administration deemphasized cost control and emphasized security.[82] A second finding came from a March 1994 focus group presented with the Clinton plan without stating that it was the Clinton plan. The group preferred that plan to other alternatives. When the group was told that it was the Clinton plan, support dropped dramatically.[83]

It should be pointed out that part of the problem with public opinion polling is that slight differences in question wording can affect the results. When asked whether the Clinton plan was better or worse than the present system, a majority (52 percent) said better. When the phrase "or don't you know enough about the plan to say" was added, only 21 percent said it was better. The percentage of those who felt that the Clinton plan was worse declined to 27 percent from 34 percent. Thus a substantial portion of those polled (52 percent) admitted ignorance of the plan.[84]

As the struggle over health care reform continued in Congress, public support for change decreased. By September 1994, only about 40 percent approved of the way President Clinton was handling the health care issue. But the opinion of other players in the health care reform debate also diminished. Robert Dole's unfavorability ratings increased by 10 points over the previous year. Strong support remained for universal coverage and the idea that the health care system was in crisis. The major targets for blame included the opposition to the Clinton plan and the high level of government regulation in the plan.[85]

Health Care Reform Defeated

While several committees in the House of Representatives passed a version of the Clinton health care reform bill, there was never a vote on the floor of the House. House Democrats, despite the crafting of a bill by House Majority Leader Richard Gephardt (D-Mo.) calling for universal coverage by 1999, never united behind a single plan.[86] By early August, House leaders decided that between Republican opposition and the hesitancy of a number of Democrats, they would let the Senate take the led.[87]

One of the interesting things that happened during deliberations over health care reform was how little of the original plan remained. President Clinton said his major concern was universal coverage. Then the question raised was what did universal mean? Was it 100 percent or would some lesser figure, such as 95 or 90 percent, be acceptable? The president agreed to a lesser figure. Lost in the debate was another major concern: controlling the cost of care.[88] But Senate Democrats were also not united. Senate Finance Committee Chairman Moynihan stated that he saw no crisis in health care that warranted emergency surgery. Several Republicans and Democrats on the Finance Committee proposed a plan that had an individual rather than an employer mandate.[89] The feeling of some of those on the committee was that even though the individual mandate was not desirable, it would help get a bill reported to the floor of the Senate. But a group of civic, consumer, and labor groups, known as the Health Care Reform Project, opposed the proposal. They wanted an employer mandate; they felt that the individual mandate would not achieve universal coverage and that middle-income families without insurance would still have financial problems.[90] At the same time, Senate Minority Leader Dole moved away from his previous advocacy of universal coverage toward a much less ambitious goal of assisting the poor in purchasing insurance and prohibiting insurance companies from covering those with previous medical conditions.[91]

It also became clear that Republicans in both the House and the Senate were opposing reform with an eye on the forthcoming November 1994 elections, a strategy that would ultimately be successful. House Minority Whip Newt Gingrich (R-Ga.) told Republicans on the Ways and Means Committee not to support any amendments that would improve the chances of a committee bill passing. Further, Gingrich told Republicans that if they supported a tax increase, one portion of the bill the Ways and Means Committee was considering, that such support could be used against them by Democrats in the elections. To a small extent, the Republican strategy backfired. Democrats who had previously been divided on a bill came to support one in a show of party unity.[92] The Republicans were emboldened in their opposition as support for the Clinton plan eroded and Democrats showed little unity.[93]

In early August, Senate Majority Leader George Mitchell (D-Me.) made one last try at a bill.[94] The Mitchell bill relied on individual mandates with the goal of having 95 percent coverage by the end of the century. The president supported the Mitchell bill.[95] Mitchell a few days later agreed to compromise with a bill being prepared by Senator Chafee.[96] After debate began on the Mitchell bill, Senate Republicans began a filibuster to prevent a vote on the floor of the Senate. Mitchell was unable to get enough votes to end debate and at one point threatened to keep the Senate in an around-the-clock session to break the filibuster.[97] Mitchell's efforts would eventually fail, and health care reform was doomed. Moderate Republicans and Democrats, in what became known as the Mainstream Group, attempted to fashion a compromise bill but got little support beyond their group.[98]

By the end of August, it became clear that health care reform could not be passed in any version. Republicans were not only opposing any reform in both the Senate and the House but were threatening to drop support for the trade agreement, the General Agreement on Tariffs and Trade (GATT), which would be debated later in the year.[99]

The November elections brought a historic Republican victory. Health care was not an important issue in the campaigns, and the Republicans gained control of both houses of Congress for the first time in forty years.[100] Perhaps most symbolic were losses by two Democrats. Jim Cooper, the author of a major alternative to the Clinton health plan in the House, lost his bid for senator from Tennessee. Harris Wofford, whose unexpected victory in the special senatorial election in Pennsylvania in 1991 sparked political movement toward health care reform, lost his effort to serve a complete term.

The Failure of Health Care Reform

> After hundreds of town hall meetings, months of congressional hearings and markups by five committees, days of Senate consideration and an unprecedented lobbying campaign by special interest groups, neither the House nor the Senate ever did vote on a health care bill. As the 103rd Congress adjourned, its unwillingness to act on what President Clinton described as his most important domestic priority stood as the most conspicuous symbol of Clinton's failure to implement the ambitious reform agenda.[101]

Why did health care reform fail to win approval in 1994?[102] A number of reasons have been put forth to explain the failure. One was the inability of the president to maintain public support, either for himself or for his reform proposal. While the initial returns from the president's September 1993 speech were quite positive, opinion polls always showed that support was tenuous. The public wanted change but was also satisfied with its care. It wanted security but feared government bureaucracy.[103]

This last point is an important one. The Clinton plan, rightly or wrongly, was characterized by opponents, such as the Health Insurance Association of America and congressional Republicans, as big government. This ran into the traditional American distrust of government, particularly at a time (1994) when government was under attack.

The president's own approval ratings also were a problem. Bill Clinton won the 1992 election but captured only 43 percent of the popular vote. During his first two years in office, his approval ratings hovered in that area, only periodically exceeding 50 percent. Questions about his character and finances (Whitewater) also affected Clinton's approval ratings. Further, during the 1992 elections, he had run behind virtually all the congressmen and senators who ran that year. He clearly had no coattails that one could cling to in 1994.[104]

The process by which the Health Security Act was formulated also may have contributed to its defeat. The 500-person task force headed by First Lady Hillary Rodham Clinton and Ira Magaziner focused on technical issues and not political feasibility.[105] It was conducted in secret and created antagonism from the beginning. The bill produced was very complex, and its complexity and length (more than 1,300 pages) did not help win it public support.[106] The administration was urged by moderates within the White House to come up with a general set of principles and goals and let Congress work out the details. Instead, the detailed, highly complex plan became a target for those opposed either to reform or to portions of it.

The administration did not respond well to attacks by interest groups, particularly via television advertisements. Nor was the administration able to portray its flexibility and willingness to negotiate.[107]

Time was also a problem.[108] The proceedings of the task force were lengthy and a bill promised in April 1993 was not unveiled under September 1993. Even then, the bill was not delivered to Congress until the next month. The anticipation and buildup that accompanied the early stages of policy formulation dissipated with delay.

Other administration priorities blocked the way.[109] In 1993, this included the big deficit-cutting budget bill and the North American Free Trade Agreement (NAFTA). In 1994, the administration's crime bill got in the way. To a certain extent, Republicans' opposition to the crime bill in the House was designed to impede passage of health care reform.

Another thing that hurt the Clinton plan was the economy. While the 1990–91 recession was over by the time of the 1992 elections, the effects of the recession were still being felt because the recovery was slow. By 1994, things had changed. The economy was growing at a good clip and inflation was low. Further, medical inflation was relatively low in 1994. Thus, Senator Dole could with some reason claim that there was no health care crisis. The slowdown in health care inflation has been attributed to the reduction in overall inflation and changes in the health care system toward managed care. The more cynical could argue that providers and insurers kept cost increases low as a means of deflating the drive for reform.[110]

Of course, a major portion of the failure is attributable to opposition on the part of interest groups, most prominently the National Federation of Independent Businesses and the Health Insurance Association of America. The financial resources devoted to the campaign for advertising, lobbying, and grassroots activity towered over those of supporters. One estimate is that interest groups spent about $300 million to oppose the Clinton plan.[111]

These groups, especially NFIB, were able to mobilize their members to contact their congressmen. NFIB was also able to convince groups that originally supported reform to come out in opposition to the Clinton plan. The AMA and the Chamber of Commerce are cases in point. Small businesses began to quit the chamber because of its support for the Health Security Act. The chamber reversed its position. Other groups that originally supported the plan, such as the Business Roundtable, eventually came out against it.[112]

Partisanship was also a problem. Democrats in both the House and Senate were divided. This was in contrast to the considerable unity among Republicans in opposition to the Clinton plan. As the Republicans saw that public support was low and that the outlook for a successful election in 1994 grew, they became less inclined to negotiate and see the passage of a bill.[113]

There was one last factor, an institutional one. The institutional perspective takes note of the structure of the American political system, such as checks and balances, separation of powers, and federalism (discussed in chapter 1), and sees how that structure affects policy debate. The system devised by the delegates to the Constitutional Convention of 1787 was designed for two purposes. The first was to create a government that could act. The second was to create barriers to precipitous action by what the Founders called "factions" (what we would call interest groups and political parties). The Founders were distrustful of democracy and sought ways to limit the power of factions and of government that could be controlled by them.

The history of attempts at health care reform and national health insurance in the twentieth century bears witness to the power of the Founders' vision of limited government. And so while other Western industrialized countries moved toward some form of national health insurance and universal coverage, the United States did not. The barriers created, especially in Congress, provided the access points for interest groups opposed to reform and made the development of broad majorities at several different points of the legislative process very difficult.

After reviewing the institutionalist argument and the history of health care reform attempts in the United States, two political scientists, Sven Steinmo and Jon Watts, predicted eight months before the Health Security Act was presented to Congress that comprehensive health care reform would fail:

> America cannot pass major comprehensive health care reform that will control costs and offer complete coverage to all Americans because her political

institutions are designed to prevent this kind of reform. To truly pass meaningful reform would require imposing costs on certain groups (factions).
Clearly the majority (faction) both want and would benefit from such a
reform. But the fragmentation of authority designed into the U.S. Constitution makes it virtually impossible for the majority's will to supersede the
minority—at least when that minority is well financed and well organized.
To overcome the opposition of the minority faction, the majority must buy
off their opposition. The effect (in the case of health care reform at least) is to
throw fat onto the inflationary fire.[114]

Picking Up the Pieces of Reform

Although comprehensive health care reform failed in 1994, that does not
mean change will not or has not come about. In this section we look at three
aspects of the future. First, we examine some suggestions for change in the
wake of the failure of 1994. Second, we look at what the states have been
doing in terms of health care reform. Finally, we explore changes in the
private sector.

Incremental Change

As argued earlier, comprehensive change is difficult, if not impossible, to
effect. To recall the quote that opened this chapter, politics is about resolving conflicts of interest and values. To that we add the institutional perspective that makes change difficult. A number of observers have looked at the
Clinton plan and the politics surrounding it and suggested alternative, less
comprehensive changes.

Writing about the time that the Clinton plan was being sent to Congress,
Stuart Butler of the Heritage Foundation asserted that the appropriate model
for a health care system was the one that federal employees and retirees
(including members of Congress) are members of: the Federal Employees
Health Benefits Program. The program allows members to choose from a
large number of plans each year, with the employee paying about one-third
of the premiums and the federal government paying the rest. Employees are
given information by private groups (such as unions) about the plans, they
see the differences in costs and services provided, and they make choices.
According to Butler, this consumer-driven competition plan restrains cost
increases and does not have the heavy-handed bureaucracy that he said was
inherent in the Clinton plan.[115]

Additionally, things could be done at the federal level that would be less
comprehensive, more incremental. These include insurance regulation, subsidies, standardizing of benefits, and state experimentation.[116] A number of
these policies were incorporated into the Mainstream Coalition's health bill

in the Senate.[117] Each of these reforms sounds good but also creates problems when taken in isolation.

Insurance regulation might take three forms. One would be to mandate community rating so that everyone would pay an average premium. This would certainly help those who are sick and/or old. Healthier, younger people would likely have to pay higher premiums and this might be a source of opposition. A second form of insurance regulation would be requiring the coverage of people with preexisting conditions and making insurance portable. That is, laws would allow insurance to be carried from job to job. Of course, one problem here is that without an employer mandate, not all jobs carry insurance as a benefit. A third possibility would be to make it easier for smaller businesses to join together to get the better insurance rates that large employers enjoy.

Another line of incremental change might provide for subsidies for those who are near the poverty line but not eligible for Medicaid and tax credits for the self-employed. One problem with subsidies is that they might induce employers to drop health insurance.

Subsidies might be provided for health care for children, sometimes called Kidcare. Here subsidies plus a requirement that employers who offer health insurance cover children might be sufficient. This would be in line with the development of Medicare: focus on a segment of the population that is needy (the estimate is 8–12 million children have either no or inadequate health insurance coverage), worthy, and relatively inexpensive to cover. This would be truly American-style incremental policymaking.[118]

Another incremental reform would be to require that insurance policies be standardized with a set of minimum benefits. This would follow along the lines of the 1990 legislation that required standardization of medigap insurance policies for Medicare recipients (see chapter 4). The experience with the medigap regulations is that, despite some problems, the options were easily understandable and therefore assisted consumer choice.[119] The major benefit of such a policy would be to end the problem of underinsurance. While insurance companies are likely to oppose such regulation on the grounds of government intrusion, the experience with medigap policies suggests that such arguments can be overcome.[120]

The final suggestion for incremental reform is to allow states to experiment and innovate. As we see shortly, while the federal government has been unable to take action on health care reform, a number of states have done so. For states to continue to innovate requires that the federal government grant them the freedom to do so. Here two federal actions are suggested. First is to grant states waivers from federal regulations, especially Medicaid.

The second, and perhaps more difficult, problem is to revisit the issue of the Employee Retirement Income Security Act (ERISA) of 1974.[121] ERISA was born out of concern for the protection of private employee pensions. How the act has been implemented and interpreted by the courts has restricted the ability of states to innovate and contributed to the insurance problem. Unlike insurance companies, employers who self-insure do not come under state insurance regulations. And so, for example, self-insured companies have dropped coverage for people who contract costly illnesses, such as AIDS. This kind of dumping means that such patients would turn to public programs such as medicaid.[122] Further, companies that self-insure do not pay taxes on premiums, nor are they required to contribute to a state fund to help the uninsured.[123] Courts have declared portions of state laws on insurance and rate setting as violating ERISA.[124]

Federalism and Health Care Reform

> Change is likely to be driven less by what Washington does than by the skyrocketing costs to states of caring for the poor under the Medicaid program and the tactics used by health maintenance organizations and insurance companies to cut health care spending. Together, the pressures on state budgets and business bottom lines are changing medical care on a level hardly envisioned when Clinton unveiled his proposals last year.[125]

Although the federal government considered health care reform in 1992–94, little was actually accomplished. In contrast, a number of states passed legislation that sought either to cover more of the population or to reform the entire system.

There are several rationales for state action. One is flexibility. States differ along many dimensions—size, economic base, urbanization, and so forth. From this perspective, a single plan from the federal government would not be appropriate for all states.[126] A second rationale is that states have an important role in health care: insurance and hospital regulation, rate regulation, licensing, delivering public services, and education and training.[127]

A third rationale for looking at states (and local governments) is that even under a national plan, the states would have an important administrative role. This is typical of other domestic policy areas, such as welfare. Medicaid, building on the welfare system, is a joint federal-state program. Under the Clinton plan, states would have an important role in designing and overseeing regional health alliances.[128]

The earliest state health reform effort was in Hawaii in 1974. Hawaii has an employer mandate, even covering part-time workers. For low-income people, there is an insurance premium subsidy. The Hawaii program, including Medicaid, covers about 93 percent of the state's population.[129]

One of the more interesting attempts at reform came when Oregon sought to impose an explicit rationing program within Medicaid. It did this by ranking some 709 medical procedures and then setting a line of what would be and would not be funded by the state. For example, medical therapy for AIDS patients was allowed, unless they were in the last six months of life. Liver transplants would be allowed for those suffering from cirrhosis of the liver unless it was related to alcohol consumption.[130] Oregon argued that this rationing scheme could cover up to 400,000 more people with the same amount of money.

The Oregon plan required a Medicaid waiver from the federal government, but the Bush administration rejected it. There were several reasons for the rejection. One was that the plan was too inflexible given the variety of medical conditions physicians are presented with. A second reason was that explicit rationing affected only Medicaid recipients. Thus the least politically powerful would bear the brunt of rationing. Third, if health care costs rose more than expected after rationing went into effect, the cutoff point would have to be drawn higher.[131]

Perhaps the most important reason was that advocacy groups and others felt that the rationing plan would discriminate against disabled persons and therefore violate the 1990 Americans with Disabilities Act. Those making this claim included pro-life groups, the liberal Children's Defense Fund, the Catholic church, and the Democratic vice-presidential candidate, Al Gore.[132]

Oregon's governor, Barbara Roberts, argued that the plan was well thought out, had participation from a wide variety of interests, and that disability groups in Oregon supported the plan. Further, she asserted that neither the General Accounting Office nor the Office of Technology Assessment (both staff arms of Congress) had raised the disabilities issue. Finally, Governor Roberts said that the Justice Department had not said how the Oregon plan might violate the act.[133] After changing the plan to meet some of the objections, the Clinton administration approved the Medicaid waiver in March 1993.[134]

By early 1994, eight states had enacted health care reform plans, some successfully, some not so successfully. One important failure was the insurance reforms enacted in New York. The combination of community rating and limitations on preexisting conditions restrictions induced healthier and younger residents to drop insurance coverage. A second failure was in Massachusetts. The state passed a comprehensive universal health care law in 1988, based on the "play-or-pay" formula, under Democratic governor Michael Dukakis. But economic problems, some opposition, and the political destruction of Dukakis after his unsuccessful campaign as the Democratic nominee for president against George Bush in 1988 led to delay in implementation of the plan until 1995. The Republican governor, William Weld, supports repeal of the law, despite popular support for it.[135]

More encompassing health care reform programs have been adopted in Florida, Minnesota, and Washington. These programs generally seek to employ both managed competition and regulation, a goal of the Clinton Health Security Act. The Florida law provides for a basic benefits package and creates eleven regional alliances similar to those in the Clinton plan.[136] The Washington law has both an individual and employer mandate, controls over insurance premiums, organized provider delivery systems, and purchasing cooperatives.[137]

The first state to implement purchasing cooperatives was California. Beginning in July 1993, small businesses began enrolling their employees into the program. There are limitations on benefits and restrictions on which providers can be chosen. A few businesses have opted out, but their costs have been higher than those participating in the alliance. As of the middle of 1994, another thirteen states were moving in this direction.[138]

One of the motives for state reform is to limit the effect of Medicaid expenditures on state budgets. One way that states have done this is to try to enroll Medicaid recipients in HMOs.[139] Such plans require Medicaid waivers from the federal government, a policy that the Clinton administration supports. Missouri, for example, is seeking such a waiver for all its Medicaid recipients, to go into effect in 1996.[140] The most drastic plan is Tennessee's proposal to withdraw entirely from Medicaid and, still in partnership with the federal government, enroll poor patients in managed care organizations.[141]

Cities and communities have also moved toward change. Rochester, New York, and Minneapolis–St. Paul have been leaders, especially in managed care and competition. Lancaster, Pennsylvania, and Mount Carmel, Illinois, are two smaller communities that developed their own plans. In Lancaster, managed care has been implemented and HMOs are growing. The two major hospitals support the change, forming integrated units of providers.[142] In Mount Carmel, a clinic has been set up to provide care for those without insurance.[143]

States and communities have thus begun to move toward reforming the health care system. Any further reform will either include other levels of government or perhaps be concentrated on states and communities. But with the elections of November 1994, when Republicans gained more control over state legislatures and captured more governors' offices, change may be impeded at the state level. There may be opposition to employer mandates and changes in ERISA.[144]

Private-Sector Changes

Apart from changes beginning to take place at the state and local levels, the private sector has begun to reform health care. Prior to President Clinton's September 1993 national address presenting his health care reform proposal, Alain Enthoven argued that the health care sector was beginning to "heal itself."[145] Employers, according to Enthoven and Singer, are making employees pay more for expensive plans, and employees are increasingly enrolling in managed care plans, such as HMOs, which are experiencing lower premium increases than the traditional fee-for-service plans.

A second change Enthoven and Singer point to is that large employers are forming purchasing cooperatives (as called for in managed competition plans such as the ones advocated by the Jackson Hole group). Perhaps most significant for the future of health care is the third change. Providers and insurers are increasingly forming integrated service plans. "The goal is to make the financing and provision of services more efficient by eliminating duplication of administrative duties, by matching the numbers of doctors and facilities to the needs of the population and by relying more on primary and preventive care."[146]

These changes seem to be fostered by the political pressure of the Clinton health plan as well as changes in the health care market.[147] As health insurance costs continue to grow, business has sought ways to restrain costs. Further, providers fear that if they do not become part of an integrated service network, they will lose patients and income. The result has been a continuing wave of mergers and acquisitions. In some cases, doctors have organized their own networks to forestall acquisition by hospitals or insurance companies. Some states have passed laws that encourage service network formation.[148]

One place where much of this is occurring is in New York City (Southern California is also active in organizing service networks). Three large teaching centers, New York Hospital–Cornell Medical Center, Columbia-Presbyterian Medical Center, and Mount Sinai Medical Center, have affiliated with smaller hospitals to form networks. The larger hospitals benefit by getting referrals from the affiliated hospitals for specialized medical care. The smaller hospitals get an important connection, resources, and inclusion in an industry that is consolidating. Further, the networks hope to attract the attention of major corporations, insurers, and HMOs.[149]

Such mergers and consolidations are occurring in smaller communities as well. In Springfield, Missouri, where the authors live, the two major hospitals, St. Johns and Cox (as well as some of the smaller ones), began buying up doctors' practices and forming managed care organizations.[150] The first HMO in Springfield appeared in 1994.

There are several problems with the these private-sector changes, especially with the service network integration. First, these changes do not help those outside the system, such as the self-employed or those working in jobs that do not offer health insurance. Thus one problem that led to the call for universal coverage remains, in the absence of government action at whatever level.[151]

A second issue is whether this integration, purchasing alliances and service networks, will reduce costs or at least reduce increases in health care costs. It is clear that health care costs for large employers such as Hewlett-Packard and Chrysler are lower.[152] But in many instances, the savings are achieved by shifting costs to those outside the system.

A third problem has to do with provider relationships (i.e., doctors and pharmacists) with networks, especially those using managed care. One way that networks operate is by buying physician practices or offering contracts to doctors and then limiting subscribers to those doctors because they offer discounts. Doctors not included are moving to be included in managed care plans. Some state laws prevent the exclusion of providers. One attempt to deal with this during the debate over health care reform in 1994 was to include a provision preempting these state laws. With the failure of health reform, preemption also died.[153]

Doctors are also concerned about the control over their medical decisions that accompanies managed care and integrated service networks. Health insurers are in essence engaged in rationing health services, much the same as Oregon has decided to do. Health plans covering about 50 million Americans use the services of a Seattle-based consulting firm to make decisions about what procedures to allow. The firm, Milliman and Robertson Inc., has developed a set of guidelines for these plans to follow. Some examples of guidelines for patients under sixty-five are refusal to allow admission to a hospital for a mastectomy, limiting hospital stays to three days for those with strokes, and limitations on tonsillectomies.[154]

Yet another concern is that these private-sector changes will lead to a reduction in consumer choice of providers. If integrated service networks buy up physician practices, that means that a doctor outside the network would not be available to operate in every community hospital. A doctor not part of an employer's plan would also not be available for the subscriber. Using doctors outside the plan generally costs considerably more money. One accusation about the Clinton Health Security Act was that it would limit choice of doctors. As we saw earlier, the Health Security Act provided for a choice of at least three health care plans, one of which was the fee-for-service plan. For many, the Clinton plan increased choice. But if employers offer only one plan and integrated service networks limit choice of providers, then consumer choice would be lessened.[155] The complaint about the Clinton plan would have been realized by the private sector. In this sense, managed competition and managed care lead to the private regulation of health care. But that regulation comes without the guarantees and rights that would accompany a public plan.[156] There may have been complaints about public bureaucracy (the health care alliances); however, we may be faced with private bureaucratic control instead.[157]

There is one last, related aspect to these private-sector changes. In 1970, the Health Policy Advisory Center (Health-PAC) published a book entitled *The American Health Empire: Power, Profits and Politics*.[158] The authors pointed out that the health care system was evolving toward integration and away from the characteristic solo-practice doctor. Given the changes in these last several years, Health-PAC must be seen as prophetic.

Conclusion

The push for health care reform and national health insurance during the first two years of the Clinton administration is another example of the failure of comprehensive change, dating back to Woodrow Wilson's administration. Despite this failure, there has been considerable reform by some states and by the private sector. The impetus for reform has been rising costs, and the effect has been to begin to change the economic incentives in health care. Consider the following:

- A majority of privately insured Americans were enrolled in managed-care plans that limit choice of doctors and treatments. Sixty-five percent of workers at medium and large companies were in such plans by 1994.
- For-profit health maintenance organizations grew so fast that they overtook nonprofit H.M.O.'s as the dominant force in managed care. Today the majority of all people enrolled in H.M.O.'s, the most common and stringent form of managed care, are in plans run by for-profit companies.
- At least three-fourths of all doctors signed contracts, covering at least some of their patients, to cut their fees and accept oversight of their medical decisions. Among doctors who work in group practices, the share of such managed-care contracts was 89 percent by 1993, up sharply from 56 percent the year before.[159]

The federal government can certainly take actions that do not impede experimentation and innovation at the state level. These include making sure that federal laws and regulations, from Medicaid to ERISA, do not interfere with new state laws. This would be a "federalist" solution to health care.[160] On the other hand, in 1995, the Clinton administration proposed federal regulation of health insurance as a means of expanding insurance coverage and easing the costs of purchasing private insurance. The proposal appears to be politically feasible, because both parties in Congress and the insurance industry appear to support the change.[161]

But with these changes, at the state level and in the private sector, are three dangers. One is that a single action (an incremental change) might be taken that produces a result opposite of what is desired. The best example of this is when New York State adopted community rating in 1993. As mentioned earlier, one likely result is that healthy and younger people will face higher rates. When they did so in New York, many dropped their insurance coverage. Because those left with insurance coverage were, on the average, sicker, the rates for everyone went up.[162] Combined with limitations on preexisting conditions, one can envision individuals and families making a yearly decision whether to purchase health insurance based on expected health needs.

A second danger is that nothing is done but restraints are put on those seeking change. This has been labeled the "triple negative health care reform": "Congress might do nothing to expand coverage, might impose strict limits on spending for Medicare and Medicaid and might hold back states trying to adopt comprehensive health programs."[163] As mentioned in chapters 3 and 4, both Congress and President Clinton have proposed significant cuts in both programs.

The third concern is that in the absence of comprehensive health care reform, what will develop, especially given private-sector changes, is a three-tiered health care system. Some poor people will have Medicaid, but many will continue to be treated by public clinics and hospitals (especially emergency rooms). The middle tier, the middle class, will be continually pushed into managed care systems. The affluent will continue to use the fee-for-service system.[164] Thus the rationalization that purchasing alliances and integrated service networks promise will still leave a very fragmented health care system.

9

Conclusion: Health Care Policy at the End of the Twentieth Century

In these final few pages, we would like to summarize the discussion of the text, focusing on the features that help explain the course of health care policy in the United States. Based on this review, we end by making some reasonably educated guesses about the future of health care policy.

We began this text by examining various factors that affect the policy-making process, whether in health care or some other policy area. Policymaking and the policies that result from that process are profoundly affected by the constitutional structure of government. In the United States, that constitutional structure creates a bias against major changes. The system of separation of powers and checks and balances creates separate institutions that share power. Chief among them is the separation between executive and legislative powers. In a parliamentary system, such as in England, the party with a majority in the legislature would be able to enact its program (party discipline is important here too). In the United States, even under conditions of party control of both Congress and the presidency, the passage of programs is hardly assured. Separation of powers creates institutional jealousies that are difficult to overcome. This is not to say that major changes cannot take place, only that they occur under constitutionally difficult circumstances.[1] And all three branches of government—executive, legislative, and judicial—are brought into policymaking.

A further constitutional feature is federalism, the division of powers between different levels of government. States (and local governments) are independent actors, and policy made at the federal level must consider its impact on states. The result of federalism and separation of powers/checks and balances is the deliberate fragmentation of power, vertically and horizontally. It would be little exaggeration to say that no other country faces as difficult a set of constitutional barriers as the United States.

A second key set of factors is the political environment, shaped by constitutional structure and the institutional environment. Fragmentation of power requires that policies be adopted as a result of consensus building, especially in legislatures. It also means that rather than adopt major reforms or new ways of doing things, we tend to adopt smaller changes, tinkering as we go along. This incremental style of decision making characterizes policymaking in health care. Numerous attempts at comprehensive change in the twentieth century have failed, most recently in 1994 (see chapter 8).

Our political philosophy or ideology has a strong promarket, antigovernment bias. Those who seek positive government action have the burden of justifying new programs and then maintaining political support for them. This antigovernment bias, among other factors, helps explain why the public sector's role in health care is limited, as compared to other countries.

The same political philosophy, and constitutional/institutional factors, allows for another important feature of our political environment: the presence of interest groups. The right to assemble, the rights of free speech and press, and the rights of association and to petition government create a constitutional basis for interest groups. Fragmentation in government, where there are multiple sources of power at different levels of government, invite interest groups to try to influence those sources of power. Recall the definition of politics offered by Lawrence Brown in the opening quote in chapter 8: politics involves the resolution of conflicts of values and interests. For every program, a set of is interests is affected by it. Interest groups seek either to defend programs that benefit them or to get rid of programs that adversely affect them. They are also prepared to defend themselves against policy proposals that would hurt them. We certainly saw the mobilization of interests in chapter 8. But this occurs in other ways as well. Medicaid, Medicare, and the planning programs of the 1960s all contained provisions in their original legislation that effectively said that the program could not interfere with the practice of medicine. The danger of interest-group activity is that once programs are enacted and entrenched, their interest-group defenders man the barricades against change. The result is what Rauch calls *demosclerosis*.[2]

All these factors help explain the peculiar nature of the health care system in the United States. It is a combination of mostly private sector, with substantial public programs and public regulation. If we were to develop a health care system from scratch, we would never produce the system we currently have.

That system has problems. Costs keep mounting, which affects governments, businesses, insurers, individuals, and providers. At the same time that the health care sector is the largest in the nation (about one-seventh of the economy), a sizable number of people have inadequate access to quality care, largely but not entirely because of lack of health insurance (about 14 percent of the population). This is compounded by developments in bio-medical technology that present ethical issues (such as what is life and is there a right to die) we have not yet and may never resolve.

Given these political features, problems, and policy failures (such as in 1994), what is the future of health care policy in the United States? It is always hazardous to go out on a limb and make projections. But certain trends seem obvious, based on our analysis in the previous eight chapters.

First, what change is likely to take place will be incremental. For example, President Clinton has proposed federal regulation of private insurance. The political system, given the fragmentation of power and the highly developed set of interest groups in health care, does not seem capable of comprehensive change. Perhaps that is good. One of the virtues of incremental change is that we tinker with the system, see how well it works, and then make needed changes. Yet there is a danger that incremental changes will affect other elements of the health care system in ways that are difficult to understand. As one example, the changes in insurance policy in New York designed to increase access to health insurance led to fewer people having insurance than before the law was passed in 1992. Maybe it is better to look at all the interconnections and ramifications at once. But who can think of them all?

A second prediction is that the twin pressures of the cost of public-sector health care programs and large budget deficits will create momentum to alter Medicaid and Medicare. Medicaid is a major item of state budgets, and the Medicare trust fund is in danger of insolvency around the turn of the century. It may be that Medicaid is easier to change because there is considerably less support for it than there is for Medicare. The numbers for both programs are daunting. There are proposals pending for over $100 billion in future spending in both programs to be cut by the year 2000. Even this change will be difficult to effect.

One last set of predictions. What changes will take place in health care will most likely be made by states and the private sector. Both are driven by the cost problem (and to some extent by problems of access). A number of states have enacted reform policies when the federal government was unable to act. The private sector, especially larger firms, are moving toward managed care and health alliances. Insurers and providers are increasingly forming provider networks. The trends are likely to continue. These two types of changes are profound, though not without danger. Those without insurance and in states that have not increased access or engaged in insurance reform will be left out. Nor is it entirely clear that health care reform can come to grips with the cost problem. And in the case of private-sector changes, it may be that what we are seeing is a buildup of private centers of power that will exert control over health care.

Notes

Chapter 1. Health Care Politics

1. Charles O. Jones, *An Introduction to the Study of Public Policy;* James E. Anderson, *Public Policy Making: An Introduction.*
2. Lawrence D. Brown, "The Formulation of Federal Health Care Policy," 48.
3. J.H.A. Brown, *The Politics of Health Care,* 15–16.
4. Susan Dentzer, "America's Scandalous Health Care," *U.S. News & World Report,* March 12, 1990, 25–30; Humphrey Taylor, "U.S. Health Care: Built for Waste," *New York Times,* April 17, 1990.
5. Walter A. Rosenbaum, *Environmental Politics and Policy,* 31.
6. James Madison, "Federalist 51," in *The Federalist Papers,* ed. Alexander Hamilton, James Madison, and John Jay.
7. Calculated from Harold W. Stanley and Richard G. Niemi, *Vital Statistics on American Politics.*
8. Lawrence D. Brown, *Health Policy in the Reagan Administration,* 32–33.
9. See Frank J. Thompson, "New Federalism and Health Care Policy," 647–699.
10. Christa Altenstetter, *Health Policy-Making and Administration in West Germany and the United States,* 26–27.
11. Ralph Huitt, "Political Feasibility," 410.
12. Lawrence D. Brown, "Formulation of Federal Health Care Policy," 53.
13. Graham Allison, *The Essence of Decision,* 163.
14. Brown, "Formulation of Federal Health Care Policy," 53
15. Charles A. Lindblom, "The Science of Muddling Through," 86.
16. Walter A. Rosenbaum, *Environmental Politics and Policy,* 36.
17. Ralph Huitt, "Political Feasibility," 410.
18. Rudolf Klein, "The Political Ideology vs. the Reality of Politics," 83.
19. S.H. Beer, *Modern British Politics,* 5.
20. Jane H. Bayes, *Ideologies and Interest-Group Politics,* 42.
21. James Madison, "Federalist 10," 77–84.
22. Theodore Lowi, "The Public Philosophy."
23. David Wilsford, *Doctors and the State,* 69.
24. Grant McConnell, *Private Power and American Democracy.*
25. Robert A. Alford, *Health Care Politics,* 15.
26. S.E. Berki, "Health Care Policy."
27. Paul Samuelson, *Economics.*
28. Victor R. Fuchs, *Who Shall Live?*

29. Alan L. Sorkin, *Health Care and the Changing Economic Environment*, xiii, 1.

30. Victor R. Fuchs, *The Health Economy*, 13.

31. Ibid., 6.

32. Joseph A. Califano, Jr., "The Health-Care Chaos," *New York Times Magazine*, March 20, 1988.

33. Gavin Mooney, *Economics, Medicine and Health Care*, 21.

34. Alan B. Cohen and Donald R. Cohodes, "Certificate of Need and Low Capital-Cost Medical Technology," 307.

35. H.V. Fineberg and H.H. Hiatt, "Evaluation of Medical Practices."

36. Fuchs, *Health Economy*, 30.

37. Katharine R. Levit et al., "National Health Expenditures, 1993," 280.

38. Ibid.

39. Hospital Insurance Association of America, *Source Book of Health Insurance Data*, 35.

40. Katharine R. Levit et al., "National Health Expenditures, 1993," 291.

41. The description that follows is derived from Office of the Federal Register, National Archives and Records Administration, *The United States Government Manual 1990/91*, 287–315.

42. Levit et al., "National Health Expenditures, 1993," 280.

43. Hospital Insurance Association of America, *Source Book of Health Insurance Data*, 38–39.

44. Ibid., 13.

45. Wesley S. Mellow, "Determinants of Health Insurance and Pension Coverage," 30–32.

46. Deborah J. Chollet, *Employer-Provided Health Benefits: Coverage, Provisions and Policy Issues*, 31.

47. Reported in "Employees Finding 'Free' Health Insurance Costly, Survey Shows," *Springfield News-Leader*, July 10, 1991.

48. *Academic American Encyclopedia* (Danbury, Conn.: Grolier, 1990).

49. Stanley Whol, M.D., *The Medical Industrial Complex*, 5.

50. Ibid., 111–117. For a detailed discussion of about thirty-five major medical corporations, see 101–176.

51. *Academic American Encyclopedia*.

52. Bruce C. Vladeck, *Unloving Care: The Nursing Home Tragedy*, 8–9.

53. Calculated from Katharine R. Levit et al., "National Health Expenditures, 1993," 292.

54. *Academic American Encyclopedia*.

55. Elisabeth Rosenthal, "Medicine Suffers as Fewer Doctors Join Front Lines," *New York Times*, May 24, 1993.

56. Ibid.

57. Katharine R. Levit, Gary L. Olin, and Suzanne W. Letsch, "Americans' Health Insurance Coverage, 1980–1991," 33.

58. Ibid.

59. Helen C. Lazenby and Suzanne W. Letsch, "National Health Expenditures, 1989," *Health Care Financing Review*, 16–17; Sally T. Burner, Daniel R. Waldo, and David R. McKusick, "National Health Expenditure Projections through 2030," 20.

60. Ibid., 19.

61. Milt Freudenheim, "Business and Health: Health Insurers Changing Role," *New York Times*, January 16, 1990; Peter Kerr, "The Changing Definition of Health Insurers," *New York Times*, May 10, 1993.

62. Spencer Rich, "Are Insurers Playing Favorites?" *Washington Post National Weekly Edition,* June 24–30, 1991, 37.

63. Katharine R. Levit et al., "National Health Expenditures, 1993," 285.

64. Robert J. Blendon, Robert Leitman, Ian Morrison, and Karen Donelan, "Satisfaction with Health Systems in Ten Nations," 188. The countries included in the study were the United States, Canada, Great Britain, West Germany, Australia, France, Sweden, Japan, Italy, and the Netherlands.

65. Milt Freudenheim, "Business and Health: Most Want U.S. to Pay the Bill," *New York Times,* July 3, 1990.

66. Richard Morin, "Americans Want Health Care to Save Lives Whatever the Cost," *Washington Post National Weekly Edition,* February 5–11, 1990, 38.

67. Ibid.

68. Cindy Jajich-Toth and Burns W. Roper, "Americans' Views on Health Care: A Study in Contradictions," 151, 153.

69. Peter Navarro, *The Policy Game: How Special Interests and Ideologues Are Stealing America.*

70. James T. Bennett and Thomas J. DiLorenzo, *Destroying America: How Government Funds Partisan Politics.*

71. Judith G. Smith, ed., *Political Brokers: Money, Organizations, Power and People.*

72. Stephen Miller, *Special Interest Groups in American Politics,* esp. 113–135.

73. H.R. Mahood, *Interest Group Politics in America: A New Intensity,* 162.

74. For a good discussion of public and private interest groups involved in the health care field and the techniques they use to influence health care politics and policies, see Paul D. Ward, "Health Lobbies: Vested Interests and Pressure Politics," 28–47; Paul J. Feldstein, "Health Associations and the Legislative Process," 223–242; James A. Morone, "The Citizen Role in Health Politics: Democratic Wishes and Sensible Reforms," 243–257.

75. *Encyclopedia of Associations 1991,* 25th ed. (New York: Gale Research, 1990).

76. Jane H. Bayes, *Ideologies and Interest-Group Politics,* 222.

77. Reported in Lynn Wagner, "Health PACs Modest Donors—Study," 4.

78. Charles R. Babcock, "Health Care Fears Open Up the Pocketbooks." *Washington Post National Weekly Edition,* June 7–13, 1993, 14.

79. Dwight L. Wilbur, "The AMA in Washington," in Douglas Carter and Philip R. Lee, *Politics of Health,* 48–60.

80. Foundation for Public Affairs, *Public Interest Profiles 1988–1989,* 302.

81. Frank D. Campion, *The AMA and U. S. Health Policy Since 1940,* 45–47.

82. Charles R. Babcock, "Health Care Fears Open Up the Pocketbooks."

83. Harold W. Stanley and Richard G. Niemi, *Vital Statistics on American Politics,* 165.

84. Charles R. Babcock, "Health Care Fears Open Up the Pocketbooks."

85. Lewis E. Weeks and Howard J. Berman, *Shapers of American Health Care Policy: An Oral History,* 195.

86. *Encyclopedia of Associations 1991,* 1414.

87. Cynthia Wallace, "Hospital PACs Ring Up More Clout," 52.

88. Clark C. Havighurst, "The Questionable Cost-Containment Record of Commercial Health Insurers," 243–245.

89. Ibid., 255.

90. Health Insurance Association of America, *Source Book of Health Insurance Data* (New York: Health Insurance Institute, 1991), 23.

91. Ibid., 1469.

92. Allen S. Meyerhoff and David A. Crozier, "Health Care Coalitions: The Evolution of a Movement," 120.

93. Julie Kosterlitz, "Softening Resistance," 66.
94. Foundation for Public Affairs, *Public Interest Profiles 1988–1989*, 333–335.
95. Ibid., 343–345.

Chapter 2. Health Care Policy in the United States

1. "A Survey of Health Care: Surgery Needed," 4–5.
2. Ibid., Also see Craig R. Whitney, "British Health Service, Much Beloved but Inadequate, Is Facing Changes," *New York Times*, June 9, 1991; Philip J. Hilts, "Demands to Fix U.S. Health Care Reach a Crescendo," *New York Times*, May 19, 1991.
3. "A Survey of Health Care," 2–3.
4. Philip J. Hilts, "Many Leave Emergency Room Needing Care," *New York Times*, August 27, 1991; David W. Baker, Carl D. Stevens, and Robert H. Brook, "Patients Who Leave a Public Hospital Emergency Department without Being Seen by a Physician," 1085–1090; Andrew Bindman, Kevin Grumbach, Dennis Keane, Loren Rauch, and John M. Luce, "Consequences of Queuing for Care at a Public Hospital Emergency Department," 1091–1096.
5. Lisa Belkin, "Hospitals Sacked, a Report Asserts," *New York Times*, October 22, 1991.
6. Robert Pear, "Health Clinics Cut Services as Cost of Insurance Soars," *New York Times*, August 21, 1991.
7. Peter Kerr, "Chain of Mental Hospitals Faces Inquiry in Four States," *New York Times*, October 22, 1991.
8. "The Health Care System Is Broken and Here Is How to Fix It," *New York Times*, July 22, 1991.
9. Anthony Lewis, "A Sick System," *New York Times*, June 3, 1991.
10. Barbara Ehrenreich, "Our Health-Care Disgrace," *Time*, December 10, 1990, 112.
11. Milton Terris, "A Wasteful System That Doesn't Work," 14–16.
12. Humphrey Taylor, "U.S. Health Care: Built for Waste," *New York Times*, April 17, 1990.
13. Susan Dentzer, "America's Scandalous Health Care," *U.S. News & World Report*, March 12, 1990, 25–30.
14. Erik Eckholm, "Rescuing Health Care," *New York Times*, May 2, 1991.
15. Lister Hill, "Health in America: A Personal Perspective," 4–5.
16. Odin W. Anderson, *Health Services in the United States: A Growth Enterprise Since 1875*, 13–15.
17. Milton I. Roemer, *An Introduction to the U.S. Health Care System*, 2nd ed., 50–51.
18. Marshall W. Raffel, *The U.S. Health System: Origins and Functions*, 534.
19. U.S. Health Resource Administration, *Health in America: 1776–1976* (Rockville, Md.: U.S. Department of Health, Education, and Welfare, 1976), 69–79.
20. Odin W. Anderson, *Health Services in the United States*, 14.
21. Daniel M. Fox, *Health Policies, Health Politics: The British and American Experience: 1911–1965*, 39.
22. Paul Starr, *The Social Transformation of American Medicine*, 117–118.
23. Ibid., 120–123.
24. Ibid., 237.
25. Milton I. Roemer, "The Politics of Public Health in the United States," 264.
26. Merton C. Bernstein and Joan Broadshaug Bernstein, *Social Security: The System That Works*, 253–254.

27. Gregg Easterbrook, "The Revolution in Medicine," *Newsweek,* January 26, 1987, 43.

28. Robert B. Greifinger and Victor William Sidel, "Three Centuries of Medical Care," 22–23.

29. Milton I. Roemer, *Introduction to the U.S. Health Care System,* 57.

30. Paul Starr, *Social Transformation of American Medicine,* 281.

31. Merton C. Bernstein and Joan Broadshaug Bernstein, *Social Security,* 256.

32. Rosemary Stevens, *In Sickness and in Wealth: American Hospitals in the Twentieth Century,* 229.

33. Merton C. Bernstein and Joan Broadshaug Bernstein, *Social Security,* 259.

34. U.S. Department of Health, Education and Welfare, *Health in America: 1776– 1976,* 124–125.

35. Rashi Fein, *Medical Care, Medical Costs: The Search for a Health Insurance Policy,* 60–61.

36. Sheri I. David, *With Dignity,* 90.

37. Ibid., 105.

38. For an excellent examination of the rhetorical debate over the issue of Medicare, see Max J. Skidmore, *Medicare and the American Rhetoric of Reconciliation.*

39. Helen Darling, "The Role of the Federal Government in Assuring Access to Health Care," 286.

40. Stephen H. Long and Russell F. Settle, "Medicare and the Disadvantaged Elderly: Objectives and Outcomes," 644.

41. Henry J. Aaron, *Serious and Unstable Condition: Financing America's Health Care,* 61.

42. Lawrence D. Brown, "Introduction to a Decade of Transition," 572.

43. Katharine R. Levit et al., "Health Care Expenditures, 1993," 285.

44. Ibid.

45. Richard M. Nixon, "Message to Congress."

46. U.S. Congress, Senate, Senator Edward M. Kennedy, remarks on introducing the Health Security Act (Senate Bill #3), 92nd Cong., 1st sess., *Congressional Record,* January 25, 1971, 284.

47. Jonas Norris, *Searching for a Cure: National Health Policy Considered,* 61.

48. Ibid., 71–72. See also Joseph L. Falkson, *HMOs and the Politics of Health Service Reform.*

49. Paul Starr, *Social Transformation of American Medicine,* 411.

50. For a more detailed and systematic analysis of the first two years of the Reagan administration's initiatives in the health area, see Lynn Etheredge, "Reagan, Congress, and Health Spending," 14–24.

51. Thomas Rice, Katherine Desmond, and Jon Gable, "The Medicare Catastrophic Coverage Act: A Post-Mortem," 76.

52. Thomas Rice and Jon Gable, "Protecting the Elderly against High Health Care Costs," 5.

53. Thomas Rice, Katherine Desmond, and Jon Gable, "Medicare Catastrophic Coverage Act," 76.

54. John T. Hanlon and George E. Picker, *Public Health: Administration and Practice,* 23.

55. Philip R. Lee and Carroll L. Estes, "New Federalism and Health Policy," 93.

56. David L. Rosenbloom, "New Ways to Keep Old Promises in Health Care," 50.

57. Bayless Manning and Bruce Vladeck, "The Role of State and Local Government in Health," 134.

58. Drew E. Altman and Douglas H. Morgan, "The Role of the State and Local Government in Health," 13–14.

59. David L. Rosenbloom, "New Ways to Keep Old Promises in Health Care," 45.

60. Richard P. Nathan et al., "Initial Effects of the Fiscal Year 1982 Reductions in Federal Domestic Spending," 315–349.

61. Frank J. Thompson, "New Federalism and Health Care Policy: States and the Old Questions," 665–666.

62. Philip R. Lee and Carroll L. Estes, "New Federalism and Health Policy," 90.

63. Joseph P. Shapiro, "How States Cook the Books," *U.S. News & World Report,* July 29, 1991, 24–25.

64. Robert Pear, "U.S. Moves to Curb Medicaid Payments for Many States," *New York Times,* September 11, 1991.

65. Rick Curtis, "The Role of the State Government in Assuring Access to Care," 277–278.

66. See John F. Holahan and Joel W. Cohen, *Medicaid: The Trade-Off between Cost-Containment and Access to Care.*

67. Helen Darling, "The Role of the Federal Government in Assuring Access to Health Care," 289.

68. Michael Specter, "Putting Michigan Hospitals on the Critical Care List," *Washington Post Weekly Edition,* June 4–10, 1990, 33; Patricia King, "The City as a Patient," *Newsweek,* February 19, 1990, 58–59; Melinda Beck, Daniel Glick, Nadine Joseph, and Peter Katel, "State of Emergency," *Newsweek,* October 14, 1991, 52–53.

69. David Mechanic, "Some Dilemmas in Health Care Policy," 8.

70. Paul Starr, *Social Transformation of American Medicine,* 419.

Chapter 3. Medicaid: Health Care for the Poor

1. Paul B. Ginsburg, "Public Insurance Programs: Medicare and Medicaid," 181.

2. Paul Starr, *The Social Transformation of American Medicine,* 368.

3. Karen Davis and Roger Reynolds, *The Impact of Medicare and Medicaid on Access to Medical Care,* 391.

4. Thomas W. Grannemann and Mark V. Pauly, *Controlling Medicaid Costs: Federalism, Competition, and Choice,* 5.

5. E. Richard Brown, "Medicare and Medicaid: Band-Aids for the Old and Poor," 60–61.

6. Paul Starr, *Social Transformation of American Medicine,* 370.

7. Saundra K. Schneider, "Intergovernmental Influences on Medicaid Program Expenditures," 756.

8. Richard E. Brown, "Medicare and Medicaid," 61.

9. Grannemann and Pauly, *Controlling Medicaid Costs,* 6.

10. Paul B. Ginsburg, "Public Insurance Programs," 183–186.

11. Saundra K. Schneider, "Intergovernmental Influences on Medicaid Program Expenditures," 757.

12. John F. Holahan and Joel W. Cohen, *Medicaid: The Trade-Off between Cost Containment and Access to Care,* 9–10.

13. Suzanne W. Letsch, Helen C. Lazenby, Katharine R. Levit, and Cathy A. Cowan, "National Health Expenditures, 1991," 13.

14. Michael Specter, "Medicaid's Crazy Quilt of Care," *Washington Post National Weekly Edition,* August 26–September 1, 1991, 33.

15. Schneider, "Intergovernmental Influences on Medicaid Program Expenditures," 757.

16. Robert J. Samuelson, "Medicaid Monster," *Washington Post National Weekly Edition,* May 12–26, 1991, 29.

17. Paul B. Ginsburg, "Public Insurance Programs," 190.

18. Karen Davis, Gerard F. Anderson, Diane Rowland, and Earl P. Steinberg, *Health Care Cost Containment,* 75–78.

19. Suzanne W. Letsch et al., "National Health Expenditures, 1991," 13.

20. Elliot J. Dubin, "Medicaid Reform: Major Trends and Issues," 7.

21. Suzanne W. Letsch et al., "National Health Expenditures, 1991," 13.

22. Elliot J. Dubin, "Medicaid Reform," 7.

23. John F. Holahan and Joel W. Cohen, *Medicaid,* 10.

24. Katharine R. Levit et al., "National Health Expenditures, 1993," 288.

25. Drew Altman, "Health Care for the Poor," 112–113.

26. George Gross, "Reagan's 'Bold' Aid Reform," 1.

27. Fred Jordan, "Governors OK Alternative Plan on Federalism," 1.

28. David L. Barnett, "Reagan's Bold New Blueprint," *U.S. News & World Report,* February 8, 1982, 20.

29. Ed Magnuson, "New Federalism or Feudalism?" *Time,* February 8, 1982, 19.

30. Philip R. Lee and Carroll L. Estes, "New Federalism and Health Policy," 100.

31. Lynn Wagner, "Access for All People," 28.

32. Ibid.

33. Julie Kosterlitz, "Middle-Class Medicaid," 2728–2731.

34. Philip R. Lee and Carroll L. Estes, "New Federalism and Health Policy," 100.

35. For a detailed analysis of the evolution of health care policy and its implications for federalism, see Frank J. Thompson, "New Federalism and Health Care Policy: States and the Old Questions," 647–669; also see Lee and Estes, "New Federalism and Health Policy," 88–102.

36. Drew E. Altman and Douglas H. Morgan, "The Role of State and Local Government in Health," 26.

37. Drew E. Altman, "Health Care for the Poor," 115.

38. Ibid.

39. Randall R. Bovbjerg and John Holahan, *Medicaid in the Reagan Era: Federal Policy and State Choices,* 30–31.

40. John F. Holahan and Joel W. Cohen, *Medicaid,* 99.

41. For a detailed look at how different states are tightening eligibility standards and cutting benefits, see Kathryn Johnson, "Major Surgery for Ailing Medicaid Program," *U.S. News & World Report,* October 17, 1983, 91–93.

42. Ibid., 35–38.

43. Joseph Newhouse et al., "Some Interim Results from a Controlled Trial of Cost Sharing in Health Insurance," 1501–1507.

44. John Holahan, "The Impact of Alternative Hospital Payment Systems on Medicaid Costs," 519–520.

45. Ronald J. Vogel, "An Analysis of Structural Incentives in the Arizona Health Care Cost-Containment System," 14.

46. Jeffrey S. McCombs and Jon B. Christianson, "Applying Competitive Bidding to Health Care," 703–721.

47. Howard E. Freeman and Bradford L. Kirkman-Liff, "Health Care under AHCCCS: An Examination of Arizona's Alternative to Medicaid," 245–266.

48. Mary Wagner, "Colorado Considers Establishing Its Own Health Plan for Needy," 5.

49. Julie Kosterlitz, "Rationing Health Care," 1590–1595.

50. William B. Schwartz and Henry J. Aaron, "The Achilles Heel of Health Care Rationing," 15; William B. Schwartz and Henry J. Aaron, *Health Care Costs: The Social Tradeoffs.*

51. Susan S. Laudicina and Brian Burwell, "Profile of Medicaid Home and Community-Based Care Waivers, 1985: Findings of a National Survey," 528–529.

52. Ibid., 544.

53. Thomas L. Friedman, "Clinton Allowing States Flexibility on Medicaid Funds," *New York Times,* February 2, 1993.

54. Donald P. Baker, "Squeezing through the Loophole in the Medicaid Law," *Washington Post National Weekly Edition,* March 2–8, 1992, 34.

55. Julie Kosterlitz, "Middle-Class Medicaid," 2728–2731.

56. Donald P. Baker, "Squeezing through the Loophole in the Medicaid Law," 34.

57. Julie Kosterlitz, "Middle-Class Medicaid," 2728–2731.

58. Rosemary G. Kern and Susan R. Windham with Paula Griswold, *Medicaid and Other Experiments in State Health Policy* 54.

59. Frank Sloan, Janet Mitchell, and Jerry Cromwell, "Physician Participation in State Medicaid Programs," 211–245.

60. Bovbjerg and Holahan, *Medicaid in the Reagan Era,* 41.

61. Thomas W. Grannemann and Mark V. Pauly, *Controlling Medicaid Costs,* 71.

62. John Holahan, "Impact of Alternative Hospital Payment Systems on Medicaid Costs," 517.

63. David A. Crozier, "State Rate Setting: A Status Report," 66–83.

64. Craig Coelen and Daniel Sullivan, "An Analysis of the Effects of Prospective Reimbursement Programs on Hospital Expenditures," 1.

65. John Holahan, "Impact of Alternative Hospital Payment Systems on Medicaid Costs," 531–532.

66. Karen Davis et al., *Health Care Cost Containment,* 85.

67. George Anders, "Many States Embrace Managed Care System for Medicaid Patients," *Wall Street Journal,* June 11, 1993.

68. General Accounting Office, *Medicaid: States Turn to Managed Care to Improve Access and Control Costs,* 4.

69. Ibid., 2–3.

70. Ibid., 5.

71. Reported in George Anders, "Many States Embrace Managed Care System for Medicaid Patients."

72. Ronda Kotelchuck, "Medicaid Managed Care: A Mixed Review," 4–11; Deborah A. Freund, et al., "Evaluation of the Medicaid Competition Demonstrations," 81; Maren D. Anderson and Peter D. Fox, "Lessons Learned from Medicaid Managed Care Approaches," 80.

73. General Accounting Office, *Medicaid,* 4.

74. George Anders, "Many States Embrace Managed Care System for Medicaid Patients."

75. Lynn Wagner, "28 States Face Potential Deficits," 2.

76. General Accounting Office, *Medicaid Expansions.*

77. Joseph P. Shapiro, "How States Cook the Books," *U.S. News & World Report,* July 29, 1991, 24–25.; William Tucker, "A Leak in Medicaid," 46–48.

78. William Tucker, "A Leak in Medicaid," 48.

79. Robert Pear, "U.S. Moves to Curb Medicaid Payments for Many States," *New York Times,* September 11, 1991.

80. Terese Hudson, "States Scramble for Solutions under New Medicaid Law," 52–56.

81. "HCFA, States Spar—Again—Over Medicaid Provider Taxes," *State Health Notes* 16, no. 200 (March 20, 1995): 1–3; Dan Morgan, "Medicaid Bills Come Home to Roost," *Washington Post National Weekly Edition,* February 6–12, 1995, 32.

82. David Durda, "Number of Medicaid Lawsuits Belies Complexities Involved in Such Filings," 31–32.

83. Robert Pear, "Ruling May Lead to Big Rise in States' Medicaid Costs," *New York Times,* July 5, 1990.

84. Ibid.

85. Robert Pear, "Suits Force U.S. and States to Pay More for Medicaid," *New York Times,* October 29, 1991.

86. Katharine R. Levit et al., "National Health Expenditures, 1993," 290–291.

87. Teresa A. Coughlin, *Medicaid Since 1980;* Intergovernmental Health Policy Project, *Expanding Access to Health Care.*

88. Deborah Stone, "Why States Can't Solve the Health Care Crisis," 51–60.

89. Robin Toner, "This time, Clinton Tries a Selective Health Care Strategy," *New York Times,* June 14, 1995; Marilyn Werber Serafini, "No Strings Attached!"

Chapter 4. Medicare: Health Care for the Elderly and Disabled

1. Paul Starr, in *The Social Transformation of American Medicine,* 240–257, argues that "ideology, historical experience, and the overall political contest" (p. 255) helps explain the failure in 1917. "Ideology" refers to the liberal emphasis on individualism. "Historical experience" refers to, at least in part, the absence of dominant purchasers. "Political context" refers to fragmentation of political power, discussed in chapter 1. A president, whether Wilson, Franklin Roosevelt, or Truman, did not by himself have sufficient power to enact national health insurance, certainly not in the face of interest-group opposition.

2. Paul Starr, *Social Transformation of American Medicine,* 266–270; Theodore Marmor, *The Politics of Medicare,* 8–9.

3. Theodore Marmor, *Politics of Medicare,* 10–11.

4. Ibid., 15–20.

5. Ibid., 20.

6. For a thorough discussion of how health policy promised not to interfere with the practice of medicine, see Elliot A. Krause, *Power and Illness: The Political Sociology of Health and Medical Care.*

7. Theodore Marmor, *Politics of Medicare,* 23.

8. Paul Starr, *Social Transformation of American Medicine,* 369.

9. This social insurance strategy as described in Medicare was a continuation of that initially incorporated into Social Security. The idea was that the program would be so popular, and everyone would have such an interest in it, that it would survive attack. That politically astute strategy seems to have worked well for both programs.

10. Frank J. Thompson, *Health Policy and the Bureaucracy: Politics and Implementation,* 155.

11. Number calculated from U.S. Bureau of the Census, *Statistical Abstract of the United States 1966,* 72.

12. Data from U.S. Bureau of the Census, *Statistical Abstract of the United States 1992,* 105.

13. Center for the Study of Social Policy, *Kids Count Data Book 1994.*

14. John T. Petrie, "Overview of the Medicare Program," 1–12.

15. The Medicare Hospital Insurance tax is listed separately from the FICA tax on pay stubs.

16. "Medicare Premiums, Deductibles Increasing in '95," *Springfield News-Leader,* December 1, 1994.

17. John T. Petrie, "Overview of the Medicare Program," 1.

18. "Medicare Premiums, Deductibles Increasing in '95."

19. The percentages are not pulled out of a hat. The Medicare fee schedule is approximately 59 percent of what private insurers pay. See Robert Pear, "Medicare Paying Doctors 59% of Insurers' Rates, Panel Finds," *New York Times*, April 5, 1994.

20. Calculated from Marilyn Moon, *Medicare Now and in the Future*, 38.

21. Randall S. Brown et al., "Do Health Maintenance Organizations Work for Medicare?" 7–23.

22. Alma McMillan, "Trends in Medicare Health Maintenance Organization Enrollment: 1986–1993," 135–146.

23. Randall S. Brown, "Do Health Maintenance Organizations Work for Medicare?"

24. Ibid., 10.

25. Ibid., 14–15.

26. Marilyn Moon, *Medicare Now and in the Future*, 98–99.

27. Charles Helbing, "Medicare Program Expenditures," 37.

28. U.S. Bureau of the Census, *Statistical Abstract of the United States 1992*, 105.

29. Marilyn Moon, *Medicare Now and in the Future*, 37–38.

30. Pamela Farley Short and Jessica Primoff Vistnes, "Multiple Sources of Medicare Supplementary Insurance," 42.

31. Ibid., 42–43.

32. OBRA was part of the deal between Congress and President Bush to reduce the budget deficit by about $500 billion over a five-year period.

33. Short and Vistnes, "Multiple Sources of Medicare Supplementary Insurance," 34.

34. Thomas Rice and Kathleen Thomas, "Evaluating the New Medigap Standardization Regulations," 194–207.

35. Julie Rovner, "Climbing Medigap Premiums Draw Attention on Hill," 527–530.

36. "Filling the Gaps in Medicare," *Consumer Reports*, August 1994, 524.

37. Ibid., 524–525.

38. Ibid., 526.

39. Thomas Rice and Kathleen Thomas, "Evaluating the New Medigap Standardization Regulations," 194–207. See also Peter D. Fox, Thomas Rice, and Lisa Alecxih, "Medigap Regulations: Lessons for Health Care Reform?" 31–48.

40. Pamela Farley Short and Jessica Primoff Vistnes, "Multiple Sources of Medicare Supplementary Insurance," 33.

41. Claudia L. Schur, Marc L. Berk, and Penny Mohr, "Understanding the Cost of a Catastrophic Drug Benefit," 90.

42. Marilyn Moon, *Medicare Now and in the Future*, 110–111.

43. Ibid.

44. Description of the benefits comes from ibid., 116–117.

45. Ibid., 118–119. The reason for the delay in benefits was to build up a reserve to begin paying for them. The precedent for this is the original Social Security Act of 1935. Payments into the trust fund began in 1936, but the first Social Security checks did not begin until 1940.

46. Marilyn Moon, *Medicare Now and in the Future*, 121.

47. Ibid., 121–123.

48. Thomas Rice, Katherine Desmond, and Jon Gabel, "Medicare Catastrophic Coverage Act: A Post-Mortem," 75–87.

49. Marilyn Moon, *Medicare Now and in the Future*, 124–127.

50. See Judith M. Feder, *Medicare: The Politics of Federal Hospital Insurance;* and Thompson, *Health Policy and the Bureaucracy*.

51. John T. Petrie and Herbert A. Silverman, "Medicare Enrollment," 1992 annual supplement, *Health Care Financing Review*, 14.

52. Charles Hebling, "Medicare Program Expenditures,"41.

53. Ibid., 26.

54. Judith M. Feder, *Medicare*, 1.

55. Theodore R. Marmor, Donald A. Wittman, and Thomas C. Heagy, "The Politics of Medical Inflation," 61–75.

56. Calculated from U.S. Bureau of the Census, *Statistical Abstract of the United States 1992*, 98, 317.

57. Marmor's theory would work best under a system of national health insurance. This is undoubtedly one reason why providers have long opposed such programs in the United States.

58. Bruce Steunwald and Frank A. Sloan, "Regulatory Approaches to Hospital Cost Containment: A Synthesis of the Empirical Evidence," 276.

59. Paul L. Joskow, "Alternative Regulatory Mechanism for Controlling Hospital Costs," 219–257.

60. For a detailed discussion and analysis of the all-payer DRG system in New Jersey, see *Bulletin of the New York Academy of Medicine* 62, no. 6 (July/August 1986). The entire issue is devoted to the discussion of New Jersey's DRG system.

61. For an excellent analysis of the political process through which the DRG system was initiated first in New Jersey and then at the federal level, see James A. Morone and Andrew B. Dunham, "Slouching toward National Health Insurance: The Unanticipated Politics of DRGs," 646–662.

62. Franklin A. Shaffer, "DRGs: History and Overview," 389.

63. E.S. Quade, *Analysis for Public Decisions*, 3rd ed., 294.

64. Bruce M. Vladeck, "Comment on Hospital Reimbursement under Medicare," 269.

65. D.A. Dolnec and C.J. Dougherty, "DRGs: The Counterrevolution in Financing Health Care," 19–29.

66. Karen Davis, Gerald F. Anderson, Diane Rowland, and Earl P. Steinberg, *Health Care Cost Containment*, 50–51.

67. Urban Institute, "Hospital Prospective Payment: Cost Control and Windfall Profits," 12–13.

68. Karen Davis et al., *Health Care Cost Containment*, 170–171.

69. Frank Sloan, Michael A. Morrisey, and Joseph Valvona, "Effects of the Medicare Prospective Payment System on Hospital Costs Containment: An Early Appraisal," 191–220.

70. Judith R. Lave, "Hospital Reimbursement under Medicare," 251–278; Donald W. Simborg, "DRG Creep: A New Hospital Acquired Disease," 1602–1604; William C. Hsiao and Daniel L. Dunn, "The Impact of DRG Payment on New Jersey Hospitals," 212–220.

71. Karen Cook et al., "A Theory of Organizational Response to Regulation: The Case of Hospitals," 193–205.

72. T.E. Parsons, "Suggestions for a Sociological Approach to a Theory of Organizations," 63–85.

73. E. Green Gay et al., "An Appraisal of Organizational Response to Fiscally Constraining Regulation: The Case of Hospitals and DRGs," 41–55.

74. John Holahan and John L. Palmer, "Medicare's Fiscal Problems: An Imperative for Reforms," 66–68.

75. Stuart H. Altman and Marc A. Rodwin, "Halfway Competitive Markets and Ineffective Regulation: The American Health Care System," 335.

76. Numbers calculated from Petrie, "Overview of the Medicare Program," 6.

77. Thomas R. Oliver, "Analysis, Advice, and Congressional Leadership: The Physician Payment Review Commission and the Politics of Medicare," 117.

78. Ibid., 120.

79. Gornick notes that the Medicare fee schedule was part of a stream of reforms that began in 1975 with the creation of an economic index to limit changes in physician charges. See Marian Gornick, "Physician Payment Reform under Medicare: Monitoring Utilization and Access," 79–80.

80. For a full chronology of theses events, see Oliver, "Analysis, Advice, and Congressional Leadership," 124–127.

81. Marilyn Moon, *Medicare Now and in the Future*, 67.

82. Ibid., 68–69.

83. Thomas R. Oliver, "Analysis, Advice, and Congressional Leadership," 163.

84. Ibid., 165–168.

85. Mark E. Miller, Stephen Zuckerman, and Michael Gates, "How Do Medicare Physician Fees Compare with Private Payers?" 25.

86. Marsha Gold et al., "Effects of Selected-Cost-Containment Efforts: 1971–1993," 198–202.

87. Joshua M. Weiner and Laurel Hixon Illston, "How to Share the Burden: Long-Term Care Reform in the 1990s," 17.

88. The 1970–1993 numbers are calculated from Katharine R. Levit et al., "National Health Expenditures, 1993, " 282–284, 288. The 2018 estimate is from Wiener and Illson, "How to Share the Burden," 17.

89. U.S. Bureau of the Census, *Statistical Abstract of the United States 1994.*

90. Testimony of Jane L. Ross, associate director of income security issues, Health, Education, and Human Services Division, General Accounting Office, "Long-Term Care: Demography, Dollars, and Dissatisfaction Drive Reform," before the Special Committee on Aging, U.S. Senate, April 12, 1994, 6.

91. Joshua Perin, "Long-Term Care Insurance: Partnership Model Offers an Option," 4–5.

92. Katharine L. Levit et al., "National Health Expenditures, 1993," 288.

93. Jane Ross, "Long-Term Care," 1.

94. Ibid.

95. Joshua M. Wiener and Laurel Hixson Illston, "Sharing the Burden," 17.

96. General Accounting Office, *Long-Term Care for the Elderly: Issues of Need, Access, and Cost.*

97. Bruce C. Vladeck, Nancy A. Miller, and Steven B. Clauser, "The Changing Face of Long-Term Care," 8, 10.

98. General Accounting Office, *Long-Term Care: Diverse, Growing Population Includes Millions of Americans of All Ages.*

99. Penelope Lemov, "Nursing Homes and Common Sense," 46.

100. The 1988 estimate is from General Accounting Office, *Long-Term Care for the Elderly,* 4. The 1994 figure is from Lemov, "Nursing Homes and Common Sense," 45.

101. Esther B. Fein, "Elderly Transfer Assets to Qualify for Medicaid," *New York Times,* September 25, 1994.

102. Penelope Lemov, "Nursing Homes and Common Sense," 45–46.

103. General Accounting Office, *Long-Term Care: Private Sector Elder Care Could Yield Multiple Benefits.*

104. Ibid., 5–10.

105. General Accounting Office, *Long-Term Care: Support for Elder Care Could Benefit the Government Workplace and the Elderly,* 6–7.

106. Penelope Lemov, "Nursing Homes and Common Sense," 47.

107. A block grant is money from, in this case, the federal government to a state, for a particular area such as caring for the elderly. The state then has freedom to allocate that money among different programs, nursing homes, community-based care, or assisted home care.

108. Lemov, "Nursing Homes and Common Sense," 48.

109. Ibid.

110. Testimony of Janet L. Shikles, director, health financing and policy issues, Human Resources Division, General Accounting Office, *Long-Term Care Insurance: Risks to Consumers Should Be Reduced,* 2.

111. Ibid., 2–3.

112. Ibid., 5–6.

113. Cited in Thomas Rice, Kathleen Thomas, and William Weissert, *The Impact of Owning Private Long-Term Care Insurance Policies on Out-of-Pocket Costs,* 7.

114. Joseph M. Wiener and Laurel Hixson Illston, "Sharing the Burden," 18.

115. Joshua Perin, "Long-Term Care Insurance," 4.

116. Ibid.

117. Sharon M. Keigher, "Health Care Reform and Long-Term Care: Uneasy Political Partners," 224–225.

118. Sharon M. Keigher, "Health Care Reform and Long-Term Care," 224. See also the Kaiser Commission on the Future of Medicaid, *Health Reform Legislation: A Comparison of Major Proposals;* Testimony of Joseph F. Delfico before the Subcommittee on Aging, Committee on Labor and Human Resources, U.S. Senate, *Long-Term Reform: Program Eligibility, States' Service Capacity, and Federal Role in Reform Need More Consideration* (General Accounting Office, April 14 , 1994); and Testimony of Mark V. Nadel before the Subcommittees on Health and the Environment and On Commerce, Consumer Protection, and Competitiveness, Committee on Energy and Commerce, U.S. House of Representatives, *Health Care Reform: Supplemental and Long-Term Care Insurance* (General Accounting Office, September 9, 1993).

119. Sharon M. Keigher, "Health Care Reform and Long-Term Care," 224; Kaiser Commission on the Future of Medicaid, *Health Reform Legislation.*

120. Spencer Rich, "For the Elderly, A Promise of More Social Security and Less Taxation," *Washington Post National Weekly Edition,* December 26, 1994–January 1, 1995, 10.

121. In 1994, Vermont considered financing long-term care through a social insurance model. See Linda Demkovich, "Vermont Takes on LTC Financing," 1–2, 8.

122. Joshua M. Wiener and Laurel Hixson Illston, "Sharing the Burden," 19–21.

123. Walter N. Leutz, Merwyn R. Greenlick, and John A. Capitman, "Integrating Acute and Long-Term Care," 58–74. The states of Massachusetts and Washington are trying to place greater emphasis on community-based care. See Donna Folkemer, "Shift to Community Long-Term Care Looms on Horizon," 1–2, 8.

124. Spencer Rich, "For the Elderly, A Promise of More Social Security and Less Taxation," 10.

125. Because so many Medicare recipients have medigap policies (about 89 percent), cost sharing is likely to have little impact on recipient use of services. See George S. Chulis, Franklin P. Eppig, Mary O. Hogan, Daniel R. Waldo, and Ross H. Arnett III, "Health Insurance and the Elderly," 111–118.

126. Robert Pear, "Medicare to Stop Pushing Patients to Enter H.M.O.'s," *New York Times,* December 27, 1993.

127. Robert Pear, "Another Set of Dire Warnings on Social Security and Medicare Trust Funds," *New York Times,* April 4, 1995.

128. Robin Toner, "This Time, Clinton Tries a Selective Health Care Strategy," *New York Times,* June 14, 1995.

129. Marilyn Werber Serafini, "Managed Medicare."

Chapter 5. Health Care and the Disadvantaged:
Falling through the Cracks

1. Elliot A. Krause, *Power and Illness: The Political Sociology of Health and Medical Care,* 146.

2. For a discussion of health care systems in other countries and lessons they might hold for the United States, see Laurence A. Graig, *Health of Nations: An International Perspective on U.S. Health Care Reform.*

3. Lu Ann Aday, "Equity, Accessibility, and Ethical Issues: Is the U.S. Health Care Reform Debate Asking the Right Questions?" 724–740. Aday briefly discusses the liberal, individual rights tradition and the communitarian tradition that underlies the notion of the common good. See also Lu Ann Aday, *At Risk in America: The Health and Health Care Needs of Vulnerable Populations in the United States.*

4. Deborah A. Stone, "The Struggle for the Soul of Health Insurance," 287–317.

5. Nancy S. Jecker, "Can an Employer-Based Health Insurance System Be Just?" 657–673. For critiques of Jecker's argument, see Joan E. Ruttenberg, "Commentary—Revisiting the Employment–Insurance Link," 675–681; and David A. Rochefort, "Commentary—The Pragmatic Appeal of Employment-Based Health Care Reform," 683–693.

6. A medigap policy is an addition to Medicare to help recipients cover costs not paid by Medicare. See chapter 4 for a discussion of medigap policies.

7. Calculated from U.S. Bureau of the Census, *Statistical Abstract of the United States 1992,* 105.

8. Calculated from ibid., 8.

9. Robert Pear, "Increase Found in Those without Health Coverage," *New York Times,* December 15, 1993.

10. Robert Pear, "Gaps in Coverage for Health Insurance," *New York Times,* March 29, 1994.

11. Diana Rowland, Barbara Lyons, Alina Salganicoff, and Peter Long, "A Profile of the Uninsured in America," 283.

12. Stephen H. Long and M. Susan Marquis, "Gaps in Employer Coverage: Lack of Supply or Lack of Demand?" 284.

13. Deborah Chollet, "Employer-Based Health Insurance in a Changing Work Force," 319–320.

14. "Eroding Employer-Based Insurance," 4.

15. Diana Rowland et al., "Profile of the Uninsured in America," 285.

16. Ibid.

17. Ibid.

18. Calculated from U.S. Bureau of the Census, *Statistical Abstract of the United States 1992,* 396.

19. For an analysis of downsizing, see Steven Pearlstein, "The Downsizing Trap," *Washington Post National Weekly Edition,* January 10–16, 1994, 8–9; Steven Pearlstein, "Recessions Fade, but Downsizings Are Forever," *Washington Post National Weekly Edition,* October 3–9, 1994, 21; and Deborah Chollet, "Employer-Based Health Insurance in a Changing Work Force," 314–315.

20. Cynthia B. Sullivan, Marianne Miller, Roger Feldman, and Bryan Dowd, "Employer-Sponsored Health Insurance in 1991," 173.

21. Milt Freudenheim, "Medical Insurance Is Being Cut Back for Many Retirees," *New York Times,* June 28, 1992.

22. Charlotte F. Muller, *Health Care and Gender,* 73.

23. Deborah Chollet, "Employer-Based Health Insurance in a Changing Work Force," 314.

24. Stephen H. Long and M. Susan Marquis, "Gaps in Employer Coverage," 284.

25. Deborah Chollet, "Employer-Based Health Insurance in a Changing Work Force," 321. See also Alan C. Monheit and Jessical Primoff Vistnes, "Implicit Pooling of Workers from Large and Small Firms," 301–314.

26. Victor Cohn, "How Can We Fix a Broken System?" *Washington Post National Weekly Edition,* February 3–9, 1992, 6–7.

27. The controversy arises because the poverty line looks only at money income, leaving out food stamps, Medicaid, housing allowance, and so forth. Adding those items in would bring more people over the poverty line, but the trends in poverty would remain more or less the same.

28. The National Commission on the State and Local Public Service, *Frustrated Federalism: Rx for State and Local Health Care Reform,* 15.

29. Fuchs argues, as many economists do, that whatever the size of the firm, employees do not pay for health insurance. Ultimately, the workers pay for it. If one considers salary (or wages) plus fringe benefits as a total work compensation package, then this may be correct (see below). Fuchs notes that between 1970 and 1990, total compensation grew by 12 percent in real dollars, while earnings fell by 6 percent. Presumably, employers can offer all compensation in the form of wages and let employees purchase what they want with it. The implication of Fuchs's analysis is that, in a sense, the size of the firm is irrelevant to whether health insurance is offered. The question is the size of total compensation and, thus, whether employees can afford it. Though Fuchs does not make this point, perhaps the major benefit from size of firm, apart from higher compensation, is the ability to buy as a group. Victor R. Fuchs, "The Clinton Plan: A Researcher Examines Reform," 102–114. One could also make the point that firms pass on only a portion of health insurance premiums to their employees. Part of the costs are captured by tax deductions. Another portion might be included in product or service prices. It is not entirely clear what portion of premiums should be considered as part of compensation.

30. See, for example, Robert Pear, "Insurance-Liability Curb Poses Problem for Bush," *New York Times,* May 19, 1992.

31. Diana Rowland et al., "Profile of the Uninsured in America," 284.

32. Ibid., 284–285.

33. Chris Hafner-Eaton, "Physician Utilization Disparities between the Uninsured and Insured: Comparisons of the Chronically Ill, Acutely Ill, and Well Nonelderly Populations," 787–782.

34. Paula Braverman, V. Mylo Schaaf, Susan Egerter, Trude Bennett, and William Schecter, "Insurance-Related Differences in the Risk of Ruptured Appendix," 444–449.

35. See David W. Baker, Carl D. Stevens, and Tobert H. Brook, "Regular Source of Ambulatory Care and Medical Care Utilization by Patients Presenting to a Public Hospital Emergency Department," 1909–1912; and Kimberly J. Rask, Mark V. Williams, Ruth M. Parker, and Sally E. McNagny, "Obstacles Predicting Lack of a Regular Provider and Delays in Seeking Care for Patients at an Urban Public Hospital," 1931–1933.

36. Joel S. Weisman, Constantine Gatsonis, and Arnold M. Epstein, "Rates of Avoidable Hospitalization by Insurance Status in Massachusetts and Maryland," 2388–2394.

37. Jack Hadley, Earl P. Steinberg, and Judith Feder, "Comparison of Uninsured and Privately Insured Hospital Patients: Condition on Admission, Resource Use, and Outcome," 374–379.

38. Jeffrey J. Stoddard, Robert F. St. Peter, and Paul W. Nweacheck, "Health Insurance Status and Ambulatory Care for Children," 1421–1425.

39. Charles Oberg, Betty Lia-Hoagberg, Ellen Hodkinson, Caterine Skovholt, and Renee Vanman, "Prenatal Care Comparisons among Privately Insured, Uninsured, and Medicaid-Enrolled Women," 533–535.

40. Paula A. Braveman, Susan Egerter, Trude Bennett, and Jonathan Showstack, "Differences in Hospital Resource Allocation among Sick Newborns According to Insurance Coverage," 3300–3308.

41. John Z. Ayanian, Betsy A. Kohler, Toshi Abe, and Arnold M. Epstein, "The Relation between Health Insurance Coverage and Clinical Outcomes among Women with Breast Cancer," 326–331.

42. Helen R. Burstin, Stuart R. Lipsitz, and Troyen A. Brennan, "Socioeconomic Status and Risk for Substandard Medical Care," 2383–2387.

43. Peter Franks, Carolyn M. Clancy, Marthe R. Gold, and Paul A. Nutting, "Health Insurance and Subjective Health Status: Data from the 1987 National Medical Expenditure Survey," 1295–1299.

44. Peter Franks, Carolyn M. Clancy, and Marthe R. Gold, "Health Insurance and Mortality: Evidence from a National Cohort," 737–741.

45. Wendy K. Zellers, Catherine G. McLaughlin, and Kevin D. Frick, "Small-Business Health Insurance," 174–180. See also Donald W. Light, "The Practice and Ethics of Risk-Related Insurance," 2503–2508.

46. See Robert S. Stern, Joel E. Weissman, and Arnold M. Epstein, "The Emergency Department as a Pathway for Admission for Poor and High-Cost Patients," 2238–2246; and Luba Vikhanski, "Emergency Departments Face a Growing Crisis in Care," 50–51.

47. See Bruce Goldfarb, "Uncompensated Care Pushes Trauma Centers Out of Business," 32; and Ellen S. Campbell, "Unpaid Hospital Bills: Evidence from Florida," 92–98.

48. Terrel W. Zollinger, Robert M. Saywell, Jr., and David K.W. Chu, "Uncompensated Hospital Care for Pregnancy and Childbirth Cases," 1017–1022.

49. Eleanor D. Kinney and Suzanne K. Steinmetz, "Notes from the Insurance Underground: How the Chronically Ill Cope," 641.

50. Thomas Rice and Kenneth E. Thorpe, "Income-Related Cost Sharing in Health Insurance," 22.

51. Deborah A. Stone, "Struggle for the Soul of Health Insurance," 290.

52. See General Accounting Office, Health Insurance: Cost Increases Lead to Coverage Limitations and Cost Shifting; Alan C. Monheit and Jessical Primoff Vistnes, "Implicit Pooling of Workers from Large and Small Firms," 301–314; Gina Kolata, "New Insurance Practice: Dividing Sick from Well," New York Times, March 4, 1992; and Gina Kolata, "The Philosophical Fight over What Insurance Should Be" New York Times, March 8, 1992.

53. Wendy K. Zellers, Catherine G. McLaughlin, and Kevin D. Frick, "Small-Business Health Insurance," 175.

54. Ibid., 174–175.

55. Ibid., 175.

56. Eleanor D. Kinney and Suzanne K. Steinmentz, "Notes from the Insurance Underground," 637.

57. See Jeffrey A. Buck and Mark S. Kamlet, "Problems with Expanding Medicaid for the Uninsured," 1–25; and Julie Kosterlitz, "Buying into Trouble," 3245–3249.

58. Jeffrey A. Buck and Mark S. Kamlet, "Problems with Expanding Medicaid for the Uninsured," 2.

59. Ibid., 3–4.

60. Ibid., 6–7.

61. Ibid., 7–12.

62. Ibid., 13–20.

63. Robert Pear, "National Health Care Policy: How Bush and Clinton Differ," *New York Times,* August 12, 1992.

64. Clifford Krauss, "Under Political Steam, Health-Care Issue Gains Wider Support in Congress," *New York Times,* January 12, 1992.

65. Michael Wines, "Bush Announces Health Plan, Filling Gap in Re-election Bid," *New York Times,* February 7, 1992.

66. Ibid.

67. Robert Pear, "President Leaves Many Areas Gray," *New York Times,* February 7, 1992.

68. Henry Simmons, "Cheaper Health Care (for the Rich)," *New York Times,* May 15, 1992.

69. Stuart M. Butler, "A Tax Reform Strategy to Deal with the Uninsured," 2541.

70. Ibid.

71. Ibid., 2541–2542.

72. Ibid., 2542.

73. Ibid.

74. Ibid., 2542–2543. The article also examines how the refundable tax credit program would reduce inflationary pressures by making consumers more cost conscious.

75. See Paul Starr, *The Social Transformation of American Medicine,* 370–372; and Karen Davis and Cathy Schoen, *Health and the War on Poverty: A Ten-Year Proposal,* 161–202.

76. Karen Davis and Cathy Schoen, *Health and the War on Poverty,* 177–185.

77. Robert Pear, "Panel Offers Health Plan to Bush on Uninsured," *New York Times,* December 20, 1991.

78. The most direct provision of health services by the federal government is the Department of Veterans Affairs Hospital System and the Public Health Service Hospitals.

79. Karen Davis and Cathy Schoen, "Universal Coverage: Building on Medicare and Employer Financing," 11–12.

80. Ibid., 12–14.

81. Sheila R. Zedlewdki, Gregory Acs, and Colin W. Winterbottom, "Play-or-Pay Employer Mandates: Potential Effects," 69.

82. See Karen Davis, "Expanding Medicare and Employer Plans to Achieve Universal Health Insurance," 2525–2528; and Davis and Schoen, "Universal Coverage," 7–20.

83. Karen Davis, "Expanding Medicare and Employer Plans to Achieve Universal Health Insurance," 2525.

84. Howard Berman, "Rochester: Community Rating = Insurance Access," 56.

85. For a discussion of the class versus race issue, see the two works by William Julius Wilson, *The Declining Significance of Race* and *The Truly Disadvantaged.*

86. David McBride, "Black America," 319–337.

87. Eli Ginzberg, "Improving Health Care for the Poor," 464.

88. U.S. Department of Health and Human Services, *Health Status of Minorities and Low-Income Groups,* 89.

89. Ibid., 99.

90. Diane Rowland and Alina Salganicoff, "Commentary: Lessons from Medicaid," 550–551.

91. Ibid., 551.

92. U.S. Department of Health and Human Services, *Health Status of Minorities and Low-Income Groups,* 131.

93. Ibid., 137.

94. Ibid., 167.

95. Ibid., 195; see also "Fighting on Two Fronts (Minorities and AIDS)," *Time,* January 25, 1993, 23; and Lu Ann Aday, *At Risk in America: The Health and Health Care Needs of Vulnerable Populations in the United States*, 52.

96. U.S. Department of Health and Human Services, *Health Status of Minorities and Low-Income Groups,* 196.

97. Ibid., 199.

98. Ibid., 325.

99. Ibid., 345.

100. Ibid.

101. Velvet G. Miller and Janis L. Curties, "Health Care Reform and Race-Specific Policies," 748.

102. Eli Ginzberg, "Improving Health Care for the Poor," 464–465.

103. Ibid., 465.

104. Ibid.

105. Durado D. Brooks, David R. Smith, and Ron J. Anderson, "Medical Apartheid: An American Perspective," 2746.

106. Ibid., 2747.

107. R. Burciaga Valdez, Hal Morgenstern, E. Richard Brown, Roberta Wyn, Wang Chao, and William Cumberland, "Insuring Latinos Against the Costs of Illness," 889–894.

108. See Fernando M. Trevino, M. Eugene Moyer, R. Burciaga Valdez, and Christine A. Stroup-Benham, "Health Insurance Coverage and Utilization of Health Services by Mexican Americans, Mainland Puerto Ricans, and Cuban Americans," 233–237; and "Hispanic Health in the United States," 248–252.

109. Helen R. Burstin, Stuart R. Lipsitz, and Troyen A. Brennan, "Socioeconomic Status and Risk for Substandard Medical Care," 2383–2387.

110. Kevin G. Volpp and J. Sanford Schwartz, "Myths and Realities Surrounding Health Reform," 1372; see also Charles N. Oberg, Betty Lia-Hoagberg, Ellen Hodkinson, Catherine Skovholt, and Renee Vanman, "Prenatal Comparisons among Privately Insured, Uninsured, and Medicaid-Enrolled Women," 533–535.

111. Diana Rowland and Alina Salganicoff, "Commentary: Lessons from Medicaid," 551.

112. Ibid.

113. Ibid., 552.

114. U.S. Department of Health and Human Services, *Health Status of Minorities and Low-Income Groups,* 647; see also Chris Hafner-Eaton, "Will the Phoenix Rise, and Where Should She Go? The Women's Health Agenda," 841–856.

115. Some of this may change with the implementation of the Family and Medical Leave Act of 1993. The act provides employees with up to twelve weeks of unpaid leave because of the birth or adoption of a child, the illness of a family member, or a death in the family.

116. U.S. Department of Health and Human Services, *Health Status of Minorities and Low-Income Groups,* 648.

117. Charlotte F. Muller, *Health Care and Gender,* 104–114.

118. Ibid., 73.

119. Carolyn M. Clancy and Charlea T. Massion, "American Women's Health Care: A Patchwork Quilt with Gaps," 1918–1920.

120. Chris Hafner-Eaton, "Will the Phoenix Rise, and Where Should She Go?" 851.

121. Ibid., 843.

122. Charles Mawrick, "Women's Health Action Plan Sees First Anniversary," 1816–1818.

123. Barbara J. Culliton, "Critics Condemn NIH Women's Study," 11.

124. The following is based on Andrew G. Kadar, "The Sex-Bias Myth in Medicine," *Atlantic Monthly* 274, no. 2 (August 1994): 66–70.

125. Ibid., 69.

126. Ibid.

127. Ibid., 70.

Chapter 6. Health Care Cost Containment

1. Karen Davis and Cathy Schoen, *Health and the War on Poverty.*

2. Robert G. Evans, "Finding the Levers, Finding the Courage: Lessons from Cost Containment in North America," 585–615.

3. Katharine R. Levit et al., "National Health Expenditures, 1993," 280.

4. Sally T. Burner, Daniel R. Waldo, and David R. McKusick, "National Health Expenditures Projections through 2030," 20.

5. Maurice McGregor, "Hospital Costs: Can They Be Cut?" 92–93.

6. W. Bryan Latham, *Health Care Costs: There Are Solutions,* 11–26; For a discussion of business attitudes toward health care costs, see Harvey M. Sapolsky et al., "Corporate Attitude toward Health Care Costs," 561–585.

7. John R. Virts and George W. Wilson, "Inflation and Health Care Prices," 88–100.

8. David Mechanic, "Some Dilemmas in Health Care Policy," 2–3.

9. James R. Jones, "Cost Pressures and Health Policy Reforms," 41.

10. Kevin Grumbach and Thomas Bodenheimer, "Reins or Fences: A Physician's View of Cost Containment," 120.

11. This is an old debate. See, for example, Charles E. Lindblom, *Politics and Markets;* Robert A. Dahl and Charles E. Lindblom, *Politics, Economics and Planning.*

12. Walter McClure, "Structural and Incentive Problems in Economic Regulation of Medical Care," 109–110.

13. Robert M. Ball, "Background of Regulation in Health Care," 8–9.

14. Mark V. Pauly, "Is Medical Care Different?" 22.

15. Theresa Varner and Jack Christy, "Consumer Information Needs in a Competitive Health Care Environment," 99–104.

16. Mark V. Pauly, "Is Medical Care Different?" 236.

17. Stephen M. Weiner, "On Public Values and Private Regulation: Some Reflections on Cost Containment Strategies," 278.

18. Stuart Altman and Sanford L. Weiner, "Regulation as a Second Best Choice," 421–447.

19. Bruce C. Vladeck, "The Market vs. Regulation: The Case for Regulation," 209–223; Bruce C. Vladeck, "Variation Data and the Regulatory Rationale," 102–109.

20. S. Breyer, "Analyzing Regulatory Failure: Mismatches, Less Restrictive Alternatives and Reform," 549–609.

21. McClure, "Structural and Incentive Problems in Economic Regulation of Medical Care," 107–144. The author outlines a series of structural and incentive problems such as diffused consumer interests versus concentrated producer interests, political setting problems, and technical content problems. For a theoretical argument against government regulation analogous to the concept of market failure, see Charles Wolf, Jr., "A Theory of Non-Market Failures," 114–123.

22. John C. Goodman, *The Regulation of Medical Care: Is the Price Too High?* 133.

23. David F. Durenberger, "The Politics of Health," 4.

24. Roger G. Noll, "The Consequences of Public Utility Regulation of Hospitals," 23–48.

25. S.E. Berki, "Health Care Policy: Lessons from the Past and Issues of the Future," 235.

26. Paul M. Ellwood, Jr., "Alternative to Regulation: Improving the Market," 49–72.

27. Alain C. Enthoven, "Competition in the Marketplace: Health Care in the 1980s," 18–19. For a more extended discussion, see Alain C. Enthoven, *Health Plan.*

28. Alain C. Enthoven, "Consumer Choice Health Plans," 650–658; 709–720.

29. Alain C. Enthoven, "Managed Competition of Alternate Delivery System," 305–321; H.E. Frech III and Paul B. Ginsburg, "Competition among Health Insurers, Revisited," 279–291.

30. Michael R. Pollard, "The Essential Role of Antitrust in a Competitive Market for Health Services," 263.

31. Ibid., 262.

32. Walter McClure, "The Competitive Strategy for Medical Care," 46.

33. Robert G. Evans, "Incomplete Vertical Integration in the Health Care Industry: Pseudomarkets and Pseudopolicies," 60–87.

34. Eli Ginzberg, "Procompetition in Health Care: Policy or Fantasy?" 386–398.

35. Jon R. Gabel and Alan C. Monheit, "Will Competition Plans Change Insurer–Provider Relationships?" 635.

36. Paul Starr, "Changing the Balance of Power in American Medicine," 170.

37. John C. Goodman, *Regulation of Medical Care,* 117–118.

38. M.S. Roemer, "Hospitals Utilization and the Supply of Physicians," 933–989.

39. Clark C. Havighurst, "Regulation of Health Facilities and Services by 'Certificate of Need,' " 1143–1233.

40. The major example of the early planning effort was the Hospital Survey and Construction Act of 1946, better known as the Hill-Burton Act.

41. For a very extensive analysis of federal and state laws and procedures in this area, see Medicine in Public Interest, *Certificate of Need: An Expanding Regulatory Concept: A Compilation and Analysis of Federal and State Laws and Procedures* (Washington, D.C.: Medicine in Public Interest, 1978); for an excellent annotated bibliography of certificate-of-need project reviews, see U.S. Department of Health, Education, and Welfare, *Certificate of Need/1122 Project Reviews: An Annotated Bibliography.*

42. Louanne Kennedy and Bernard M. Baruch, "Health Planning in an Age of Austerity," 233.

43. Judith Gelman, *Competition and Health Planning,* 11. Also see D.S. Salkever and T.W. Bice, "The Impact of Certificate of Need Controls on Hospital Investment," 185–214.

44. David Salkever and Thomas Bice, *Hospital Certificate-of-Need Controls: Impact on Investment, Costs and Use,* 75.

45. Clark C. Havighurst, "Regulation of Health Facilities and Services by 'Certificate of Need,' " 1143–1233; John C. Goodman, *Regulation of Medical Care,* 121.

46. David Salkever and Thomas Bice, *Hospital Certificate-of-Need Controls,* 16; William J. Bicknell and Diana C. Walsh, "Critical Experiences in Organizing and Administering a State Certificate-of-Need Program," 29–45.

47. Theodore Marmor and James Morone, "HSAs and the Representation of Consumer Interests: Conceptual Issues and Litigation Problems," 117–128.

48. Lewin and Associates, Inc., *Evaluation of the Efficiency and Effectiveness of the Section 1122 Review Process,* 1–17.

49. Bruce Vladeck, "Interest Group Representation and the HSAs: Health Planning and Political Theory," 23–29.

50. Stephen S. Mick and John D. Thompson, "Public Attitude toward Health Planning under the Health Systems Agencies," 783–800.

51. Lynn Etheredge, "Reagan, Congress and Health Spending," 16.

52. Richard L. Johnson, "Should Hospital Planning Continue to Be Regulated?" 90.

53. U.S. Congress, Congressional Budget Office, *The Impact of PSROs on Health-Care Costs: Update of CBO's 1979 Evaluation.* The other studies by the CBO using data for earlier years had come to similar conclusions.

54. John C. Goodman, *Regulation of Medical Care,* 126–127.

55. Charlotte L. Rosenberg, "Why Doctor-Policing Laws Don't Work," 84–96; John Varlova, "A $2.2 Million Lesson in the Perils of Peer Review," 56–61; Robert Cassidy, "Can You Really Speak Your Mind in Peer Review?" 246–262.

56. Lynn Etheredge, "Reagan, Congress and Health Spending," 16.

57. "PROs: Peering Harder in the '90s," *Hospitals,* February 5, 1989, 42–46.

58. Ibid.

59. General Accounting Office, *Medicare PROs: Extreme Variation in Organizational Structure and Activities.*

60. Lawrence D. Brown, "Introduction to a Decade of Transition," 569–583.

61. Richard McNeil, Jr., and Robert E. Schlenker, "HMOs, Competition and Government," 195–224.

62. See Joseph L. Falkson, *HMOs and the Politics of Health Service Reform.*

63. U.S. Department of Health, Education, and Welfare, *Toward a Comprehensive Health Policy for the 1970s: A White Paper.*

64. John K. Iglehart, "The Federal Government as Venture Capitalist: How Does It Fare?" 656–666.

65. Paul M. Ellwood, "Health Maintenance Strategy," 291–298; Clark C. Havighurst, "Health Maintenance Organizations and the Market for Health Services," 716–795.

66. Joseph L. Falkson, "Market Reform, Health Systems, and HMOs," 218.

67. Arnold J. Rosoff, "Phase Two of the Federal HMO Development Program: New Directions After a Shaky Start," 209–243.

68. Ibid.

69. Karen Davis et al., *Health Care Cost Containment,* 135.

70. Roger Feldman, John Kralewski, and Bryan Dowd, "Health Maintenance Organizations: The Beginning or the End?" 191–211.

71. Alan L. Hillman, "Financial Incentives for Physicians in HMOs: Is There a Conflict of Interest?" 1734–1748.

72. Donald W. Moran, "HMOs, Competition, and the Politics of Minimum Benefits," 190–208.

73. Alan L. Sorkin, *Health Care and the Changing Economic Environment,* 124; Harold S. Luft, *Health Maintenance Organizations: Dimensions of Performance;* Harold S. Luft, "How Do Health Maintenance Organizations Achieve Their Savings? Rhetoric and Evidence," 1336–1343.

74. Sorkin, *Health Care and the Changing Economic Environment,* 119, 124; Harold S. Luft, "Trends in Medical Costs: Do HMOs Lower the Rate of Growth?" 1–16; William G. Manninh et al., "A Controlled Trial of the Effects of a Prepaid Group Practice on Use of Services," 1505–1510; J.E. Ware et al., "Comparison of Health Outcomes at a Health Maintenance Organization with Those of Fee-for-Service Care," 1017–1022; Group Health Association of America, *HMO Industry Profile: Utilization Pattern* (Washington, D.C., 1988).

75. Harold S. Luft, Susan C. Maerki, and Joan B. Trauner, "The Competitive Effects of Health Maintenance Organizations: Another Look at Evidence from Hawaii, Rochester, and Minneapolis/St. Paul," 625–658.

76. Sorkin, *Health Care and the Changing Economic Environment,* 128; Marie L.F. Ashcraft and S.E. Berki, "Health Maintenance Organizations as Medicaid Providers," 122–131. The authors argue that HMOs have no incentives to enroll Medicaid beneficiaries and Medicaid beneficiaries have no incentives to enroll in HMOs.

77. Gail Wilensky and L. Rossiter, "Patient Self-Selection in HMOs," 66–80.

78. Stanley B. Jones, "Multiple Choice Health Insurance: The Lessons and Challenges to Private Insurers," 161–166; Ira Strumwasser et al., "The Triple Option Choice: Self Selection Bias in Traditional Coverage, HMOs, and PPOs," 432–441; Harold S. Luft and R.H. Miller, "Patient Selection in a Competitive Health Care System," 97–119.

79. F.J. Hellinger, "Selection Bias in Health Maintenance Organizations: Analysis of Recent Evidence," 55–63; Mark S. Blumberg, "Health Status and Health Care Use by Type of Private Health Coverage," 633–655.

80. Jeffrey Merrill and Catherine McLaughlin, "Competition versus Regulation: Some Empirical Evidence," 613–623.

81. Roger Feldman et al., "The Competitive Impact of Health Maintenance Organizations on Hospital Finances: An Exploratory Study," 675–697; Allan N. Johnson and David Aquilina, "The Competitive Impact of Health Maintenance Organizations and Competition on Hospitals in Minneapolis/St. Paul," 659–674.

82. Jack Hadley and Katherine Swartz, "The Impact of Hospital Costs between 1980 and 1984 of Hospital Rate Regulation, Competition, and Change in Health Insurance Coverage," 35–47.

83. Harold S. Luft, "Trends in Medical Care Costs," 1–17.

84. Karen Davis, *Health Care Cost Containment,* 132–134.

85. W. P. Welch, "The New Structure of Individual Practice Associations," 723–739.

86. Lawrence D. Brown, "Competition and Health Cost Containment: Cautions and Conjectures," 157–158.

87. Peter Kerr, "The Changing Definition of Health Insurers," *New York Times,* May 10, 1993.

88. J.H.A. Brown, *The Politics of Health Care,* 27.

89. Odin Anderson et al., *HMO Development: Patterns and Prospects,* 146.

90. Lawrence D. Brown, "Competition and Health Care Policy: Experience and Expectations," 51.

91. Katharine R. Levit et al., "National Health Expenditures, 1993," 285.

92. Ibid., 26.

93. Robert M. Gibson et al., "National Health Expenditures, 1983," 22.

94. Bruce Steunwald and Frank A. Sloan, "Regulatory Approaches to Hospital Cost Containment: A Synthesis of the Empirical Evidence," 276.

95. Paul L. Joskow, "Alternative Regulatory Mechanism for Controlling Hospital Costs," 219–257.

96. For a detailed discussion and analysis of the all-payer DRG system in New

Jersey, see *Bulletin of the New York Academy of Medicine* 62, no. 6. The entire issue is devoted to the discussion of New Jersey's DRG system.

97. For an excellent analysis of the political process through which the DRG system was initiated first in New Jersey and than at the federal level, see James A. Morone and Andrew B. Dunham, "Slouching toward National Health Insurance: The Unanticipated Politics of DRGs," 646–662.

98. Bruce C. Vladeck, "Comment on Hospital Reimbursement under Medicare," 269.

99. D.A. Dolnec and C.J. Dougherty, "DRGs: The Counterrevolution in Financing Health Care," 19–29.

100. Frank A. Sloan, "Government and the Regulation of Hospital Care," 196–201.

101. Kenneth J. Meir, *Regulation: Politics, Bureaucracy and Economics*, 1.

102. Franklin A. Shaffer, "DRGs: History and Overview," 389.

103. E.S. Quade, *Analysis for Public Decisions*, 3rd ed., 294

104. Karen Davis et al., *Health Care Cost Containment*, 50–51.

105. Urban Institute, "Hospital Prospective Payment: Cost Control and Windfall Profits," 12–13.

106. Karen Davis et al., *Health Care Cost Containment*, 170–171.

107. Frank Sloan, Michael A. Morrisey, and Joseph Valvona, "Effects of the Medicare Prospective Payment System on Hospital Costs Containment: An Early Appraisal," 191–220.

108. Judith R. Lave, "Hospital Reimbursement under Medicare," 251–78; Donald W. Simborg, "DRG Creep: A New Hospital Acquired Disease," 1602–1604; William C. Hsiao and Daniel L. Dunn, "The Impact of DRG Payment on New Jersey Hospitals," 212–220.

109. Karen Cook et al., "A Theory of Organizational Response to Regulation: The Case of Hospitals," 193–205.

110. T.E. Parsons, "Suggestions for a Sociological Approach to a Theory of Organizations," 63–85.

111. E. Green Gay et al., "An Appraisal of Organizational Response to Fiscally Constraining Regulation: The Case of Hospitals and DRGs," 41–55.

112. John Holahan and John L. Palmer, "Medicare's Fiscal Problems: An Imperative for Reforms," 66–68.

113. Stuart H. Altman and Marc A. Rodwin, "Halfway Competitive Markets and Ineffective Regulation: The American Health Care System," 335.

114. Sun Valley Forum on National Health, Harrison Conference Center, "The Role of State and Local Government in Health," 134.

115. Helen C. Lazenby and Suzanne W. Letsch, "National Health Expenditures, 1989," 14, 23.

116. For a detailed analysis of the evolution of health care policy and its implications for federalism, see Frank J. Thompson, "New Federalism and Health Care Policy: States and the Old Questions," 647–669.

117. David A. Crozier, "State Rate Setting: A Status Report," 66–83.

118. Alfonso Esposito et al., "Abstracts of State Legislated Hospital Cost-Containment Programs," 129.

119. Harold Cohen, "State Rate Regulation," in Institute of Medicine, *Controls on Health Care*, 123–135.

120. Craig Coelen and Daniel Sullivan, "An Analysis of the Effects of Prospective Reimbursement Programs on Hospital Expenditures," 1.

121. Samuel A. Mitchell, "Issues, Evidence, and the Policymaker's Dilemma," 84–98.

122. David Rosenbloom, "New Ways to Keep Old Promises in Health Care," 53.

123. Frank A. Sloan, "Reviews: An Economist," 115.

124. See Spencer Rich, "How One State Holds Down Costs in Its Hospitals," *Washington Post National Weekly Edition,* December 21–27, 1992, 33–34.

125. Ronald J. Vogel, "An Analysis of Structural Incentives in the Arizona Health Care Cost-Containment System," 14.

126. Jeffrey S. McCombs and Jon B. Christianson, "Applying Competitive Bidding to Health Care," 703–721.

127. Drew E. Altman and Douglas H. Morgan, "The Role of State and Local Government in Health," 26.

128. Henry J. Aaron and William B. Schwartz, *The Painful Prescription: Rationing Hospital Care.*

129. Paul T. Menzel, *Strong Medicine: The Ethical Rationing of Health Care.*

130. Victor Cohn, "Rationing Medical Care," *Washington Post National Weekly Edition,* August 13–19, 1990, 11.

131. John Kitzhaber, "A Healthier Approach to Health Care," 59–65; Timothy Egan, "Oregon Shakes Up Pioneering Health Plan for the Poor," *New York Times,* February 22, 1991; Patrick O'Neill, "Oregon's Health Care Rationing Plan Causing Fight," 17–21; Melinda Beck and Nadine Joseph, "Not Enough for All: Oregon Experiments with Rationing Health Care," *Newsweek,* May 14, 1990, 53–54; and B. Drummond Ayres Jr., "States Hustle to Adopt Health-Care Overhauls," *New York Times,* April 25, 1993.

132. Julie Kosterlitz, "Rationing Health Care," 1590–1595.

133. William B. Schwartz and Henry J. Aaron, "The Achilles Heel of Health Care Rationing"; William B. Schwartz and Henry J. Aaron, *Health Care Costs: The Social Tradeoffs.*

134. Cited in Frank Swoboda, "The Mercury Rises for Health Care Costs," *Washington Post National Weekly Edition,* February 4–10, 1991, 21.

135. Julie Kosterlitz, "Softening Resistance," 64–68.

136. Frank Swoboda, "A Surgical Strike against Corporate Health Care Costs: Firms Try Managed Plans to Remedy Soaring Expenses," *Washington Post National Weekly Edition,* February 19–25, 1990, 20.

137. Harvey M. Sapolsky et al., "Corporate Attitude toward Health Care Costs," 561–585.

138. John K. Iglehart, "Health Care and American Business," 120–124.

139. Eileen J. Tell, Marilyn Falik, and Peter D. Fox, "Private-Sector Health Care Initiatives: A Comparative Perspective from Four Communities," 372.

140. Much of the discussion that follows is derived from Sean Sullivan, *Managing Health Care Costs: Private Sector Innovations;* Davis, *Health Care Cost Containment;* and Tell, Falik, and Fox, "Private-Sector Health Care Initiatives," 357–379.

141. Joseph P. Newhouse et al., "Some Interim Results from a Controlled Trial of Cost Sharing in Health Insurance," 1501–1507.

142. Karen Davis et al., *Health Care Cost Containment,* 125–126.

143. Milt Freudenheim, "Employers Winning Wide Leeway to Cut Medical Insurance Benefits," *New York Times,* March 29, 1992.

144. Milt Freudenheim, "Medical Insurance Is Being Cut Back for Many Retirees," *New York Times,* June 28, 1992.

145. Karen Davis et al., *Health Care Cost Containment,* 115–116.

146. Annetta Miller and Elizabeth Bradburn, "Shape Up—Or Else," *Newsweek,* July 1, 1991, 42–43.

147. Robert Pear, "U.S. Is to Argue Employers Can Cut Health Insurance," *New York Times,* October 16, 1993.

148. Spencer Rich, "The Doctor Will See You Now at the Corporate, In-House Clinic," *Washington Post National Weekly Edition,* June 10–16, 1991, 22.

149. E.R. Brooks et al., "Does Free Care Improve Adult Health?" 1426–1434; Jack Hadley, *More Medical Care: Better Health?;* N. Lurie, "Termination from Medical: Does It Affect Health?" 480–484.

Chapter 7. Health Care Technology

1. John K. Kerr and Richard Jelinek, "Impact of Technology in Health Care and Health Administration: Hospitals and Alternative Care Delivery Systems," 5–10.

2. D.W. Hill, "25 Years of Medical Technology," 242–243.

3. Joseph D. Bronzino, Vincent H. Smith, and Maurice L. Wade, *Medical Technology and Society: An Interdisciplinary Perspective,* 34.

4. Paul E. Kalb, "Controlling Health Care Costs by Controlling Technology: A Private Contractual Approach," 1112.

5. Julie Kosterlitz, "Paying for Miracles," 1967.

6. Paul E. Kalb, "Controlling Health Care Costs by Controlling Technology," 1112.

7. Eli Ginzberg, "High-Tech Medicine and Rising Health Care Costs," 1820.

8. Kevin W. Wildes, "Health Reform and the Seduction of Technology," 30.

9. Virginia Lotlarz, "History of Medical Techology in the United States," 233–236.

10. Ibid.

11. Howard S. Berlinger, *Strategic Factors in U.S. Healthcare: Human Resources, Capital, and Technology,* 112.

12. Burton A. Weisbrod, "The Nature of Technological Change: Incentives Do Matter!" 10.

13. Mary-Lan Kambert, "High-Tech Health Care: Medical Devices and Treatments for the Future—and Present," 4–9.

14. Ibid.

15. Kevin W. Wildes, "Health Reform and the Seduction of Technology," 30.

16. Lewis Thomas, *The Lives of a Cell.*

17. Ibid., 37.

18. Jonas Morris, *Searching for a Cure: National Health Policy Considered,* 197.

19. Quoted in ibid., 198.

20. Lewis Thomas, *Lives of a Cell,* 40.

21. "Health Care Dollars," *Consumer Reports,* July 1992, 435–448.

22. Eli Ginzberg, "High-Tech Medicine and Rising Health Care Costs," 1821.

23. Frans F.H. Rutten and Gouke J. Bonsel, "High Cost Technology in Health Care: A Benefit or a Burden?" 567.

24. Ibid., 570.

25. David H. Freed, "Toward Redefining Expectations about Medical Technology," 22.

26. Victor R. Fuchs, *The Health Economy;* Annetine Gelijns and Nathan Rosenberg, "The Dynamics of Technological Change in Medicine," 28–46.

27. Burton A. Weisbrod, "Nature of Technological Change," 25–26.

28. Ibid., 27.

29. John Nyman, "Costs, Technology, and Insurance in the Health Care Sector," 108–109.

30. N. Kane and P. Manoukian, "The Effect of the Medicare Prospective Payment System on the Adoption of New Technology: The Case of Cochlear Implants," 1378–1383.

31. Paul F. Griner, "New Technology in the Hospital," 123–132; Gerald F. Anderson and Earl Steinberg, "Role of the Hospital in the Acquisition of Technology," 61–70.

32. David H. Freed, "Toward Redefining Expectations about Medical Technology," 23.

33. Jason H. Sussman, "Financial Considerations in Technology Assessment," 33.

34. Eric J. Cassell, "The Sorcerer's Broom: Medicine's Rampant Technology," *Hastings Center Report* 23, no. 6 (November–December 1993): 32–39.

35. David H. Freed, "Toward Redefining Expectations about Medical Technology," 23–24; Charles E. Phelps and Stephen T. Parente, "Priority Setting in Medical Technology and Medical Practice Assessment," 703–723.

36. Bruce J. Hillman, "Physicians' Acquisition and Use of New Technology in an Era of Economic Constraints," 133–149; A. Mark Fendrick and J. Sanford Schwartz, "Physicians' Decisions Regarding the Acquisition of Technology," 71–84.

37. A. Everette James et al., "The Diffusion of Medical Technology," 150–155.

38. David H. Freed, "Toward Redefining Expectations about Medical Technology," 21–28.

39. Robert H. Blank, *Rationing Medicine,* 4–5.

40. John W. Melski, "Price of Technology: A Blind Spot," 1517.

41. William R. Davis, "Medical Technology Investing in the '90s," 35.

42. G. Lawrence Atkins and John L. Bauer, "Taming Health Care Costs Now," 56.

43. Dale A. Rublee, "Medical Technology in Canada, Germany, and the United States: An Update," 114–115.

44. Julie Kosterlitz, "Paying for Miracles," 1967–1971.

45. Mary-Lan Kambert, "High-Tech Health Care," 8.

46. Sara Collins, "Saving Lives Isn't Cheap," *U.S. News & World Report,* June 7, 1993, 57.

47. Robert Rhodes, *Health Care: Politics, Policy and Distributive Justice: The Ironic Triumph,* 76.

48. Ibid.

49. Julie Kosterlitz, "Paying for Miracles," 1969.

50. Sara Collins, "Saving Lives Isn't Cheap," 56.

51. Henry J. Aaron, *Serious and Unstable Condition: Financing America's Health Care,* 26.

52. Ibid., 48.

53. General Accounting Office, *Hospital Costs: Adoption of Technologies Drives Cost Growth,* 2.

54. Julie Kosterlitz, "Paying for Miracles," 1967–1971.

55. Paul E. Kalb, "Controlling Health Care Costs by Controlling Technology," 1114–1118.

56. G.G. Jaros and D.A. Boonzaier, "Cost Escalation in Health-Care Technology—Possible Solutions," 422.

57. Paul E. Kalb, "Controlling Health Care Costs by Controlling Technology," 1112.

58. Geoffrey Cowley, "What High Tech Can't Accomplish," *Newsweek,* October 4, 1993, 60.

59. Ibid.

60. Julie Kosterlitz, "Paying for Miracles," 1967.

61. Geoffrey Cowley, "What High Tech Can't Accomplish," 62.

62. Frans F.H. Rutten and Gouke J. Bonsel, "High Cost Technology in Health Care," 570.

63. William B. Schwartz, "In the Pipeline: A Wave of Valuable Medical Technology," 70–79.

64. "High Tech Medicine for the 90s," 18; Mary Wagner, "Weighing the Cost of New Technology," 43–58; Henry C. Alder, "Technology Assessment: A Vital Tool for Managers" (Update on Technology Diffusion), 56–57; Suzanna Hoppszallern, Christine Hughes, and Robert A. Zimmerman, "MRI Acquisition: How Appropriate Is It for Hospitals?" 58.

65. "Cost/Benefits of High-Tech Medicine," 16.

66. H. David Banta and Hindrik Vondeling, "Strategies for Successful Evaluation and Policy-Making toward Health Care Technology on the Move: The Case of Medical Lasers," 1663–1674.

67. Kathryn S. Taylor, "Technology's Next Test: Regional Systems Laying Groundwork for Post-Reform Technology Planning," 42–44.

68. Patricia Huston, "Is Health Technology Assessment Medicine's Rising Star?" 1839.

69. Richard A. Merrill, "Regulation of Drugs and Devices: An Evolution," 47–69.

70. Richard A. Rettig, "Medical Innovation Fuels Cost Containment," 16.

71. Anne O. Kilpatrick, Krishna S. Dhir, and John M. Sanders, "Health Care Technology Assessment: A Policy Planning Tool," 61.

72. David Banta and Stephen B. Thacker, "The Case for Reassessment of Health Care Technology: Once Is Not Enough," 235.

73. Victor R. Fuchs, "The New Technology Assessment," 673.

74. David M. Eddy, "Connecting Value and Costs: Whom Do We Ask, and What Do We Ask Them?" 1737–1739.

75. Charlotte Muller, "Objective Health Care Technology Evaluation—It Isn't Easy," 121–124.

76. Ibid., 124–130.

77. Julie Kosteritz, "Paying for Miracles," 1967–1971.

78. Ibid.

79. Frans F.H. Rutten and Gouke J. Bonsel, "High Cost Technology in Health Care," 574–575.

80. Renaldo N. Battista, "Health Care Technology Assessment: Linking Science and Policy Making," 461–462.

81. Charles E. Lindblom, "The Science of Muddling Through," 79–88.

82. Wouter Van Rossum, "Decision-Making and Medical Technology Assessment," 107–124.

83. Victor R. Fuchs, "New Technology Assessment," 676.

84. Frans F.H. Rutten and Gouke J. Bonsell, "High Cost Technology in Health Care," 571–573.

85. Alexander Morgan Capron, "Biomedical Technology and Health Care: Transforming Our World," 1–10; Joseph C. d'Oronzio, "Bioethics and the Body Politic," 300–301; Margot C.J. Mabie, *Bioethics and the New Medical Technology;* John Harris, *Wonderwoman and Superman: The Ethics of Human Biotechnology.*

86. Robert H. Blank, "Introduction," vii–xiv.

87. Donald VanDeVeer, "Introduction," 20.

88. Martin A. Strosberg, Joshua M. Wiener, Robert Baker, and I. Alan Fein, eds., *Rationing America's Medical Care: The Oregon Plan and Beyond,;* Norman Daniels, "Rationing Fairly: Programmatic Consideration," 224–233.

89. Julie Johnsson, "High-Tech Health Care: How Much Can We Afford?" 80;

Robert Wright, "The Technology Time Bomb," 25–30; Lowell C. Kruse, "Some Thoughts about Resource Allocation in Health Care," 15–16.

90. Henry J. Aaron and William B. Schwartz, "Rationing Health Care: The Choice Before Us," 418.

91. Henry J. Aaron and William B. Schwartz, *The Painful Prescription: Rationing Hospital Care,* esp. 29–56.

92. Eli Ginzberg, "Balancing Dollars and Quality," 4.

93. John F. Kilner, "Age as a Basis for Allocating Lifesaving Medical Resources: An Ethical Analysis," 405–423.

94. Daniel Callahan, "Why We Must Set Limits."

95. "Bioethics: Private Choice and Common Good," *Hastings Center Report* 24, no. 3 (May 1, 1994): 28.

96. Daniel Callahan, *Setting Limits: Medical Goals in an Aging Society.*

97. Daniel Callahan, *What Kind of Life: The Limits of Medical Progress.*

98. John F. Kilner, *Who Lives? Who Dies? Ethical Criteria in Patient Selection;* John F. Kilner, *Life on the Line: Ethics, Aging, Ending Patients' Lives, and Allocating Vital Resources.*

99. Paul T. Menzel, *Strong Medicine: The Ethical Rationing of Health Care;* Robert H. Blank, *Rationing Medicine.*

100. Norman L. Cantor, *Advance Directives and the Pursuit of Death with Dignity.*

101. Jerry Buckley, "How Doctors Decide Who Shall Live, Who Shall Die," *U.S. News & World Report,* January 11, 1990, 50–58.

102. Philip G. Peters, Jr., "The Constitution and the Right to Die," 13.

103. Gregory E. Pence, *Classic Cases in Medical Ethics,* 2nd ed., 41–47; Maggie Shreve and June Isaacson Kailes, "The Right to Die or the Right to Community Support," 11–15.

104. Marcia Angell, "Prisoners of Technology: The Case of Nancy Cruzan," 1227.

105. Gilbert Meilaender, "The Cruzan Decision: 9.5 Theses for Discussion," 3–5.

106. Richard A. McCormick, "Clear and Convincing Evidence: The Case of Nancy Cruzan," 10–12; Peters, "The Constitution and the Right to Die," 13–16.

107. "Who Should Live—or Die? Who Should Decide?" Interview with Yale Kamisar, professor of law at the University of Michigan Law School.

108. Thomas M. Garrett, Harold W. Baillie, and Rosellen M. Garrett, *Health Care Ethics: Principles and Problems,* 115–117.

109. Nancy Gibbs and Andrea Sachs, "Love and Let Die: In an Era of Medical Technology, How Are Patients and Families to Decide Whether to Halt Treatment—or Even to Help Death Along?" *Time,* March 19, 1990, 66.

110. Ibid., 64.

111. "Oregon's Assisted Suicide Law Stokes the Fires of Controversy," 1.

112. Ibid.

113. Thomas M. Garrett, Harold W. Baillie, and Rosellen M. Garrett, *Health Care Ethics,* 132–133.

114. Linda R. Shaw et al., "Ethics of Lung Transplantation with Live Donors," 678–681; General Accounting Office, *Heart Transplants: Concerns about Cost, Access, and Availability of Donor Organs;* Keith J. Mueller, "Organ Transplant Legislation," 143–165; Thomas M. Garrett, Harold W. Baillie, and Rosellen M. Garrett, *Health Care Ethics,* esp. chap. 9, "Ethics of Organ Transplants," 177–197.

115. Mark Nichols, "Tinkering with Mother Nature: A Controversial Report on Reproductive Technologies," 38–40; Mary S. Henifin, "New Reproductive Technologies: Equity and Access to Reproductive Health Care," 61–74; Melinda Beck and Geoffrey Cowley, "Mother Nature?" *Newsweek,* January 17, 1994, 54–57; Gina Kolata, "Repro-

ductive Revolution Is Jolting Old Views," *New York Times,* January 11, 1994; Thomas M. Garrett, Harold W. Baillie, and Rosellen Garrett, *Health Care Ethics,* esp. chap. 8, "New Methods of Reproduction," 160–176; Janice G. Raymond, *Women as Wombs: Reproductive Technologies and the Battle over Women's Freedom;* John A. Robertson, *Children of Choice: Freedom and the New Reproductive Technologies;* Marilyn Strathern, *Reproducing the Future: Essays on Anthropology, Kinship and the New Reproductive Technologies);* Elain H. Baruch, Amadeo F. D'Adamo, Jr., and Joni Seager, eds., *Embryos, Ethics, and Women's Rights: Exploring the New Reproductive Technologies*; Paul Lauritzen, *Pursuing Parenthood: Ethical Issues in Assisted Reproduction.*

116. Robyn Y. Nishimi, "From the Congressional Office of Technology Assessment," 2911.

117. Lynn Gillam, "Bioethics and Public Policy in Australia," 97.

118. Judith Miller, "What to Do Until the Philosopher Kings Come: Bioethics and Public Policy in Canada," 93–95.

119. Cynthia B. Cohen and Elizabeth L. McCloskey, "Private Bioethics Forums: Counterpoint to Government Bodies," 283–289.

120. Kathi E. Hanna, Robert M. Cook-Degan, and Robyn Y. Nishimi, "Finding a Forum for Bioethics in U.S. Public Policy," 205–219.

121. Ira H. Carmen. "Bioethics, Public Policy and Political Science," 80.

Chapter 8. Reforming the System

1. Lawrence D. Brown, "Politics, Money, and Health Care Reform," 175.

2. Deborah A. Stone, "When Patients Go to Market: The Workings of Managed Competition," 111.

3. See Elliott A. Krause, *Power and Illness: The Political Sociology of Health and Medical Care;* Betty Leyerle, *The Private Regulation of American Health Care;* and Paul Starr, *The Social Transformation of American Medicine.*

4. It is an extraordinary coincidence that *The Wealth of Nations,* which extolled the virtues of free markets, appeared in the same year as the Declaration of Independence, which declared humanity's freedom.

5. Frederick Hayek, *The Road to Serfdom.*

6. Milton Friedman, *Capitalism and Freedom.*

7. As we see, this traditional structure is becoming less prominent, largely because of the press of cost increases.

8. See Mark V. Pauly, *Medical Care at Public Expense: A Study in Applied Welfare Economics,* 42–45.

9. Though, given the earlier statement, it might be more correct to argue that providers were both the demand and the supply side.

10. See Patricia Bauman, "The Formulation and Evolution of the Health Maintenance Organization Policy, 1970–1973," 129–142; and Joseph L. Falkson, *HMOs and the Politics of Health System Reform.*

11. Alain C. Enthoven, "Consumer-Choice Health Plans (First of Two Parts)," 650–658, and "Consumer-Choice Health Plans (Second of Two Parts)," 709–720; Alain C. Enthoven, *Health Plan: The Only Practical Solution to the Soaring Cost of Medicare Care.*

12. This is based on Mark E. Rushefsky, "A Critique of Market Reform in Health Care: The 'Consumer-Choice Health Plan,' " 724–725.

13. See, for example, Elizabeth Wehr, "Competition in Health Care: Would It Bring

Costs Down?" 1587–1595; and Linda E. Demkovich, "Adding Competition to the Health Industry," 1796–1800.

14. Clark C. Havighurst, *Deregulating the Health Care Industry*.

15. For an evaluation of the California program, see General Accounting Office, *Health Insurance: California Public Employees' Alliance Has Reduced Recent Premium Growth*.

16. Robert Reinhold, "A Health-Care Theory Hatched in Fireside Chats," *New York Times*, February 10, 1993. See also Alain C. Enthoven, "The History and Principles of Managed Competition," 24–48.

17. See Alain Enthoven and Richard Kronick, "A Consumer-Choice Health Plan for the 1990s: Universal Health Insurance in a System Designed to Promote Quality and Economy (First of Two Parts)," 29–37; Alain Enthoven and Richard Kronick, "A Consumer-Choice Health Plan for the 1990s: Universal Health Insurance in a System Designed to Promote Quality and Economy (Second of Two Parts)," 94–101; Alain C. Enthoven, "Universal Health Insurance through Incentives Reform," 2532–2536; and Alain E. Enthoven and Richard Kronick, "Will Managed Competition Work? Better Care at Lower Cost," *New York Times*, January 25, 1992.

18. Alain E. Enthoven and Richard Kronick, "A Consumer-Choice Health Plan for the 1990s," pt. 1, 31.

19. This is a variation of the play-or-pay rule and contains an employer mandate.

20. The managed competition plan has some resemblance to the German system, whereby Sickness Funds negotiate with organizations of providers.

21. John D. Rockefeller IV, "The Pepper Commission Report on Comprehensive Health Care," 1005–1007.

22. John Kingdon argues that political and problem factors are the most important in placing an item on the governmental agenda. See John W. Kingdon, *Agendas, Alternatives, and Public Policies*.

23. Adam Clymer, "Democrats Call Town Meetings on Health Care," *New York Times*, December 22, 1991.

24. Michael Wines, "Bush Announces Health Plan, Filling Gap in Re-Election Bid," *New York Times*, February 7, 1992.

25. Robert Pear, "President Leaves Many Areas Gray," *New York Times*, February 7, 1992.

26. Robert Pear, "Doctors's Group Offers Plan to Curb Health-Care Costs," *New York Times*, September 15, 1992.

27. Quoted in Robert Pear, "Conflicting Aims in Health Lobby Stall Legislation," *New York Times*, March 18, 1992.

28. Ibid.

29. Jonathan Rauch, *Demosclerosis: The Silent Killer of American Government*. See also Mancur Olson, *The Logic of Collective Action: Public Goods and the Theory of Groups*, and *The Rise and Decline of Nations: Economic Growth, Stagflation, and Social Rigidities*.

30. Clifford Krauss, "Democrats Offer a Health-Care Plan," *New York Times*, June 26, 1992.

31. "Conservative Democrats Offer Health-Care Plan," *Springfield News-Leader*, September 17, 1992.

32. See "Editorial: The Bush-Clinton Health Reform," *New York Times*, October 10, 1992; and Robert Pear, "Bush and Clinton Aren't Saying It, but Health-Care Taxes Are Likely," *New York Times*, October 18, 1992.

33. See Robert Pear, "In Shift, Insurers Ask U.S. to Require Coverage for All," *New York Times*, December 3, 1993; and Peter Kerr, "Insurers Stand to Profit Big from a Health Care Overhaul," *New York Times*, December 4, 1992.

34. Adam Clymer, "Americans Have High Hopes for Clinton, Poll Finds," *New York Times,* January 19, 1993.

35. Robin Toner, "Support Is Found for Broad Change in Health Policy," *New York Times,* April 6, 1993.

36. Richard Morin, "Even Doctors Are on the Health Reform Bandwagon," *Washington Post National Weekly Edition,* April 19–25, 1993, 37.

37. David Wessel and Gerald F. Seib, "Clinton Had Devised His Health Package Before the Inaugural," *Wall Street Journal,* September 22, 1993.

38. James Fallows, "A Triumph of Misinformation," 28. The book was the first edition of Paul Starr, *The Logic of Health Care Reform: Why and How the President's Plan Will Work.*

39. This was mostly a political complaint. Whatever plan the president proposed would have to be approved by Congress, where the deliberations were open. This is opposed to situations during the Reagan and Bush administrations where secret meetings with industry were held that affected regulations and would not be subject to open meetings or congressional oversight at a later time. On this point, see Richard Nathan, *The Administrative Presidency;* and Charles Tiefer, *The Semi-Sovereign Presidency: The Bush Administration's Strategy for Governing without Congress.* On the openness of the task force to outside views, see Fallows, "Triumph of Misinformation," 28–30.

40. Adam Clymer, "Clinton Asks Backing for Sweeping Change in the Health System," *New York Times,* September 23, 1993.

41. White House House Domestic Policy Council, *The President's Health Security Act: The Clinton Blueprint,* 21–22.

42. The following description is based on Patrick Rogers, "Healthtown, U.S.A.," *Newsweek,* October 4, 1993, 44–45.

43. Alice M. Rivlin, David M. Cutler, and Len M. Nichols, "Financing, Estimation, and Estimation Effects," 31.

44. See Walter A. Zelman, "The Rationale behind the Clinton Health Reform Plan," 20–21. See, in general, Starr, *Logic of Health Care Reform.*

45. Paul Starr, *Logic of Health Care Reform,* 101.

46. Ibid, 102.

47. See Steven Pearlstein and Dana Priest, "Some Spoonfuls of Sugar Help the Medicine Go Down with Special Interests," *Washington Post National Weekly Edition,* September 27–October 3, 1993, 7.

48. William Schneider, "Health Care Reform: What Went Right," 2404.

49. Richard E. Cohen, "Ready, Aim, Reform," 2582.

50. James Fallows, "Triumph of Misinformation," 30.

51. Julie Kosterlitz, "Winners and Losers," 2938–2941.

52. Milt Freudenheim, "Changing the Fortunes of the Medical Business," *New York Times,* September 19, 1993. See also David S. Broder, "Of Gored Oxen and Health Care," *Washington Post National Weekly Edition,* January 17–23, 1994, 4.

53. Richard E. Cohen, "Ready, Aim, Reform," 2584.

54. See Robert Pear, "Analysis Says Cost of Health Effort Is Underestimated," *New York Times,* December 9, 1993. See also John F. Sheils and Lawrence S. Lewin, "Perspective: Alternative Estimate: No Pain, No Gain," 50–55.

55. Robert Pear, "Early Doubts on Health, Papers Show," *New York Times,* September 8, 1993. See also Steven Greenhouse, "Many Experts Say Health Plan Would Fall Far Short on Savings," *New York Times,* September 21, 1993.

56. Quoted in Jodie T. Allen, "New Blue Smoke and Mirrors," *Washington Post National Weekly Edition,* February 21–27, 1994, 23.

57. Alain Enthoven, "Why Not the Clinton Health Plan?" 129–135.

58. Paul Starr, "Why the Clinton Plan Is Not the Enthoven Plan," 136–140.

59. The following two paragraphs are based on the Kaiser Commission on the Future of Medicaid, *Health Reform Legislation: A Comparison of Major Proposals.*

60. Cosponsorship is an indicator of support for a proposal.

61. Adam Clymer, "Many Health Plans, One Political Goal," *New York Times,* October 17, 1993.

62. Julie Kosterlitz, "Health Lobby Cranks Up Its Postage Meter."

63. Katharine Q. Seelye, "Lobbyists Are the Loudest in the Health Care Debate," *New York Times,* August 16, 1994. See also Neil A. Lewis, "Medical Industry Showers Congress with Lobby Money," *New York Times,* December 13, 1993.

64. Clifford Krauss, "Lobbyists of Every Stripe on Health Care Proposals," *New York Times,* September 24, 1993.

65. Ibid.

66. Elizabeth Kolbert, "Health Plan Foes Try Campaign-Style Ads," *New York Times,* October 21, 1993.

67. Robin Toner, "Highlighting Fears about the Clinton Health Plan," *New York Times,* February 1, 1994.

68. Robin Toner, "Ads Are Potent Weapon in Health Care Struggle," *New York Times,* February 1, 1994. For a critique of the HIAA ad campaign, see Julie Kosterlitz, "Harry, Louise and Doublespeak," 1542.

69. One could argue that changes occurring in the health care system will in fact reduce choice more than the Clinton plan would have, had it gone into effect.

70. Steven Waldman and Bob Cohn, "Health Care Reform: The Lost Chance," *Newsweek,* September 19, 1994, 32.

71. "Spin Doctors Wreck Harry and Louise," *New York Times,* July 8, 1994.

72. Robin Toner, "Ads Are Potent Weapons in Health Care Struggle."

73. "Muddling through the Message," *Newsweek,* October 11, 1993, 44.

74. Robin Toner, "Ad Drive Opens for Canadian-Style Health Care," *New York Times,* May 3, 1994.

75. Kathleen Hall Jamieson, "When Harry Met Louise," *Washington Post National Weekly Edition* 11, no. 43, August 22–28, 1994, 29.

76. Adam Clymer, "Debate on Health Care May Depend on 'Crisis,' " *New York Times,* January 17, 1994.

77. Richard Morin, "Is There a Health Care Crisis? Yes and No," *Washington Post National Weekly Edition,* February 21–27, 1994, 37.

78. William Schneider, "Health Care: So Where's the Crisis?" 1378.

79. Robin Toner, "Poll on Changes in Health Care Finds Support amid Skepticism," *New York Times,* September 22, 1993. See also Toner, "Support Is Found for Broad Change in Health Policy."

80. Robert J. Blendon, quoted in Richard Morin, "Health Care Reform, Yes, but Not at Any Price," *Washington Post National Weekly Edition,* January 10–16, 1994, 37.

81. David S. Broder and Richard Morin, "Clinton's Health Plan: A Turn for the Worse," *Washington Post National Weekly Edition,* March 7–13, 1994, 15. See also Adam Clymer, "Poll Finds Public Still Doubtful over Costs of Clinton Health Plan," *New York Times,* March 15, 1994.

82. James Fallows, "Triumph of Misinformation," 30.

83. Ibid., 37.

84. See Richard Morin, "Don't Know Much about Health Care Reform," *Washington Post National Weekly Edition,* March 14–20, 1994, 37. See also Richard Morin, "A Bitter Pill to the Public," *Washington Post National Weekly Edition,* March 28–April 3, 1994, 37. This lack of information about policy issues is a fairly common finding. On

the importance of looking at question wording to get a real sense of changes in public mood, see James A. Stimson, *Public Opinion in America: Moods, Cycles, and Swings.*

85. Robin Toner, "Health Impasse Sours Voters, New Poll Finds," *New York Times,* September 13, 1994.

86. Robin Toner, "House Democrats Unveil Proposal for Health Bill," *New York Times,* July 30, 1994; and Katharine Q. Seelye, "Some House Democrats Like Plan but Not Political Risks," *New York Times,* July 30, 1994.

87. Adam Clymer, "House Is Letting Senate Go First on Health Care," *New York Times,* August 5, 1994.

88. Robert Pear, "Cost Is Obscured in Health Debate," *New York Times,* August 7, 1994.

89. Adam Clymer, "Centrists on Senate Panel Near Compromise on Health Care Bill," *New York Times,* June 23, 1994.

90. See Adam Clymer, "Blind Eye Now, Eyeing Victory Later," *New York Times,* June 24, 1994; and Robin Toner, "Health Coalition Strongly Opposes Compromise Plan," *New York Times,* June 24, 1994.

91. Adam Clymer, "Dole Gathering Broad Backing for a G.O.P. Health Care Plan," *New York Times,* June 30, 1994.

92. Adam Clymer, "G.O.P. in the House Trying to Block Health Care Bill," *New York Times,* June 17, 1994.

93. Julie Kosterlitz, "Brinksmanship," 1648.

94. Adam Clymer, "Senate Leader Unveils His Plan for Health Care," *New York Times,* August 3, 1994.

95. Michael Wines, "Clinton Puts Onus for Health Care on Republicans," *New York Times,* August 4, 1994.

96. Adam Clymer, "Mitchell Sees Room for Dealing on Rival Health Care Proposals," *New York Times,* August 13, 1994.

97. Adam Clymer, "Mitchell Announces Plan to End G.O.P.'Filibuster' on Health Bill," *New York Times,* August 16, 1994.

98. Robert Pear, "Diverse Elements Criticize 'Mainstream' Senate Plan," *New York Times,* August 21, 1994.

99. See Todd S. Purdum, "Clinton's Allies on Health Concede that Broad Plan Is All but Dead This Year," *New York Times,* August 27, 1994; and Adam Clymer, "Clinton Is Urged to Abandon Fight over Health Bill," *New York Times,* September 21, 1994.

100. Adam Clymer, "Defying Omens, Health Care Drops from Campaign Stage," *New York Times,* October 22, 1994.

101. Dana Priest and Michael Weisskopf, "Death from a Thousand Cuts," *Washington Post National Weekly Edition,* October 17–23, 1993, 9.

102. For a discussion of the failure of health care reform on the part of sympathetic observers, see James Fallows, "A Triumph of Misinformation"; and Paul Starr, "What Happened to Health Care Reform?" 20–31.

103. Richard Morin, "A Health Care Reform Post-Mortem," *Washington Post National Weekly Edition,* September 12–18, 1994, 37.

104. Helen Dewar, "Health Care's Real Issue: November," *Washington Post National Weekly Edition,* July 11–17, 1994, 12–13.

105. Dana Priest and Michael Weisskopf, "Death from a Thousand Cuts." Though see James Fallows, "Triumph of Misinformation."

106. See Stuart M. Butler, "Rube Goldberg, Call Your Office," *New York Times,* September 28, 1993; and Steven Waldman, "How Clinton Blew It," *Newsweek,* June 27,

1994, 28. One could argue that the health care system envisioned by the plan was no more and perhaps even less complex than the current system. That assertion was never made by the Clinton forces or its allies.

107. Adam Clymer, "Hillary Clinton Says Administration Was Misunderstood on Health Care," *New York Times,* October 3, 1994. See also E.J. Dionne, Jr., "Clinton's Health Care Crisis," *Washington Post National Weekly Edition,* March 14–20, 1994, 29.

108. Adam Clymer, Robert Pear, and Robin Toner, "For Health Care, Time Was a Killer," *New York Times,* August 29, 1994.

109. James Fallows, "Triumph of Misinformation," 30–32.

110. David S. Hilzenrath, "Health Care Costs' Double-Edged Sword," *Washington Post National Weekly Edition,* December 27, 1993–January 2, 1994, 22. There Is some precedent for this. In the late 1970s, President Carter proposed legislation that would result in some federal controls over hospitals. The health care sector promised to restrain inflation through what became known as the Voluntary Effort. While Carter was president, medical inflation was restrained. With Carter's defeat in 1980, the Voluntary Effort was dropped.

111. Steven Waldman and Bob Cohn, "Health Care Reform: The Lost Chance," *Newsweek,* September 19, 1994, 28.

112. Ibid., 32.

113. James Fallows, "Triumph of Misinformation," 36–37.

114. Sven Steinmo and Jon Watts, "It's the Institutions, Stupid: Why Comprehensive Health Reform Fails in America."

115. Stuart M. Butler, "Rube Goldberg, Call Your Office."

116. Adam Clymer, "With Health Overhaul Dead, a Search for Minor Repairs," *New York Times,* August 28, 1994.

117. Ibid.; and Robert Pear, "Clintons Should Address Health Care One Issue at a Time, Experts Suggest," *New York Times,* October 10, 1994.

118. E.J. Dionne, Jr., "Start with Kidcare," *Washington Post National Weekly Edition,* September 5–11, 1994, 28.

119. Peter D. Fox, Thomas Rice, and Lisa Alecxih, "Medigap Regulation: Lessons for Health Care Reform," 31–48.

120. Adam Clymer, "With Health Overhaul Dead, a Search for Minor Repairs."

121. Linda Demkovich, "ERISA: States Push to Raze the Biggest Barrier to Health Reform," 1–2, 7.

122. Robert Pear, "Insurance-Liability Curb Poses Problem for Bush," *New York Times,* May 19, 1992.

123. Milt Freudenheim, "States Seek Aid for the Uninsured," *New York Times,* June 23, 1994.

124. James W. Fossett, "Cost Containment and Rate Setting," 74–75.

125. Dan Morgan, "While Washington Fiddles, the States March On," *Washington Post National Weekly Edition,* October 10–16, 1994, 47.

126. Harry Nelson, *Federalism in Health Reform: Views from the States That Could Not Wait,* 1.

127. National Commission on the State and Local Public Service, *Frustrated Federalism: Rx for State and Local Health Care Reform.*

128. John J. DiIulio, Jr., and Richard Nathan, "Introduction," in DiIulio and Nathan, (eds.), *Making Health Reform Work,* 3.

129. Harry Nelson, *Federalism in Health Reform,* 9. See also Deanne Neubauer, "Hawaii: A Pioneer in Health System Reform," 31–39.

130. Robert Pear, "Plan to Ration Health Care Is Rejected by Government," *New York Times,* August 4, 1992.

131. Robert Pear, "Too-Bitter Medicine," *New York Times,* August 5, 1992.

132. Ibid.

133. Barbara Roberts, "Bush Blows It on Health Care," *New York Times,* August 11, 1992.

134. John K. Iglehart, "Health Care Reform: The States," 78.

135. Ibid., 75.

136. Ibid., 76; and Nelson, *Federalism in Health Reform,* 8.

137. Robert Crittenden, "Managed Competition and Premium Caps in Washington State," 82–88.

138. Michelle Quinn, "California's Health Pool: Limits, but Lower Rates," *New York Times,* June 11, 1994.

139. General Accounting Office, *Medicaid: States Turn to Managed Care to Improve Access and Control Costs.*

140. Bill Foreman, "HMO Would Give Treatment to All Medicaid Patients," *Springfield News-Leader,* March 22, 1995.

141. See Penelope Lemov, "States and Medicaid: Ahead of the Feds," 27–28; Penelope Lemov, "An Acute Case of Health Care Reform," 44–50; and Stuart Schear, "A Medicaid Miracle?" 294–298.

142. Dale Russakoff, "When Health Care Reform Hits Home," *Washington Post National Weekly Edition,* October 25–31, 1993, 31–32.

143. Melinda Henneberger, "Self-Help Overhaul of Health Care," *New York Times,* May 6, 1994.

144. Dan Morgan, "State Health Care Goes on the Critical List," *Washington Post National Weekly Edition,* December 5–11, 1994, 31; see also "Elections: What Impact on Health Care Reform?" 4–5.

145. Alain C. Enthoven and Sara J. Singer, "Health Care Is Healing Itself," *New York Times,* August 17, 1993.

146. Ibid.

147. Jolie Solomon, "Why Wait for Hillary?" *Newsweek,* June 28, 1993, 38–40.

148. Robert Pear, "Health Industry Is Moving to Form Service Networks," *New York Times,* August 21, 1993.

149. Elisabeth Rosenthal, "Big Hospitals in New York Recruiting Affiliates," *New York Times,* April 4, 1994.

150. Bill Foreman, "Buying Up Doctors," *Springfield News-Leader,* June 26, 1994; Dan Morgan, "The Rise of Corporate Medicine," *Washington Post National Weekly Edition,* June 20–26, 1994, 6–7.

151. George Anders and Hilary Stout, "As Clinton Plan Falters, Health Care Is Shaped by the Private Sector," *Wall Street Journal,* August 26, 1994.

152. Ibid.

153. Milt Freudenheim, "Doctors Are Sparring with Insurers over Right to Join Health Networks," *New York Times,* July 12, 1994.

154. Allen R. Myerson, "Helping Health Insurers Say No," *New York Times,* March 20, 1995.

155. Robin Toner, "Ills of Health System Outlive Debate on Care," *New York Times,* October 2, 1994.

156. Betty Leyerle, *Private Regulation of American Health Care.*

157. Julie Kosterlitz, "Signs of Life in the Wreckage," 2484. See also Julie Kosterlitz, "Unmanaged Care," 2903–2907.

158. Barbara Ehrenreich and John Enrenreich, *The American Health Empire: Power, Profits and Politics.*

159. Erik Eckholm, "While Congress Remains Silent, Health Care Transforms Itself," *New York Times,* December 18, 1994.

160. Jerry L. Mashaw and Theodore R. Marmor, "The States as Health Care Labs," *New York Times,* August 18, 1993. See also Dan Morgan, "Health Care Reform via the Back Door," *Washington Post National Weekly Edition,* November 28–December 4, 1994, 32.

161. Robert Pear, "Clinton Proposes U.S. Rules for Private Health Insurance," *New York Times,* June 15, 1995.

162. Adam Clymer, "With Health Overhaul Dead, a Search for Minor Repairs."

163. Robert Pear, "Clintons Should Address Health Care One Issue at a Time."

164. Robin Toner, "Ills of Health System."

Chapter 9. Conclusion: Health Care Policy at the End of the Twentieth Century

1. For a discussion of how major changes can occur, see Frank R. Baumgartner and Bryan D. Jones, *Agendas and Instability in American Politics;* and John W. Kingdon, *Agendas, Alternatives, and Public Policies.*

2. Jonathan Rauch, *Demosclerosis: The Silent Killer of American Government.*

Selected Bibliography

Aaron, Henry J. *Serious and Unstable Condition: Financing America's Health Care.* Washington, D.C.: Brookings Institution, 1991.

Aaron, Henry J., and William B. Schwartz. *The Painful Prescription: Rationing Hospital Care.* Washington, D.C.: Brookings Institution, 1984.

———. "Rationing Health Care: The Choice Before Us." *Science* 247, no. 4941 (January 26, 1990): 418–422.

Aday, Lu Ann. *At Risk in America: The Health and Health Care Needs of Vulnerable Populations in the United States.* San Francisco: Jossey-Bass, 1993.

———. "Equity, Accessibility, and Ethical Issues: Is the U.S. Health Care Reform Debate Asking the Right Questions?" *American Behavioral Scientist* 36, no. 6 (July/August 1993): 724–740.

Alder, Henry C. "Technology Assessment: A Vital Tool for Managers." *Hospitals* 65, no. 8 (April 20, 1991): 56–57.

Alford, Robert A. *Health Care Politics: Ideological and Interest Group Barriers to Reform.* Chicago: University of Chicago Press, 1975.

Allison, Graham. *The Essence of Decision.* Boston: Little, Brown, 1971.

Altenstetter, Christa. *Health Policy-Making and Administration in West Germany and the United States.* Beverly Hills: Sage, 1974.

Altman, Drew E. "Health Care for the Poor." *Annals of the American Academy of Political and Social Sciences* 468 (July 1983): 103–121.

Altman, Drew E., and Douglas H. Morgan. "The Role of the State and Local Government in Health." *Health Affairs* 2, no. 4 (Winter 1983): 7–31.

Altman, Stuart H., and Marc A. Rodwin. "Halfway Competitive Markets and Ineffective Regulation: The American Health Care System." *Journal of Health Politics, Policy and Law* 13, no. 2 (Summer 1988): 323–339.

Altman, Stuart H., and Sanford L. Weiner. "Regulation as a Second Best Choice." In Bureau of Economics, U.S. Federal Trade Commission, *Competition in the Health Care Sector: Past, Present, and Future,* 421–427. Washington, D.C.: Government Printing Office, 1978.

Anderson, Gerald F., and Earl P. Steinberg. "Role of the Hospital in the Acquisition of Technology." In *Adopting New Medical Technology,* ed. Annetine C. Gelijns and Holly V. Dawkins, 61–70. Washington, D.C.: National Academy Press, 1994.

Anderson, James E. *Public Policy Making: An Introduction.* 2nd ed. New York: Holt, Rinehart and Winston, 1979.

Anderson, Maren D., and Peter D. Fox. "Lessons Learned from Medicaid Managed Care Approaches." *Health Affairs* 71 (Spring 1987).

Anderson, Odin W. *Health Services in the United States: A Growth Enterprise Since 1875.* Ann Arbor, Mich.: Health Administration Press, 1985.

Anderson, Odin W., et al. *HMO Development: Patterns and Prospects.* Chicago: Pluribus Press, 1985.

Angell, Marcia. "Prisoners of Technology: The Case of Nancy Cruzan." Editorial. *New England Journal of Medicine* 322, no. 17 (April 26, 1990): 1226–1228.

Ashcraft, Marie L.F., and S.E. Berki. "Health Maintenance Organizations as Medicaid Providers." *Annals of the American Academy of Political and Social Science* 468 (July 1983): 122–131.

"A Survey of Health Care: Surgery Needed." *The Economist,* July 6, 1991, 4–5.

Atkins, G. Lawrence, and John L. Bauer. "Taming Health Care Costs Now." *Issues in Science and Technology* 9, no. 2 (Winter 1992): 54–60.

Ayanian, John Z., Betsy A. Kohler, Toshi Abe, and Arnold M. Epstein. "The Relation between Health Insurance Coverage and Clinical Outcomes among Women with Breast Cancer." *New England Journal of Medicine* 329, no. 5 (July 29, 1993): 326–331.

Baker, David W., Carl D. Stevens, and Robert H. Brook. "Patients Who Leave a Public Hospital Emergency Department without Being Seen by a Physician." *Journal of American Medical Association* 266, no. 8 (August 28, 1991): 1085–1090.

————. "Regular Source of Ambulatory Care and Medical Care Utilization by Patients Presenting to a Public Hospital Emergency Department." *Journal of the American Medical Association* 271, no. 24 (June 22, 1994): 1909–1912.

Ball, Robert M. "Background of Regulation in Health Care." In Institute of Medicine, *Controls of Health Care,* 3–22. Washington, D.C.: National Academy of Sciences, 1975.

Banta, David H., and Stephen B. Thacker. "The Case for Reassessment of Health Care Technology: Once Is Not Enough." *Journal of the American Medical Association* 2654, no. 2 (July 11, 1990): 235–240.

Banta, David H., and Hindrik Vondeling. "Strategies for Successful Evaluation and Policy-Making toward Health Care Technology on the Move: The Case of Medical Lasers." *Social Science and Medicine* 38, no. 12 (1994): 1663–1674.

Baruch, Elain H., Amadeo F. D'Adamo, Jr., and Joni Seager, eds. *Embryos, Ethics, and Women's Rights: Exploring the New Reproductive Technologies.* New York: Haworth Press, 1988.

Battista, Renaldo N. "Health Care Technology Assessment: Linking Science and Policy Making." *Canadian Medical Association Journal* 146, no. 4 (February 15, 1992): 461–462.

Bauman, Patricia. "The Formulation and Evolution of the Health Maintenance Organization Policy, 1970–1973." *Social Science and Medicine* 10 (March–April 1976): 129–142.

Baumgartner, Frank R., and Bryan D. Jones. *Agendas and Instability in American Politics.* Chicago: University of Chicago Press, 1993.

Bayes, Jane H. *Ideologies and Interest-Group Politics.* Novato, Calif.: Chandler and Sharp, 1982.

Beer, S.H. *Modern British Politics.* London: Faber and Faber, 1965.

Bennett, James T., and Thomas J. DiLorenzo. *Destroying America: How Government Funds Partisan Politics.* Washington, D.C.: CATO Institute, 1985.

Berki, S.E. "Health Care Policy: Lessons from the Past and Issues of the Future." *Annals of the American Academy of Political and Social Science* 468 (July 1983): 231–246.

Berlinger, Howard S. *Strategic Factors in U.S. Healthcare: Human Resources, Capital, and Technology.* Boulder, Colo.: Westview Press, 1987.

Berman, Howard. "Rochester: Community Rating = Insurance Access." *Hospitals* 66, no. 20 (October 20, 1992): 56.

Bernstein, Merton C., and Joan Broadshaug Bernstein. *Social Security: The System That Works.* New York: Basic Books, 1988.

Bicknell, William J., and Diana C. Walsh. "Critical Experiences in Organizing and Administering a State Certificate-of-Need Program." *Public Health Reports* 91 (January/February 1976): 29–45.

Bindman, Andrew, Kevin Grumbach, Dennis Keane, Loren Rauch, and John M. Luce. "Consequences of Queuing for Care at a Public Hospital Emergency Department." *Journal of American Medical Association* 266, no. 8 (August 28, 1991): 1091–1096.

Blank, Robert H. *Rationing Medicine.* New York: Columbia University Press, 1988.

————. "Introduction." In *Biomedical Technology and Public Policy,* ed. Robert H. Blank and Miriam K. Mills, vii–xv. New York: Greenwood Press, 1989.

Blank, Robert H., and Mills, Miriam K., eds. *Biomedical Technology and Public Policy.* New York: Greenwood Press, 1989.

Blendon, Robert J., Robert Leitman, Ian Morrison, and Karen Donelan. "Satisfaction with Health Systems in Ten Nations." *Health Affairs* 9, no. 2 (Summer 1990): 185–192.

Blumberg, Mark S. "Health Status and Health Care Use by Type of Private Health Coverage." *Milbank Memorial Fund Quarterly/Health and Society* 58, no. 4 (Fall 1980): 633–655.

Bovbjerg, Randall R., and John Holahan. *Medicaid in the Reagan Era: Federal Policy and State Choices.* Washington, D.C.: Urban Institute Press, 1982.

Braveman, Paula A., Susan Egerter, Trude Bennett, and Jonathan Showstack. "Differences in Hospital Resource Allocation among Sick Newborns According to Insurance Coverage." *Journal of the American Medical Association* 266, no. 23 (December 18, 1991): 3300–3308.

Braveman, Paula A, V. Mylo Schaaf, Susan Egerter, Trude Bennett, and William Schecter. "Insurance-Related Differences in the Risk of Ruptured Appendix." *New England Journal of Medicine* 333, no. 7 (August 18, 1994): 444–449.

Breyer, S. "Analyzing Regulatory Failure: Mismatches, Less Restrictive Alternatives and Reform." *Harvard Law Review* 92, no. 1 (1979): 549–609.

Bronzino, Joseph D, Vincent H. Smith, and Maurice L. Wade. *Medical Technology and Society: An Interdisciplinary Perspective.* Cambridge, Mass.: MIT Press, 1990, p. 34.

Brooks, Durado D., David R. Smith, and Ron J. Anderson. "Medical Apartheid: An American Perspective." *Journal of the American Medical Association* 266, no. 9 (November 20, 1991): 2746, 2747.

Brooks, E.R., et al. "Does Free Care Improve Adult Health?" *New England Journal of Medicine* 309, no. 23 (1983): 1426–1434.

Brown, J.H.A. *The Politics of Health Care.* Cambridge, Mass: Ballinger, 1978.

Brown, Lawrence D. "The Formulation of Federal Health Care Policy." *Bulletin of the New York Academy of Medicine* 54, no. 1 (January 1978).

————. "Competition and Health Cost Containment: Cautions and Conjectures." *Milbank Memorial Fund Quarterly/Health and Society* 59, no. 2 (Spring 1981): 145–189.

————. "Competition and Health Care Policy: Experience and Expectations." *Annals of the American Academy of Political and Social Science* 468 (July 1983): 48–59.

————. *Health Policy in the Reagan Administration: A Critical Appraisal.* Washington, D.C.: Brookings Institution, 1984.

————. "Introduction to a Decade of Transition." *Journal of Health Politics, Policy and Law* 11, no. 4 (1986): 569–583.

————. "Politics, Money, and Health Care Reform." *Health Affairs* 13, no. 2 (Spring 1994): 175.

Brown, Randall S., et al. "Do Health Maintenance Organizations Work for Medicare?" *Health Care Financing Review* 15, no. 1 (Fall 1993): 135–146.

Brown, Richard E. "Medicare and Medicaid: Band-Aids for the Old and Poor." In *Reforming Medicine: Lessons of the Last Quarter Century,* ed. Victor W. Sidel and Ruth Sidel, 50–76. New York: Pantheon, 1984.

Buck, Jeffrey A., and Mark S. Kamlet. "Problems with Expanding Medicaid for the Uninsured." *Journal of Health Politics, Policy and Law* 18, no. 1 (Spring 1993): 1–25.

Burner, Sally T, Daniel R. Waldo, and David R. McKusick. "National Health Expenditures Projections through 2030." *Health Care Financing Review* 14, no. 1 (Fall 1992): 1–29.

Burstin, Helen R., Stuart R. Lipsitz, and Troyen A. Brennan. "Socioeconomic Status and Risk for Substandard Medical Care." *Journal of the American Medical Association* 268, no. 17 (November 4, 1994): 2383–2387.

Butler, Stuart M. "A Tax Reform Strategy to Deal with the Uninsured." *Journal of the American Medical Association* 265, no. 19 (May 15, 1991): 2541–2543.

Callahan, Daniel. *Setting Limits: Medical Goals in an Aging Society.* New York: Simon and Schuster, 1987.

———. "Why We Must Set Limits." In *A Good Old Age? The Paradox of Setting Limits,* ed. Paul Homer and Martha Holstein, 23–43. New York: Simon and Schuster, Inc., 1990.

———. "Bioethics: Private Choice and Common Good." *Hastings Center Report* 24, no. 3 (May 1, 1994): 28–31.

———. *What Kind of Life: The Limits of Medical Progress.* Washington, D.C.: Georgetown University Press, 1995.

Campbell, Ellen S. "Unpaid Hospital Bills: Evidence from Florida." *Inquiry* 29, no. 1 (Spring 1992): 92–98.

Campion, Frank D. *The AMA and U.S. Health Policy Since 1940.* Chicago: University of Chicago Press, 1984.

Cantor, Norman L. *Advance Directives and the Pursuit of Death with Dignity.* Indianapolis: Indiana University Press, 1993.

Capron, Alexander Morgan. "Biomedical Technology and Health Care: Transforming Our World." *Southern California Law Review* 65, no. 1 (November 1, 1991): 1–10.

Carmen, Ira H. "Bioethics, Public Policy and Political Science." *Politics and Life Sciences* 13, no. 1 (February 1, 1994): 79–81.

Carter, Douglas, and Philip R. Lee, eds. *Politics of Health.* Huntington, N.Y.: Robert F. Krieger, 1979.

Cassell, Eric J. "The Sorcerer's Broom: Medicine's Rampant Technology." *Hastings Center Report* 23 (November–December 1993): 32–39.

Cassidy, Robert. "Can You Really Speak Your Mind in Peer Review?" *Medical Economics* 61 (January 23, 1984): 246–262.

Center for the Study of Social Policy. *Kids Count Data Book 1994.* Washington, D.C., 1994.

Chollet, Deborah J. *Employer-Provided Health Benefits: Coverage, Provisions and Policy Issues.* Washington, D.C.: Employees Benefit Research Institute, 1984.

———. "Employer-Based Health Insurance in a Changing Work Force." *Health Affairs* 13, no. 1 (Spring 1994): 313–326.

Chulis, George S., Franklin P. Eppig, Mary O. Hogan, Daniel R. Waldo, and Ross H. Arnett III. "Health Insurance and the Elderly." *Health Affairs* 12, no. 1 (Spring 1993): 111–118.

Clancy, Carolyn M., and Charlea T. Massion. "American Women's Health Care: A Patchwork Quilt with Gaps." *Journal of the American Medical Association* 268, no. 14 (October 24, 1992): 1918–1920.

Coelen, Craig, and Daniel Sullivan. "An Analysis of the Effects of Prospective Reimbursement Programs on Hospital Expenditures." *Health Care Financing Review,* Winter 1981.

Cohen, Alan B., and Donald R. Cohodes. "Certificate of Need and Low Capital-Cost Medical Technology." *Milbank Memorial Fund Quarterly/Health and Society* 60, no. 2 (Spring 1982): 307–328.

Cohen, Cynthia B., and Elizabeth L. McCloskey. "Private Bioethics Forums: Counterpoint to Government Bodies." *Kennedy Institute of Ethics Journal* 4, no. 2 (September 1, 1994): 283–289.

Cohen, Harold. "State Rate Regulation." In *Controls on Health Care,* ed. Institute of Medicine, 123–135. Washington, D.C.: National Academy of Sciences, 1975.

Cohen, Richard E. "Ready, Aim, Reform." *National Journal* 25, no. 44 (October 30, 1993): 2581–2586.

Cook, Karen, et al. "A Theory of Organizational Response to Regulation: The Case of Hospitals." *Academy of Management Review* 8, no. 2 (1983): 193–205.

"Cost/Benefits of High-Tech Medicine." *Health Systems Review* 25, no. 1 (January 1, 1992): 16–18.

Coughlin, Teresa A. *Medicaid Since 1980: Costs, Coverage, and the Shifting Alliance between the Federal Government and the States.* Washington, D.C.: Urban Institute Press, 1994.

Crittenden, Robert. "Managed Competition and Premium Caps in Washington State," *Health Affairs* 12, no. 2 (Summer 1993): 82–88.

Crozier, David A. "State Rate Setting: A Status Report." *Health Affairs* 1, no. 2 (Summer 1982): 66–83.

Culliton, Barbara J. "Critics Condemn NIH Women's Study." *Nature* 366, no. 6450 (November 4, 1993): 11.

Curtis, Rick. "The Role of the State Government in Assuring Access to Care." *Inquiry* 23, no. 1 (Fall 1986): 277–285.

Dahl, Robert A. and Charles E. Lindblom. *Politics, Economics and Planning.* New York: Harper & Row, 1953.

Daniels, Norman. "Rationing Fairly: Programmatic Consideration." *Bioethics* 7, no. 2/3 (April 1, 1993): 224–233.

Darling, Helen. "The Role of the Federal Government in Assuring Access to Health Care." *Inquiry* 23, no. 1 (Fall 1986): 286–295.

David, Sheri I. *With Dignity: The Search for Medicare and Medicaid.* Westport, Conn.: Greenwood Press, 1985.

Davis, Karen. "Expanding Medicare and Employer Plans to Achieve Universal Health Insurance." *Journal of the American Medical Association* 265, no. 19 (May 15, 1991): 2525–2528.

Davis, Karen, Gerard F. Anderson, Diane Rowland, and Earl P. Steinberg. *Health Care Cost Containment.* Baltimore: John Hopkins University Press, 1990.

Davis, Karen, and Roger Reynolds. *The Impact of Medicare and Medicaid on Access to Medical Care.* Washington, D.C.: Brookings Institution, 1977.

Davis, Karen, and Cathy Schoen. *Health and the War on Poverty: A Ten-Year Proposal.* Washington, D.C.: Brookings Institution, 1978.

———. "Universal Coverage: Building on Medicare and Employer Financing." *Health Affairs* 13, no. 2 (Spring 1994): 7–20.

Davis, William R. "Medical Technology Investing in the '90s." *Medical World News* 33, no. 11 (November 1992): 35.

Demkovich, Linda E. "Adding Competition to the Health Industry." *National Journal* 11 (October 27, 1979): 1796–1800.

————. "Vermont Takes on LTC Financing." *State Health Notes* 15, no. 175 (March 7, 1994): 1–2, 8.

————. "ERISA: States Push to Raze the Biggest Barrier to Health Reform," *State Health Notes* 15, no. 192 (November 14, 1994): 1–2, 7.

————. "HCFA, States Spar—Again—Over Medicaid Provider Taxes," *State Health Notes* 16, no. 200 (March 20, 1995): 1–3.

DiIulio, John J., Jr., and Richard P. Nathan, eds. *Making Health Reform Work: The View from the States.* Washington, D.C.: Brookings Institution, 1994.

Dolnec, D.A., and C.J. Dougherty. "DRGs: The Counterrevolution in Financing Health Care." *Hasting Center Report* 15, no. 3 (June 1985): 19–29.

d'Oronzio, Joseph C. "Bioethics and the Body Politic." *Cambridge Quarterly of Health Care Ethics* 3, no. 2 (1994): 300–301.

Dubin, Elliot J. "Medicaid Reform: Major Trends and Issues." *Intergovernmental Perspective* 18, no. 2 (Spring 1992).

Durda, David. "Number of Medicaid Lawsuits Belies Complexities Involved in Such Filings." *Modern Health Care* 21, no. 8 (February 25, 1991): 31–32.

Durenberger, David F. "The Politics of Health." In *Competition in the Marketplace: Health Care in the 1980s,* ed. James R. Gay and Barbara J. Sax Jacobs, 4. New York: Spectrum Publications, 1982.

Eddy, David M. "Connecting Value and Costs: Whom Do We Ask, and What Do We Ask Them?" *Journal of the American Medical Association* 254, no. 13 (October 3, 1990): 1737–1739.

Ehrenreich, Barbara, and John Ehrenreich. *The American Health Empire: Power, Profit and Politics.* New York: Vintage Books, 1970.

"Elections: What Impact on Health Care Reform?" *State Health Notes* 15, no. 194 (December 12, 1994): 4–5.

Ellwood, Paul M., "Health Maintenance Strategy." *Medical Care* 9 (May/June 1971): 291–298.

————. "Alternative to Regulation: Improving the Market." In Institute of Medicine, *Controls on Health Care,* 49–72. Washington, D.C.: National Academy of Sciences, 1975.

Enthoven, Alain C. "Consumer Choice Health Plans." *New England Journal of Medicine* 298 (March 23, 1978): 650–658.

————. "Consumer Choice Health Plans." *New England Journal of Medicine* 298 (March 30, 1978): 709–720.

————. *Health Plan: The Only Practical Solution to the Soaring Cost of Medicare Care.* Reading, Mass.: Addison-Wesley, 1980.

————. "Competition in the Marketplace: Health Care in the 1980s." In *Competition in the Marketplace: Health Care in the 1980s,* ed. James R. Gay and Barbara J. Sax Jacobs, 11–19. New York: Spectrum Publications, 1982.

————. "Managed Competition of Alternate Delivery System." *Journal of Health Politics, Policy and Law* 13, no. 2 (Summer 1988): 305–321.

————. "Universal Health Insurance through Incentives Reform." *Journal of American Medical Association* 265, no. 19 (May 15, 1991): 2532–2536.

————. "The History and Principles of Managed Competition." *Health Affairs* 12 (Supplement 1993): 24–48.

————. "Why Not the Clinton Health Plan?" *Inquiry* 31, no. 2 (Summer 1994): 129–135.

Enthoven, Alain C., and Richard Kronick. "A Consumer-Choice Health Plan for the 1990s: Universal Health Insurance in a System Designed to Promote Quality and Economy" (first of two parts). *New England Journal of Medicine* 320, no. 1 (January 5, 1989): 29–37.

————. "A Consumer-Choice Health Plan for the 1990s: Universal Health Insurance in a System Designed to Promote Quality and Economy" (second of two parts). *New England Journal of Medicine* 320, no. 2 (January 12, 1989): 94–101.

"Eroding Employer-Based Insurance." *CDF Reports* 15, no. 5 (April 1994): 4.

Esposito, Alfonso, et al. "Abstracts of State Legislated Hospital Cost Containment Programs." *Health Care Financing Review* 4, no. 2 (December 1982): 129–158.

Etheredge, Lynn. "Reagan, Congress and Health Spending." *Health Affairs* 2, no. 1 (Spring 1983): 14–24.

Evans, Robert G. "Incomplete Vertical Integration in the Health Care Industry: Pseudomarkets and Pseudopolicies." *Annals of the American Academy of Political and Social Science* 468 (July 1983): 60–87.

————. "Finding the Levers, Finding the Courage: Lessons from Cost Containment in North America." *Journal of Health Politics, Policy and Law* 11, no. 4 (1986): 585–615.

Everette, James A., et al. "The Diffusion of Medical Technology: Free Enterprise and Regulatory Models in the USA." *Journal of Medical Ethics* 17, no. 3 (1991): 150–155.

Falkson, Joseph L. *HMOs and the Politics of Health Service Reform.* Chicago: American Hospital Association and Robert J. Brady, 1980.

————. "Market Reform, Health Systems, and HMOs." *Policy Studies Journal* 9, no. 2 (1980–81): 213–220.

Fallows, James. "A Triumph of Misinformation," *Atlantic Monthly* 275, no. 1 (January 1995): 26–37.

Feder, Judith M. *Medicare: The Politics of Federal Hospital Insurance.* Lexington, Mass.: D.C. Heath, 1977.

Fein, Rashi. *Medical Care, Medical Costs: The Search for a Health Insurance Policy.* Cambridge: Harvard University Press, 1986.

Feldman, Roger, John Kralewski, and Bryan Dowd. "Health Maintenance Organizations: The Beginning or the End?" *Health Research Service* 24, no. 2 (June 1989): 191–211.

Feldman, Roger, et al. "The Competitive Impact of Health Maintenance Organizations on Hospital Finances: An Exploratory Study." *Journal of Health Politics, Policy and Law* 10 (Winter 1986): 675–697.

Feldstein, Paul J. "Health Associations and the Legislative Process." In *Health Politics and Policy,* ed. Theodore J. Litman and Leonard S. Robins, 223–242. New York: Wiley, 1984.

Fendrick, Mark A., and J. Sanford Schwartz. "Physicians' Decisions Regarding the Acquisition of Technology." In *Adopting New Medical Technology,* ed. Annetine C. Gelijns and Holly V. Dawkins, 71–84. Washington, D.C.: National Academy Press, 1994.

Fineberg, H.V., and H.H. Hiatt. "Evaluation of Medical Practices: The Case for Technology Assessment." *New England Journal of Medicine* 301, no. 20 (1979): 1086–1091.

Folkemer, Donna. "Shifts to Community Long-Term Care Looms on Horizon." *State Health Notes* 15, no. 184 (July 11, 1994): 1–2, 8.

Fossett, James W. "Cost Containment and Rate Setting." In *Making Health Reform Work: The View from the States,* ed. John J. DiIulio, Jr., and Richard P. Nathan, 60–84. Washington, D.C.: Brookings Institution, 1994.

Foundation for Public Affairs. *Public Interest Profiles 1988–1989.* Washington, D.C.: Congressional Quarterly, 1988.

Fox, Daniel M. *Health Policies, Health Politics: The British and American Experience: 1911–1965.* Princeton: Princeton University Press, 1986.

Fox, Peter D., Thomas Rice, and Lisa Alecxih. "Medigap Regulation: Lessons for Health Care Reform." *Journal of Health Politics, Policy and Law* 20, no. 1 (Spring 1995): 31–48.

Franks, Peter, Carolyn M. Clancy, and Marthe R. Gold. "Health Insurance and Mortality: Evidence from a National Cohort." *Journal of the American Medical Association* 270, no. 6 (August 11, 1993): 737–741.

Franks, Peter, Carolyn M. Clancy, Marthe R. Gold and Paul A. Nutting. "Health Insurance and Subjective Health Status: Data from the 1987 National Medical Expenditure Survey." *American Journal of Public Health* 83, no. 9 (September 1993): 1295–1299.

Frech, H.E., III, and Paul B. Ginsburg. "Competition among Health Insurers, Revisited." *Journal of Health Politics, Policy and Law* 13, no. 2 (Summer 1988): 279–291.

Freed, David H. "Toward Redefining Expectations about Medical Technology." *Trends in Health Care, Law and Ethics* 9, no. 2 (Spring 1994): 21–28.

Freeman, Howard E., and Bradford L. Kirkman-Liff. "Health Care under AHCCCS: An Examination of Arizona's Alternative to Medicaid." *Health Services Research* 20, no. 3 (August 1985): 245–266.

Freund, Deborah A., et al. "Evaluation of the Medicaid Competition Demonstrations." *Health Care Financing Review* 11 (Winter 1989): 81–97.

Friedman, Milton. *Capitalism and Freedom*. Chicago: University of Chicago Press, 1962.

Fuchs, Victor R. *The Health Economy*. Cambridge: Harvard University Press, 1986.

———. "The New Technology Assessment." *New England Journal of Medicine* 323, no. 19 (September 6, 1990): 673–677.

———. "The Clinton Plan: A Researcher Examines Reform." *Health Affairs* 13, no. 1 (Spring 1994): 102–114.

———. *Who Shall Live? Health, Economics and Social Choice*. New York: Basic Books, 1995.

Gabel, Jon R., and Alan C. Monheit. "Will Competition Plans Change Insurer-Provider Relationships?" *Milbank Memorial Fund Quarterly/Health and Society* 61, no. 4 (Fall 1983): 614–640.

Garrett, Thomas M., Harold W. Baillie, and Rosellen M. Garrett. *Health Care Ethics: Principles and Problems*, 115–133. Englewood Cliffs, N.J.: Prentice Hall, 1989.

Gavin, Mooney. *Economics, Medicine and Health Care*. New Jersey: Humanities Press, 1986.

Gay, E. Green, et al. "An Appraisal of Organizational Response to Fiscally Constraining Regulation: The Case of Hospitals and DRGs." *Journal of Health and Social Behavior* 30, no. 1 (March 1989): 41–55.

Gelijns, Annetine, and Nathan Rosenberg. "The Dynamics of Technological Change in Medicine." *Health Affairs* 13, no. 3 (Summer 1994): 28–46.

Gelman, Judith. *Competition and Health Planning*. An Issue Paper. Bureau of Economics, U.S. Federal Trade Commission. Washington, D.C.: Government Printing Office 1982.

General Accounting Office. *Medicare PROs: Extreme Variation in Organizational Structure and Activities*. Washington, D.C.: Government Printing Office, November 1988.

———. *Long-Term Care for the Elderly: Issues of Need, Access, and Cost*. Washington, D.C.: Government Printing Office, 1988.

———. *Heart Transplants: Concerns about Cost, Access, and Availability of Donor Organs*. GAO/HRD, 89–61. Washington, D.C.: Government Printing Office, May 1989.

———. *Health Insurance: Cost Increases Lead to Coverage Limitations and Cost Shifting*. Washington, D.C.: Government Printing Office, 1990.

———. *Medicaid Expansions*. Washington, D.C.: Government Printing Office, June 1991.

————. *Hospital Costs: Adoption of Technologies Drives Cost Growth.* Washington, D.C.: Government Printing Office, September 1992.

————. *Health Insurance: California Public Employees' Alliance Has Reduced Recent Premium Growth.* Washington, D.C.: General Accounting Office, 1993.

————. *Medicaid: States Turn to Managed Care to Improve Access and Control Costs.* Gaithersburg, Md.: General Accounting Office, March 1993.

————. *Long-Term Care: Diverse, Growing Population Includes Millions of Americans of All Ages.* Washington, D.C.: General Accounting Office, 1994.

————. *Long-term Care: Private Sector Elder Care Could Yield Multiple Benefits.* Washington, D.C.: Government Printing Office, 1994.

————. *Long-Term Care: Support for Elder Care Could Benefit the Government Workplace and the Elderly.* Washington, D.C.: Government Printing Office, 1994.

Gibson, Robert M., and Daniel R. Waldo. "National Health Expenditures, 1980." *Health Care Financing Review* 3, no. 1 (September 1981): 1–54.

Gibson, Robert M., et al. "National Health Expenditures, 1983." *Health Care Financing Review* 6, no. 2 (Winter 1984): 1–29.

Gillam, Lynn. "Bioethics and Public Policy in Australia." *Politics and Life Science* 13, no. 1 (February 1, 1994): 87–88.

Ginsburg, Paul B. "Public Insurance Programs: Medicare and Medicaid." In *Health Care in America: The Political Economy of Hospitals and Health Insurance,* ed. H.E. Frech III, 179–215. San Francisco: Pacific Research Institute for Public Policy, 1988.

Ginzberg, Eli. "Procompetition in Health Care: Policy or Fantasy?" *Milbank Memorial Fund Quarterly/Health and Society* 60, no. 3 (Summer 1982): 386–398.

————. "Balancing Dollars and Quality." *Midwest Medical Ethics* 5, no. 4 (Fall 1989): 1–5.

————. "High Tech Medicine and Rising Health Care Costs." *Journal of the American Medical Association* 263, no. 13 (April 4, 1990): 1820–1822.

————. "Improving Health Care for the Poor." *Journal of the American Medical Association* 271, no. 6 (February 9, 1994): 464.

Gold, Marsha, et al. "Effects of Selected Cost-Containment Efforts: 1971–1993." *Health Care Financing Review* 14, no. 3 (Spring 1993): 183–225.

Goldfarb, Bruce. "Uncompensated Care Pushes Trauma Centers Out of Business." *Medical World News* 33, no. 4 (April 1992): 32.

Goodman, John C. *The Regulation of Medical Care: Is the Price Too High?* San Francisco: Cato Institute, 1980.

Gornick, Marian. "Physician Payment Reform under Medicare: Monitoring Utilization and Access." *Health Care Financing Review* 14, no. 3 (Spring 1993): 77–96.

Graig, Laurence A. *Health of Nations: An International Perspective on U.S. Health Care Reform.* Washington, D.C.: CQ Press, 1993.

Grannemann, Thomas W., and Mark V. Pauly. *Controlling Medicaid Costs: Federalism, Competition, and Choice.* Washington, D.C.: American Enterprise Institute for Public Policy Research, 1983.

Green, Gay, et al. "An Appraisal of Organizational Response to Fiscally Constraining Regulation: The Case of Hospitals and DRGs." *Journal of Health and Social Behavior* 30, no. 1 (March 1989): 41–55.

Greifinger, Robert B., and Victor William Sidel. "Three Centuries of Medical Care." In *Medical Care in the United States,* ed. Eric F. Oatman, 12–26. New York: H.W. Wilson Company, 1978.

Griner, Paul F. "New Technology Adoption in the Hospital." In *Technology and Health Care in an Era of Limits,* ed. Annetine C. Gelijns, 123–132. Washington, D.C.: National Academy Press, 1992.

Gross, George. "Reagan's 'Bold' Aid Reform." *Nation's Cities Weekly* 5, no. 5 (February 1, 1982): 1, 8.

Grumbach, Kevin, and Thomas Bodenheimer. "Reins or Fences: A Physician's View of Cost Containment." *Health Affairs* 9, no. 4 (Winter 1990): 120–126.

Hadley, Jack. *More Medical Care: Better Health?* Washington, D.C.: Urban Institute Press, 1982.

Hadley, Jack, Earl P. Steinberg, and Judith Feder. "Comparison of Uninsured and Privately Insured Hospital Patients: Condition on Admission, Resource Use, and Outcome." *Journal of the American Medical Association* 265, no. 3 (January 19, 1991): 374–379.

Hadley, Jack, and Katherine Swartz. "The Impact of Hospital Costs between 1980 and 1984 on Hospital Rate Regulation, Competition, and Change in Health Insurance Coverage." *Inquiry* 26, no. 1 (Spring 1989): 35–47.

Hafner-Eaton, Chris. "Physician Utilization Disparities between the Uninsured and Insured: Comparisons of the Chronically Ill, Accutely Ill, and Well Nonelderly Populations." *Journal of the American Medical Association* 269, no. 6 (February 10, 1993): 787–782.

Hafner-Eaton, Chris. "Will the Phoenix Rise, and Where Should She Go? The Women's Health Agenda." *American Behavioral Scientist* 36, no. 6 (July/August 1993): 841–856.

Hamilton, Alexander, James Madison, and John Jay. *The Federalist Papers.* New York: New American Library, 1961.

Hanlon, John T., and George E. Picker. *Public Health: Administration and Practice.* St. Louis: C.V. Mosby, 1974.

Hanna, Kathi E., Robert M. Cook-Deegan, and Robyn Y. Nishimi. "Finding a Forum for Bioethics in U.S. Public Policy." *Politics and Life Sciences* 12 (1993): 205–219.

Harris, John. *Wonderwoman and Superman: The Ethics of Human Biotechnology.* New York: Oxford University Press, 1992.

Havighurst, Clark C. "Health Maintenance Organizations and the Market for Health Services." *Law and Contemporary Problems* 35, no. 1 (Autumn 1970): 716–795.

———. "Regulation of Health Facilities and Services by 'Certificate of Need.' " *Virginia Law Review* 59, no. 7 (October 1973): 1143–1233.

———. *Deregulating the Health Care Industry.* Cambridge, Mass.: Ballinger, 1982.

———. "The Questionable Cost-Containment Record of Commercial Health Insurers." In *Health Care in America: The Political Economy of Hospital and Health Insurance,* ed. H.E. Frech III, 221–258. San Francisco: Pacific Research Institute for Public Policy, 1988.

Hayek, Frederick. *The Road to Serfdom.* Chicago: University of Chicago Press, 1944.

Helbing, Charles. "Medicare Program Expenditures." *Health Care Financing Review,* 1992 Annual Supplement, 26–41.

Hellinger, F.J. "Selection Bias in Health Maintenance Organizations: Analysis of Recent Evidence." *Health Care Financing Review* 9, no. 2 (1987): 55–63.

Henifin, Mary S. "New Reproductive Technologies: Equity and Access to Reproductive Health Care." *Journal of Social Issues* 49, no. 2 (Summer 1993): 61–74.

"High Tech Medicine for the '90s." *Health Systems Review* 25, no. 1 (January 1, 1992): 18.

Hill, D.W. "25 Years of Medical Technology." *British Journal of Hospital Medicine* 46 (October 1991): 242–243.

Hill, Lister. "Health in America: A Personal Perspective." In U.S. Department of Health, Education and Welfare, *Health in America: 1776–1976.* Washington, D.C.: Government Printing Office, 1976.

Hillman, Alan L. "Financial Incentives for Physicians in HMOs: Is There a Conflict of Interest?" *New England Journal of Medicine* 317, no. 27 (December 31, 1987): 1734–1748.

Hillman, Bruce J. "Physicians' Acquisition and Use of New Technology in an Era of Economic Constraints." In *Technology and Health Care in an Era of Limits*, ed. Annetine C. Geligns, 133–149. Washington, D.C.: National Academy Press, 1992.

Holahan, John. "The Impact of Alternative Hospital Payment Systems on Medicaid Costs." *Inquiry* 25, no. 4 (Winter 1988): 519–520.

Holohan, John F., and Joel W. Cohen. *Medicaid: The Trade-Off between Cost-Containment and Access to Care*. Washington, D.C.: Urban Institute Press, 1986.

Holohan, John, and John L. Palmer. "Medicare's Fiscal Problems: An Imperative for Reforms." *Journal of Health Politics, Policy and Law* 13, no. 1 (Spring 1988): 66–68.

Hoppszallern, Suzanna, Christine Hughes, and Robert A. Zimmerman. "MRI Aquisition: How Appropriate Is It for Hospitals?" *Hospitals* 65, no. 8 (April 20, 1991): 58.

Hospital Insurance Association of America. *Source Book of Health Insurance Data*. Washington, D.C.: Hospital Insurance Association of America, 1990.

Hsiao, William C., and Daniel L. Dunn. "The Impact of DRG Payment on New Jersey Hospitals." *Inquiry* 24, no. 3 (1987): 212–220.

Hudson, Terese. "States Scramble for Solutions under New Medicaid Law." *Hospitals* 66, no. 11 (June 5, 1992): 52–56.

Huitt, Ralph. "Political Feasibility." In *Policy Analysis in Political Science*, ed. Ira Sharkansky. Chicago: Markham, 1970.

Huston, Patricia. "Is Health Technology Assessment Medicine's Rising Star?" *Canadian Medical Association Journal* 147, no. 12 (December 15, 1992): 1839–1841.

Iglehart, John K. "The Federal Government as Venture Capitalist: How Does It Fare?" *Milbank Memorial Fund Quarterly/Health and Society* 59, no. 4 (Fall 1980): 656–666.

———. "Health Care and American Business." *New England Journal of Medicine* 306, no. 2 (1981): 120–124.

———. "Health Care Reform: The States." *New England Journal of Medicine* 330, no. 1 (January 6, 1994): 75–79.

Intergovernmental Health Policy Project. *Expanding Access to Health Care: An Overview of 1992 State Legislation*. Washington, D.C.: George Washington University Press, 1993.

Jajich-Toth, Cindy, and Burns W. Roper. "Americans' Views on Health Care: A Study In Contradictions." *Health Affairs* 9, no. 4 (Winter 1990): 149–157.

James, A. Everette. et al. "The Diffusion of Medical Technology: Free Enterprise and Regulatory Models in the USA." *Journal of Medical Ethics* 17 (1991): 150–155.

Jaros, G.G., and D.A. Boonzaier. "Cost Escalation in Health-Care Technology—Possible Solutions." *South African Medical Journal* 83, no. 6 (June 1, 1993): 420–422.

Jecker, Nancy S. "Can An Employer-Based Health Insurance System Be Just?" *Journal of Health Care Politics, Policy and Law* 18, no. 3 (Fall 1993): 657–673.

Johnson, Allan N., and David Aquilina. "The Competitive Impact of Health Maintenance Organizations and Competition on Hospitals in Minnneapolis/St. Paul." *Journal of Health Politics, Policy and Law* 10, no. 4 (Winter 1986): 659–674.

Johnson, Richard L. "Should Hospital Planning Continue to Be Regulated?" *Health Affairs* 2, no. 1 (Spring 1983): 83–91.

Johnsson, Julie. "High-Tech Health Care: How Much Can We Afford?" *Hospitals* 65, no. 16 (August 20, 1991): 80.

Jones, Charles O. *An Introduction to the Study of Public Policy*. North Scituate, Mass: Duxbury Press, 1978.

Jones, James R. "Cost Pressures and Health Policy Reforms." *Health Affairs* 1, no. 3 (Summer 1982): 39–47.

Jones, Stanley B. "Multiple Choice Health Insurance: The Lessons and Challenges to Private Insurers." *Inquiry* 27, no. 2 (Summer 1990): 161–166.

Jordan, Fred. "Governors OK Alternative Plan on Federalism." *Nation's Cities Weekly* 5, no. 5 (March 1, 1982): 1, 9.

Joskow, Paul L. "Alternative Regulatory Mechanism for Controlling Hospital Costs." In *A New Approach to the Economics of Health Care,* ed. Mancur Olson, 219–257. Washington, D.C.: American Enterprise Institute for Public Policy Research, 1981.

Kaiser Commission on the Future of Medicaid. *Health Reform Legislation: A Comparison of Major Proposals.* Henry J. Kaiser Family Foundation, January 1994.

Kalb, Paul E. "Controlling Health Care Costs by Controlling Technology: A Private Contractual Approach." *Yale Law Journal* 99, no. 4 (March 1990): 1109–1126.

Kambert, Mary-Lan. "High Tech Health Care: Medical Devices and Treatments for the Future—and Present." *Current Health* 16, no. 8 (April 2, 1990): 4–9.

Kamisar, Yale. "Who Should Live—or Die? Who Should Decide?" An interview with Professor Kamisar at the University of Michigan Law School. *Trial* 27, no. 12 (December 1, 1991): 20–26.

Kane, N., and P. Manoukian. "The Effect of the Medicare Prospective Payment System on the Adoption of New Technology: The Case of Cochlear Implants." *New England Journal of Medicine* 321 (1989): 1378–1383.

Keigher, Sharon M. "Health Care Reform and Long-Term Care: Uneasy Political Partners." *Health and Social Work* 19, no. 3 (August 3, 1994): 223–226.

Kennedy, Edward M. "Remarks on Introducing the Health Security Act." *Congressional Record,* January 25, 1971.

Kennedy, Louanne, and Bernard M. Baruch. "Health Planning in an Age of Austerity." *Policy Studies Journal* 9, no. 2 (Special #1, 1980–81): 232–241.

Kern, Rosemary G., and Susan R. Windham, with Paula Griswold. *Medicaid and Other Experiments in State Health Policy.* Washington, D.C.: American Enterprise Institute for Public Policy Research, 1986.

Kerr, John K., and Richard Jelinek. "Impact of Technology in Health Care and Health Administration: Hospitals and Alternative Care Delivery Systems." *Journal of Health Administration Education* 8, no. 1 (Winter 1990): 5–10.

Kilner, John F. "Age as a Basis for Allocating Lifesaving Medical Resources: An Ethical Analysis." *Journal of Health Politics, Policy and Law* 13, no. 3 (Fall 1988): 405–423.

———. *Who Lives? Who Dies? Ethical Criteria in Patient Selection.* New Haven: Yale University Press, 1991.

———. *Life on the Line: Ethics, Aging, Ending Patients' Lives, and Allocating Vital Resources.* Grand Rapids, Mich.: W.B. Eerdmans, 1992.

Kilpatrick, Anne O., Krishna S. Dhir, and John M. Sanders. "Health Care Technology Assessment: A Policy Planning Tool." *International Journal of Public Administration* 14, no. 1 (1991): 59–82.

Kingdon, John W. *Agendas, Alternatives, and Public Policies.* Boston: Little, Brown, 1984.

Kinney, Eleanor D., and Suzanne K. Steinmetz. "Notes From the Insurance Underground: How the Chronically Ill Cope." *Journal of Health Politics, Policy and Law* 19, no. 3 (Fall 1994): 637–641.

Kitzhaber, John. "A Healthier Approach to Health Care." *Issues in Science and Technology* 7, no. 2 (Winter 1991): 59–65.

Klein, Rudolf. "The Political Ideology vs. the Reality of Politics: The Case of Britain's Health Services in the 1980s." *Milbank Memorial Fund Quarterly/Health and Society* 62, no. 1 (Winter 1984).

Kosterlitz, Julie. "Buying into Trouble," *National Journal* 20, no. 57 (December 31, 1988): 3245–3249.

———. "Rationing Health Care." *National Journal* 22, no. 26 (June 30, 1990): 1590–1595.

———. "Softening Resistance." *National Journal* 23, no. 2 (January 12, 1991): 64–68.

———. "Paying for Miracles." *National Journal* 25, no. 32 (August 7, 1993): 1967–1971.

———. "Health Lobby Cranks Up Its Postage Meter." *National Journal* 25, no. 42 (October 16, 1993).

———. "Winners and Losers." *National Journal* 25, no. 50 (December 11, 1993).

———. "Brinkmanship." *National Journal* 26, no. 28 (July 9, 1994): 1648.

———. "Harry, Louise and Doublespeak." *National Journal* 26, no. 26 (June 25, 1995): 542.

———. "Signs of Life in the Wreckage," *National Journal* 26, no. 43 (October 22, 1994).

———. "Unmanaged Care," *National Journal* 26, no. 50 (December 10, 1994): 2903–2907.

Kotelchuck, Ronda. "Medicaid Managed Care: A Mixed Review." *Health/PAC Bulletin* 22, no. 3 (Fall 1992): 4–11.

Krause, Elliott A. *Power and Illness: The Political Sociology of Health and Medical Care.* New York: Elsevier, 1977.

Krauss, Clifford. "Under Political Steam, Health-Care Issue Gains Wider Support in Congress." *New York Times,* January 12, 1992.

Kruse, Lowell C. "Some Thoughts about Resource Allocation in Health Care." *Midwest Medical Ethics* 5, no. 4 (Fall 1989): 15–16.

Ladenheim, Kala, *Expanding Access to Health Care: An Overview of 1992 State Legislation.* Washington, D.C: Intergovernmental Health Policy Project, George Washington University, 1993.

Latham, Bryan W. *Health Care Costs: There Are Solutions.* New York: American Management Association, 1983.

Laudicina, Susan S., and Brian Burwell. "Profile of Medicaid Home and Community-Based Care Waivers, 1985: Findings of a National Survey." *Journal of Health Politics, Policy and Law* 13, no. 3 (Fall 1988): 528–529.

Lauritzen, Paul. *Pursuing Parenthood: Ethical Issues in Assisted Reproduction.* Bloomington: Indiana University Press, 1993.

Lave, Judith R. "Hospital Reimbursement under Medicare." *Milbank Memorial Fund Quarterly/Health and Society* 62, no. 2 (1984): 251–278.

Lazenby, Helen C., and Suzanne W. Letsch. "National Health Expenditures, 1989." *Health Care Financing Review* 12, no. 2 (Winter 1990): 1–26.

Lee, Philip R., and Carroll L. Estes. "New Federalism and Health Policy." *Annals of the American Academy of Political and Social Science* 468 (July 1983): 88–102.

Lemov, Penelope. "States and Medicaid: Ahead of Feds," *Governing* 6, no. 10 (July 1993): 27–28.

———. "An Acute Case of Health Care Reform," *Governing* 7, no. 8 (May 1994): 44–50.

———. "Nursing Homes and Common Sense." *Governing* 7, no. 10 (July 1994): 44–49.

Letsch, Suzanne W. Calculated from "Data Watch: National Health Care Spending in 1991." *Health Affairs* 12, no. 1 (Spring 1993): 94–110.

Letsch, Suzanne W., Helen C. Lazenby, Katharine R. Levit, and Cathy A. Cowan.

"National Health Expenditures, 1991." *Health Care Financing Review* 14, no. 2 (Winter 1992): 1–30.

Leutz, Walter N., Merwyn R. Greenlick, and John A. Capitman. "Integrating Acute and Long-Term Care." *Health Affairs* 13, no. 4 (Fall 1994): 58–74.

Levit, Katharine R. "National Health Expenditures, 1993." *Health Care Financing Review* 16, no. 1 (Fall 1994): 280.

Levit, Katharine R., Gary L. Olin, and Suzanne W. Letsch. "Americans' Health Insurance Coverage, 1980–1991." *Health Care Financing Review* 14, no. 1 (Fall 1992): 31–57.

Levit, Katharine R., Arthur L. Sensebig, Cathy A. Cowen, Helen C. Lazenby, Patricia A. McDonnell, Darleen K. Won, Lekha Sivarajan, Jean M. Stiller, Carolyn S. Donham, and Madie S. Stewart. "National Health Expenditures, 1993." *Health Care Financing Review* 16, no. 1 (Fall 1994): 247–294.

Lewin and Associates, Inc. *Evaluation of the Efficiency and Effectiveness of the Section 1122 Review Process.* Springfield, Va.: National Technical Information Service, 1975.

Leyerle, Betty. *The Private Regulation of American Health Care.* Armonk, N.Y.: M.E. Sharpe, 1994.

Light, Donald W. "The Practice and Ethics of Risk-Related Insurance." *Journal of the American Medical Association* 267, no. 18 (May 13, 1992): 2503–2508.

Lindblom, Charles A. "The Science of Muddling Through." *Public Administration Review* 19 (Spring 1959): 79–88.

Lindblom, Charles E. *Politics and Markets: The World's Political Economic System.* New York: Basic Books, 1977.

Long, Stephen H., and M. Susan Marquis. "Gaps in Employer Coverage: Lack of Supply or Lack of Demand?" *Health Affairs* 12 (Supplement 1993): 282–293.

Long, Stephen H., and Russell F. Settle. "Medicare and the Disadvantaged Elderly: Objectives and Outcomes." *Milbank Memorial Fund Quarterly (Health and Society)* 62, no. 4 (Fall 1984): 609–656.

Lotlarz, Virginia. "History of Medical Technology in the United States." *Clinical Laboratory Science* 4, no. 4 (July/August 1991): 233–236.

Lowi, Theodore. "The Public Philosophy: Interest Group Liberalism." *American Political Science Review* 61, no. 1 (March 1967): 5–24.

Luft, Harold S. "How Do Health Maintenance Organizations Achieve Their Savings? Rhetoric and Evidence." *New England Journal of Medicine* 298, no. 24 (1978): 1336–1343.

———. "Trends in Medical Costs: Do HMOs Lower the Rate of Growth? *Medical Care* 18, no. 1 (1980): 1–16.

———. *Health Maintenance Organizations: Dimensions of Performance.* New York: Wiley, 1981.

Luft, Harold S., Susan C. Maerki, and Joan B. Trauner. "The Competitive Effects of Health Maintenance Organizations: Another Look at Evidence from Hawaii, Rochester, and Minneapolis/St. Paul." *Journal of Health Politics, Policy and Law* 10, no. 4 (Winter 1986): 625–658.

Luft, Harold S. and R.H. Miller, "Patient Selection in a Competitive Health Care System." *Health Affairs* 7, no. 3 (1988): 97–119.

Lurie, N. "Termination from Medical: Does It Affect Health?" *New England Journal of Medicine* 311, no. 7 (1984): 480–484.

Mabie, Margot C.J. *Bioethics and the New Medical Technology.* New York: Atheneum, 1993.

McBride, David. "Black America: From Community Health Care to Crisis Medicine." *Journal of Health Politics, Policy, and Law* 18, no. 2 (Summer 1993): 319–337.

McClure, Walter. "Structural and Incentive Problems in Economic Regulation of Medical Care." *Milbank Memorial Quarterly/Health and Society* 59, no. 2 (Spring 1981): 107–144.

———. "The Competitive Strategy for Medical Care." *Annals of the American Academy of Political and Social Science* 469 (July 1983): 30–47.

McCombs, Jeffrey S., and Jon B. Christianson. "Applying Competitive Bidding to Health Care." *Journal of Health Politics and Law* 12, no. 4 (Winter 1987): 703–721.

McConnell, Grant. *Private Power and American Democracy.* New York: Knopf, 1966.

McCormick, Richard A. "Clear and Convincing Evidence: The Case of Nancy Cruzan." *Midwest Medical Ethics* 6, no. 4 (Fall 1990): 10–12.

McGregor, Maurice. "Hospital Costs: Can They Be Cut?" *Milbank Memorial Fund Quarterly/Health and Society* 59, no. 1 (Winter 1981): 89–98.

McMillan, Alma. "Trends in Medicare Health Maintenance Organization Enrollment: 1986–1993." *Health Care Financing Review* 15, no. 1 (Fall 1993): 135–146.

McNeil, Richard, Jr., and Robert E. Schlenker. "HMOs, Competition and Government." *Milbank Memorial Fund Quarterly/Health and Society,* 53, no. 1 (Spring 1975): 195–224.

Mahood, H.R. *Interest Group Politics in America: A New Intensity.* Englewood Cliffs, N.J.: Prentice Hall, 1990.

Manning, Bayless, and Bruce Vladeck. "The Role of State and Local Government in Health." *Health Affairs* 2, no. 4 (Winter 1983): 134–140.

Manninh, William G., et al. "A Controlled Trial of the Effects of a Prepaid Group Practice on Use of Services." *New England Journal of Medicine* 310, no. 23 (June 1984): 1505–1510.

Marmor, Theodore. *The Politics of Medicare.* Chicago: Aldine, 1973.

Marmor, Theodore, and James Morone. "HSAs and the Representation of Consumer Interests: Conceptual Issues and Litigation Problems." *Health Law Project Library Bulletin* 4 (April 1979): 117–128.

Marmor, Theodore R., Donald A. Wittman, and Thomas C. Heagy. "The Politics of Medical Inflation." In *Political Analysis and American Medical Care,* ed. Theodore R. Marmor. Cambridge, England: Cambridge University Press, 1983.

Mawrick, Charles. "Women's Health Action Plan Sees First Anniversary." *Journal of the American Medical Association* 268, no. 14 (October 14, 1992): 1816–1818.

Mechanic, David. "Some Dilemmas in Health Care Policy." *Milbank Memorial Fund Quarterly/Health and Society* 59, no. 1 (Winter 1981): 1–14.

Meilaender, Gilbert. "The Cruzan Decision: 9.5 Theses for Discussion." *Midwest Medical Ethics* 6, no. 4 (Fall 1990): 3–5.

Meir, Kenneth J. *Regulation: Politics, Bureaucracy and Economics.* New York: St. Martin's Press, 1985.

Mellow, Wesley S. "Determinants of Health Insurance and Pension Coverage." *Monthly Labor Review,* 105, no. 5 (May 1982): 30–32.

Melski, John W. "Price of Technology: A Blind Spot." *Journal of the American Medical Association* 267, no. 11 (March 18, 1992): 1516–1518.

Menzel, Paul T. *Strong Medicine: The Ethical Rationing of Health Care.* New York: Oxford University Press, 1990.

Merrill, Jeffrey and Catherine McLaughlin. "Competition versus Regulation: Some Empirical Evidence." *Journal of Health Politics, Policy and Law* 10, no. 4 (Winter 1988): 613–623.

Merrill, Richard A. "Regulation of Drugs and Devices: An Evolution." *Health Affairs* 13, no. 3 (Summer 1994): 47–69.

Meyerhoff, Allen S., and David A. Crozier. "Health Care Coalitions: The Evolution of a Movement." *Health Affairs* 3, no. 1 (Spring 1984): 120–127.

Mick, Stephen S., and John D. Thompson. "Public Attitude toward Health Planning under the Health Systems Agencies." *Journal of Health Politics, Law and Policy* 9, no. 4 (Winter 1984): 783–800.

Miller, Judith. "What to Do until the Philosopher Kings Come: Bioethics and Public Policy in Canada." *Politics and the Life Sciences* 13, no. 1 (February 1, 1994): 93–95.

Miller, Mark E., Stephen Zuckerman, and Michael Gates. "How Do Medicare Physician Fees Compare with Private Payers?" *Health Care Financing Review* 14, no. 3 (Spring 1993): 25–39.

Miller, Stephen. *Special Interest Groups in American Politics.* New Brunswick, N.J.: Transaction, 1985.

Miller, Velvet G., and Janis L. Curties. "Health Care Reform and Race-Specific Policies." *Journal of Health Politics, Policy and Law* 18, no. 3 (Fall 1993): 748.

Mitchell, Samuel A. "Issues, Evidence, and the Policymaker's Dilemma." *Health Affairs* 1, no. 3 (Summer 1982): 84–98.

Monheit, Alan C., and Jessica Primoff Vistnes. "Implicit Pooling of Workers from Large and Small Firms." *Inquiry* 13, no. 1 (Spring 1994): 301–314.

Moon, Marilyn. *Medicare Now and in the Future.* Washington, D.C.: Urban Affairs Press, 1993.

Mooney, Gavin. *Economics, Medicine and Health Care.* Atlantic Highlands, N.J.: Humanities Press, 1986.

Moran, Donald W. "HMOs, Competition, and the Politics of Minimum Benefits." *Milbank Memorial Fund Quarterly/Health and Society* 59, no. 2 (Spring 1981): 190–208.

Morone, James A., and Andrew B. Dunham. "Slouching toward National Health Insurance: The Unanticipated Politics of DRGs." *Bulletin of the New York Academy of Medicine* 62, no. 6 (July/August 1986): 646–662.

Morris, Jonas. *Searching for a Cure: National Health Policy Considered.* New York: Pica Press, 1984.

Mueller, Keith J. "Organ Transplant Legislation." In *Biomedical Technology and Public Policy,* ed. Robert H. Blank and Miriam K. Mills, 143–165. New York: Greenwood Press, 1989.

Muller, Charlotte. *Health Care and Gender.* New York: Russell Sage Foundation, 1990, 73.

———. "Objective Health Care Technology Evaluation—It Isn't Easy." *Social Work in Health Care* 16, no. 1 (1991): 119–132.

Nathan, Richard. *The Administrative Presidency.* New York: Wiley, 1983.

Nathan, Richard P., et al. "Initial Effects of the Fiscal Year 1982 Reductions in Federal Domestic Spending." In *Reductions in U.S. Domestic Spending: How They Affect State and Local Governments,* ed. John W. Ellwood, 315–349. New Brunswick, N.J.: Transaction, 1982.

National Commission on the State and Local Public Service. *Frustrated Federalism: Rx for State and Local Health Care Reform.* Albany, N.Y.: Nelson A. Rockefeller Institute of Government, 1993, p. 15.

Navarro, Peter. *The Policy Game: How Special Interests and Ideologues Are Stealing America.* New York: Wiley, 1984.

Nelson, Harry. *Federalism in Health Reform: Views from the States That Could Not Wait.* New York: Milbank Memorial Fund, 1994.

Neubauer, Deanne. "Hawaii: A Pioneer in Health System Reform." *Health Affairs* 12, no. 12 (Spring 1993): 3–39.

Newhouse, Joseph P., et al. "Some Interim Results from a Controlled Trial of Cost

Sharing in Health Insurance." *New England Journal of Medicine* 305, no. 25 (December 1981): 1501–1507.

Nichols, Mark. "Tinkering with Mother Nature: A Controversial Report on Reproductive Technologies." *Maclean's* 106, no. 48 (November 29, 1993): 38–40.

Nishimi, Robyn Y. "From the Congressional Office of Technology Assessment." *Journal of the American Medical Association* 270, no. 24 (December 22, 1993): 2911.

Nixon, Richard M. "Message to Congress." *Weekly Compilation of Presidential Documents.* Washington, D.C.: Office of the Register, February 18, 1971.

Noll, Roger G. "The Consequences of Public Utility Regulation of Hospitals." In Institute of Medicine, *Controls on Health Care,* 23–48. Washington, D.C.: National Academy of Sciences, 1975.

Norris, Jonas. *Searching for a Cure: National Health Policy Considered.* New York: PICA Press, 1984.

Nyman, John. "Costs, Technology, and Insurance in the Health Care Sector." *Journal of Policy Analysis and Management* 10, no. 1 (Winter 1991): 106–111.

Oberg, Charles, Betty Lia-Hoagberg, Ellen Hodkinson, Catherine Skovholt, and Renee Vanman. "Prenatal Care Comparisons among Privately Insured, Uninsured, and Medicaid-Enrolled Women." *Public Health Reports* 105, no. 5 (September/October 1990): 533–535.

Office of the Federal Register, National Archives and Records Administration. *The United States Government Manual 1990/91.* Washington, D.C.: Government Printing Office, 1990.

Oliver, Thomas R. "Analysis, Advice and Congressional Leadership: The Physician Payment Review Commission and the Politics of Medicare." *Journal of Health Politics, Policy and Law* 18, no. 1 (Spring 1993): 113–174.

Olson, Mancur. *The Logic of Collective Action: Public Goods and the Theory of Groups.* Cambridge: Harvard University Press, 1965.

———. *The Rise and Decline of Nations: Economic Growth, Stagflation, and Social Rigidities.* New Haven: Yale University Press, 1983.

O'Neill, Patrick. "Oregon's Health Care Rationing Plan Causing Fight." *Health Career News* (September 12, 1990): 17–21.

"Oregon's Assisted Suicide Law Stokes the Fires of Controversy." *State Health Notes,* February 20, 1995, 1–3.

Parsons, T.E. "Suggestions for a Sociological Approach to a Theory of Organizations." *Administrative Science Quarterly* 1 (1956): 63–85.

Pauly, Mark V. *Medical Care at Public Expense: A Study in Applied Welfare Economics.* New York: Praeger, 1971.

———. "Is Medical Care Different?" In Bureau of Economics, U.S. Federal Trade Commission, *Competition in the Health Care Sector: Past, Present and Future,* 19–48. Washington, D.C.: Government Printing Office, 1978.

———. "Is Medical Care Different? Old Questions, New Answers." *Journal of Health Politics, Policy and Law* 13, no. 2 (Summer 1988): 227–237.

Pear, Robert. "Another Set of Dire Warnings on Social Security and Medicare Trust Funds." *New York Times,* April 4, 1995.

———. "Clinton Proposes U.S. Rules for Private Health Insurance." *New York Times,* June 15, 1995.

Pence, Gregory E. *Classic Cases in Medical Ethics,* 2nd. ed. New York: McGraw Hill, 1995, 41–47.

Perin, Joshua. "Long-Term Care Insurance: Partnership Model Offers an Option." *State Health Notes* 15, no. 193 (November 28, 1994): 4–5.

Peters, Philip G., Jr. "The Constitution and the Right to Die." *Midwest Medical Ethics* 6, no. 4 (Fall 1990): 13–16.

Petrie, John T. "Overview of the Medicare Program." *Health Care Financing Review,* 1992 Annual Supplement, 1–14.

Phelps, Charles E., and Stephen T. Parente. "Priority Setting in Medical Technology and Medical Practice Assessment." *Medical Care* 28, no. 8 (August 1990): 703–723.

Pollard, Michael R. "The Essential Role of Antitrust in a Competitive Market for Health Services." *Milbank Memorial Fund Quarterly/Health and Society* 59, no. 2 (Spring 1981): 256–268.

Quade, E.S. *Analysis for Public Decisions,* 3rd ed. New York: Elsevier, 1989.

Raffel, Marshall W. *The U.S. Health System: Origins and Functions.* New York: Wiley, 1980.

Rask, Kimberly J., Mark V. Williams, Ruth M. Parker, and Sally E. McNagny. "Obstacles Predicting Lack of a Regular Provider and Delays in Seeking Care for Patients at an Urban Public Hospital." *Journal of the American Medical Association* 271, no. 24 (June 22, 1994): 1931–1933.

Rauch, Jonathan. *Demosclerosis: The Silent Killer of American Government.* New York: Times Books, 1994.

Raymond, Janice G. *Women as Wombs: Reproductive Technologies and the Battle over Women's Freedom.* San Francisco: Harper, 1993.

Rettig, Richard A. "Medical Innovation Duels Cost Containment." *Health Affairs* 13, no. 3 (Summer 1994): 7–27.

Rhodes, Robert P. *Health Care: Politics, Policy and Distributive Justice: The Ironic Triumph.* New York: SUNY Press, 1992, 76.

Rice, Thomas, Katherine Desmond, and Jon Gable. "The Medicare Catastrophic Coverage Act: A Post-Mortem." *Health Affairs* 9, no. 3 (Fall 1990): 75–87.

Rice, Thomas, and Jon Gable. "Protecting the Elderly against High Health Care Costs." *Health Affairs* (Fall 1986).

Rice, Thomas, and Kathleen Thomas. "Evaluating the New Medigap Standardization Regulations." *Health Affairs* 11, no. 1 (Spring 1992): 194–207.

Rice, Thomas, Kathleen Thomas, and William Weissert. *The Impact of Owning Private Long-Term Care Insurance Policies on Out-of-Pocket Costs.* Washington, D.C.: American Association of Retired Persons, 1989, 7.

Rice, Thomas, and Kenneth E. Thorpe. "Income-Related Cost Sharing in Health Insurance." *Health Affairs* 12, no. 1 (Spring 1993): 22.

Rivlin, Alice M., David M. Cutler, and Len M. Nichols. "Financing Estimation, and Estimation Effects." *Health Affairs* 13, no. 1 (Spring 1994): 30–49.

Robertson, John A. *Children of Choice: Freedom and the New Reproductive Technologies.* Princeton.: Princeton University Press, 1994.

Rochefort, David A. "Commentary—The Pragmatic Appeal of Employment-Based Health Care Reform." *Journal of Health Care Politics, Policy and Law* 18, no. 3 (Fall 1993): 683–693.

Rockefeller, John D., IV. "The Pepper Commission Report on Comprehensive Health Care." *New England Journal of Medicine* 323, no. 14 (October 4, 1990): 1005–1007.

Roemer, Milton I. "Hospitals Utilization and the Supply of Physicians." *Journal of the American Medical Association* 178, no. 1 (December 1961): 933–989.

———. "The Politics of Public Health in the United States." In *Health Politics and Policy,* ed. Theodore J. Litman and Leonard S. Robins, 261–273. New York: Wiley, 1984.

———. *An Introduction to the U.S. Health Care System,* 2nd ed. New York: Springer, 1986.

Rosenbaum, Walter A. *Environmental Politics and Policy.* Washington, D.C.: CQ Press, 1985.

Rosenberg, Charlotte L. "Why Doctor-Policing Laws Don't Work." *Medical Economics* 61 (March 5, 1984): 84–96.

Rosenbloom, David. "New Ways to Keep Old Promises in Health Care." *Health Affairs* 2, no. 4 (Winter 1983): 41–53.

Rosoff, Arnold J. "Phase Two of the Federal HMO Development Program: New Directions after a Shaky Start." *American Journal of Law and Medicine* 1, no. 2 (Fall 1975): 209–243.

Ross, Jane L. "Long-Term Care: Demography, Dollars, and Dissatisfaction Drive Reform." Testimony before the Special Committee on Aging, U.S. Senate. General Accounting Office, Washington, D.C., April 12, 1944, 1–6.

Rovner, Julie. "Climbing Medigap Premiums Draw Attention on Hill." *Congressional Quarterly Weekly Report* (February 17, 1990): 527–530.

Rowland, Diana, Barbara Lyons, Alina Salganicoff, and Peter Long. "A Profile of the Uninsured in America." *Health Affairs* 13, no. 2 (Spring 1994): 283–289.

Rowland, Diana, and Alina Salganicoff. "Commentary: Lessons from Medicaid—Improving Access to Office-Cased Physician Care for the Low-Income Population." *American Journal of Public Health* 84, no. 4 (April 1994): 550–551.

Rublee, Dale A. "Medical Technology in Canada, Germany, and the United States: An Update." *Health Affairs* 13, no. 4 (Fall 1994): 113–117.

Rushefsky, Mark E. "A Critique of Market Reform in Health Care: The 'Consumer-Choice Health Plan.' " *Journal of Health Politics, Policy and Law* 5, no. 4 (Winter 1981): 720–741.

Rutten, Frans F.H., and Gouke J. Bonsel. "High Cost Technology in Health Care: A Benefit or a Burden?" *Social Science and Medicine* 35, no. 4 (1992): 567–577.

Ruttenberg, Joan E. "Commentary—Revisiting the Employment-Insurance Link." *Journal of Health Care Politics, Policy and Law* 18, no. 3 (Fall 1993): 675–681.

Salkever, David, and Thomas Bice. "The Impact of Certificate of Need Controls on Hospital Investment." *Milbank Memorial Fund Quarterly/Health and Society* 54, no. 1 (Spring 1976): 185–214.

————. *Hospital Certificate-of-Need Controls: Impact on Investment, Costs and Use.* Washington, D.C.: American Enterprise Institute for Public Policy Research, 1979, 75.

Samuelson, Paul. *Economics.* New York: McGraw-Hill, 1970.

Sapolsky, Harvey M., et al. "Corporate Attitude toward Health Care Costs." *Milbank Memorial Fund Quarterly/Health and Society* 59, no. 4 (Fall 1981): 561–585.

Schear, Stuart. "A Medicaid Miracle?" *National Journal* 27, no. 5 (February 4, 1995): 294–298.

Schneider, Saundra K. "Intergovernmental Influences on Medicaid Program Expenditures." *Public Administration Review* 48, no. 4 (July/August 1988): 756–763.

Schneider, William. "Health Care Reform: What Went Right." *National Journal* 25, no. 40 (October 2, 1993): 2404.

————. "Health Care: So Where's the Crisis?" *National Journal* 26, no. 24 (June 11, 1994): 1378.

Schur, Claudia L., Marc L. Berk, and Penny Mohr. "Understanding the Cost of a Catastrophic Drug Benefit." *Health Affairs* 9, no. 3 (Fall 1990): 88–100.

Schwartz, William B. "In the Pipeline: A Wave of Valuable Medical Technology." *Health Affairs* 13, no. 3 (Summer 1994): 70–79.

Schwartz, William B., and Henry J. Aaron. *Health Care Costs: The Social Tradeoffs.* Washington, D.C.: Brookings Institution, 1985.

————. "The Achilles Heel of Health Care Rationing." *New York Times*, July 9, 1990, A15.

Serafini, Marilyn Werber. "Managed Medicare." *National Journal* 27, no. 15 (April 15, 1995): 920–923.

————. "No Strings Attached!" *National Journal* 27, no. 20 (May 20, 1995): 1230–1234.

Shaffer, Franklin A. "DRGs: History and Overview." *Nursing and Health Care*, September 1983, 389.

Shaw, Linda R., et al. "Ethics of Lung Transplantation with Live Donors." *The Lancet* 338, no. 8768 (September 14, 1991): 678–681.

Shear, Jeff. "The Big Fix." *National Journal* 27, no. 12 (25 March 1995): 734–738.

Sheils, John F., and Lawrence S. Lewin. "Perspective: Alternative Estimate: No Pain, No Gain." *Health Affairs* 13, no. 1 (Spring 1993): 50–55.

Sheri, David I. *With Dignity: The Search for Medicare and Medicaid*. Westport, Conn.: Greenwood Press, 1985.

Shikles, Janet L. *Long-Term Care Insurance: Risks to Consumers Should Be Reduced*. Testimony of director, health financing and policy issues, Human Resources Division. General Accounting Office. Washington, D.C., 1991, p. 2.

Short, Pamela Farley, and Jessica Primoff Vistnes. "Multiple Sources of Medicare Supplementary Insurance." *Inquiry* 29 (Spring 1992): 33–43.

Shreve, Maggie, and June Isaacson Kailes. "The Right to Die or the Right to Community Support." *Midwest Medical Ethics* 6, nos. 2 and 3 (Spring/Summer 1990): 11–15.

Silverman, Herbert A. "Medicare-Covered Skilled Nursing Facility Services, 1967–88." *Health Care Financing Review* 12, no. 3 (Spring 1991): 103–108.

Simborg, Donald W. "DRG Creep: A New Hospital Acquired Disease." *New England Journal of Medicine* 304, no. 26 (1981): 1602–1604.

Skidmore, Max J. *Medicare and the American Rhetoric of Reconciliation*. University: University of Alabama Press, 1970.

Sloan, Frank A. "Government and the Regulation of Hospital Care." *Journal of American Economic Review* 72 (May 1982): 196–201.

————. "Reviews: An Economist." *Health Affairs* 1, no. 3 (Summer 1982): 113–118.

Sloan, Frank, Janet Mitchell, and Jerry Cromwell. "Physician Participation in State Medicaid Programs." *Journal of Human Resources* 13 (Supplement 1978): 211–245.

Sloan, Frank, Michael A. Morrisey, and Joseph Valvona. "Effects of the Medicare Prospective Payment System on Hospital Costs Containment: An Early Appraisal." *Milbank Memorial Fund Quarterly/Health and Society* 66, no. 2 (1988): 191–220.

Smith, Adam. *An Inquiry into the Nature and Causes of the Wealth of Nations: A Concordance*. Savage, Md.: Roman and Littlefield, 1993.

Smith, Judith G., ed. *Political Brokers: Money, Organizations, Power and People*. New York: Liveright, 1972.

Sorkin, Alan L. *Health Care and the Changing Economic Environment*. Lexington, Mass: D.C. Heath, 1986.

Stanley, Harold W., and Richard G. Niemi. *Vital Statistics on American Politics*. Washington, D.C.: CQ Press, 1988.

Starr, Paul. "Changing the Balance of Power in American Medicine." *Milbank Memorial Fund Quarterly/Health and Society* 58 (Winter 1980): 170.

————. *The Social Transformation of American Medicine*. New York: Basic Books, 1982.

————. *The Logic of Health Care Reform: Why and How the President's Plan Will Work*. New York: Penguin Books, 1994.

————. "Why the Clinton Plan Is Not the Enthoven Plan." *Inquiry* 31, no. 2 (Summer 1994): 136–140.

————. "What Happened to Health Care Reform?" *American Prospect,* no. 20 (Winter 1995): 20–31.

Steinmo, Sven, and Jon Watts. "It's the Institutions, Stupid! Why Comprehensive National Health Insurance Always Fails in America." *Journal of Health Politics, Policy, and Law* 20, no. 2 (Summer 1995): 329–372.

Stern, Robert S., Joel E. Weissman, and Arnold M. Epstein. "The Emergency Department as a Pathway for Admission for Poor and High-Cost Patients." *Journal of the American Medical Association* 266, no. 16 (October 23, 1991): 2238–2246.

Steunwald, Bruce, and Frank A. Sloan. "Regulatory Approaches to Hospital Cost Containment: A Synthesis of the Empirical Evidence." In *A New Approach to the Economics of Health Care,* ed. Mancur Olson. Washington, D.C.: American Enterprise Institute for Public Policy, 1981.

Stevens, Rosemary. *In Sickness and in Wealth: American Hospitals in the Twentieth Century.* New York: Basic Books, 1989.

Stimson, James A. *Public Opinion in America: Moods, Cycles, and Swings.* Boulder, Colo.: Westview Press, 1991.

Stoddard, Jeffrey J., Robert F. St. Peter, and Paul W. Nweacheck. "Health Insurance Status and Ambulatory Care for Children." *New England Journal of Medicine* 330, no. 20 (May 19, 1994): 1421–1425.

Stone, Deborah A. "When Patients Go to Market: The Workings of Managed Competition." *American Prospect* 13 (Spring 1993).

————. "The Struggle for the Soul of Health Insurance." *Journal of Health Politics, Policy and Law* 18, no. 2 (Summer 1993): 287–317.

Strathern, Marilyn. *Reproducing the Future: Essays on Anthropology, Kinship and the New Reproductive Technologies.* New York: Routledge, Chapman and Hall, 1992.

Strosberg, Martin A., Joshua M. Wiener, Robert Baker, and I. Alan Fein, eds. *Rationing America's Medical Care: The Oregon Plan and Beyond.* Washington, D.C.: Brookings Institution, 1992.

Strumwasser, Ira, et al. "The Triple Option Choice: Self Selection Bias in Traditional Coverage, HMOs, and PPOs." *Inquiry* 26 (Winter 1989): 432–441.

Sullivan, Cynthia B., Marianne Miller, Roger Feldman, and Bryan Dowd. "Employer-Sponsored Health Insurance in 1991." *Health Affairs* 11, no. 4 (Winter 1992): 173.

Sullivan, Sean. *Managing Health Care Costs: Private Sector Innovations.* Washington, D.C.: American Enterprise for Public Policy Research, 1984.

Sun Valley Forum on National Health, Harrison Conference Center. "The Role of State and Local Government in Health." *Health Affairs* 2, no. 4 (Winter 1983): 134–139.

Sussman, Jason H. "Financial Considerations in Technology Assessment." *Topics in Health Care Financing* 17, no. 3 (Spring 1991): 30–41.

Taylor, Kathryn S. "Technology's Next Test: Regional Systems Laying Groundwork for Post-Reform Technology Planning." *Hospitals and Health Networks* 67, no. 11 (June 5, 1993): 42–44.

Tell, Eileen J., Marilyn Falik, and Peter D. Fox. "Private-Sector Health Care Initiatives: A Comparative Perspective from Four Communities." *Milbank Memorial Fund Quarterly/Health and Society* 62, no. 3 (Summer 1984): 357–379.

Terris, Milton. "A Wasteful System That Doesn't Work." *The Progressive* (October 1990): 14–16.

Thomas, Lewis. *The Lives of a Cell.* New York: Bantam Books, 1975.

Thompson, Frank J. *Health Policy and the Bureaucracy: Politics and Implementation.* Cambridge, Mass.: MIT Press, 1981.

————. "New Federalism and Health Care Policy: States and the Old Questions." *Journal of Health Politics, Policy and Law* 11, no. 4 (Tenth Anniversary issue, 1986): 647–669.

Tiefer, Charles. *The Semi-Sovereign Presidency: The Bush Administration's Strategy for Governing without Congress.* Boulder, Colo.: Westview Press, 1994.

Toner, Robin. "This time Clinton Tries a Selective Health Care Strategy." *New York Times,* 14 June, 1995.

Trevino, Fernando M., M. Eugene Moyer, R. Burciaga Valdez, and Christine A. Stroup-Benham. "Health Insurance Coverage and Utilization of Health Services by Mexican Americans, Mainland Puerto Ricans, and Cuban Americans." *Journal of the American Medical Association* 265, no. 2 (January 9, 1991): 233–237.

————. "Hispanic Health in the United States." *Journal of the American Medical Association* 265, no. 2 (January 9, 1991): 248–252.

Tucker, William. "A Leak in Medicaid." *Forbes* 148, no. 1 (July 8, 1991): 46–48.

Urban Institute. "Hospital Prospective Payment: Cost Control and Windfall Profits." *Policy and Research Report,* Winter 1988: 12–13.

U.S. Bureau of the Census. *Statistical Abstract of the United States 1966.* Washington, D.C.: Government Printing Office, 1966.

————. *Statistical Abstract of the United States 1992.* Washington, D.C.: Government Printing Office, 1992.

————. *Statistical Abstract of the United States.* Washington, D.C.: Government Printing Office, 1994.

U.S. Congress, Congressional Budget Office. *The Impact of PSROs on Health-Care Costs: Update of CBO's 1979 Evaluation.* Washington, D.C.: Government Printing Office, 1981.

U.S. Department of Health, Education, and Welfare. *Certificate of Need/1122 Project Reviews: An Annotated Bibliography.* Washington, D.C.: Government Printing Office, 1977.

————. *Toward a Comprehensive Health Policy for the 1970s: A White Paper.* Washington, D.C.: Government Printing Office, 1971.

U.S. Department of Health and Human Services. *Health Status of Minorities and Low-Income Groups,* 3rd edition. Washington, D.C.: Government Printing Office, 1991.

Valdez, R. Burciaga, Hal Morgenstern, E. Richard Brown, Roberta Wyn, Wang Chao, and William Cumberland. "Insuring Latinos Against the Costs of Illness." *Journal of the American Medical Association* 269, no. 7 (February 17, 1993): 889–894.

VanDeVeer, Donald. "Introduction." In *Health Care Ethics: An Introduction,* ed. Donald VanDeVeer and Tom Regan, 3–57. Philadelphia: Temple University Press, 1987.

Van Rossum, Wouter. "Decision-making and Medical Technology Assessment: Three Dutch Cases." *Knowledge in Society* 4, nos. 1/2 (September 1991): 107–124.

Varlova, John. "A $2.2 Million Lesson in the Perils of Peer Review." *Medical Economics* 61 (December 24, 1984): 56–61.

Varner, Theresa, and Jack Christy. "Consumer Information Needs in a Competitive Health Care Environment." *Health Care Financing Review,* Annual Supplement 1986, 99–104.

Vikhanski, Luba. "Emergency Departments Face a Growing Crisis in Care." *Medical World News* 33, no. 3 (March 1992): 50–51.

Virts, John R., and George W. Wilson. "Inflation and Health Care Prices." *Health Affairs* 3, no. 1 (Spring 1984): 88–100.

Vladeck, Bruce C. "Interest Group Representation and the HSAs: Health Planning and Political Theory." *American Journal of Pubilc Health* 67, no. 1 (January 1977): 23–29.

————. *Unloving Care: The Nursing Home Tragedy.* New York: Basic Books, 1980.

————. "The Market vs. Regulation: The Case for Regulation." *Milbank Memorial Fund Quarterly/Health and Society* 59, no. 2 (Spring 1981): 209–223.

————. "Comment on Hospital Reimbursement under Medicare." *Milbank Memorial Fund Quarterly/Health and Society* 62, no. 2 (Spring 1984): 269–278.

————. "Variation Data and the Regulatory Rationale." *Health Affairs* 3, no. 2 (Summer 1984): 102–109.

Vladeck, Bruce C., Nancy A. Miller, and Steven B. Clauser. "The Changing Face of Long-Term Care." *Health Care Financing Review* 14, no. 4 (Summer 1993): 5–23.

Vogel, Ronald J. "An Analysis of Structural Incentives in the Arizona Health Care Cost-Containment System." *Health Care Financing Review* 5, no. 4 (Summer 1984): 13–32.

Volpp, Kevin G., and J. Sanford Schwartz. "Myths and Realities Surrounding Health Reform." *Journal of the American Medical Association* 271, no. 17 (May 4, 1994): 1372.

Wagner, Lynn. "Access for All People." *Modern Healthcare* 19, no. 30 (July 28, 1989): 28.

————. "Health PACs Modest Donors—Study." *Modern Healthcare,* September 24, 1990.

————. "28 States Face Potential Deficits." *Modern Healthcare* 21, no. 1 (January 7, 1991).

Wagner, Mary. "Weighing the Cost of New Technology." *Modern Healthcare* 18, no. 47 (November 18, 1988): 43–58.

————. "Colorado Considers Establishing Its Own Health Plan for Needy." *Modern Healthcare* 22, no. 16 (April 20, 1992): 5.

Wallace, Cynthia. "Hospital PACs Ring Up More Clout." *Modern Healthcare* 12, no. 10 (October 1982): 52–53.

Ward, Paul D. "Health Lobbies: Vested Interests and Pressure Politics." In *Politics of Health,* ed. Douglass Carter and Philip R. Lee, 28–47. Huntington, N.Y.: Robert F. Krieger, 1979.

Ware, J.E., et al. "Comparison of Health Outcomes at a Health Maintenance Organization with Those of Fee-for-Service Care." *Lancet* 1 (May 1986): 1017–1022.

Weeks, Lewis E., and Howard J. Berman. *Shapers of American Health Care Policy: An Oral History.* Ann Arbor, Mich.: Heath Administration Press, 1985.

Wehr, Elizabeth. "Competition in Health Care: Would It Bring Costs Down?" *Congressional Quarterly* 37, no. 31 (August 4, 1979): 1587–1595.

Weiner, Joshua M., and Laurel Hixon Illston. "How to Share the Burden: Long-Term Care Reform in the 1990s." *Brookings Review* 12, no. 2 (Spring 1994): 16–21.

Weiner, Stephen M. "On Public Values and Private Regulation: Some Reflections on Cost Containment Strategies." *Milbank Memorial Fund Quarerly/Health And Society* 59, no. 2 (1982): 269–296.

Weisbrod, Burton A. "The Nature of Technological Change: Incentives Do Matter!" In *Adopting New Medical Technology: Medical Innovation at the Crossroads,* ed. Annetine C. Gelijns and Holly V. Dawkins, 25–26. Washington, D.C.: National Academy Press, 1994.

Weisman, Joel S., Constantine Gatsonis, and Arnold M. Epstein, "Rates of Avoidable Hospitalization by Insurance Status in Massachusetts and Maryland." *Journal of the American Medical Association* 268, no. 17 (November 4, 1992): 2388–2394.

Welch, W.P. "The New Structure of Individual Practice Associations." *Journal of Health Politics, Policy and Law* 12, no. 4 (Winter 1987): 723–739.

White House Domestic Policy Council. *The President's Health Security Act: The Clinton Blueprint.* New York: Times Books, 1993.

Index

About the Authors

Kant Patel (Ph.D., University of Houston) is a professor of political science at Southwest Missouri State University. He has published numerous articles in the field of health care, public policy, and American politics.

Mark E. Rushefsky (Ph.D., SUNY/Binghamton) is a professor of political science at Southwest Missouri State University. He is the author of *Making Cancer Policy* (1986) and *Public Policy in the United States: Toward the Twenty-First Century,* 2d ed. (1995). He has also contributed articles and chapters on health care and environment policies.

Medford/Somerville Campus Map

...mic Buildings

Alumnae Hall	J9	
Alumni House	F9	
Anderson Hall	J7	
Arena Theater	H10	
Bacon Hall	M7	
Ballou Hall	F7	
Barnum Hall	F7	
Baronian Field House	J11	
Bendetson Hall	F6	
Blakeslee House	B8	
Bolles House	J8	
Bookstore	G9	
550 Boston Ave.	M8	
Braker Hall	H6	
Bray Lab	L7	
Bromfield House		
16 Dearborn Rd.	L8	
Bromfield-Pearson	K7	
Cabot Intercultural		
Center	E7	
6-8 Capen St.	C4	
Catholic Center		
58 Winthrop St.	B3	
Central Heating Plant	G5	
Central Services Bldg.	L7	
Cohen Arts Center	J9	
Computer User		
Center	G10	
Costume Shop	H10	
Cousens Gymnasium	J4	
Curtis Hall	J6	
89-91 Curtis St.	C10	
126-128 Curtis St.	B9	
Dana Biology Lab	E7	
Dewick Hall	F10	
East Hall	G6	
Eaton Hall	H7	
Eliot-Pearson Child		
Study Center	J1	
Eliot-Pearson School	J1	
Goddard Chapel	G7	
Goddard Hall	E7	
Halligan Hall	J4	
Hamilton Pool	J3	
Hayes House	B8	
Hooper Infirmary		
134 Professors Row	C9	
Jackson Gymnasium	H10	
Lane Hall	E5	
Lincoln Filene Center	H6	
MacPhie Hall	F10	
Mayer Campus		
Center	G9	
Michael Chemical		
Research Lab	G10	
Miner Hall	H7	

48	Mugar Hall	D7
49	Office Services Bldg.	J5
50	108 Packard Ave.	E10
51	112 Packard Ave.	E10
52	120 Packard Ave.	E9
53	Packard Hall	F6
54	Paige Hall	H6
55	Pearson Chemical	
	Lab	G10
56	72 Professors Row	F8
	Dearborn House	
57	128 Professors Row	C9
58	Research Building	K6
59	Robinson Hall	J7
60	20 Sawyer Ave.	D9
61	28 Sawyer Ave.	D9
62	Sawyer House	B9
63	Scene Shop	M7
64	Sweet Hall	G5
66	11 Talbot Ave.	J8
67	55 Talbot Ave.	H9
68	97 Talbot Ave.	F9
69	44 Teele Ave.	C11
70	Wessell Library	H7

Residences

101	Anthony House	
	14 Professors Row	J8
102	Bartol House	
	37 Sawyer Ave.	C9
103	16 Bellevue St.	C4
117	Blakeley Hall	D7
104	Bush Hall	F10
105	Capen House	
	8 Professors Row	J8
108	Carmichael Hall	C6
109	Carpenter House	
	8 Winthrop St.	B6
110	Chandler House	
	125 Powder	
	House Blvd.	E11
111	90-94 Curtis St.	B10
112	114 Curtis St.	
	Sigma Pi Epsilon	B9
113	176 Curtis St.	B6
114	Davies House	
	13 Sawyer Ave.	D9
115	12 Dearborn Rd.	L8
116	Fairmont House	
	21-23 Fairmount St.	D5
118	Hall House	
	98 Packard Ave.	E10

119	Haskell Hall	G11
120	Hill Hall	E4
121	Hillside Dormitory	F5
122	Hillside House	
	32 Dearborn Rd.	K8
123	Hodgdon Hall	F10
124	Houston Hall	D7
125	Latin Way Dorm	G11
126	Lewis Hall	E10
127	McCollester House	
	28 Capen St.	A5
128	Metcalf Hall	F9
129	Miller Hall	D6
130	Milne House	
	8-10 Whitfield Rd.	E10
131	Theta Chi	E10
132	Theta Delta Chi	E9
133	President's House	
	161 Packard Ave.	E8
134	20 Professors Row	H8
135	Provost's House	
	48 Professors Row	G8
136	Zeta Psi	E9
137	Sigma Nu	E9
138	Delta Tau Delta	D9
139	Chi Omega	D9
140	Delta Upsilon	D9
141	134 Professors Row	
	Alpha Tau Omega	C9
142	Richardson House	H8
143	14 Sawyer Ave.	
	Alpha Phi	D9
144	36 Sawyer Ave.	D9
145	44 Sawyer Ave.	C9
146	45 Sawyer Ave.	C9
147	50 Sawyer Ave.	C9
148	Schmalz House	
	9-11 Whitfield Rd.	C9
149	Start House	
	17 Latin Way	G9
150	Stratton Hall	H9
151	9-11 Sunset Rd.	B7
152	13 Talbot Ave.	J9
153	15 Talbot Ave.	J9
154	101 Talbot Ave.	F9
155	Tilton Hall	F11
156	Tousey House	
	14 Edison Ave.	A5
157	West Hall	E6
158	25 Whitfield Rd.	D10
159	Wilson House	B8
160	10 Winthrop St.	B6
161	43-45 Winthrop St.	C4
162	44-46 Winthrop St.	B4
163	Wren Hall	C5
164	Wyeth House	D10